THE FAMILY
PREPAREDNESS
BUYER'S
GUIDE

THE FAMILY PREPAREDNESS BUYER'S GUIDE

THE BEST SURVIVAL GEAR, TOOLS, AND WEAPONS FOR YOUR SKILLS AND BUDGET

EDITORS OF LIVING READY

LR

LIVING READY BOOKS
IOLA, WISCONSIN
www.LivingReadyOnline.com

Contents

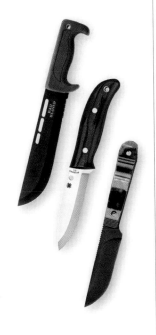

Introduction

Preparedness requires you to ask yourself many difficult questions. *How would my family survive with no power or water for a week? Where would I go if a storm or fire destroyed my home? How would I collect my children from school in the midst of a security emergency?*

Preparedness also allows you to remove some of the fear brought on by these questions. When you identify the potential threats and emergencies you may some day face, you can construct well thought-out responses that will help you survive, and maybe even thrive, despite the chaos around you.

One of the keys to being prepared is to have the things you need for survival well ahead of an emergency or disaster. This book will help you identify the survival supplies and gear you need to complete your family preparedness plans.

The feature articles in each chapter explain the importance of each type of gear and demonstrate how to effectively use it in survival situations. The Buyer's Guides in each chapter list specifications for dozens of survival products so you can quickly and easily compare among various manufactures and models. Products are listed in order by price from least expensive to most expensive (based on MSRP at time of printing) so you can evaluate what you are getting for your money and choose the gear that is best for your needs, your skills, and your budget.

When you are prepared, you're not just hoping for the best, you're planning for the best possible outcome no matter what life throws at you.

CHAPTER ONE

Survival Kits

Survival kits are an essential part of any preparedness plan. When a disaster strikes, you don't want to be caught empty handed. This chapter explains the many types of emergency survival kits you will want to build including home survival kits, go bags, everyday carry gear, and of course, bug out bags. Vehicle kits are also covered—and not just for cars. Kits for trucks, ATVs, and boats are also included.

While building your own kits is ideal (you can customize each kit for your specific needs), there are many pre-assembled survival kits on the market and the Buyer's Guide to Prepackaged Survival Kits found in this chapter details the contents of many of these kits. Use this information to decid which kit is right for you, or use it as a guide for what to include in your own custom-built kit. You could also use a pre-made kit as the core of your survival kit and add to it to meet all of your unique survival needs.

30 Items for a Home Survival Kit

BY PAT MCHUGH

This home survival kit can help you in a bug-in situation or you can easily grab it on your way out of your house if you are in a forced evacuation situation. Store the items for this kit in a 5-gallon bucket that has a lid (available at home improvement stores). A small plastic trash can with a good lid and handles also works. Place tape on the bucket and mark on the tape the date you last filled it with the items below. The contents of the kit need to be inspected and/or rotated and replaced every three to six months.

Contents for Home Survival Kit:

1. Flashlights: At least two of them without batteries inserted.
2. Batteries for flashlights: At least 3 sets for each light (watch expiration dates on package)
3. Small roll of duct tape
4. Pair of work gloves
5. Basic tools
6. At least four chemical light sticks (8-12 hour variety)
7. Portable radio (batteries out)
8. Two sets of radio batteries (again, watch the dates)
9. Small, basic First Aid kit
10. Roll of toilet paper
11. Toothbrushes
12. Toothpaste
13. Small bar of soap
14. Washcloths
15. Moist towelettes (e.g., Wet Wipes)
16. Bottled water (rotate every six months). Stack bottles around perimeter of bucket. Water is heavy, but necessary and could be a scarce commodity in a shelter.
17. A 32-oz. wide mouth polycarbonate water bottle (e.g., Nalgene bottle) in case you have to secure water in a shelter. Fill this bottle with as many travel-sized personal toiletries as you can.
18. Save a small eyedropper-type bottle and fill it with household bleach (replace every six months). You can use the bleach to disinfect your drinking water. 1 quart water = 2 bleach drops if water is clear, 4 drops if water is cloudy.

6 HOME SURVIVAL KIT ESSENTIALS YOU'LL FORGET

Think fast. The time it took to read that sentence is how long you'll have to think when disaster hits. If you have a survival kit already prepared, you're doing better than most people.

However, there are five essential items that won't be in that home survival kit because you use them every day. Don't forget them.

1. PERSONAL DOCUMENTS
Since you live in a disaster prone area, get all personal papers such as personal identification items, deeds, bank books, check books, insurance papers, agents' phone numbers, car titles in one place so you can take them if you have to evacuate. Have them stored in a plastic folder so it's a grab and go.

2. PERSONAL MEDICATION
Keep an empty zip-lock poly bag stored inside your medicine cabinet. Place all your personal medications in it and take with you when it is time to evacuate. For help in times of panic, write beforehand on the bag with a marker or make a list of the items you really need to put in this bag when the time comes.

3. GLASSES/CONTACTS
Don't forget your extra set of glasses or contacts.

4. CELL PHONE CHARGER
Most of us have cell phones today, make sure you have a car recharging unit to take with you so you will be able to recharge the phone battery from any car lighter or 12V socket. Electricity outlets may not be readily available for your home plug-in recharger.

5. EXTRA SET OF CLOTHES
If you have the room in your vehicle's trunk, put in an extra set of work type clothes like jeans, t-shirts, and clean socks.

6. A SURVIVAL KNIFE
Unless you carry one every day, the *Gun Digest* editors recommend keeping a knife set aside just for emergencies. Don't forget it. As they say, "your knife is your life." Select a knife that is durable, portable, reliable and affordable. See chapter 8 for more about selecting a survival knife.

19. A few high-energy food bars/candy/mints (watch expiration dates)
20. Pre-sweetened iced tea packets or drink mix, maybe even some dry soup mix.
21. Small pocket stove and solid fuel tablets stored in a metal camper's cup to use over the flame.
22. Small, hard plastic cups
23. Individual packets of sugar, salt and pepper
24. Emergency survival blanket (e.g., SPACE Brand all weather blankets)
25. Draw-top kitchen trash bags
26. Contact list: written on a piece of paper taped to the bottom of the lid. On the list include: Phone numbers and addresses of your out-of-state family-friends, your home/car insurance policy # and agent contact #.
27. Pen and a notebook—you will need it.
28. Pre-paid calling card
29. Some cash as credit cards and your ATM will be useless.
30. Entertainment/comfort item: deck of playing cards, reading material, puzzle books; small toy for young children.

THREE REASONS TO MAKE YOUR OWN SURVIVAL KIT

BY JOHN D. MCCANN

There are many types of commercial survival kits available on the market today. Some of these kits are well made. Some are sufficient. And some are lacking in serious survival components.

Although many of these survival kits provide the basics, the quality of the components must fit the selling price of the kit.

In other words, the components may not be chosen based on the quality of the item but on the price of the item. The total price of the items in the kit must fit within the overall selling price that allows the kit to be affordable.

I'm not opposed to commercial survival kits, but there are three reasons I prefer DIY survival kits.

REASON 1: QUALITY.

Oftentimes a commercial kit does not provide the highest quality of components. I have always felt that you should spend as much as you can afford on components for your personal survival kit.

After all, you might depend on your kits for survival, and therefore, this is no place to be frugal.

REASON 2: INSIGHT.

I believe that a survival kit should be designed on an item-by-item basis. In this manner, you are familiar with the individual components.

By packaging your own survival kit, you also know where each item is in an emergency. When you buy a kit that is prepacked, you lose the flexibility of choosing a container that offers you the space for those extra items you desire.

If you do purchase a prepackaged survival kit, be sure you become familiar with it before you need it.

REASON 3: IT'S EASY.

Making your own personal survival kit is not difficult. You can choose your own container and components, and customize it for your needs.

The Go Bag Defined

WHAT IS IN A GO BAG DEPENDS ON WHO YOU ARE AND WHERE YOU'RE GOING

BY JAMES CARD

We've heard of bug-out bags and 72-hour bags. But what is a go bag? Let's define what a go bag is in the following scenario. A massive storm has struck your community. There is plenty of chaos and wreckage. The power is out and streets are blocked by flooding and down trees making vehicles useless. You have to leave your home but you're not bugging out. You have to check on your grandma who lives four miles away on the other side of town. Night is coming. She could need help or she might be fine. You grab your go bag and start the trek into the dark streets.

Most go bags are small sized. They could take the form of a messenger bag, a small backpack, a fanny pack, a camera case or a soft-sided attaché. They cannot be too big because go bags are about going. You're on the move and cannot be weighed down by unnecessary stuff.

What is the necessary stuff? Mostly the basics: a multi-tool, a water bottle, flashlight, a mini-first aid kit, an emergency repair kit, and a fire-starting device. The contents of the go bag should be tweaked to suit your lifestyle and surroundings. If you live in the tropics, bug spray is a good addition. If you're an urban dweller, extra subway cards or tokens are a smart choice. Mostly what is inside a go bag is a personal choice and should reflect the tools that you will need to handle most emergencies that you could encounter in your day-to-day life.

Firearms: if you are committed to the concealed carry lifestyle, a go bag isn't the best place for a handgun. The best place for it is holstered on your side where you have trained yourself to draw the weapon from that position. It is always there and the motion is automatic. Also, by putting it in a go bag, you risk leaving the go bag unattended and thereby the weapon could fall into the wrong hands.

The most important thing inside of a go bag is emptiness. Leave a good amount of space open. It could be for a notebook computer, extra water bottles, a change of clothes or cookies for grandma.

THE GERBER GO BAG

Gerber Tactical teamed up with a number of other companies to create their version of a Go Bag. Did they get it right? Let's go through the checklist of contents.

GERBER MULTI-PLIER 600 SIGHT TOOL
A good and obvious choice. Multi-tools should be a standard component of any go bag.

GERBER DPSF FOLDING KNIFE
An excellent choice but not for the go bag. This tough, lock-back knife is so lightweight and easy to handle that it is better suited to ride clipped to your pants' pocket rather than tucked away inside a bag. It will get more use and the multi-tool in the go bag has a back-up knife anyway.

GERBER RECON-M TASK LIGHT
It's a great little flashlight for small tasks. Flashlight aficionados will argue about how much illumination power one needs but in the case of a go bag, smaller is better.

FROGLUBE CLP
FrogLube is known as a quality bio-based cleaner, lubricant and preservative used for firearms. It's a great choice, but is it necessary to carry around an entire bottle of it? A smaller-sized disposable packet would be a perfect addition—just enough to get the job done.

POCKET REF
A fat, yet shirt pocket-sized reference book by Thomas J. Glover. It is one of the oddest books you have ever seen. It contains plumbing info, chemistry tables, mathematical conversion charts, first aid tips, and more Wikipedia-like info than you can imagine. Is such a book a useful item in a go bag? It is the kind of book that you could carry around for 20 years, never reference it, and then one day it offers a tidbit of information that saves your life.

ALUMINUM WATER BOTTLE
A great choice and the latch-hook bottle top is a nice touch.

RITE IN THE RAIN NOTEBOOK
A slam-dunk choice. These notepads are great for preserving your scribbles even after getting wet, and notepads should always be in everyone's go bag.

MAXPEDITION MONGO VERSIPACK
This bag was designed to be a go bag. It is of rugged construction and meant to be used and abused. It rides well on your hip, has accessible pockets and enough room to leave some empty space for swapping out items as your needs change.

Everyday Carry Gear

BY JAMES NOWKA

Everyday carry, or EDC, gear is what we take with us every day, just in case.

For some, everyday carry gear is just a cell phone and a credit card. For me, I carry a simple grouping of tools that over the years have evolved into this emergency preparedness checklist.

The evolution started a long time ago with a pocket knife and grew into a refined collection that can help me solve most simple problems that crop up during my typical day. Depending on what my immediate plans are, I might add to this everyday carry gear with a small hatchet, a bigger knife or a bigger gun.

This emergency preparedness checklist contains enough to stop a fight, not what I would take to war. Here's my emergency preparedness checklist of everyday carry gear:

- Larger knife with a lock and at least a 3.5-inch blade that can be opened with one hand
- Pocketknife (small slip joint or traditional jack knife)
- Pocket tool carried in a pouch on my belt
- Small single-cell CR123A flashlight
- Small pocket compass
- Pen and pad of waterproof paper
- Paracord survival bracelet
- Belt (nylon web riggers type with steel buckle)
- Cash
- Sunglasses
- Small wind-proof lighter
- Watch
- Handgun

These 13 everyday carry gear items will be on my person on any given day. I carry these things because I am comfortable knowing I can mitigate many of the issues I might encounter.

Making Vehicle Kits

BY JOHN D. MCCANN

There are many types of vehicle survival kits. They can be broken down into the type of vehicle that is being used, the activity being performed, and the environment in which the activity is being conducted. Of course, we always know the type of vehicle for which the kit is being made. We normally know the activity we plan on performing, such driving a car into the country, taking a truck off road, fishing with a boat, whitewater rafting, or maybe flying for fun. However, we cannot always be certain of the environment; therefore, we need to plan for the worst so we don't have to hope for the best.

Vehicle kits will be broken down into the following categories for ease of discussion:

- Automobile Survival Kits
- Truck Survival Kits
- Boat Survival Kits
- Aircraft Survival Kits
- Snowmobile Survival Kits
- ATV Survival Kits

Each type of vehicle kit should include items or equipment that will not only provide you with the personal survival items you need (which should be in your personal survival kit and carried in the vehicle), but also those necessary to fix or repair the type of vehicle you are using, to supplement your personal items and provide additional equipment for the specific activity in which you are involved. And because you are using a vehicle, you can carry larger items, or more items, than with a personal kit.

Obviously, your personal survival kit is the basis for your survival. Although you should always carry at least a mini kit on your person, a small, medium, or large kit can be left in a car or truck. Even an aircraft and larger boats should have a designated survival kit. But when you get into smaller modes of transportation such as canoes, kayaks, snowmobiles, or ATVs, you will need to remember to include one of your survival kits as the personal survival component of the overall kit.

You should keep in mind that a vehicle can also provide various emergency survival items itself. Most cars and trucks have a rearview or side mirror, which can be broken off in an emergency and used as a signal mirror. Vehicles are full of wires that can be used for lashing, and seating material and carpets can be used for protection and insulation from the cold. The list could go on and on, but always examine what you have (thinking outside the box) and determine how it might be used for other than which it was originally intended.

AUTOMOBILE SURVIVAL KITS

As mentioned above, you should have a personal survival kit that goes with you when you get out of the vehicle. You should also have equipment that can be used to repair your vehicle. This should include a spare tire, jack, and lug wrench, in the event you get a flat tire. Additional tools for minor repairs should also be considered, such as screwdrivers, pliers, a hammer, and a hacksaw. Jumper cables, a tow cable or strap, tire chains (if in an extremely snowy area), and possibly some small replacement parts such as fan belts and radiator hoses should be carried. A shovel can be extremely useful in many situations and a small ax or saw can assist removing a tree across the road.

Safety items should always be maintained in your vehicle. These items would include flares, a reflective safety vest, heavy work gloves, and a brightly colored flag to hang of your side mirror to warn of an emergency situation.

For personal survival, a container of water (as large a container as is practical, or several smaller bottles) should be carried. Keep in mind that if you are in an area where the temperature goes down below freezing, you should carry the water in a metal canteen or other type of container that can be placed over a fire or stove to melt the water (or melt snow into water).

Some extra food, rain gear, a first aid kit, some survival blankets, a regular blanket, and some duct tape are also items that should be included. In cold regions, you should also carry extra clothing. If you normally wear dress shoes for work, a pair of hiking shoes or boots should be kept in your vehicle. If you have to leave your vehicle and walk, you won't want to be wearing dress shoes. In the winter, I carry a pair of winter boots, especially when I'm working in a suit and tie with dress shoes. I also carry a winter parka, as a dress trench coat only goes so far in a blizzard.

For emergency communications, you should have a cell phone. At one time vehicle cell phones were permanently mounted in the vehicle, but today everybody has a handheld device so if you have to leave the vehicle, the phone can go with you. The same is true for CB radios. There are vehicle-mounted units, but you can get handheld units that can be used in or out of the vehicle. If you are an Amateur Radio operator, you should have a portable. Multipurpose is always the way to go.

If room is available, there are some additional items that could prove useful. These could include a 12-volt emergency power supply, a power inverter, a portable compressor, a small survival stove, and a metal cup or pot to boil water, cook food, or melt snow for water.

AUTOMOBILE SURVIVAL KIT

TOOLS

- ☐ Jack
- ☐ Lug wrench
- ☐ Screwdrivers
- ☐ Pliers
- ☐ Hammer
- ☐ Hacksaw
- ☐ Jumper cables
- ☐ Tow cable or strap
- ☐ Tire chains (in snowy areas)
- ☐ Shovel
- ☐ Small ax or saw

PARTS

- ☐ Spare tire
- ☐ Fan belts
- ☐ Radiator hoses

SAFETY ITEMS

- ☐ Flares
- ☐ Reflective safety vest
- ☐ Heavy work gloves
- ☐ Brightly colored flag

SURVIVAL

- ☐ Container of water
- ☐ Extra food
- ☐ Rain gear
- ☐ First aid kit
- ☐ Survival blankets
- ☐ Regular blanket
- ☐ Duct tape
- ☐ Extra clothing (in cold weather)
- ☐ Hiking shoes / winter boots
- ☐ Cell phone

MISCELLANEOUS

- ☐ 12-volt emergency power supply
- ☐ Power inverter
- ☐ Portable compressor
- ☐ Small survival stove
- ☐ Metal cup or pot

TRUCK SURVIVAL KIT

Use the automobile survival kit checklist and add the following items.

TOOLS

- ☐ Tow strap
- ☐ Recovery straps
- ☐ Portable come-along (a.k.a. power puller)
- ☐ D-shackles
- ☐ Snatch-block pulleys
- ☐ Heavy work gloves
- ☐ High-Lift jack
- ☐ Permanently mounted winch

Of course, the size of your vehicle limits the amount of equipment and supplies that you can carry. However, with a little innovative effort, you will be surprised at how much stuff you can store in a small amount of space. Remember to select items that will serve more than one purpose, reducing the overall package.

TRUCK SURVIVAL KITS

When I speak of trucks, I'm talking about personal transportation vehicles, such as pickups and SUVs. Some pickups and SUVs are four-wheel drive, and if you go off road, you need even more equipment than if you stay on normal roads.

Obviously, trucks have more room than automobiles, which means your equipment can be stored in a larger bag or container, or you can segregate items into containers of various sizes. Some trucks have room to build a container, such as a box, in the back or behind the seat to contain your survival gear.

The first thing you need to include is your personal survival kit. I recommend a medium or large kit for a truck, especially if you go off road. All the items discussed for automobiles would also be appropriate for a truck kit. However, with the additional room, you can increase the amount of food and water, as well as some additional equipment to assist in getting unstuck (again, especially for those going off road).

Some handy items for a truck are a tow strap, some recovery straps, a por-table come-along (also known as a power puller), D-shackles, snatch-block pulleys, and some heavy work gloves. If your vehicle is high, you also might consider a High-Lift jack. Another nice but expensive (especially if you don't do a lot of off-roading) piece of equipment is a permanent winch mounted on the truck.

I try to keep the same supplies in my truck at all times, adding special items as needed for specific trips. I keep a bag that carries a blanket, some rope, two MREs, a 32-ounce Nalgene bottle with an Alpine cup on the bottom, an Esbit stove with four solid fuel cubes, a Sierra survival stove (see chapter 8), duct tape, parachute cord, a Mora knife, an original Becker BK-3 Tac Tool and BK-7 Combat Utility knife, a radio with a wind charger, a small compressor, work gloves, five light sticks, a poncho, and three large contractor bags.

I have a flashlight mounted to the dash of my truck and a fire extinguisher mounted to the center console. A rescue tool for cutting the seat belt and breaking the window is mounted to the headliner between the two front seats so either the driver or passenger can reach it. A head lamp is kept in the glove box, which is especially handy for changing a tire at night.

A 12-volt power unit with jumper cables and an AC voltage regulator are also part of my normal equipment, along with a 2.5-gallon water container. This container is nice, as it is half the size of most heavy-duty water containers, making it easier to carry.

Additional equipment includes a small bag with rain gear, hat, and gloves. I also keep a folding shovel (and a collapsible snow shovel in the winter), a hatchet, a Sawvivor saw, and a tool kit. These are my tools for various emergency chores. I also keep a tow strap, D-Shackles, a come-along, and a Hi-Lift X-TREME jack. A large first aid kit is always present as are a roll of duct tape, some flares, and an emergency vest and flag. When driving in the back country, I also carry my M6 survival rifle with a built-in survival kit.

BOAT SURVIVAL KITS

The type and size of boat will dictate what type of boat kit is required. For the purpose of this discussion, we are mainly concerning ourselves with smaller boats such as canoes, kayaks, inflatables, and small fishing boats used for freshwater adventures.

Keeping in mind that when you are on the water with a boat kit, there is equipment essential to this type of transportation. First, your personal survival kit should be in a waterproof container. If you want to carry a kit that is not normally waterproof, either place it in a waterproof container or double-bag it in freezer bags, placing the first one upside down in the second.

You should carry an additional waterproof bag or container with an extra set of clothes and a towel. They make a very lightweight towel called the "pack-towel" that can be packed down very small. Emergency rations should also be a part of this additional container.

Your next piece of gear should be a personal floatation device (PFD). Try to get one with several pockets that either zip or have Velcro fasteners. Include emergency devices in these pockets such as a strobe, signal mirror, and signal flares. I have D-rings on mine and attach a survival whistle to one of them on the outside. Also add a fire-starter kit, a survival blanket, and a flashlight. A quality knife in a sheath should be attached to the outside. If there is room, add some energy bars. The idea is that if you fall overboard and lose your other equipment (I'm not talking about the ocean here, but fresh water), you should have on you the essentials to survive. Fire starting is important because you want to get warm and dry as quickly as possible.

For the boat itself, you should have an extra paddle (tied inside the boat), a throw bag (for tossing to a person overboard), and something with which to bail water, or a small bilge pump. A roll of duct tape is also a good idea, as it can be used to help repair the boat as well as a broken paddle.

All gear and equipment placed in the boat should be secured by tying it down. If the boat is capsized, you don't want your stuff floating downstream, or worse, sinking.

If you are on a wilderness trip, you might consider a weapon. The Henry US Survival rifle discussed at the end of chapter 8 would be a good choice, as the entire rifle is stored in a flotation stock, making it ideal for waterborne operations. A larger fishing kit would also be a good choice since you are already on water, and catching fish would be a readily available food source.

AIRCRAFT SURVIVAL KITS

A survival kit for an aircraft should be able to accommodate the amount of people on the aircraft. An individual kit is not required for each person, but the total equipment available should be able to provide for everyone. Of course, if you are flying, you will have a personal survival kit with you. But you can't always count on everyone else being as prudently equipped.

All survival gear, excluding your personal kit, should be stored in either a large pack or carry bag that can be readily transported away from the aircraft in the event that is necessary, such as the threat of fire or explosion.

At least one good fire-starting kit should be incorporated with the minimum of a magnesium fire starter, waterproof/windproof matches, a lighter, some candles, and fire starters such as cotton balls saturated in petroleum jelly or Tinder-Quik fire starter tabs. A good quality waterproof flashlight with extra batteries should be available for the minimum of every other person.

There should be a supply of drinking water and emergency food and rations, again, for the amount of people present. Include bouillon cubes, tea or coffee bags, and sugar. A stove, such as an Esbit Pocket Stove, and cooking utensils should also be included, with at least one cup for each person. Include several water bags for storage, as well as a means to purify water.

BOAT SURVIVAL KIT

Secure all gear by tying it down
- ☐ Extra paddle
- ☐ Throw bag
- ☐ Bucket or small bilge pump
- ☐ Roll of duct tape
- ☐ Waterproof container for personal survival kit
- ☐ Personal floatation device (PFD) with zipping pockets

IN PFD
- ☐ Strobe light
- ☐ Signal mirror
- ☐ Signal flares
- ☐ Survival whistle
- ☐ Fire-starter kit
- ☐ Survival blanket
- ☐ Flashlight
- ☐ Knife in sheath (attached to the outside)
- ☐ Energy bars

IN SEPARATE WATERPROOF CONTAINER
- ☐ Extra set of clothes
- ☐ Pack towel
- ☐ Emergency rations

SNOWMOBILE/ATV SURVIVAL KIT
- ☐ Basic repair parts and tools
- ☐ Extra gas and oil
- ☐ Tow rope
- ☐ Cold weather survival kit
- ☐ Extra warm clothes
- ☐ Tube tent or lightweight tarp
- ☐ Survival sleeping bag or small sleeping bag
- ☐ Backpacking stove
- ☐ Emergency rations
- ☐ Snow shovel
- ☐ Snowshoes

In addition to emergency sleeping bags (or real sleeping bags if room is available) and parachute cord, tube tents or other types of emergency shelter should be available for everyone on board.

A good-sized fixed-blade survival knife, and a machete or ax should be included in the kit along with a folding saw, a survival saw, and a multipurpose tool. Some additional repair tools to include are a hacksaw, vise grip pliers, and a good quantity of duct tape.

A first aid kit that can handle the number of people present and any severe injuries that may result from a crash landing should be part of the package. This kit should also include lip balm, sunscreen, insect repellent, and a head net for each person.

Signaling devices should include at least one signal mirror, a survival whistle, signal flares, a strobe light, and a signal panel and flagging tape. If there is room available, a couple of whistles and signal mirrors would be better. A good-quality orienteering compass should be included for navigation.

For food collection, include a freshwater fishing kit, some SpeedHooks, several survival yo-yos, a gill net, and some commercial snares or snare wire.

Finally, include some aluminum foil, toilet paper, a sewing kit and a survival manual. If a weapon is desired, the Henry US Survival Rifle would be ideal, as well as the M6 Scout rifle.

SNOWMOBILE SURVIVAL KITS

I've talked to numerous people who drive snowmobiles and it never ceases to amaze me how many don't carry a survival kit, even though they travel at relatively high speeds over various terrain for ten or more miles. I ask what happens if they break down ten miles out in the woods, and they respond that they never really thought about it. This is when a survival kit is important. To build a serviceable snowmobile kit, a personal survival kit would be your starting point, adding additional items as indicted below.

Of course, you should have repair items to keep your machine going if it breaks down. This would include basic repair parts and tools, extra gas and oil, and a tow rope if you are out with more than one machine.

If you are snowmobiling, you are out in a cold conditions, so you should have a survival kit that will help you survive that environment. A rack of some type on your snowmobile may be handy to accommodate additional gear. Extra warm clothes are important, especially if you have to spend a night in the wilderness. To protect you from the elements, include shelter options, such as a tube tent or lightweight tarp. If room allows, a small one-man tent would also be a great advantage. A survival sleeping bag would be a minimum; a small sleeping bag would be better.

A small stove is needed to melt snow into drinking water, and some emergency rations are needed to keep your energy level up in the cold. Snowshoes and a collapsible snow shovel should be attached somewhere to your snowmobile. If you end up having to walk out, you will be glad you have the snowshoes.

ATV SURVIVAL KITS

ATVs (all-terrain vehicles) are similar to snowmobiles, as they are often used as recreational vehicles. Although ATVs are taken out into the wilderness, I often get the same response from owners questioned about survival kits: "What survival kit?"

A survival kit for an ATV should be similar to that for a snowmobile. Repair parts and tools, extra gas and oil, and a tow rope are a must. If you don't have a winch on the machine, you might consider a small come-along to get yourself out of a sticky situation. There are many types of ATV racks that provide extra storage space for carrying gear.

You still need a good personal kit, with additions to the shelter and emergency food or rations section. Unless you take your ATV out in the snow, you should trade the snow shovel for a folding shovel, and leave out the snowshoes.

Additional clothing should depend on the environment and season. Carry extra water and something in which to cook in addition to a first aid kit. Don't take a chance. If you break down and have to spend a night in the wilderness, be prepared.

SUMMARY OF VEHICLE KITS

While there are some similarities between the different vehicle survival kits, there is gear that is specific to the type of vehicle being used. Always remember to keep the environment, number of people, and weather conditions in mind when venturing out. Some gear will provide for all of these factors, while some items must be specifically chosen to serve in certain circumstances.

Vehicle kits are not difficult to make. Plan for the worst, and be prepared to survive! Find more survival kit packing instructions in *Build the Perfect Survival Kit* by John D. McCann available at store.livingreadyonline.com.

Packing Car Kits
for Temperature Variations

BY BEN SOBIECK

It's always great when readers of Living Ready's magazine and newsletter write in with questions. If the staff can't answer them, we usually know someone else with the right know-how. Jeff W. lives near Chicago, where the winters can get brutally cold. The summers can get just as hot. This makes it tough to balance the items in his car survival kit, or "go bag" as he calls it.

With the winter approaching, he wrote in with this question. It's a really good one:

When talking about go bags, most people think of being fully prepared for 72 hours or more. Up here north of Chicago, if I leave my bags in the car for a long shopping stop everything will freeze solid in the winter, and the inside of the vehicle will get north of 140 degrees in the summer.

Anything in a pressurized can, such as Fix-a-Flat, would not only freeze, but you run a real risk of it exploding along with your other supplies. Any cans of food, even solids like candles, can break to pieces at the slightest bump.

In the summer, you have chances of your food spoiling or melting, fire starters possibility causing a fire, not to mention ammo and other flammables causing a fire.

Plus, all these huge swings in temperatures have to even affect items like tents, freeze-dried food, and other equipment shortening their life span also.

I have several go bags, but I really can't see a safe way to carry them on a regular basis in the above conditions in my vehicles. I guess you could always only carry the items that travel safely under the above conditions but that could leave you very short on supplies when you really need them.

GEMENACOM/SHUTTERSTOCK.COM

I'm sorry but I can't figure an easy way around this issue.

Here was my suggestion:

You need two bags. One goes in the cab with you. The other one goes in the trunk.

The items that need to stay warm in the winter or cool in the summer (like a can of Fix-a-Flat) go in the bag in the front. That air will be conditioned to be cooler or warmer depending on the season. Even if you don't have AC, body heat or rolled down windows can help a lot.

The bag in the trunk is for things that need to stay out of the sun during the summer, aren't as sensitive to temperatures in the winter or just should stay in the trunk.

Our readers offered these suggestions:

There are a few things you can do to keep the internal temps down in your car during the summer. 1) Put one of those reflective shades in your windshield during the day. Not only will your car stay cooler but your interior will stay in good condition and resist fading & cracking a lot longer. 2) Tint your windows. Most newer vehicles come with tinted windows right from the factory, and this helps a lot. 3) Install window visors like those from Ventvisor (by Lund). They will allow you to leave you windows very slightly cracked to allow the heat to escape without having to worry about weather or prying eyes. Your car will still get hot inside, but, short of leaving the windows open or the top down, there's nothing you can do about that.

During the winter you can pack your cold-sensitive items into a small cooler and bring them inside with you at night to warm up. That's really about all you can do. Soft-sided coolers pack easier within your vehicle.

Winter Driving Kit
Checklist

FOOD & WATER
- ☐ Gallon jug(s) of water
- ☐ Energy snacks with long shelf life
- ☐ MREs (Meals Ready to Eat)
- ☐ Backpaker stove with cooking pot, fuel
- ☐ Coffee, tea and cocoa packets
- ☐ Instant soup mix

TOOLS
- ☐ Jumper cables
- ☐ Solar battery charger
- ☐ Multi-tool knife
- ☐ Paracord
- ☐ Flashlight and headlamp
- ☐ Spare batteries
- ☐ Compass
- ☐ Seatbelt cutter/window breaker
- ☐ First aid kit
- ☐ Whistle
- ☐ Cell-phone charger
- ☐ Matches and lighters

WARMTH
- ☐ Space blankets for each passenger
- ☐ Sleeping bag and blankets
- ☐ Chemical handwarmers
- ☐ Extra warm clothing

SANITATION & SANITY
- ☐ Urine container for emergencies
- ☐ Wet wipes
- ☐ Toilet paper
- ☐ Books
- ☐ Deck of cards

GETTING UNSTUCK
- ☐ Bags of sand or kitty litter
- ☐ Folding snow shovel
- ☐ Winter boots
- ☐ Tire chains
- ☐ Tow straps
- ☐ Warm work gloves
- ☐ Tire-in-a-can
- ☐ Ice scraper
- ☐ Lock de-icer
- ☐ Spare keys
- ☐ Extra gasoline in approved container
- ☐ Basic tool kit (wrenches, pliers, etc.)
- ☐ Strobe light or road flares

BAD CHOICE: CANDLES
There is the ventilation problem but there is another concern: Where do you put the candle? On your dashboard where it will burn scorch marks on the windshield glass? On the armrest where it will most likely get bumped? On an uneven car seat where it will be unstable? Consider all of the flammable materials in cars. It is a disaster waiting to happen.

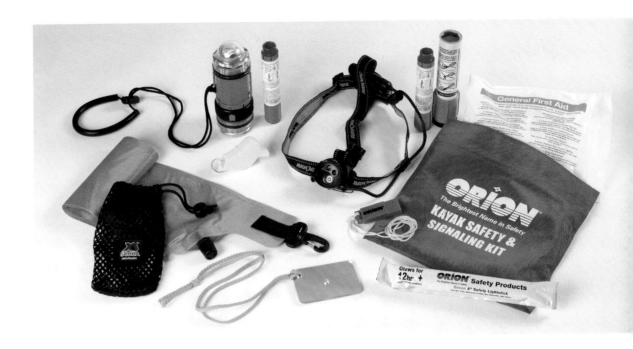

What's in Your
Ditch Bag?

A DITCH BAG NEED NOT HAVE A LOT OF STUFF. IF IT'S SMALLER IT WILL BE MORE CONVENIENT TO FIND THE ITEMS YOU NEED WHEN YOU'RE IN THE WATER.

BY DAVE MULL

A ditch bag is essential boating safety gear. This small kit should contain a variety of signaling equipment you can use while in the water if you are forced to evacuate your boat. Here's what to keep in it.

ORION RED AERIAL SIGNAL

Nothing signals distress better than a red flare headed for the heavens. It will get other boaters headed your way and possibly encourage land-bound observers to call for help. Fully functional flares are your best chance to be seen by others in the vicinity.

2-IN-1 STROBE AND LED TORCH

If you're in the water after dark, a strobe will help rescuers pinpoint your location.

RAYOVAC SPORTSMAN HEADLIGHT

This is a good one because it also has a strobe function, and if your boat sinks around other boats (such as trolling in the same large area), the flashes will lead rescuers to your location and the light will stand out among all the white navigation lights on other boats. The light is handy for other fishing and cruising tasks in the dark, and it's already on your head if you have to ditch.

XS SCUBA ORANGE INFLATABLE TUBE

When you're in the water with just your head above the water, you are very difficult to see. This inflatable tube attaches to your PFD and sticks well above the water surface—much easier to see than your bobbin' noggin alone.

ORION ORANGE SMOKE SEARCH AND RESCUE SIGNAL

This is a good tool for getting found from a distance and from the air.

WHISTLES

Whereas voices might be drowned out by engine noise on passing boats, a whistle might just pierce the rumble. It's also a tool for helping rescuers find you in the dark. Give one to your companion for added volume.

GREEN 6" SAFETY LIGHT STICK

This might be the only thing a passing boat can see if you're in the water between sunset and sunrise.

SIGNAL MIRROR

The bright reflection of the sun can alert other boats and people on shore of your dilemma. It's a simple, easy-to-carry tool that I wish I'd had when I was in the water.

GENERAL FIRST AID KIT

This is handy to have aboard when you don't sink—and if you get rescued and have cuts or abrasions, there's no guarantee your rescuers will have one with antibiotic salve or bandages. Might as well come aboard with your own.

Summer Survival Kit
Checklist and Maintenance Reminders

BY BEN SOBIECK

This summer survival kit checklist is adapted from a 1981 U.S. Army manual titled, *Checklist for Individual Hot Climate Survival Kit*. It contains a list of items and maintenance tips for those items. It's basic, but should provide ideas to get started.

No matter the summer survival kit checklist you use, keep two things in mind.

First, although it's always important, water plays an even greater role in a summer survival kit. The old adage of "one gallon per person per day" may not be enough, especially if travel by foot is involved.

Second, and less obvious, is to remember that hot days can still have cold nights. In a desert survival situation, for example, temperatures can plummet at night. A light sleeping bag may seem like overkill, but it won't be when the mercury hits the 40s.

SUMMER SURVIVAL KIT CHECKLIST

- ☐ **Tarp:** Check for holes, cuts, frays, tears, burns, loose or broken stitching, damaged grommets.
- ☐ **Magnetic Compass:** Is it cracked or have a broken dial face? Test operation.
- ☐ **Insect Headnet and/or Body Net:** Are there holes or tears in netting, broken or loose stitching, missing or broken elastic headband, loose or missing grommets.
- ☐ **Plastic Fork/Spoon/Knife:** Replace any that are cracked or broken.
- ☐ **Reversible Sun Hat:** Check for Cuts, frays, tears, broken or loose stitching.
- ☐ **First Aid Kit:** Make sure all components are secure and not expired.
- ☐ **Survival Manual/Book**
- ☐ **Matches in Waterproof Container:** Check for failures in container, broken or wet matches.
- ☐ **Non-Perishable Food Items:** Replace spoiled or expired food; look for tears in packaging
- ☐ **Signaling Mirror:** Check for scratches, chips, cracks, distortions.
- ☐ **Rescue Whistle:** Check for cracked or missing components, obstructions in mouthpiece.
- ☐ **Tool Kit (including firestarting gear):** Check for damage or corrosion to tools, dull edges, dry tinder.
- ☐ **Fishing Tackle (line & lures):** Check for corrosion, old line, dull hooks.
- ☐ **Water Containers (1 plastic, 1 metal, 1 collapsible):** Check for dents, leaks.
- ☐ **Water Disinfectant (iodine tablets, etc.):** Check for expiration, damaged packaging.
- ☐ **Frying Pan/Pot:** Check for rust, corrosion, cracks, buckling.
- ☐ **Sunscreen Lotion:** Check for damage to container, expiration of contents.
- ☐ **Pocket Knife:** Look for rust, corrosion, missing components, dull edges.
- ☐ **Light Sleeping Bag:** Check for tears, rodent damage, broken zipper, broken clasps.

How to Evacuate
without Losing It All

BY JAMES D. NOWKA

Both natural and man-made disasters can force you to evacuate your home. A good preparedness plan will help you limit the emotional distress an emergency situation could bring to your life. No one can pack up every last bit of his belongings before evaculating. People can, however, carry along their most cherished pieces. It's a matter of setting some clear priorities.

Think about the small and lightweight items you might tuck away for the ride with an ultimate focus on what's most meaningful. Those planning for evacuation should consider the real possibility of returning from an event and finding nothing left.

Furniture, clothing, vehicles and all types of household goods can be replaced. Those forced from their homes, however, aren't going to replace those heirloom pieces of jewelry that were handed down in the family from generation to generation. Should flooding or a fire strike, no insurance company could restore the children's first-grade school pictures or Dad's collection of World War II medals.

It's an interesting exercise to go through the home and determine those items that truly mean the most. It's also an important one. Families should keep those small, important items in a safe where they're protected every day and easy to grab when a situation requires a quick move.

Preppers should assemble a checklist so they're not struggling to remember every last thing amid the stress of that ticking clock. You should keep a storage bin or some other means of collection at the ready for quick packing of those irreplaceable goods whether it's a few photo albums, jewelry or any number of documents.

Preppers might invest in a decent photo scanner. They're fairly inexpensive and good investments from the standpoint of emotional well-being. Photos are crucial pieces of our families' stories. In the event of any disaster, scanned images would provide one less cause for stress, worry or mourning. Certainly, it's not the same to have a digital file as that original picture of your great grandmother on century-old photo paper, but something is always better than nothing.

You might store the images on CDs, DVDs or a flash drive. Some people have cloud-based accounts. It would make sense to send copies to other family members or put copies in the safe deposit box. Any of those options would provide yet one more assurance those photos are always safe and available regardless of what this unpredictable world could bring.

Electronic files might very well fall among your irreplaceable items in this digital world. In an evacuation, those who work from laptops could easily grab their computers before fleeing. Those who own desktop computers might not do the same. People should back up their files. Digital storage is inexpensive and grows cheaper by the year. It's a good idea, whether for laptop or desktop, at any point and for reasons well beyond the chance of disaster.

I keep a loose-leaf binder in my safe containing clear, plastic pages in which I can store any number of those irreplaceable certificates, awards and other pieces of my story. For many, high school or university diplomas aren't hanging on display. They're nonetheless important recognitions, pieces of our histories and items that

folks would feel terrible about losing to a disaster. I keep another binder containing other important documents ranging from vehicle titles and mortgage papers to life insurance policies and passports.

Preppers might keep a notebook in the safe or elsewhere that's in easy reach in the event of evacuation that includes contact information for everyone they owe money to or otherwise engage in business. The notebook might include account numbers in addition to phone numbers. It's a small step that could make life that much easier when away.

Certainly, the power company and mortgage company would have the ability to look up your account information, but that bit of preparation is going to make things more convenient. The notebook would serve as a reference that would eliminate any concerns about forgetting something important. Any bit of efficiency that's put in place beforehand is going to go a long way to providing some ease amid difficulty.

It's smart to keep some cash in a safe that isn't touched and there for the taking in the event of an evacuation. It's really up to each person as to how much he is able to put away and how much he would feel comfortable carrying. It would make sense to have $100 available for each member of the family. It's a contingency that recognizes credit cards aren't foolproof. In the midst of emergencies, you might find businesses that are able to keep their doors open but lost the computers and can't make credit card transactions. Every business takes cash.

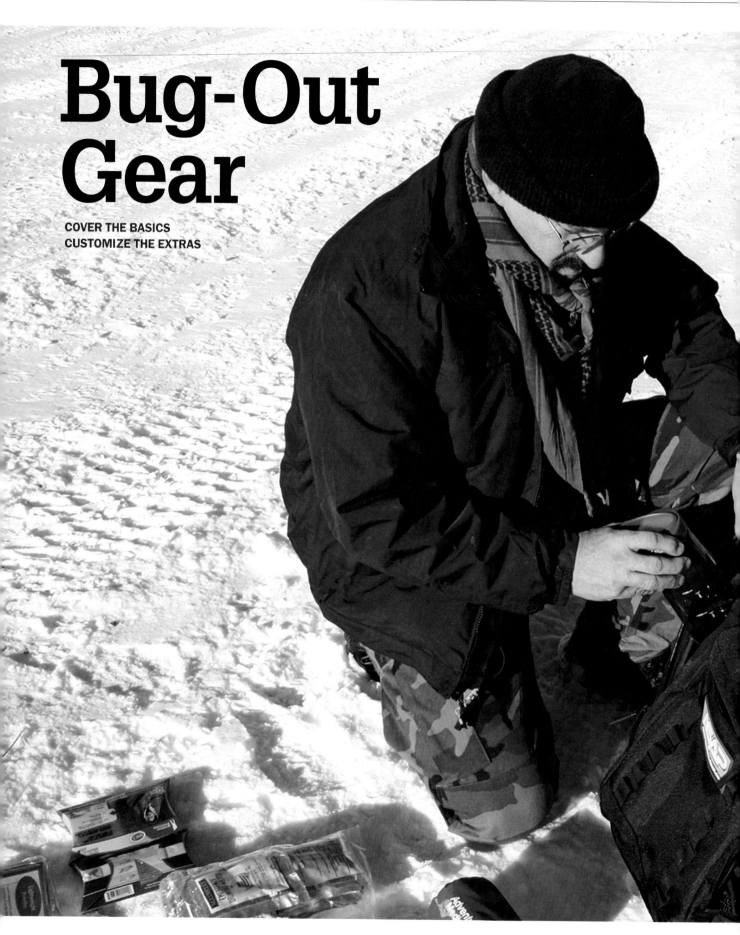

Bug-Out Gear

COVER THE BASICS
CUSTOMIZE THE EXTRAS

The bag comes loaded with essentials that can be added to. Some of the tools are a Super Leatherman tool, Bushnell GPS, light sticks, flashlight/solar radio, two portable shelters, space blankets, ponchos and food for 72 hours.

BY DAVE MORELLI

There is a lot of talk these days about putting together some sort of bug-out pack. I agree it is a good idea to be prepared for emergency, but there are a host of ideas as to what a bug-out pack is for.

Lots of folks that think they could throw a minimal pack on their back and disappear from civilization and live happily ever after. The problem is only a few can do it. An argument could be made that the wise woodsman could make a living following these folks and using what they left behind after they expire. Whatever your reason is to bug out, having some minimal stuff and (most importantly) the knowledge to use it will be a deciding factor in your final outcome.

There are some good reasons to bug out and the bag should be planned for a particular reason. Still, there are some things that should be in any bug-out bag, no matter what, because these items are instrumental to survival.

Some sort of fire starter is paramount especially in cooler weather. It stays cold for a long time up here in the Idaho mountains. It may be spring where you are, right now, but I'm still looking at winter conditions, so I prepare for the worst. Water is also key, but it is heavy to carry. So you should carry some and plan to get more on the fly. You'll need enough food to get you by until you can find more. A good knife, a small hatchet, fishing supplies, some first aid stuff, a couple space blankets, some plastic garbage bags (these can be used for a variety of functions), a GPS (and batteries) or a map and compass, flashlight (and batteries) and some method of purifying water. Some sort of firearm would make me feel better if I was stranded in the woods. If I was building a bag for the unlikely event of dealing with civil unrest, I would elevate the weaponry on the priority list.

But the reality is that you'll be grabbing your bug-out bag to help you get out of the way of a violent storm or wildfire. Or you will have it in your vehicle in case you get stuck or stranded. This bug out would be a temporary situation and may only last until you could get to safety, are found by rescuers or in a serious situation, reach a gathering station of displaced people.

Your location and community will play a big part in planning what to have in the bag. How long might you be on the move until you get to safety? What services are going to be available at that safe place? What time of the year will you be moving and how? Will there be obstacles along the way such as bridges out, hostiles, or unplanned challenging travel routes? No single bag set up could cover all the possibilities; so a bag that covers as many of the necessities for an estimated period of time to get to the next stage of safety is a good place to start. If your location leaves you with the possibility of being stranded for longer periods, you need to take this into consideration.

A situation involving a long stretch without power or road blockages thanks to storms could cause long delays in supplies getting to your area. Your bug-out bag may be better used to wait out the situation in your home. Hopefully, you have some emergency supplies for this situation but the bug-out bag still needs to be ready should some reason force you from the shelter.

There would be a ton of chatter if we started the discussion on which firearm to bug out with. I can already hear the gears turning. We all have a variety of firearms available and some are favorites we take everywhere we go. I would leave the firearm selection until I was running out the door. The situation or reason I was bug-

ging out may play a big role in what type of firearm would be the better choice. I always have a handgun on me so I would imagine it would be coming along just because.

Will the bug out gun fill a defensive role or will it be used for food gathering? I realize that the roles are interchangeable but some guns are better for some purposes. More important is to consider what would be the best for a variety of situations and which one you will grab without too much thought as the disaster happens.

As important as a defensive firearm is, the risk of starving to death or succumbing to exposure is probably more of a threat than getting into a firefight with a panic-stricken mob, especially if you use some evasive tactics in your bug out.

Planning with the Rule of Threes in mind will help you prioritize. You can live three minutes without air, three hours without shelter, three days without water, three weeks without food, and three months without sex. I am living proof you can stretch the three months out much longer.

I believe the minimum bug-out pack should have at least three days or 72 hours of supplies for each member of the family. I would also put my areas of importance based on the Rule of Threes, even though that's more of a survival priority, it puts things in perspective. When the situation deteriorates, like situations often do, three days of water will get you farther than all the food in the world.

You can put your bug-out bag together from scratch in a quality pack or you can buy the ready-made bag. Another option is to buy the Ready Bag and add to it. The

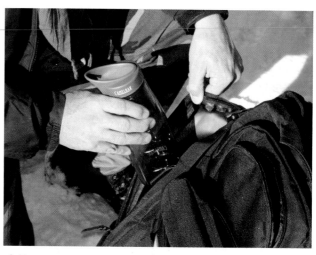

The water envelopes are good emergency water but the CamelBak bottle that comes with the bag can be refilled along the way and it fits right into one of the convenient pockets on the bag.

problem with buying the Ready Bag is you don't really know if the gear will be adequate until it is too late and if you use the Ready Bag to test it out you will have to replace the contents before you need them.

I checked out a bug-out bag from ASAP Survival Gear. They have many selections but this was a 72-hour, two-person bag. It comes with a lot of necessities but also includes a book and CD called Your Survival by Dr. Bob Arnot. This book and CD will definitely add to your knowledge when you are adding to your bag. It goes over many types of disasters and gives you an idea of what might be important to have in that situation.

The supplies come in a pack that I really liked. The pockets and zippered pouches were of adequate size and positioned for efficient utility. Things that you might want to access quickly without digging through the pack like a GPS can be kept in a properly sized pocket. It also had a generous amount of extra room for additional supplies like clothes, medications, and extra food. This bag is designed for the scenario where you are leaving on foot or it can accompany the other supplies packed in a truck or SUV bug-out vehicle.

The bag also comes with a multipurpose radio powered by a solar panel or a crank that can be used as a cell phone charger. The unit also has a light that is powered by the crank or the solar panel and has several weather channels. Also in the bag is a water bottle, space blankets and individual shelters, headlamp, fire starter, a complete first aid kit, ponchos, and a Bushnell Backtrack GPS. The first aid kit is well stocked and has some common medications you would use in the field. Along with common first aid items, there is a book on wilderness medicine and a small roll of duct tape. There is also room to include personal medications.

Light is always a useful commodity and the kit has several light sticks for instant light and a Leatherman Super Tool for common chores.

The kit comes with a 72-hour supply of food and water for two people. The water is in four-ounce foil envelopes, 36 to a bag. That's roughly 144 ounces of water for two people for 72 hours. I think it would work out a little light for two people over 72 hours and I would carry more water or at least have a plan to get it on the move. The bag also has a 32-ounce water bottle from Camelbak that can be filled and refilled when water comes available. Remember, you've only got three days without water.

The food contained in the pack made up of cubes is best described as a food-like substance. But it actually tastes pretty good. The ration calls for one cube three times a day. Each bar provides 400 calories, giving you 1,200 calories per day. I would imagine it would be enough to survive on but I would add some munchies to my bag. MREs or food from the grocery store in aluminum envelopes instead of cans would last a long time and would add some enjoyment to surviving. If you went with the supermarket type you could buy MRE heaters to warm them up if you couldn't make a fire.

There are a variety of long-lasting snacks that can be added to this bug-out bag and it is big enough to accommodate some extra rationing. I would also try to put a change of clothes in the bag and maybe some extra socks and gloves. There may be other medications and supplies that will be needed for each individual according to the circumstances.

You can also set up a bug-out bag from scratch, tailoring it to your specific purpose. For me, it would have to be a dire circumstance for me to leave my home on foot, especially in winter. It is just too far to go to get anywhere that would be safer. I most likely will be leaving in a vehicle and will have the luxury of packing a little heavier. A duffle bag with clothing and food and several cases of bottled water are in my storeroom ready for a bug out. These supplies need to be kept in a safe place and easily retrieved when it is time. Although the food should be rotated for freshness, the supply should be separate from the regular pantry. This will assure the rations will be adequate when the emergency unfolds.

The idea of the bug-out bag is to have some motility in case the best thing to do is get moving. The idea is to be ready for a catastrophe that might keep you from getting to the store. I live in a remote place and it is common to always have a little more supplies in case a winter storm keeps us from the market or the power goes down for a few days. We live on the end of the grid and it is not uncommon to lose power here. Being prepared means having the things needed to survive through an interruption of necessary services. It is also good to include bugging out as part of that plan.

Whatever the situation that presents it is wise to consider the circumstances that might apply to the area in which you live and prepare for them. Having supplies on hand for a minor emergencies is a good start, but disasters happen quickly and without notice. Having a plan can mean the difference between life and death should the poop hit the propeller. Whatever your bug-out vehicle is, foot or motor, set up and give some thought to the things that will come in handy.

Think of a bug-out bag as a bag that holds multiple bags. Keep the bag organized by grouping gear into various pouches. Transparent bags are good for at-a-glance identification of contents.

Choose the Best Pack for Your Bug-Out Bag

BY CREEK STEWART

You have numerous style options available when you select your pack. I have experimented with, used, and tested countless pack styles in environments all over the world—from single-sling backpacks to duffle bags and everything in between. In my opinion, every Bug-Out Bag (BOB) must be a backpack with two shoulder straps. Here's why:

- A backpack is designed to distribute weight evenly—thus reducing fatigue from extended use.
- Backpacks allow your hands to be free for other tasks. Limiting the use of your hands is a huge compromise you make when carrying a hand-held-style kit such as a duffle bag.
- Backpacks offer a more streamlined contour, which allows for less restricted travel.
- A backpack is strapped and attached to you, which reduces incidence of loss.

BACKPACK STYLES

There are literally thousands of backpacks available from hundreds of different manufacturers and retailers. Choosing only one can be a daunting task, but it's your first very important decision in building your BOB. Function and comfort are your two top priorities. The guidelines on the following pages will help you wade through the sea of choices. Almost all backpacks fall into one of three main categories.

Frameless

These packs are typically the smallest and offer the least support. They are also the cheapest both to manufacture and to buy. I don't recommend using a frameless pack as a primary BOB. Save these for going on a picnic or to the beach, not for hauling life-sustaining survival supplies.

External Frame

I own many external-frame backpacks, and I like this style very much. External-frame packs are known for their performance with heavy loads. They do a great job of distributing weight to your hips, which helps to reduce fatigue in your shoulders, upper body, and back. Because the pack is mounted to a frame and not directly against your back, this style also offers excellent air circulation, which you will appreciate in hot weather.

External-frame packs can feel "shifty" and top heavy because the weight is mounted slightly away from your back. They also tend to feel slightly bulky as compared to other styles. My personal BOB was an external frame pack for a very long time. This style works well as a BOB.

Internal Frame

Most of the backpacks you will find for sale are internal-frame style packs. The rigid support system that gives the backpack structure and shape is built into the pack body. These supports can be plastic, metal, or even foam. Internal-frame packs are very popular with adventure sports enthusiasts because of their sleek, agile appearance. They are close-fitting and hug very snuggly to the body, which causes poor air circulation—the number one frustration with this style of backpack. This can be annoying in warmer climates.

The form-fitting nature also reduces load shifting, which helps with balance—especially on rough, uneven terrain. These packs are very maneuverable and also are easier to store in your home because they typically have a smaller overall footprint.

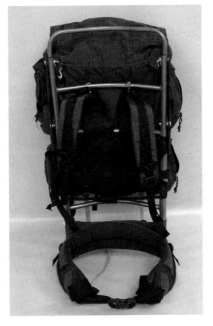
⚠ External frame backpack

Internal-frame packs make excellent BOBs. My current BOB is an internal-frame pack.

SIZE DOES MATTER
Balancing Act

Choosing your BOB pack size is a balancing act between comfort and necessity. It needs to be large enough to contain a certain amount of necessary gear while still remaining comfortable and manageable during extended periods of use.

Follow Your Gut

Choosing the right pack is a gut feeling. There are no right or wrong answers, only shades of gray. Your pack shouldn't be too small, and it shouldn't be too large.

Some of my students collect all of their Bug-Out gear first and save the pack decision for last. This is certainly an option. Choose a medium-size pack that feels right and looks appropriate on your body frame.

Seeking Help

Don't order your pack online! Many specialty outdoor and camping stores (especially independently owned stores) will help you find backpacks tailored to your size and weight. Some packs can even be

⚠ Closeup of external frame backpack

⚠ Internal frame backpack

heat molded to your specific form, which is a pricey but cool feature.

Retailers can add weight bags to the pack while you are in the store to give you an idea of how the pack wears and feels when loaded. When asking for help, a good rule of thumb is to tell the store associate that you are taking a three- to five-day backpacking trip. This will help narrow the field into the size category that is appropriate.

Making the Wrong Decision

Choosing the wrong pack can have painful consequences. There is nothing more miserable than hiking all day with an uncomfortable and ill-fitting backpack. And, packs are expensive. When buying a backpack, make sure there is a satisfaction guarantee and warranty. If you use it and don't like it, return it!

Hey! They've Got Stuff!

Building a "tricked out" looking Bug-Out Bag is a bad idea. You might as well put a bull's-eye on your back.

It's human nature to show off our cool stuff. Resist the urge and be humble when it comes to your BOB. It's good practice to ask yourself, "What can I do to look less prepared?" Supplies of all kinds will be at a premium in any disaster scenario, and you will be carrying an incredibly valuable assortment of merchandise on your back. If you choose to share, that's great, but being forced to share is something totally different.

Desperation can bring out the worst in people, and you will have enough problems without sending signals to "scavenging opportunists" that you and your family are stocked with survival rations.

Rioting, looting, mugging, and pillaging are all very common (guaranteed) in disaster emergencies. Do yourself a favor and keep your BOB low-key.

KEY FEATURES OF A BOB
Durable Construction

Not to state the obvious, but the pack you choose needs to be built and designed to take abuse. Some telltale signs of a well-constructed backpack are reinforced seams and double stitching.

No cheap zippers are allowed! If it has zippers, make sure they are good ones. Some packs have water-tight zippers. This is a great feature.

Compartmentalized

Choosing a BOB that has defined compartments helps to organize gear and facilitates quick access to important items. Sifting through a pack with one cavernous compartment is not only frustrating, but also inefficient.

Being organized is extremely important. In time-sensitive situations, such as signaling for rescue, your level of orga-

---

DOES YOUR BUG-OUT BAG HAVE A CONCEALED CARRY WEAPON INSIDE?

BY KEVIN D. MICHALOWSKI

Bug-out bags are an important part of an emergency preparedness plan. What you need to pack in your bag really depends on what you expect. For me, a bug out bag requires some sort of firearm or spare ammo. When things are very bad, people might want to fight. They might want to take what is yours. The only thing that stops a bad guy with a gun is a good guy with a gun. So…

Rule #1: Have a gun. Be trained in its use. Be familiar with its operation. Know its capabilities and, perhaps most importantly, be mentally ready to use it.

Rule #2: Have a trauma kit. An exchange of gunfire usually means someone is going to need medical help. If that someone is someone you want to save you will likely need, at the bare minimum a tourniquet, a compress dressing, first aid tape or wrap, bandage material or surgical sponges and gloves.

Beyond that, your bug-out kit is yours to develop as you wish. I have one kit made just in case I have an active shooter situation in my jurisdiction. This kit is made up of a Level III plate carrier with extra soft armor, four magazines for the AR-15, a Tops Pry Knife to help open doors and a trauma kit on the back. I can put the plate carrier right over my uniform, thus giving me added ballistic protection and the tools I need to stop the threat and render aid.

I also have various other kits in various locations that will provide me things like extra ammo for my duty sidearm, a multi-tool, first aid gear, and flex cuffs. There is another kit in which I keep a spare sidearm, ammo, a trauma pack (are you noticing a trend on the trauma kit theme here?), flashlight, knife, multi-tool and more. And I have one of the Mossberg JIC shotguns in a tube, loaded up with extra ammo, first aid gear, a knife or three, a water filter, and sheet of heavy plastic for a basic tent. I think I'm ready.

A good handgun and a stout knife are very important tools. Keep them both handy with your other must-have items in the bug-out bag.

---

nization can change the course of your entire experience.

Water Resistant

Wet gear, clothing, and bedding can be deadly in certain conditions and down right miserable in all conditions. Choose a pack constructed from waterproof or water-resistant material. Some packs have built-in rain covers.

I've learned from outdoor experience to line my BOB with a construction-grade trash bag as an added layer of water-proof security. I suggest you do the same.

Pack Support

Choose a BOB with padded shoulder straps. Thin shoulder support straps can cause blisters and sores over long distances.

Many medium- to large-sized backpacks have built-in hip belts that help distribute the pack load to your hips rather than on your shoulders and upper body. A hip belt can drastically reduce shoulder and neck fatigue by supporting up to 90 percent of a pack's weight and centering that weight nearer the center of mass. For extended carry, I wouldn't even consider a pack without a hip belt unless I had no choice.

FOR FAMILIES, DOES EVERYONE NEED A BOB?

All family members need to be considered in a Bug-Out disaster evacuation. There are certain considerations that must be addressed when it comes to Bugging Out with children, the elderly and even pets.

The Primary Bug-Out Bag

If you're single, this is the only pack that concerns you. Families will also have only one primary BOB. This pack contains all of the essential survival tools for the family along with the user's personal items. This is the one pack you don't want to leave home without in the event of a disaster Bug Out. This pack is carried by the group's strongest and most able-bodied adult.

Additional Adult Packs

Additional adults include all able persons eleven years of age and older. These packs should contain only personal survival items such as water, food, clothing, hygiene items, and bedding. Anything else is optional. All of the group's survival gear, such as shelter, fire building tools, etc., will be carried in the Primary BOB. The style of this pack does not need to be as functional or elaborate of the Primary BOB because it will weigh significantly less. A basic, frameless school-style backpack will work just fine.

Youth Packs

The general age range for a youth pack is six to ten years old. These should contain only light-weight items such as clothing, hygiene items, bedding, and maybe a small toy. All other survival essentials, such as food and water, will need to be split among adult packs or carried in the primary BOB.

Children Under Six Years Old

It's unrealistic to expect to bug out on foot while carrying not only the necessary survival gear but also a small child or children. This situation exceeds most adult's physical limitations and just isn't practical. If you have small children who are unable to travel independently, purchase a wagon or stroller to use specifically in the event of a Bug Out.

Not only can a pull-behind wagon transport small children, but it can also help carry other gear as well. From the tra-ditional Radio Flyer to more rugged off-road models, many different wagon styles are available. Your local lawn and garden center will offer several options. Wagons can be stowed in the trunk or mounted to a car roof rack in the event of Bugging Out in a vehicle.

A rugged, three-wheeled, collapsible stroller is also a great "infant-toting" alternative. These are light-weight and very quick to deploy. The three-wheeled models are better suited for rough terrain and faster travel. Many styles also have storage areas as well. Don't even consider the four-wheeled options with the cheap plastic wheels.

For even greater mobility, consider a baby backpack. This pack style integrates a seat and harness for toting small children and many also have sizable compartments and extra lashing points for gear. A pack like this could serve as both an additional adult pack and a baby hauler.

Disasters often disrupt transportation systems such as roads, trains, buses, and subways. Road closures, traffic jams, and fuel shortages can force you to travel by foot. Having a Bug-Out wagon or stroller at the ready can make this possibility much more practical.

Elderly and Disabled

When Hurricane Katrina struck the United States in 2005, hundreds of elderly and disabled people were left behind and consequently died in the disaster's aftermath. To a certain extent, the elderly and disabled must be treated in the same way as small children. You need to be prepared to transport them and their personal survival supplies.

Never bug out with a battery-powered wheelchair or mobility device. Insufficient resources to recharge batteries can leave you stuck with few options. Without a charge, these modern contraptions are bulky and virtually impossible to move. A traditional push-powered wheelchair should be on hand and ready to use in the event of a Bug-Out. BOBs can be mounted to the wheelchair for assisted travel.

In the event that vehicle travel is not possible, a manual push wheelchair might be the only solution that allows an elderly or disabled person to continue on a Bug-Out journey with you. Please give yourself this option. You cannot carry them.

STOCKING YOUR PACK

Up to this point, building your own BOB has been fairly conceptual—mainly defining expectations about the build. From here on out, this is a hands-on project. It's time to start collecting gear to stock your Bug-Out Bag. And, it's time to begin understanding this gear and start learning how to use it. This is the fun part. There are twelve supply categories that need to be considered when stocking your Bug-Out Bag. They are:

- Water and hydration
- Food and food preparation
- Clothing
- Shelter and bedding
- Fire
- First aid
- Hygiene
- Tools
- Lighting
- Communications
- Protection and self-defense
- Miscellaneous supplies

Find detailed Bug-Out Bag packing instructions in *Build the Perfect Bug Out Bag* by Creek Stewart, available at store.livingreadyonline.com.

Buyer's Guide to Backpacks

Pricing key (based on manufacturer's suggested retail price):

$ = $50–$75
$$ = $76–$100
$$$ = $101–$125
$$$$ = $126–$150
$$$$$ = $151–$200
$$$$$$ = $201–$250

INTERNAL FRAME

Manufacturer/Model: Columbia Sportswear Treadlite 16 L
Price: $
Weight: 29 oz.
Frame Type: internal
Load Type: panel-loading
Fixed capacity: (Cubic inches): 610

Manufacturer/Model: The Coleman Company, Inc./ RTX 3100
Price: $
Weight: 22 oz.
Frame Type: internal
Load Type: panel-loading
Expandable Capacity: (Cubic inches): 1,831

Manufacturer/Model: Equinox/Ultralite Parula Day Pack
Price: $
Weight: 7 oz.
Frame Type: internal
Load Type: top-loading
Fixed capacity: (Cubic inches): 1,050

Manufacturer/Model: ARC'TERYX/ Cierzo 18
Price: $
Weight: 9 oz.
Frame Type: internal
Load Type: top-loading
Fixed capacity: (Cubic inches): 1,098

Manufacturer/Model: Kelty/Redstart 28
Price: $
Weight: 24 oz.
Frame Type: internal
Load Type: panel-loading
Fixed capacity: (Cubic inches): 1,700

Manufacturer/Model: Black Diamond Equipment/Magnum
Price: $
Weight: 14 oz.
Frame Type: internal
Load Type: top-loading
Fixed capacity: (Cubic inches): 1,098

Manufacturer/Model: Eureka! /Panther Peak 30L
Price: $
Weight: 38 oz.
Frame Type: internal
Load Type: panel-loading
Fixed capacity: (Cubic inches): 1,830

Manufacturer/Model: Grivel/Air Tech 28
Price: $
Weight: 23.8 oz.
Frame Type: internal
Load Type: top-loading
Fixed capacity: (Cubic inches): 1,709

Manufacturer/Model: High Sierra Sport Company/Cirque 30
Price: $
Weight: 39 oz.
Frame Type: internal
Load Type: panel-loading
Fixed capacity: (Cubic inches): 1,831

Manufacturer/Model: Boreal/Dakota 28
Price: $$
Weight 40.5 oz.
Frame Type: internal
Load Type: panel-loading
Fixed capacity: (Cubic inches): 1,709

Manufacturer/Model: Deuter USA/Race
Price: $$
Weight: 20 oz.
Frame Type: internal
Load Type: panel-loading
Fixed capacity: (Cubic inches): 610

Manufacturer/Model: High Peak USA/ Phantom 45+10
Price: $$
Weight: 4 lbs. 8 oz.
Frame Type: internal
Load Type: top-loading
Expandable capacity: (Cubic inches): 3,000-3,700

Manufacturer/Model: Cabela's/Cabela's Ridgeline 60-Liter Pack
Price: $$$
Weight: 3 lbs. 10 oz.
Frame Type: internal
Load Type: top-loading
Fixed capacity: (Cubic inches): 3,612

Manufacturer/Model: Bergans of Norway/Skarstind 22 L
Price: $$$
Weight: 13 oz.
Frame Type: internal
Load Type: hybrid
Fixed capacity: (Cubic inches): 1,200

Manufacturer/Model: Backcountry Access/Stash 30
Price: $$$$
Weight: 46.5 oz.
Frame Type: internal a-frame
Load Type: panel-loading
Fixed capacity: (Cubic inches): 1,830

Manufacturer/Model: Jandd Mountaineering/Har Lit Packer
Price: $$$$
Weight: 3 lbs. 6 oz.
Frame Type: internal
Load Type: panel-loading
Fixed capacity: (Cubic inches): 2,250

Manufacturer/Model: Eddie Bauer/First Ascent Alchemist 30
Price: $$$$
Weight: 3 lbs. 4 oz.
Frame Type: internal (removable)
Load Type: hybrid
Fixed capacity : (Cubic inches): 1,831

Manufacturer/Model: Eastern Mountain Sports/Cirque
Price: $$$$
Weight: 3 lbs. 6 oz.
Frame Type: internal
Load Type: top-loading
Fixed capacity: (Cubic inches): 2,746

Manufacturer/Model: ALPS Mountaineering/Orizaba 3300
Price: $$$$
Weight: 3 lbs. 9 oz.
Frame Type: internal
Load Type: top and panel-loading
Fixed capacity: (Cubic inches): 3,300

Manufacturer/Model: CamelBak/Highwire 25
Price: $$$$
Weight: 2 lbs. 3 oz.
Frame Type: internal
Load Type: top-loading
Fixed capacity: (Cubic inches): 1,343

Manufacturer/Model: Mountain Equipment Co-op (MEC)/Alpinelite 75
Price: $$$$$
Weight: 4 lbs. 8 oz. (smallest)
Frame Type: internal
Load Type: hybrid
Fixed capacity: (Cubic inches): 4,455; 4,577; 4,760
Sizes available: 3

Manufacturer/Model: Backcountry Access/Stash 40
Price: $$$$$
Weight: 3 lbs. 2 oz.

Frame Type: internal
Load Type: panel-loading
Fixed capacity: (Cubic inches): 2,440

Manufacturer/Model: The North Face/Terra 65
Price: $$$$$
Weight: 4 lbs. 5 oz.; 4 lbs. 7 oz.
Frame Type: internal
Load Type: hybrid
Expandable Capacity: (Cubic inches): 3,906; 4,028
Sizes available: 2

Manufacturer/Model: Six Moon Designs/Flight 40
Price: $$$$$
Weight: 30 oz.; 32 oz.
Frame Type: internal
Load Type: top-loading
Fixed capacity: (Cubic inches): 2,700; 2,900
Sizes available: 2

Manufacturer/Model: Exped/Mountain Lite 30
Price: $$$$$
Weight: 35 oz.
Frame Type: internal
Load Type: top-loading
Fixed capacity: (Cubic inches): 1,831

Manufacturer/Model: Montbell North America/Alpine Pack 50
Price: $$$$$
Weight: 3 lbs. 9 oz.
Frame Type: internal
Load Type: top-loading
Fixed capacity: (Cubic inches): 3,051

Manufacturer/Model: Gossamer Gear/Gorilla Ultralight Backpack
Price: $$$$$
Weight: 25 oz.; 26 oz.; 28 oz.
Frame Type: internal
Load Type: top-loading

Expandable Capacity: (Cubic inches): 3,000
Sizes available: 3

Manufacturer/Model: Deuter/Futura Pro 36
Price: $$$$$
Weight: 3 lbs. 11 oz.
Frame Type: internal
Load Type: top-loading
Expandable Capacity: (Cubic inches): 2,197

Manufacturer/Model: Wenger/Almer 30 L
Price: $$$$$$
Weight: 3 lbs. 5 oz.
Frame Type: internal
Load Type: top-loading
Fixed capacity: (Cubic inches): 1,950

Manufacturer/Model: Macpac/Torlesse 35
Price: $$$$$$
Weight: 45 oz.
Frame Type: internal
Load Type: top-loading
Fixed capacity: (Cubic inches): 2,136

WOMEN'S PACKS, INTERNAL FRAME

Manufacturer/Model: Kelty/Redstart 23 W
Price: $
Weight: 20 oz.
Frame Type: internal
Load Type: panel-loading
Fixed capacity: (Cubic inches): 1,400

Manufacturer/Model: Kelty/Redtail 22 W
Price: $
Weight: 22 oz.
Frame Type: internal
Load Type: panel-loading
Fixed capacity: (Cubic inches): 1,350

Pricing key (based on manufacturer's suggested retail price):

$ = $50–$75
$$ = $76–$100
$$$ = $101–$125
$$$$ = $126–$150
$$$$$ = $151–$200
$$$$$$ = $201–$250

Manufacturer/Model: L.L. Bean/Lily 18
Price: $
Weight: 23 oz.
Frame Type: internal
Load Type: panel-loading
Expandable Capacity: (Cubic inches): 1,143

Manufacturer/Model: Columbia Sportswear/Vixen 22
Price: $
Weight: 38 oz.
Frame Type: internal
Load Type: top-loading
Fixed capacity: (Cubic inches): 1,334

Manufacturer/Model: Marmot/Kompressor Plus
Price: $
Weight: 12 oz.
Frame Type: internal
Load Type: top-loading
Fixed capacity: (Cubic inches): 1,220

Manufacturer/Model: Black Diamond Equipment/Pulse
Price: $
Weight: 30 oz.; 32 oz.
Frame Type: internal
Load Type: panel-loading
Fixed capacity: (Cubic inches): 1,220; 1,340
Sizes available: 2

Manufacturer/Model: Gregory/Women's Maya
Price: $$
Weight: 19 oz.
Frame Type: internal

Load Type: panel-loading
Fixed capacity: (Cubic inches): 976

Manufacturer/Model: Osprey/Sirrus 24
Price: $$$
Weight : 37 oz.
Frame Type: internal
Load Type: panel-loading
Fixed capacity: (Cubic inches): 1,343; 1,465
Sizes available: 2

Manufacturer/Model: The North Face/W Surge ll
Price: $$$
Weight: 45 oz.
Frame Type: internal
Load Type: panel-loading
Fixed capacity: (Cubic inches): 1,648

Manufacturer/Model: Low Alpine/Airzone Centro ND 30
Price: $$$
Weight: 43 oz.
Frame Type: internal
Load Type: top-loading
Fixed capacity: (Cubic inches): 1,830

Manufacturer/Model: Deuter USA/ACT Trail 28SL
Price: $$$
Weight: 45 oz.
Frame Type: internal
Load Type: hybrid
Fixed capacity: (Cubic inches): 1,710

Manufacturer/Model: JanSport/JanSport Cienega
Price: $$$
Weight: 32 oz.
Frame Type: internal
Load Type: top-loading
Fixed capacity: (Cubic inches): 1,952

Manufacturer/Model: Granite Gear/Taku 24
Price: $$$
Weight: 38 oz.
Frame Type: internal
Load Type: panel-loading
Fixed capacity: (Cubic inches): 1,460

Manufacturer/Model: Vaude/Maremma 28
Price: $$$$
Weight: 40 oz.
Frame Type: internal
Load Type: top-loading
Fixed capacity: (Cubic inches): 1,710

Manufacturer/Model: CamelBak/Aventura 22
Price: $$$$
Weight: 37 oz.
Frame Type: internal
Load Type: panel-loading
Fixed capacity: (Cubic inches): 1,159

Manufacturer/Model: Gregory Mountain Products/Jade 33
Price: $$$$
Weight: 42 oz.; 45 oz.
Frame Type: internal
Load Type: panel-loading
Fixed capacity: (Cubic inches): 2,014; 2,136
Sizes available: 2

Manufacturer/Model: GoLite/Quest
Price: $$$$
Weight: 3 lbs. 10 oz.
Frame Type: internal
Load Type: top-loading
Expandable Capacity: (Cubic inches): 3,965
Sizes available: 2

Manufacturer/Model: Boreas Gear/Buttermilks Women's
Price: $$$$$
Weight: 2 lbs. 13 oz.; 2 lbs. 14 oz.; 2 lbs. 14 oz.
Frame Type: internal
Load Type: top-loading
Fixed capacity: (Cubic inches): 2,320; 2,441; 2,441
Sizes available: 3

Manufacturer/Model: Bergans of Norway/Helium Lady 55 L
Price: $$$$$
Weight: 41 oz.
Frame Type: internal

Load Type: hybrid

Fixed capacity: (Cubic inches): 3,350

Manufacturer/Model: Millet/UBIC 30 LD – Women's

Price: $$$$

Weight: 42 oz.

Frame Type: internal

Load Type: top-loading

Fixed Capacity: (Cubic inches): 1,831

Manufacturer/Model: Eagle Creek/ Rincon Vita 75 L

Price: $$$$$$

Weight: 5 lbs. 6 oz.

Frame Type: internal

Load Type: panel-loading

Expandable capacity:(Cubic inches): 3,540-4,740

Manufacturer/Model: ARC'TERYX/ Altra 33 Women's

Price: $$$$$$

Weight: 37 oz.; 39 oz.; 41 oz.

Frame Type: internal

Load Type: top-loading

Expandable Capacity: (Cubic inches): 2,014; 2,136; 2,258

Sizes available: 3

Buyer's Guide to Prepackaged Survival Kits

Pricing key (based on manufacturer's suggested retail price):

$ = under $25
$$ = $26–$50
$$$ = $51–$100
$$$$ = $101–$150
$$$$$ = $151–$200

GENERAL SURVIVAL

Manufacturer/model: Survive Outdoors Longer®/Survival Medic (Adventure Medical Kits –AMK)

Price: $

Weight: 4 oz.

Dimensions: 6" × 5.5" × 1"

Use: Fire, first-aid, shelter, navigation, signaling

Container type: Ultra-light, pocket-sized, waterproof pouch

Contents:
1 - SOL™ Emergency Blanket, 56" × 84"
1 - Fire Lite™ Sparker
4 - Tinder Quik™
1 - Slim Rescue Howler™ Whistle
1 - Compass, Button, Liquid Filled
1 - Duct Tape, 2" × 26"
1 - SOL™ Survival Instructions
2 - Antiseptic Towelettes

1 - Ibuprofen (200mg), Pkg./2
1 - Triple Antibiotic Ointment, 0.5g
1 - Bandage, Adhesive, Fabric, Knuckle
2 - Bandage, Adhesive, Fabric, 1" × 3"
1 - Safety Pin

Manufacturer/model: American Medical Kits (AMK)/Pocket Medic

Price: $

Weight: 3.2 oz.

Dimensions: 5" × 5.25" × 1"

Use: First-aid

Container type: Ultralight, waterproof pouch

Contents:
1 - Dressing, Gauze, Sterile, 2" × 2", Pkg./2
4 - Bandage, Adhesive, Fabric, 1" × 3"
2 - Bandage, Adhesive, Fabric, Knuckle
2 - Bandage, Butterfly Closure
3 - Antiseptic Wipe
1 - Triple Antibiotic Ointment, Single Use
1 - Moleskin, Pre-Cut & Shaped (14 pieces)
2 - Ibuprofen (200 mg), Pkg./2
1 - After Bite® Wipe
1 - Splinter Picker/Tick Remover Forceps
2 - Safety Pins

Manufacturer/model: Guardian Survival Mini, Model: GDSKMK

Price: $

Weight: 2 lbs.

Dimensions: 7" × 6" × 4"

Use: Food, water, light&fire, signaling, shelter

Container type: Small, durable bag with blue carabineer

Contents:
1- 4 oz. Water Pouch
1 - 400 Calorie Cherry Food Bar
1 - 24 Hour Emergency Glow Stick
1 - 5 -in-1 Survival Whistle
1 - Box of Waterproof Matches
1 - Rechargeable Squeeze Flashlight
1 - Emergency Poncho w/ Hood
1 - Emergency Survival Blanket
1 - Full Body Warmer
1 - Multi Function Swiss Army Style Knife
1 - Sewing Kit

Manufacturer/model: Survive Outdoors Longer®/Scout (Adventure Medical Kits –AMK)

Price: $$

Weight: 5.4 oz.

Dimensions: 3.75" × 6" × 1"

Use: Signaling, shelter, fire, navigation

Container type: Small, professional-grade RF-welded, waterproof bag

Contents:

- 1 – Duct Tape, 2" × 50"
- 1 – Compass, Button, Liquid Filled
- 1 - Fire Lite™ Sparker
- 1 - Survival Fishing and Sewing Kit
- 1 - Survive Outdoors Longer Survival Blanket 96" × 60"
- 1 - Mini Rescue Flash™ Signal Mirror
- 1 - Slim Rescue Howler™ Whistle
- 1 - Tinder Quik™

Manufacturer/model: Vigilant Trails/ Survival Kit, Trekker-513

Price: $$

Weight: 12.2 oz.

Dimensions: 5" × 3.5" × 1.5"

Use: Fire, First-Aid, Food, Shelter, Signaling, Water

Container type: crush proof metal

Contents:

- 1 – Vigilant Trails Survival Guide
- 1 – Crush Proof Metal Container (4.75" × 3.38" × 1.5")
- 1 – Nylon Compression Strap with Integrated Emergency Whistle
- 1 – Flint Fire Starter with Steel Scraper
- 8 – Storm, Wind & Water Proof Matches
- 1 – Match Striker
- 1 – Fresnel Magnifier ×3 Power (3" × 2")
- 5 – Fire Starter Tinder Tabs
- 1 – Matchbook (20 Matches)
- 1 – Emergency Space Blanket (84" × 52")
- 1 – Shatter Proof Emergency Signal Mirror with Sighting Hole
- 2 – Liquid Filled Compass (20mm)
- 1 – Airline Tubing (2' × 0.19")
- 5 – Water Purification Tablets
- 2 – Coffee Filter
- 1 – Liter Plastic Bag (re-sealable)
- 1 – Clear Plastic Sheet (42" × 31")
- 1 – Lock back Knife, Single-handed Opening (5" overall length)
- 1 – Stainless Steel Surgical Blade
- 1 – Stainless Steel Needle (3")
- 1 – Pencil (3.5")
- 1 – Olive Drab Paracord (5')
- 4 – Heavy Duty Plastic Zip Ties

- 1 – Heavy Duty #69 Nylon Thread (10')
- 3 – Size 2 Nickel Plated Steel Safety Pins
- 1 – Vitamin A & D Ointment (Petroleum Jelly, 5 gram tube)
- 2 – Antiseptic Povidone-Iodine Pads
- 2 – Alcohol Prep Pads
- 3 – Sterile Strip Bandages (1" × 3")
- 3 – Butterfly Bandages (0.38" × 1.8")
- 1 – Sterile Patch Bandage (2" × 3")
- 1 – P-38 G.I. Can Opener
- 1 – Mini LED Flashlight (water resistant housing, includes 2- CR2016 batteries)
- 1 – Insect Sting Wipe with Lidocaine
- 1 – First Aid Burn Cream
- 3 – Split Rings (10mm)
- 4 – 100% Cotton Balls
- 1 – 24 Gauge Bronze Snare Wire (5')
- 1 – Fishing Kit:
  - 3 – #7 Split Shot Sinkers
  - 3 – Size 10 Gold Treble Hooks
  - 6 – BB Split Shot Sinkers
  - 1 – 50', #6 Fishing Line
  - 3 – Foam Floats / Hook Protectors
  - 3 – Artificial Worms (3")

Manufacturer/model: Survival Resources™/PTSK-24003 Pocket Tin Survival Kit™

Price: $$

Weight: 3.5 oz.

Dimensions: 3 .75" × 2.38" × 0.88" deep

Use: Fire, signaling, navigation, food, water

Container type: Small, sturdy tin container

Contents:

- 1 - Spark-Lite™ Firestarter - Orange
- 6 - Tinder-Quick™ Fire Tabs
- 1 - AMK Mini Rescue-Flash™ Signal Mirror
- 1 - Fox 40® Micro Whistle – Orange
- 1 - 20mm Button Compass
- 1 - 10' Type III, 7 Strand, Parachute Cord
- 1 - Fishing Kit, In Small Vial
- 1 - 50' - 20 lb. Braided Fishing Line
- 1 - 6' Brass Snare Wire
- 1 - Folding Razor Knife

- 1 - Folding Pocket Saw
- 1 - Fresnel Magnifier
- 1 - Duct Tape Flat Pack - 2" × 50" - Blaze Orange
- 7 - Safety Pins - 2 #1 and 3 #00
- 1 - Sewing Needle
- 2 - Waterproof Paper - 2.13" × 2.75"
- 1 - Mini Pencil

Manufacturer/model: Survival Resources™/NPSK-24010 Neck Pouch Survival Kit™

Price: $$

Weight: 2.4 oz.

Dimensions: 5.5" (4.5" inside) × 4" × 0.75"

Use: Fire, signaling, navigation, food

Container type: Small, 5.2 mil. clear, zip-closure pouch, with grommets

Contents:

- 1 - Spark-Lite™ Firestarter – Orange
- 6 - Tinder-Quick™ Fire Tabs
- 1 - AMK Mini Rescue-Flash™ Signal Mirror
- 1 - Fox 40® Micro Whistle – Orange
- 1 - 20mm Button Compass
- 1 - 10' Type III, 7 Strand, Parachute Cord
- 1 - Fishing Kit, In Small Vial
- 1 - 50' - 20 lb. Braided Fishing Line
- 1 - 6' Brass Snare Wire
- 1 - Fresnel Magnifier
- 1 - Duct Tape Flat Pack - 2" × 50" - Blaze Orange
- 7 - Safety Pins - 2 #1 and 3 #00
- 1 - Sewing Needle
- 2 - Waterproof Paper - 2.125" x 2.75"
- 1 - Mini Pencil

Manufacturer/model: Guardian Survival Gear/Model: GDSKGK

Price: $$

Weight: 10 lbs.

Dimensions: 15" × 12" × 6"

Use: Food, water, light/fire, shelter, signaling, first aid

Container type: Multi-pocket backpack

Contents:

- 6 - 400 Calorie Food Bars (2,400 Calories)
- 6 - 4 oz. Water Pouches

10 - Water Purification Tablets - each tablet purifies 1 liter of water
1 - AM/FM Radio with Batteries and Headphones
1 - Rechargeable Squeeze Flashlight - 3 LED flashlight
1 - 5-in-1 Survival Whistle
1 - Box of Waterproof Matches
1 - Emergency Survival Blanket
1 - Emergency Poncho with Hood
1 - N95 Respirator Dust Mask - NIOSH approved
3 - Pocket Tissues packets
3 - Wet Naps
1 - 37 Piece First Aid Kit
1 - Deck of Playing Cards

Manufacturer/model: Survive Outdoors Longer®/Hybrid 3 Kit (Adventure Medical Kits –AMK)
Price: $$$
Weight: 20 oz.
Dimensions: 7" × 6" × 2.5"
Use: First aid, fire, signaling, shelter
Container type: Ultra-light, nylon bag with detachable pouch
Contents:
4 - Bandage, Adhesive, Fabric, 1" × 3"
2 - Bandage, Adhesive, Fabric, Knuckle
4 - Bandage, Butterfly Closure
1 - Bandage, Conforming Gauze, 2"
2 - Dressing, Gauze, Sterile, 4" × 4", Pkg. / 2
2 - Dressing, Gauze, Sterile, 2" × 2", Pkg./2
2 - Dressing, Gauze, Sterile, 3" × 3", Pkg./2
2 - Dressing, Non-Adherent, Sterile, 3" × 4"
1 - Gloves, Nitrile (Pair) with Hand Wipe
1 - Moleskin, Pre-Cut & Shaped (14 pieces)
1 - Duct Tape, 2" × 50"
3 - Cable Ties, 4"
3 - Cable Ties, 8"
1 - EMT Shears, 4"
1 - Splinter Picker/Tick Remover
5 - Safety Pins
2 - After Bite Wipe

2 - Antihistamine (Diphenhydramine 25 mg)
4 - Ibuprofen (200 mg), Pkg./2
1 - Detachable Bag, Pocket Size, Nylon
2 - Aluminum Foil, Heavy Duty, 3 Sq. Ft.
1 - Compass, Button, Liquid Filled
1 - Fire Lite™ Sparker
1 - Headlamp, 2 Watt LED w/ headband - 25 Hour
1 - SOL Survival Blanket 96" × 60"
1 - Mini Rescue Flash™ Signal Mirror
1 - Slim Rescue Howler™ Whistle
4 - Nylon Cord, #18, Braided, (10' 100 lb. test)
4 - Tinder Quik™
3 - Antiseptic Wipes
1 - Povidone Iodine, 0.75 oz.
1 - Tape, 0.5" × 10 Yards
1 - Skin Tac Adhesive Wipes
2 - Triple Antibiotic Ointment, Single Use

Manufacturer/model: Survival Resources™/the SKP-24007 Survival Kit Pouch™
Price: $$$$
Weight: 1 lb., 6 oz.
Dimensions: 7" × 6" × 2.25"
Use: Fire, shelter, navigation, signaling, food
Container type: Weather/water proof, clear, re-sealable pouch
Contents:
1 - Mini-Match™ Firestarter
1 - Spark-Lite™ Firestarter – Orange
8 - Tinder-Quick™ Fire Tabs
1 - AMK Rescue-Flash™ Signal Mirror
1 - Fox 40® Micro Whistle – Orange
1 - Suunto Partner A-10 Baseplate Compass
1 - AMK 2 Person Heat Sheet
1 - Emergency Poncho
1 - Emergency Sunglasses
1 - Head-Net
1 - Survival Bandana
1 - 25' Type III, 7 Strand, Parachute Cord
1 - Fishing Kit, Emergency, Small
1 - 20' Brass Snare Wire
1 - Gerber LST Lock-Blade Knife

1 - Commando Wire Saw
1 - Folding Pocket Saw
1 - Emergency Survival Pocket Guide
1 - Fresnel Magnifier
1 - Duct Tape Flat Pack - 2" × 50" - Blaze Orange
1 - Waterproof Mini Notebook
1 - 4 Square Feet Aluminum Foil
1 - Vial with Sewing Needles & Sewing Awl
1 - Bobbin of Heavy Duty Sewing Thread
7 - Safety Pins - 3 #1 and 4 #00
1 - Golf Pencil

BUG-OUT KIT

Manufacturer/model: Survivalkit.com/ Ultimate Bug Out Kit with Premium Bag
Price: $$$$$
Weight: 42 lbs.
Dimensions: 20" × 11" × 7"
Use: Water, food, first aid, hygiene kit, shelter, fire
Container type: Durable backpack with 6 external pockets & laptop compartment
Contents:
6 - Boxes of Aqua Blox Water Boxes
6 - 400 Calorie Food Bars - total of 2,400 Calories
10 - Water Purification Tablets - each tablet purifies 1 liter of water
1 - Dynamo 4-in-1 Flashlight, contains a Flashlight, Radio, Siren and a Charger
1 - 30 Hour Emergency Candle
1 - 12 Hour Green Emergency Glow Stick
1 - Box of Waterproof Matches
1 - Emergency Survival Sleeping Bag
1 - 20 Hour Body Warmer
1 - Orange Poncho with Hood
1 - N95 NIOSH Dust Mask
1 - Roll of Duct Tape
1 - 50' of Nylon Rope
1 - 16 Function Swiss Army Style Knife
1 - 6' × 8' Blue Tarp
1 - Waste Bag

Pricing key (based on manufacturer's suggested retail price):

$ = under $25
$$ = $26–$50
$$$ = $51–$100
$$$$ = $101–$150
$$$$$ = $151–$200

1 - Multi-Function Shovel that comes with a nail puller, hatchet edge, saw edge, hammer, wrench with 3 different sizes, a bottle opener, a water filled compass, a waterproof container. Inside the waterproof container you will find a box of matches, 2 nails, a sharp razor blade, fishing line, bobbers, and hooks

3 - Pocket Tissue Packs
1 - 57 Piece Deluxe First Aid Kit
1 - Deck of Playing Cards
1 - NotePad for taking notes
1 - Pencil
1 - 24 Piece Deluxe Hygiene Kit

FIRE-MAKING KITS

Manufacturer/model: Vigilant Trails/ Survival Fire Kit, Model: Firebug-713
Price: $
Weight: 9.2 oz.
Dimensions: 4.75" × 1.75"
Use: Fire
Container type: Screw top, crush resistant, metal
Contents:

1 – Vigilant Trails Survival Fire Guide
1 – Crush Proof Metal Container (4.75" × 1.75")
1 – Parabolic Solar Fire Starter
1 – 100% Cotton Muslin Draw String Bag (4" × 6")
10 – Storm, Wind & Water Proof Matches
1 – Match Striker
1 – Fresnel Magnifier ×4 Power (3" × 2")
8 – Fire Starter Tinder Tabs
2 – Matchbook (20 Matches)

1 – Flint Fire Starter w/ Steel Scraper
1 – Flint and Magnesium Fire Starter w/Steel Scraper
1 – Petroleum Jelly
8 – 100% Cotton Balls
5 – Burlap Tinder Pads
2 – Emergency Candles
1 – Paracord (6')

FISHING KITS

Manufacturer/model: Vigilant Trails/ Pocket/Survival Fishing Kit
Price: $
Weight: 1 lb.
Dimensions: Kit comes in a 4 mil. thick bag
Use: Fishing kit
Container type: Heavy duty reusable, resealable plastic bag
Contents:

1 - VIGILANT TRAILS Fishing Guide
1 - Heavy Duty Re-usable and Re-sealable Plastic Bag (4 mil thick)
1 - VIGILANT TRAILS Large Hand Line Winder (red or blue)
1 - 8 lb., Clear Monofilament Fishing Line (150')
1 - Lockback Knife (5" overall, colors will vary)
3 - Artificial Worms (3")
1 - Crawfish Lure (1.5")
1 - Flat Tail Finesse Worm (4")
1 - Ring Grub (2.5")
1 - Curly Tail Football Grub (1.5")
1 - Snap-on Cigar Fishing Float (1.5")
2 - Nylon Coated Wire Leaders (9" and 11.5")
2 - Egg Sinkers (0.5 oz.)
1 - Mustad Treble Hook (size 6)
1 - Eagle Claw Gold Treble Hook (size 10)
2 - Barrel Swivels (size 7)
2 - Eagle Claw Split Shot Sinkers (size 7)
4 - Eagle Claw BB Split Shot Sinkers
10 - Eagle Claw Single Shank Hooks (sizes 3–12, one of each)

FIRST AID KITS

Manufacturer/model: Vigilant Trails/ First Aid Kit—Outdoor Sports Edition
Price: $
Weight: 7.4 oz.
Dimensions: 5" × 3.5" × 1 ⅞"
Use: First Aid
Container type: Small, crush-proof, plastic container
Contents:

1 – Plastic Container (3.5" × 4.75" × 1.75")
1 – Vigilant Trails First Aid Guide
1 – Stainless Steel Tweezers (3.5")
1 – Stainless Steel Wire Scissors (4")
4 – Stainless Steel Safety Pin (1.5")
1 – Stainless Steel Surgical Blade
1 – Adhesive Tape (0.5" × 2.5 yards)
1 – BugX Insect Repellent Towelette
1 – IvyX Post Contact Cleanser Towelette
1 – Sun X SPF 30+ Sunscreen Towelette
4 – Insect Sting Wipe with Lidocaine
4 – Water Jel First Aid Burn Cream
1 – Moleskin (2" × 3")
10 – Cotton Swabs (3")
4 – Aspirin (325mg, 2-pk)
3 – Diphen Antihistamine (25mg HCI)
3 – Diotame Bismuth Subsalicylate (2-pk, chewable)
2 – Electrolyte Replacement (2-pk)
1 – Vitamin A & D Ointment (Petroleum Jelly)
8 – Adhesive Fabric Bandages (1" × 3")
5 – Adhesive Butterfly Bandages (0.38" × 1.75")
2 – Adhesive Knuckle Bandages (1.5" × 3")
2 – Adhesive Patch Bandages (2" × 3")
2 – Antiseptic Povidone-Iodine Pads
2 – Isopropyl Alcohol Prep Pads (70%)
2 – BZK Cleansing Towelette (5.5" × 8", BZK 1:750)
4 – Gauze Pads (2" × 2"), 12 ply
2 – Hydrocortisone Cream 1%
2 – Triple Antibiotic Cream

PET FIRST AID

Manufacturer/model: Vigilant Trails/ Pet First Aid Kit, Including: Venom Extraction Pump

Price: $$

Weight: 2 lbs.

Dimensions: 5.5" × 6.5" × 2.5"

Use: Pet First Aid, venom kit, signaling

Container type: Small, crush and dust proof, plastic container with rubber gasket

Contents:

1 – Vigilant Trails Pet First Aid Guide
1 – Crush, Dust Proof Plastic Container w/Rubber Gasket
2 – Blue Nitrile Examination Gloves
1 – Stainless Steel Tweezers (3.5")
1 – Stainless Steel Wire Scissors (4")
4 – Stainless Steel Safety Pins (size 2)
1 – Aluminum Whistle
8 – Cotton Tipped Applicators (3")
4 – Cotton Balls
1 – Adhesive Tape (0.5" × 2.5 yards)
1 – Elastic Bandage w/metal clips, 100% latex free (2" × 5 yards)
1 – Roll Gauze, Highly Absorbent, Sterile (2" × 4 yards)
1 – Self Adherent Elastic Wrap, won't stick to fur (1" × 5 yards, colors vary)
2 – Paw Tip Adhesive Knuckle Bandages (1.5" × 3")
2 – Large Patch Bandages (2" × 3")
4 – Gauze Pads, 12 ply (2" × 2")
1 – 5cc/ml Syringe without needle
4 – BZK Cleansing Towellets
4 – Isopropyl Alcohol 70% Prep Pads
4 – Antiseptic Povidone Iodine Prep Pads
4 – Junior Tongue Depressors (5.5")
4 – Diphen Antihistamine (25mg HCl, 2-pk)
4 – Water Jel First Aid Burn Cream
4 – Insect Sting Wipes with Lidocaine
2 - Vitamin A & D Ointment (Petroleum Jelly)
1 – Snake Bite / Venom Kit
1 – Certi-suction Venom Extraction Pump w/Adapter
1 – Safety Razor
1 – Antiseptic Povidone-Iodine Pads
1 – BZK Cleansing Towelette
1 – Diphen Antihistamine (25mg HCl, 2-pk)
1 – Insect Sting Wipe w/Lidocaine
1 – Stainless Steel Surgical Blade

Choose the Best
Bug-Out
Vehicle

BY CREEK STEWART

The term "Bugging Out" refers to the decision to abandon your home due to an unexpected emergency situation, whether a natural disaster or one caused by man. The thought of having to evacuate your home due to a sudden and imminent threat is not at all unrealistic. The reality is that sudden and uncontrollable events of nature and man do happen.

Whether you live in a high-rise loft in New York City or in the cornfields of Indiana, there is undisputable evidence that a disaster may one day force you to evacuate your home. As I always say, "It's not IF but WHEN." It happens to tens of thousands of people every year all over the world. Many do not make it out of the disaster zone in time and suffer incredible loss, including death. "Not making it" is due to either bad planning or bad luck and you can't control luck. Although, I argue that the study of survival skills helps to "make your own luck." The what ifs in life are someone else's reality and your turn could be next. Just having a Bug-Out Bag is not sufficient. All of the guns, bullets, food storage, survival skills, and seeds in the world will be of no use if you can't escape the disaster to begin with. If your Bug Out Plan does not include a Bug Out Vehicle of some kind, then it is incomplete and, quite frankly, reckless.

Arguably, the most important aspect of surviving a sudden large-scale disaster is the ability to quickly, effectively, and

safely get away from it. Only in the movies do people outrun a disaster on foot. In the real world, your best option is to "out-wit" and "out-smart" a disaster by using every tool at your disposal, which includes a Bug-Out Vehicle (BOV), a vehicle equipped to quickly transport you to safety.

A BOV's primary function is to get you, your loved ones, and your supplies from ground zero to your Bug-Out Location (BOL). It is a means to an end, not the end itself. I don't view a BOV as a long-term survival location. It is not a BOL. Some people view a BOV as the means of escape and also the final destination—a mobile BOL if you will. Are they right? Yes. Am I right? Yes. How? It's okay to have different opinions about a BOV. This article is my opinion. We can all learn from each other. My BOV's single purpose is to get me and my stuff from point A to point B.

Choosing a BOV is not an easy decision and should not be taken lightly. It is one of your most important survival tools. Any survival tool that your life depends on should be given thoughtful consideration. At the end of the day, BOV selection is driven by lifestyle.

Choosing the perfect BOV for your lifestyle involves many different factors including some that aren't so exciting. Just as you would never choose a spouse based on looks alone, don't fall in love with a BOV's appearance. Oftentimes, "cool" isn't

practical. Is it possible? Absolutely. But it's certainly not guaranteed and is actually so unimportant that it doesn't even make my list of deciding factors. When it comes to a BOV, function always trumps the cool factor.

As a guy, I certainly struggle with this. I want a cool-looking BOV just as much as the next guy but I'm smart enough to understand that "cool" means zilch when

it comes to life-saving benefits. After you get past the initial disappointment that you can't make a BOV decision based on looks alone, what follows are your core deciding factors.

WHAT CAN YOU AFFORD?

Yes, this first section is all about the Benjamins. A handful of companies design and manufacture vehicles I consider to be "dream" BOVs. Some of these are tailored specifically to the military and security industries. Others are targeted to outdoor adventure and off-road enthusiasts. All of them are expensive. Because of the price tag, high-end BOVs have an exclusive clientele. Take the UNICAT for example. At over half a million dollars, it is one of the most expensive and feature-rich BOVs on the planet. Its list of capabilities is stag-

▲ Too much gear for this BOV

gering. Would I like to have it? Heck yeah. Can I afford it? Heck no.

The reality is that for most of us, budget is the number one deciding factor that affects our BOVs. It will control much of the decision-making process as you work within the confines of what you can afford. However, a little creativity can make a small budget go a long way. In my book, *Build the Perfect Bug Out Vehicle*, I discuss several ways to add great features on a tight budget.

The good news is that if you can afford just one mode of transportation then you can afford a BOV. You don't necessarily need to purchase a separate vehicle that is solely dedicated to Bugging Out. The term *Everyday Driver* refers to a vehicle that you drive every day. Yes, your everyday driver can also be your BOV.

Having a BOV that is also your Everyday Driver does have certain advantages. First, if you drive it every day then you know that vehicle more intimately than

you know a vehicle you drive only on occasion. This means you already know how it handles in rain, snow, mud, ice and other conditions that you experience on a regular basis. You've used the drive-thru at the bank enough times to know what kind of clearances you need without having to get out and check. You are familiar with the vehicle's sounds and know its quirks and limitations. You have a working relationship with your Everyday Driver that will always be more intimate than with a vehicle you use much less frequently. You also know the vehicle is in good working order.

For a long time, I had a 1972 Ford Bronco dedicated as my BOV. I rarely drove it and I can't tell you how many times the battery was dead when I tried to start it. This is a classic example of how an awesome dedicated BOV can end up being worthless in a time of immediate need. Dedicated BOVs absolutely require routine attention and maintenance.

WHERE DO YOU LIVE?

Where you live weighs in heavily on your BOV decision. It's not practical for someone in Manhattan who has limited space and no parking to buy a large SUV. If a large-scale disaster strikes Manhattan, do you really think everyone is going to be able to drive out anyway? They'd have better luck catching a seat on a flying pig. This is true for all large cities. An urbanite's best BOV option may be a pedal-powered cargo bike. It can fit in an apartment, can carry a Bug-Out Bag and a few other necessities (like Fido) and can weave in and out of jam-packed traffic lines that plug limited exit routes. On the other hand, someone living in a more rural area doesn't have the same set of limitations and would definitely be better served with a four-wheel drive vehicle of his or her choice.

Similarly, weather in northern Minnesota poses an entirely different set of concerns than the weather in south Florida. This may seem like common sense, but one of the worst decisions I've ever made was when I bought a two-wheel drive truck in Indiana. That thing would get stuck on wet pavement. A new two-wheel drive was the same price as a used four-wheel drive, and I let form trump function. Rookie mistake.

WHO'S RIDING WITH YOU?

Who you live with affects your BOV options. Not only must your BOV safely fit the people and animals you intend to save, but it must also accommodate their Bug-Out Bags and any additional supplies you intend to pack, such as strollers, wagons, fuel, water, wheelchair(s), etc. Yes, a large SUV will fit six people. But will it fit six people, a child seat, a golden retriever, five Bug Out Bags, a stroller, and a cooler of food? I don't know. Even if the answer is no, the vehicle might still work. Additional exterior storage might be necessary. Sometimes it's the simple oversights that have the worst consequences. Preplanning is critical.

WHERE ARE YOU GOING?

I believe that no Bug-Out Plan is complete without a predetermined survival destination—your Bug-Out Location (BOL). The details of this location may affect the type of BOV you should choose. I know a guy whose Bug-Out Location is on an island in the ocean. He actually has two BOVs. One is a truck to get him to the dock. The other is a sailboat to get him to the island. Obviously, his BOL dictates his BOV. I also have a friend whose BOL is at the end of a fourteen mile road (road in an exaggeration) near the top of a mountain that is only passable with a four-wheel drive vehicle. His vehicle must have four-wheel drive. A BOL that's one thousand miles away (not recommended) may require a more fuel-efficient vehicle than one that is two hundred miles away. Does your BOL limit the kind of BOV you can choose?

THREE PACKING STRATEGIES

Before you consider a variety of products, tools, and supplies to include in your BOV, you need to start defining what kind of BOV packer you are. There are three strategies to consider and none of them are wrong. It will help if you decide early on in the process which one you are most comfortable with.

Build Strategy 1: BOB Heavy

This category is for those of you who feel you have pretty much everything you need for a 72-hour Bug Out packed in your Bug-Out Bag. You do not see a need to pack more survival tools, food, water or supplies in your Bug-Out Vehicle. After all, that's what a Bug-Out Bag is for, right? A BOV is simply a mode of transportation from Point A to Point B, nothing more and nothing less.

Build Strategy 2: BOV Heavy

This category is for those of you who see a Bug-Out Vehicle as another LAYER of security and choose to pack redundant survival tools, food, water and supplies inside even though you already have those items packed into your Bug-Out Bag. You have decided to reserve your Bug-Out Bag as a last ditch effort and don't want to break into it until you are officially on foot. In essence, you look at your BOV as another really big Bug-Out Bag. You plan on using the resources in your BOV first – before you open your BOB. Note: This is the category that I fall into.

Build Strategy 3: BOB/BOV Hybrid

Most people will find themselves most comfortable with this strategy. For some reason or other (maybe time or budget) you don't want to pack a bunch of redundant items in your BOV that you already have in your BOB. You may decide to pack some redundant items but certainly not everything. Your BOV isn't an entirely independent second layer, but rather a great spot to pack EXTRA stuff that you couldn't fit into your BOB; like more water, a bigger shelter and some extra clothes. You have no problem with using items out of your Bug-Out Bag while traveling in your Bug-Out Vehicle.

Your lifestyle will help you choose a general type of vehicle to use for bugging out. You need a vehicle you can afford, works with your environment, accommodates your full load (of people and supplies), and gets you where you need to go.

But lifestyle details aren't the only factors to consider when choosing a BOV. The attributes of the BOV itself are equally important. Two people can choose the same type of BOV, but outfit them to perform very differently. The devil is in the details.

Find detailed Bug-Out Vehicle outfitting and packing instructions in *Build the Perfect Bug Out Vehicle* by Creek Stewart, available at store.livingreadyonline.com.

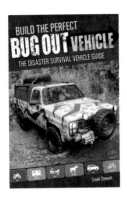

The Back-Up Bike

BY JACKIE MUSSER

It's easy to imagine a scenario when traveling by bicycle would be more advantageous than traveling by car—fuel shortages, road closures and traffic jams, just to name a few. A back-up bike can help you quickly and safely get from point A to point B. Like all survival gear, a back-up bike needs to be packed and prepared at all times so it's ready for use at a moment's notice. This guide will help you select and equip a bike strong enough to get you through an emergency.

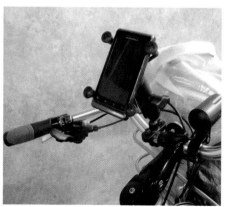

COMMUNICATIONS AND NAVIGATION

Smartphone Handlebar Mount Even if the grid is down, it's still a great idea to carry a cell phone. You may make it to an area with cell service, in which case you can use your smartphone for navigation, communications and information. This cell phone mount is from Ram Mounts (rammount.com).

2-Way Radio or Handheld CB Radio This is an excellent backup that will work even if the grid is down. This set is from midlandusa.com.

GO THE DISTANCE

Whether you are using your back-up bike in an evacuation or as temporary transportation during a public transit shut down or fuel shortage, you need a bike that can cover a lot of ground in a short amount of time.

Kelly Sullivan, owner of Bishop's Bicycles in Milford, Ohio, recommends the Allegro X Sport by Jamis Bicycles (jamisbikes.com). "It's an awesome bike for the person who needs solid transportation under unknown conditions," he says.

What makes it so awesome? The wheels are 700c, the same wheel diameter as a road bike, and bigger wheels mean more speed. The double-wall rims will support the extra weight of your gear, and the disc brakes give you the extra stopping power you need when carrying a heavy load. It has a front shock in case you need to hop a curb or go off road. You can add a rack system to the back to hold your gear, and it sets the rider upright.

"By sitting up a little higher, you have a really good sightline of your surroundings—traffic, pedestrians, potholes," says Sullivan.

Mountain bikes seem like a rugged, logical choice for a back-up bike, but if you plan to travel on roads you may want to think again. "A mountain bike tire has a lug pattern that makes it great for riding off-road in the dirt, but makes it cumbersome

to ride on the pavement," Sullivan says. If you need to cover a lot of ground fast, he recommends finding a bike that performs well on pavement but has some off-road capabilities as well. "You want a quality bike that is dependable that you can pedal for who knows how many days and how far," he adds.

CARRY THE LOAD

If you're looking to carry a lot of extra gear or even another person (or two), you may want to consider a cargo bike. This is the approach survival expert Creek Stewart, author of *Build the Perfect Bug Out Bag*, has taken with his back-up bike.

"I wanted a bike that could handle more cargo than just my bug-out bag," Stewart says. "I wanted the option to pack extra water, survival tools and even food. Traditional bikes just are not designed for this. I tried but was never happy with the results."

Stewart has outfitted a Mundo by Yuba Bicycles, (yubabikes.com), as his back-up bike. With the front cargo basket, integrated rear rack, and side-loaders, there's plenty of room for survival equipment. You can also customize the bike and add an additional adult passenger seat or up to two child seats.

The Mundo's large stainless steel cargo frame is designed to balance and distribute large amounts of weight. Though the

bike alone weighs in at nearly 50 pounds, Stewart says he has easily peddled the bike with an additional 300 pounds of weight on it. The bike has 21 speeds making it easier to shift gears and haul big loads.

Stewart's favorite part about the bike is that the frame is electric conversion ready, and Yuba sells an electric motor that can be installed on it. "For those worried about hauling the extra cargo, the electric motor option takes the work out of hills and long treks," Stewart says.

KEEP IT ROADWORTHY

Your back-up bike needs to be ready at a moment's notice, so regular maintenance is a must. And when you are riding in unknown conditions or for an unknown length of time you need to be prepared for any potential problems. Sullivan says there are three things all cyclists should do

STORAGE

Durable Storage Panniers Waterproof panniers offer even more protection for your gear. There's a wide price range for panniers. For the budget-conscious, Sullivan recommends panniers by Axiom Performance Gear (axiomgear.com). For high-end panniers, he recommends Arkel brand (arkel-od.com). The panniers pictured are from Yuba Bicycles (yubabikes.com).

Bug-Out Bag This bag is strapped to the cargo area using straps from looprope.com. Your bug-out bag will include most of the supplies you need for your journey.

WATER

Photo 1. Bulk water storage Take advantage of your bike's extra-hauling capabilities and carry extra water with you. A six-gallon water tote is stored in one of the cargo panniers.

Photo 2. Water bottle with frame mounted storage This set is from Klean Kanteen (kleankanteen.com). The bottle is all metal so it can be used to boil water should the need arise.

SHELTER

Tent and Ground Pad Strapped to cargo area (if this isn't already in your bug-out bag): Straps used are from looprope.com.

CLOTHING

Photo 3. Extra clothing in dry bag This bag is a SealLine brand waterproof dry bag.

FOOD

Case of MREs Again, take advantage of the extra space and stow extra food in the cargo panniers. Find MREs on MRE-meals.net.

TOOLS

Bicycle Tire Pump

Photos 4 and 5. Front-mounted headlamp The headlamp pictured is the Defender Bike Light from Gotham Bicycle Defense Industries (bikegotham.com). It's specifically designed to be theft resistant. "The technology and quality of lights have come up and the new technology has brought the price down," Sullivan says. He recommends the urban 550 headlight and VIS 180 taillight, both from Light and Motion (lightandmotion.com). Both use a lithium-ion cell battery than can be charged using a USB cable or solar attachment.

Photo 6. Survival Knife and Sheath Strapped to frame for easy access. This knife and sheath is from hedgehogleatherworks.com.

Photo 7. Paracord Have 100-feet wrapped around frame for easy storage.

Photo 8. SLIME Tire Sealant Tire-Patch Kit and Universal Bicycle Multi-Tool in an easy-access under-the-seat storage case.

Photo 9. Machete Strapped to Bike Frame Most useful for clearing debris from your path, but can also be used for self-defense, and looks intimidating. This is a Smith & Wesson Guide Master Machete.

Photo 10. Camouflaged-colored tarp

Photo 11. Bolt Cutters This handy tool will let you navigate through fences or gates.

Photo 12. 4' × 12' Seine Net This is a multifunctional piece of gear that can be used as a hammock, a seine for gathering fish and a makeshift ghillie tarp if you add leaves, sticks and grasses to it.

Photo 13. Crovel Survival Shovel This multipurpose tool is great for digging, chopping, hammering, prying and even self-defense. It's available from gearup-center.com.

Photo 14. Take-Down Recurve Bow With 3 three-piece take-down arrows stored in pannier storage bags. Perfect for hunting. You don't have to worry about running out of ammo, and the silent arrows won't draw unwanted attention.

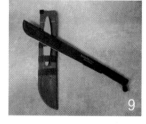

DEFENSE

Photo 1. Self-Defense Pepper Spray With Wall Mount Hub, the pepper spray pictured is the Tornado 5-in-1 (gettornado.com), and includes a built-in alarm and strobe light.

Photo 2. Ram Hand Gun Holster Handlebar Mount Available from rammount.com.

Photo 3. Glock 19 With extra magazines and ammo.

Photo 4. Cable bike lock

7 QUESTIONS TO ASK WHEN PURCHASING A BACK-UP BIKE

1. WHAT IS THE WHEEL SIZE?
Mountain bikes typically have 26-inch wheelbases. Wheelbases on road bikes are larger (approximately 29 inches) and follow a French sizing system. In this system, the standard road bike wheelbase is 700c. Bigger wheels make it easier for the bike to roll, and you'll cover more ground faster.

2. WHAT TYPE OF RIMS ARE ON THE BIKE?
Bicycle rims can be single wall, double wall or triple wall. Sullivan recommends at least double wall rims on a bug-out bike to support the added weight you will carry.

3. IS THE BIKE CAPABLE OF TAKING ON A RACK TO HOLD YOUR GEAR?
You need a place to strap on your Bug-Out Bag and/or to add panniers or a saddlebag.

4. WHAT IS THE BRAKESET ON THE BIKE?
A bug-out bike needs strong braking ability because of the additional weight. Sullivan recommends disc brakes. Keep in mind that mechanical disc brakes are easier to repair on the fly than hydraulic disc brakes.

5. WHAT IS THE TOTAL WEIGHT OF THE BIKE BEFORE ADDING ANY GEAR?
The heavier the bike, the harder you'll have to pedal.

6. IS THE GEAR RATIO COMPATIBLE WITH THE CYCLIST?
You need to find a gear ratio in which it's easy for you to pedal while your bike is fully loaded.

7. IS THE BIKE THE RIGHT FIT FOR THE CYCLIST?
"The fit is key," says Sullivan. "You want to go into the shop and ride it."

to keep their bikes on the road and avoid potential maintenance issues:

1. Do a pre-ride safety check every time you use the bike. Check the air pressure in the tires, check the brakes and make sure the chain is lubed. "When you take time to look over your bike, that ensures you're going to have a maintenance-free ride," Sullivan says.

2. Carry a saddle or seat bag that contains a spare inner tube, a tire pump, two tire levers and a small tool kit. "This kit allows you to be self-sufficient," Sullivan says. If you pull a trailer behind your bike include a spare inner tube for the trailer tires as well.

3. Know how to fix a flat tire on your bike. As with all skills, practice makes perfect. Bishop's Bicycles offers tire repair clinics at its store in Milford. Check with independent bicycle shops in your area to see if these types of classes are available near you.

Whatever style back-up bike you choose, be sure it's the right fit for you and that you can easily pedal (or at least push it) for long periods of time. Practice riding with the bike fully loaded so you have a realistic understanding of the bike's (and your own) capabilities. Trial runs will help you determine how to pack the bike for optimal balance and weight distribution.

Jackie Musser is the Senior Content Producer for Living Ready.

CHAPTER TWO

Emergency Shelter, Fire and Clothing

The rule of threes is an important survival concept. The first of these rules is: You can survive for three hours without adequate shelter. Three hours—that's all it takes for hypothermia to kill you. And the threat of hypothermia isn't limited to winter weather and cold climates. In wet, windy conditions hypothermia can set in at temperatures as high as 50 degrees F.

This chapter details heating options for sheltering at home without power. It also covers sheltering options for a bug-out situation, including how to dress for survival, and how to select tents, sleeping bags and sleeping pads for bug-out travel.

We also cover emergency fire starting supplies. Fire is one of the most primitive survival tools, but it remains one of the most valuable. Fire has so many survival functions—cooking, signaling, light, drying clothes, making tools, to name a few—that it could be placed in nearly any chapter of this guide. We've chosen to include it in the shelter chapter because fire is one of the greatest tools you can use to prevent hypothermia.

Sheltering in without Power
in the Winter and Summer

BY JAMES D. NOWKA

Power outages are common, and as recent disasters have proven, they can last weeks. Having the right gear can mean the difference from between minor inconvenience and major catastrophe for your family and your home.

STAYING WARM IN WINTER

Preparing for and getting through a stay-in-place, cold weather emergency should start with recognition that gas and electrical hook-ups haven't been around forever. People throughout history made it through the worst weather that nature could bring. Those of us living today can do the same, but we could better do so by envisioning the misery of having to get through unprepared. Listen to the gut and get the right backups in place.

The furnace is a wonderful and often reliable appliance, but it's nonetheless one that's far too often taken for granted. Those who live in climates that experience below-freezing temperatures for nearly half of the calendar year might re-assess the wisdom of relying on a single tool to provide for adequate warmth and safety. It might not be a matter of disaster. Machines fall into disrepair. The one major snowstorm that knocks out the substation could just as quickly remind families of the need for a back-up plan.

Better yet, those folks should take initiative and consider their options before any winter event cuts off their gas or electricity. A boxer wouldn't require a punch to the face to know the wisdom of putting up some guard. Many of the provisions families could take to keep the family safe in such circumstances make good sense and for reasons well beyond the scope of preparedness. Winter can be a drain on the wallet. It's less so for homes that are properly put together to account for the cold.

Assuring the home has a good degree of insulation would keep the heat inside and the cold beyond its walls. Every degree of heat within would be important should a family lose its furnace at a time of need. It's a project that stands to save a family some significant money through even the calmest of winters. The furnace doesn't have to work as hard if the house isn't so quickly giving up all the warmth the furnace produces.

If you are totally without power in you home during winter, these devices can help provide heat.

Fireplace

It's a shame that fireplaces are less often included in newly built homes. They provide a great source of heat and a cozy gathering point for the family. A fireplace certainly could become an option for some of those living in homes without. Many, though, might find themselves limited by finances or the lack of any good wall place that could accommodate one.

Wood or Pellet Stoves

Wood stoves would also take some effort and investment, but they are often far more feasible than the traditional fireplace. They're functional. It's a matter of warmth before décor. A stove would certainly provide a great deal of warmth to a home, whether during an outage or otherwise.

Many people have invested in the more modern pellet stoves. They burn compressed wood. They do so efficiently and without a lot of mess or effort. Models are available that would open the option to those with even the smallest of homes.

You could purchase a window-mount model that's no different size-wise than the room air conditioners so many have. They're options that would take some spending on the front end, but they would also come to save the family some money in the long run. When used regularly, traditional wood stoves and pellet stoves of any type would take some of the heating burden off of the furnace.

Buddy Heaters

Those who aren't in the right place to make a big initial investment in a good secondary heat source could still assemble smaller and less pricey options to provide a little warmth should Mother Nature put the family in a tough spot. Buddy heaters, which operate on propane, are safe for indoor use in an emergency and would give the family the ability to warm up a room. They typically sell for about $100. Smaller models run less. The bigger models with all the bells and whistles would cost more.

Aladdin Lamps

An Aladdin lamps is a tool that goes back more than a century. It played a big role in American life in the era just before electrical power became commonplace in the average home.

The technology might be antiquated when viewed against all our modern wonders, but there's little better to have in the home when electricity fails and a family is stuck with the capabilities that their ancestors had 100 years back. It's a great light source. An Aladdin lamp would provide 60 watts of light. It's enough for you to see your way around. They provide some good reading light.

For preppers, it offers much more. One Aladdin lamp provides 2,200 BTUs of heat. It's enough warmth to take the chill off of a 10-by-10 room.

Aladdin lamps are still manufactured and out there in the marketplace. You might also keep watch at flea markets, garage sales or second-hand stores. The antique versions are bound to look nicer and would likely come at a lesser expense. The lamp that's a century old will still work and offer the same level of function as the new model just unpacked from its box. Any family would be wise to have several around the home to account for light and a means to pick up the temperature.

Sunlight

The sun is a tremendous source of heat. If you're without a main source of heat, opening up the shades in a room when the sun is full on would allow the sun to provide some warmth. It's often enough to raise the home's temperature by a few degrees for as long as the light persists. Closed the blinds after the sun has past to provide more insulation against the window glass.

Those left in the cold, whether prepared or not, shouldn't panic regardless of how bitter the outdoor temperatures have become. The home might lose some comfort, but it would remain a viable refuge from however cold it is outdoors. Those without the right tools would have a tougher time, but it would take some time before survival becomes an issue.

Bundle Up Indoors

Get out your long underwear and dress in lots of layers. Keep your coat on and wrap in blankets. You may not always be comfortable, but you will certainly survive.

Be Safe

Even if you are struggling through the cold, keep some basic safety considerations in mind. Charcoal is certainly a tremendous and inexpensive heat source

common to most households, though it's never to be burned inside the home. The risk of carbon monoxide poisoning would put the family at far greater risk than would any temperature regardless of how uncomfortable anyone is becoming. Those completely helpless to temperature would die in three hours. Carbon monoxide poisoning could kill within minutes. Generators are never to be used inside the home and for the very same reason.

If you don't have a back-up heat source, you would want to take the steps necessary to assure the pipes don't burst. Should cold persist, you would want to shut down the water and then drain off what's left inside. It would often take a couple of weeks of pretty miserable temperatures to reach that point.

STAYING COOL IN THE SUMMER

Good shelter, as it pertains to heat concerns, can get a bit trickier when viewed from a disaster situation. You could hope a disaster wouldn't happen in conjunction with temperatures of 100 degrees or more. Preppers, however, don't rely on hope. You might not be able to avoid the heat. You could all the same maintain health and safety.

You could then rely on a variety of methods beyond those that require electricity to keep the family safe. Again, people didn't always have those tools to rely upon. Our forefathers made it through the hottest, most miserable of days. So can those of us living today.

Keep the Sun Out

Simple science provides some possibilities. Just as it's wise to open the shades for the sun's warmth in winter's cold, it's just as smart to pull them closed on the hottest days.

Stay on the Ground Floor

We all know that heat rises. Those with nothing else might find some bit of relief by sticking to the lowest floors of the

home. Those who have basements could set up living spaces and ride out a heat wave down there.

Keep Windows Closed

Many people crank open their windows on the hot days in the hopes of catching some breeze from time to time. It might sound strange, but you would do more harm than good in doing so during the daytime. Those who have an indoor temperature that's lesser than that of the outside air would only serve to let more heat into the home. You could rely on that breeze and some ventilation when the sun falls and temperatures drop if only even slightly during the overnight hours.

Keep your Body Cool

Methods of maintaining proper cool in the hottest of temperatures would go well beyond the home itself. You should be mindful of your body's needs and place proper priority on temperature when it's due. It's wise to limit physical exertion at the hottest times of the day. Even if you have a lot of storm damage to clean up, limit when you work. At a time of dangerous temperatures, all of those tasks that come to bear during a disaster aftermath might be better accomplished in the earliest hours of morning or the late hours of evening. It might be smarter to get your rest in during the hottest hours that come in mid to late afternoon.

Drink a lot of fluids. Water needs would be far greater than what a person would consume on the average day. You shouldn't wait until you're thirsty. Water is a tremendous resource for cooling in ways beyond hydration. Those who can't power up the air conditioner could cool their bodies with cold baths and showers at several points during the day. In between, you might keep the skin dampened with a towel. The water's evaporation from the skin, in the same fashion as sweat, would serve to cool the body.

Woodstove Simplicity

THIS FIXTURE OF THE HOME BRINGS WARMTH IN MULTIPLE WAYS

BY BRETT LAIDLAW

The freak May storm started as snow, then turned to a depressing rain. The freezing rain that followed was worse, but then it turned back to snow, then a spell of sleet, before it settled on snow, which then fell for two days in a manner almost Biblical. We watched our hillsides, only recently greening after numerous April snows, disappear again under featureless white.

On the second morning of the storm, as I went to fill the kettle for tea, the clock display on the kitchen range began to flicker ominously. Odd beeps and buzzes issued from smoke detectors. Then there was silence, and on the clock face, darkness. The snow was bending over trees and snapping off branches all over western Wisconsin and the power lines went with them as they fell.

Briefly I pondered the paradox of an endless winter in an age of global warming. Then I turned my mind back to tea, and carried the kettle into the living room and set it on the woodstove. No power? No problem. In the stove there were still embers from last night's fire, and with a careful arrangement of kindling, and some strategic puffing, soon I had a good flame going. If we had had to rely on the LP furnace, we'd have been without heat, never mind tea; but with our new woodstove and dry wood in the box, we'd be fine until the thaw.

We had only had the stove for a few months, and already it was hard to imagine life without it. It had become like a member of the family—the good sort, the honor student offspring, not the slacker son squatting in the basement. It's hard to overstate the impact that becoming "woodstove people" has had on our lives. What did we do in the evening before we discovered the world's greatest entertainment center, flames dancing behind glass? How had we deprived our taste buds of the splendor that is a venison goulash simmered at ideal braising temperature for hours on a January afternoon? And though our house before the woodstove was more than livable, how had we done without the unifying function that is the hearth? Hearth and heart may not share an etymological root, but they ought to.

There are trade-offs. You don't hit a button and receive instant heat, nor can you program the woodstove to magically spring to life and warm the house before you venture out from under the comforter. But in many ways, I've come to appreciate the slower pace of life with a woodstove. While I wait for the red kettle to whistle, I can do some stretching on the rug in front of the stove (first claiming a little space from the dogs, who since day one had assumed a very proprietary attitude about their spots in front of the fire). And once the tea has steeped, it stays nice and warm on the shelf at the back of the stove.

We didn't buy the woodstove for any principled reasons; frankly we just thought it would be cool to have one—and, with 20 wooded acres on our property, we had the means to fuel it. It simply made sense to use this energy resource, which is, literally, right outside our back door. But the May storm and loss of electricity, which lasted more than 24 hours, showed us how important a degree of energy independence can be, especially for rural folk. I like that this form of energy is renewable and sustainable. As we harvest mostly small dead oaks, it's a fairly carbon-neutral way to heat. I also like the simplicity of it, the direct connection to our land that it provides.

While heating with wood may be simple and direct, it is by no means easy. There's that old saying that heating with wood warms you twice, but whoever came up with it apparently could not count past two. How does wood heat warm you? Let me count the ways: trudging up the hill

with the chainsaw, and then the actual cutting, which will work up a sweat. Loading the rounds to haul them to the house, then unloading, splitting, and stacking; filling the woodbox by the house, and stocking the wood basket by the stove. Phew. Only then do we get to appreciate the actual warmth of the fire, and then finally, one's cockles are warmed by the comforting view of the entrancing flames.

Heating with wood is definitely a life-style choice, one that many people we know in this rural part of our state have made. When we were trying to decide what kind of stove to buy, we put out a query on the email share list that folks use to look for feeder pigs, offer eggs for sale, that sort of thing. We heard from a lot of people, and many different stove brands were mentioned—Jotul, Vermont Castings, Pacific Energy, Hearthstone. A clear consensus emerged: they loved them. Their own stoves, whatever the make and model, they loved them. Sure, they had some quibbles—the cooking surface on this one could be better, would be nice if that one accommodated a bigger log. But it was clear that in the woodstove and the rural mindset, here was a perfect meeting of sensibility and technology.

I couldn't end this ode to the stove without a few words about how beautiful it is to cook on a woodstove, since not one hour of the day passes when I don't give some thought to what we're having for dinner. Here again, much of the appeal is in the simple, rustic nature of this age-old device. It's very much a slow-food way of cooking, ideal for the kinds of long-simmered dishes that we tend to crave after brisk activity in the cold (like, say, chopping firewood). It excels at cast iron cookery, producing superb pancakes and frittatas. Meats and hearty vegetables, slowly pan-roasted, develop deep, savory flavors, and cheap, flavorful cuts like beef short ribs, oxtails, or pork shoulder braise to succulence while the cooking aromas fill the house. And while we have scrupulously heeded the manufacturer's admonition that "Under no circumstances should

Although having a huge stockpile of firewood gives a person a great sense of fuel security, modern woodstoves are incredibly fuel efficient. Depending on the size of the home, some woodstoves only need a few chunks of wood to get the entire house warmed up. The end result is that your wood supply lasts longer.

you attempt to barbecue in this heater," we have found that root vegetables wrapped in foil, set in the stove away from the hottest flame, cook to a beautifully caramelized turn in just around 30 minutes.

There's really no off-season when you heat your home with wood. By the time the heating season ends, it's time to make wood for next winter. Some might find it oppressive to be reminded of winter in the shank of summer, but I actually appreciate the way it brings the seasons together. It's a satisfying feeling to watch the woodpile grow, to know that there will be plenty of dry fuel when the cold weather returns. As a born-and-bred Son of the North, I look forward to those late summer and early autumn nights, when you pull out the sweaters and wool socks again, and a fire in the hearth makes everything seem just right. Likewise, winter days and deep snow are nothing to dread when you can step into the skis for a glide through the woods, ending in a swift flight down the hayfield hill, and come inside to that enveloping warmth, and the aromas of something good simmering on the woodstove.

Still, to everything its season—if we have more blossoms than snowflakes next May, I'll be okay with that.

The Ultimate
Firewood Stash

NOT ALL FIREWOOD IS CREATED EQUAL
YOUR GUIDE TO THE SWEETEST-BURNING WOOD IN THE FOREST

BY JAMES CARD

One of my friends once said as he looked over his personal library, "When I have a lot of good books I feel wealthy." I feel the same way about firewood but different types of firewood have different characteristics. Some burn fast with intense heat and some burn slow and ooze heat throughout the night. Others kick off too many sparks or smoke. Some wood such as hickory or maple, are great for smoking meats while evergreens like pine or spruce will leave your pork chop with a Pine-Sol flavor.

It's good to have a hefty stack of firewood on hand even if you do not heat your home with it. It's good to have around for backyard campfires and for daylong barbecue parties. If there is a power outage for a few days, who cares? It means you get to have a few days of camaraderie around the campfire with family and neighbors and get to dine on lots of wood-smoked meats and aluminum foil dinners. And don't forget the marshmallows.

FAST FACTS: WOOD HEAT & COOKING GUIDE

Species	Heat	Lbs./cord	Ease of Lighting	Coaling Qualities	Sparks	Fragrance
Alder	Med-Low	2540	Fair	Good	Moderate	Slight
Apple	High-Med	4400	Difficult	Excellent	Few	Excellent
Ash	High	3440	Fairly diff.	Good-Exc.	Few	Slight
Beech	High	3760	Difficult	Excellent	Few	Good
Birch (White)	Med	3040	Easy	Good	Moderate	Slight
Cherry	Med	2060	Difficult	Excellent	Few	Excellent
Elm	High	2260	Very diff.	Good	Very Few	Fair
Hickory	Very High	4240	Fairly diff.	Excellent	Moderate	Excellent
Ironwood	Very High	4000	Very diff.	Excellent	Few	Slight
Locust (Black)	Very High	3840	Difficult	Excellent	Very Few	Slight
Madrone	High	4320	Difficult	Excellent	Very Few	Slight
Maple (Red)	High-Med	3200	Fairly diff.	Excellent	Few	Good
Maple (Sugar)	High	3680	Difficult	Excellent	Few	Good
Mesquite	Very High	N/A	Very diff.	Excellent	Few	Excellent
Oak (Live)	Very High	4600	Very diff.	Excellent	Few	Fair
Oak (Red)	High	3680	Difficult	Excellent	Few	Fair
Oak (White)	Very High	4200	Difficult	Excellent	Few	Fair
Pecan	High	N/A	Fairly diff.	Good	Few	Good
Walnut	High-Med	N/A	Fairly diff.	Good	Few	Fair

THE TOP PICKS

You should have a mix of firewood for different purposes. Use fast-burning wood like aspen and pine for cheery campfires that provide comfort against the darkness. Use wood from the oak family for heavy-duty, long-burning heat. And then there is the top-shelf wood, the kind of wood that has both excellent heat radiation and sweet-flavored smoke for cooking. Keep this separate from the others and use it sparingly. It's too good to waste for frivolous burning.

APPLE

Apple, like many fruit-bearing trees such as black cherry, have excellent all-around qualities. If you live near an orchard, ask the farmer if you can help out with pruning and can keep the limbs.

MAPLE AND HICKORY

Two of the gold standards among pro-barbecue teams. Both species are plentiful and widespread across much of North America.

MESQUITE

Nicknamed "Texas Ironwood," this tough tree is plentiful in the American southwest. It has long-burning coals and a lovely smoke flavor.

The Essential Bug Out
Fire-Starting Kit

BY CREEK STEWART

The ability to create fire is quite possibly the most important survival skill on earth. Fire has been the core of survival since the beginning of time. It allows a survivalist to accomplish a huge variety of life-sustaining tasks. In certain situations, fire may be your only way to stave off severe cold and control your body's core temperature. The heat from a fire not only provides warmth, but it can be used to dry clothes, shoes, and gear.

A fire kit is an essential piece of survival equipment that you should carry with you at all times. That may sound extreme, but if you have a basic lighter and some pocket lint, you have a very basic fire kit.

In your Bug-Out Bag, fire items should be stored in their own waterproof kit to protect them from water and moisture. You can use a vast number of containers for your fire kit. Several practical examples are:

- sealed aluminum containers with o-ring
- watertight bags, boxes, and tubes
- non-watertight containers with contents packed in resealable bags

Regardless of the container style and size you choose, practice identifying this kit inside of your BOB in complete darkness or while blindfolded. You could very well need to find and use this kit in low-light circumstances. Again, disasters don't present ideal environments. Prepare for the worst and anything better is a bonus.

Because fire is such an important survival resource, I encourage redundancy when it comes to packing fire-making tools and supplies in your BOB. Your BOB fire kit should contain two main fire-making components:

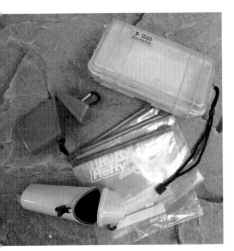
▲ Pelican Case and Resealable Bags

1. ignition sources
2. fire-starting tinder

IGNITION SOURCES

Pack a minimum of three ignition sources. I can justify this redundancy because the cost and weight of each one is very minimal.

Ignition Source 1: Cigarette Lighter

Lighters are cheap, lightweight, reliable, easy-to-use, long-lasting and extremely effective. I carry one lighter in my waterproof fire kit and two more in separate spots on my BOB. Lighters do have certain limitations. They don't function well in extreme cold or when wet.

Ignition Source 2: Waterproof Strike Anywhere Matches

Regular matches are just too vulnerable to moisture. Be sure to pack a dozen or so waterproof strike anywhere matches stored in a sealed match case. You can purchase both in the camping section of any outdoor store or even a big-box discount retail store.

FERROCERIUM AND MISCHMETAL FIRE STARTER RODS

BY JOHN D. MCCANN

I would like to attempt to clarify the confusion often surrounding the terms "ferrocerium" and "mischmetal" when it comes to various fire starters.

My wife, who speaks fluent German, voiced confusion to the term mischmetal as it relates to ferrocerium. She explained that the term mischmetal is from the German word Mishmetall, meaning mixed metal, and that since a ferrocerium rod is made of a mixture of metal, by definition it is a mischmetal rod.

So I did a little digging and she is right. But the terms have taken on their own vernacular by the survival/fire-starting community. The terms are used to distinguish the difference between two types of fire-starting rods or tools.

WHAT ARE MISCHMETAL AND FERROCERIUM?

A mischmetal, also known as cerium mischmetal, is an alloy of rare earth elements, namely those from the lanthanum series. The resultant mischmetal by itself is too soft to use as a flint, such as used in a lighter.

Therefore, it is blended with iron oxide and magnesium oxide. The resulting man-made material is called ferrocerium — probably because of the addition of the iron (ferro) and the mischmetal (cerium), hence ferrocerium—and will produce sparks to ignite tinder when scraped by a sharp edge, usually a piece of steel.

The scraper is called a striker. For years, this was the only type of spark-producing fire-starting device that came in a rod form, and was termed a ferrocerium rod or a mischmetal fire starter.

THE NEW MISCHMETAL ROD

Enter the twenty-first century and a desire for a hotter fire starter rod. A new fire starter rod is introduced and it is called a mischmetal rod. I know, I know, but what can I say.

This rod allows the user to obtain both a sufficient ignition spark and an ample shower of hot burning flakes of magnesium used to ignite tinder.

Without getting too technical, this is done by lowering the iron content and increasing the magnesium content. The increased amount of magnesium, relative to the decreased iron content, results in a softer rod.

The pieces that are scraped off are larger and, after being ignited by the sparks, continue to burn after leaving the rod.

HOW DO THE TWO PERFORM?

For the purpose of this article, a ferrocerium rod (also known as a ferro rod) is harder and gives lots of sparks, but the sparks don't continue to burn.

A mischmetal rod gives large burning chunks of magnesium that continue to burn after leaving the rod.

WHICH ONE IS RIGHT FOR YOU?

I, being old school, still prefer the ferrocerium rod. It is hard and, in my opinion, lasts much longer than a mischmetal rod. A ferro rod only gives you sparks, but hot sparks, and they have always been adequate for me to ignite tinder. The sparks are fairly easy to aim into a tinder pile.

I have found that the large burning pieces of magnesium scraped off the mischmetal rod are more difficult to aim and the rods wear down in a much shorter time than a ferro rod.

However, when the hot burning pieces of magnesium do find their way into the tinder, they burn longer, and will even ignite a piece of paper (a ferro rod won't do that). To make an intelligent decision, experiment with both and determine which is best for you.

▲ Strike Anywhere Matches and Waterproof Container

Ignition Source 3: Fire Steel Striking Rod

The technical name for this product is a ferrocerium rod. Many people also use the name ferro rod or metal match. A fire steel can generate sparks at over 2,000 degrees F when scraped with a metal striker or the back of your survival knife. There are many different styles of fire steel sparkers. Generally, they all work using the same principle.

A fire steel can generate sparks even in damp and wet conditions. An average fire steel can be used thousands of times and is an excellent survival ignition source. Striking these sparks into prepared fire tinder is a very effective fire-starting technique and one that I use almost exclusively while in the bush. The fire steel I carry is one made by Kodiak Firestarters. They manufacture a fire steel that is mounted to a small bar of magnesium. Of course, you can use the fire steel alone to ignite dry tinder in reasonable conditions just as you would any ferro rod. However, if your conditions or fire-starting tinder aren't ideal, you can scrape off shavings from the built-in magnesium bar into a small pile with your knife or the included striker tool and use these shavings as tinder. Magnesium shavings ignite with just a spark and burn at over 5,000 degrees F. It's hard not to get a fire going with a small burning pile of metal! These integrated fire steels are a little pricier but the added bonus of built-in magnesium

fire-starting material is worth the extra few dollars and ounces. This is an ignition source and fire-starting tinder in one compact package.

FIRE-STARTING TINDER

The ignition source is only half of the fire-starting equation. In a Bug-Out scenario, I want guaranteed fire. This means I need a guaranteed ignition source and some fire-starting tinder that is guaranteed to light when I hit it with one of my ignition devices. The only guaranteed fire tinder is the tinder that you pack with you. Although natural fire-starting materials exist, certain weather conditions

can make finding dry, flammable fire tinder very difficult. Below are several great BOB fire tinder options. I recommend you pack at least two of these.

WetFire Fire-Starting Tinder

WetFire is a brand name, store-bought fire tinder available at most outdoor retailers. It is undeniably the best fire starter available. It will light with just a spark in almost any weather condition. It will even light and burn while floating in water.

It's a remarkable product and makes a very reliable BOB fire-starting pack item.

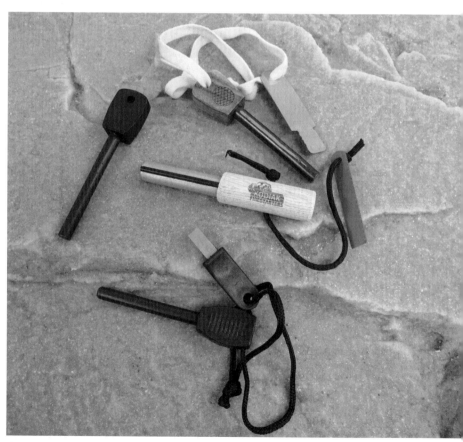

▲ Several Ferrocerium Rods including Kodiak Firestarter

WetFire Burning in Water

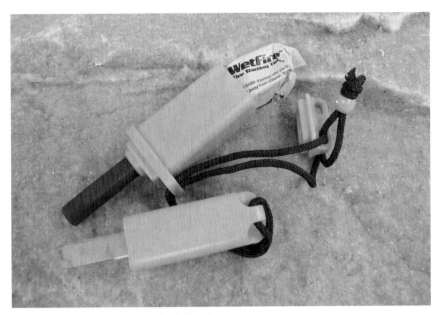
StrikeForce Fire Starter From ForgeSurvivalSupply.com

WetFire tablets will burn approximately two to three minutes and come individually wrapped in a waterproof package. With this burn time, you can even burn a WetFire tablet as the fuel source in an Esbit stove mentioned in chapter four, making these tablets a good multi-use item.

A tablet of WetFire also fits into the handle of the StrikeForce Fire Starter. This is an excellent tool that includes a ferro rod and striker built into a durable plastic housing with a compartment that fits one cube of WetFire. This makes for a very compact all-inclusive, fire-starting package.

Steel Wool

Common steel wool is one of the best fire-starting materials available. The smallest spark will ignite the thin metal fibers into a smoldering ember that burns at a very high temperature. The smoldering steel wool can then be used to ignite combustible tinder, such as dried grass, leaves, paper, etc. Steel wool is readily available at any hardware and grocery store. It is also very cheap.

Like WetFire tinder, steel wool burns even when damp. Even if it's soaking wet, you can shake it out and ignite it within a few seconds. You can pack a good amount of steel wool in a very small container and it doesn't have an expiration date. Steel wool will ignite and smolder even in freezing conditions.

PET Balls

One of best fire starters I've ever used can be made at home in just a few minutes and costs virtually nothing. This homemade tinder only requires two ingredients: petroleum jelly and either cotton balls or dryer lint. (PET is short for petroleum—hence the name PET Balls.)

These are very easy to make. Simply saturate a cotton ball or comparable-sized chunk of dryer lint with a quarter-sized scoop of petroleum jelly.

Then, mix it in thoroughly so that all of the fibers are coated.

Lastly, roll each chunk into little balls and store them in a watertight container or resealable bag.

The petroleum jelly acts as a fire extender. It becomes a fuel source and turns the cotton/lint into a makeshift wick that will light with just a spark and then burn for several minutes. Without the petroleum jelly, the burn time would be just a few seconds—drastically reducing your window of opportunity to get a healthy fire going. In addition, the petroleum jelly helps to waterproof the cotton/lint as well. Petroleum jelly can also be mixed with natural tinder such as dried grass, cattail down, or milkweed down with similar success.

For this reason, I always travel with a tube of Carmex lip balm, a petroleum-jelly-based product that can easily be used as a fire extender in an emergency.

To use a PET Ball, pull it apart to separate and expose the fine fibers. This increases surface area and facilitates airflow. Then, simply strike it with a spark from a fire steel or light it with a match or lighter and get ready to place small kindling on the flame.

Find more fire building instructions in *Build the Perfect Bug Out Bag* by Creek Stewart, available at store.livingreadyonline.com.

Dress for Survival

BY CREEK STEWART

Hypothermia is the number one killer in outdoors settings. By definition, hypothermia is when a person's core body temperature drops dangerously low. Hypothermia sets in with exposure to cold weather and is intensified by wind and water. Hypothermia leads to heart and respiratory failure and eventually death. Low temperatures, wind, and moisture make a lethal combination for the ill-prepared.

The exact opposite, hyperthermia also ranks high as an outdoor killer. Hyperthermia occurs when someone's core body temperature rises dangerously high. When left untreated for even a short period of time, hyperthermia is debilitating and lethal.

Proper clothing is your first line of defense against overexposure to the elements—hot or cold. You're especially at risk of exposure when traveling by foot in the aftermath of a disaster. Consequently, clothing is a very important survival gear category. It's not very exciting but it's important. Children and the elderly are even more susceptible to exposure, so pay special attention to ensure their clothing needs are met.

WEATHER APPROPRIATE

If you live in northern Minnesota, your clothing needs are going to be vastly different from someone who lives in southern Florida. Because there are so many different weather regions all over the world, clothing is a somewhat personalized supply category. Common sense is required. I conduct a biannual review of my Bug Out Bag and change out my clothing items every November for the onset of winter and every May for the onset of spring and summer. If you live in an area with distinct seasons, I suggest you follow a similar clothing review/replacement schedule. You will not have time to think about what clothing items to take when a disaster strikes.

CLOTHING SPECIFICATIONS

Whether you are selecting survival clothing for a Bug-Out Bag or dressing for an outdoor activity such as hiking, hunting or boating, remember rule number one: Stay away from cotton. On the scale of available fabrics, cotton is probably the worst for survival. Cotton is like a sponge—it retains moisture and is slow to dry. It's also bulky.

In survival situations, you need fabrics that wick moisture away and that are fast drying. In cold temperatures, these are especially important qualities. The best survival fabrics are wool and wool blends, fleeces, nylons, and polyesters.

Following is a quick list of attributes your survival wardrobe should possess:

- quick-drying
- moisture-wicking
- durable
- nonrestrictive
- loose-fitting
- muted colors (just in case you need to hide)

Excellent All-Season Survival Clothing Options

Light-Weight Long-Sleeve Shirt: Regardless of the season, full coverage protects from weather exposure and insects.

Mid-Weight Fleece: Fleece is lightweight and very packable and its good practice to carry one in any weather condition. Even in warm climates, a mid-weight fleece can be useful on chilly nights.

Moisture-Wicking Short Sleeve Undershirt: The word "wicking" refers to a fabric's ability to draw moisture away from your body to evaporate more quickly. Wicking fabrics are light-weight and fast drying. They help regulate your body temperature more efficiently.

Nonrestrictive Long Pants: No jeans allowed! Cotton-denim jeans are your worst enemy when wet. When selecting a fabric for pants, my favorites are light-weight wool blends or polyester-nylon blends.

Light-weight Crushable Brimmed Hat: This style hat can be a lifesaver in protecting your head and face from elements, such as sun, wind, and rain. A severe sunburn can turn into a serious medical crisis without proper care. I recently planned a 120-mile canoe trip through the state of

Outer Shell

Balaclava Face Mask

Indiana. One of the guys had to cut the trip short because of an extreme blistering sunburn on his face. A "Boonie" style hat could have prevented this.

PROTECTING YOUR FEET

I can't stress enough how important it is to have proper foot protection. If you are Bugging Out on foot, your feet are your only means of transportation. If your feet give out and you can't walk, your bug out is over. You're stuck where you are. Take care of your feet and they will take care of you.

Wool Socks

To ensure my feet are properly taken care of, I pack three extra pairs of wool hiking socks. Don't pack socks made from any other material! Wool is naturally breathable. This allows for better airflow, which helps to prevent blisters. Prolonged hiking can really give your socks a workout. Wool excels in hard-use environments because of it's durability and resiliency. I prefer the brand SmartWool. They are a little expensive but worth every penny. Below are some specific features/benefits of SmartWool socks:

- made from top quality no-itch Merino wool
- blended with elastic and nylon which helps to hold shape even with extended wear and washings

- Merino wool properties regulate temperature and moisture, which helps to reduce foot odor

When you have extra socks, you can switch them out regularly if your feet are damp or wet (whether it's sweat or outside moisture). You can dry used socks by keeping them close to your body or by hanging them off your pack. I keep an extra carabiner clipped to the outside of my BOB for just this purpose.

Hiking Boots

Get a pair of durable, waterproof, ankle-high hiking boots. There are many different styles and brands that will work just fine. These don't need to be packed inside your BOB but should be kept very close to it as you will be wearing these boots in the event of a Bug Out. Break them in! Don't plan on wearing a new pair of hiking boots in a disaster Bug Out. You could potentially be walking for several days with a twenty- to thirty-pound backpack. Your BOB boots need to be broken in, tested, proven, and comfortable.

COLD WEATHER ESSENTIALS

Bugging Out in cold weather adds to the severity of any disaster. The 2011 Tōhoku earthquake and tsunami in Japan forced thousands of people to Bug Out in freezing conditions. Many of these people fled

into the mountains with only what they could carry.

Ideally, you will be wearing most of the items listed below in a cold weather Bug Out.

These are items that don't necessarily need to be kept in your BOB year-round.

The key to warmth is layering, not one bulky parka or snowsuit. Layering is incredibly effective because it creates dead air space between the layers of clothing. Heat stays trapped within that air space. Layering also lets you to control your body temperature by adding and shedding clothing items as necessary. I've spent days at a time in temperatures below 10 degrees F with the following layering system.

Outer Shell

Your outermost layer is the outer shell. An outer shell is critical to any cold weather layering system. It has two primary functions:

- wind break
- rain protection

Wind and rain can turn even moderately cold weather into a hypothermic situation. Protecting your core from these elements is critical and that's what your outer shell will do. It is a protection layer, not an insulating layer, so your shell should not be big and bulky. This shell could be a waterproof rain jacket. Be sure

THE VERSATILE SHEMAGH

This large square scarf is similar to a bandana but much larger—typically around 40" × 40". It can be used for hundreds of different survival applications. A few are photographed here.

△ Cordage for Tripod

△ Face and Head Protection

△ First Aid Arm Sling

SHEMAGH SLING PACK

Through a series of folds and rolls, a shemagh can also function as a makeshift sling- pack to tote additional supplies.

△ Makeshift Sling Pack: Step 1

△ Makeshift Sling Pack: Step 2

△ Makeshift Sling Pack: Step 3

it has a hood. In most conditions, you will only need a shell for your upper body. In extreme conditions, outer shell pants would be a great idea. This depends on where you live.

Heavy Fleece (Rated 300-Weight Fleece) or Wool Sweater

Beneath the outer shell is a rated 300-weight fleece. This is an upper-body warmth layer that is especially important in low temperatures. The structure of fleece fabric allows for trapped air within the fibers. It has excellent insulation properties. A heavy wool sweater is also an excellent choice. Wool is hands down the best survival fabric on the planet. Wool's biggest drawback is that it can be bulky.

Mid-weight Fleece (Rated 200-Weight Fleece)

Beneath the rated 300-weight fleece is a rated 200-weight fleece. This, too, is an upper-body warmth layer. A mid-weight fleece is the most popular weight. It can easily be used as an outer layer in moderate temperatures, but is very well suited for layering. This is the layer I shed most often while adventuring in cold weather environments. If you are starting to sweat,

then you need to shed layers or reduce your physical exertion. Sweating moisture into your clothing can kill you. Cold temperatures and damp clothing is the perfect recipe for hypothermia.

Light-Weight Wicking Base Layer

The base layer is the layer of clothing against your skin. In cold temperatures, I wear both upper- and lower-body base layers. The function is to hold and trap warmth. Choose a base layer made from a wicking fabric designed to draw moisture away from your body. It should be breathable, stretchy, and very comfortable. No

RAIN PONCHO SURVIVAL SHELTER

The military-style rain poncho can also be used as an emergency survival shelter. Here are three different configurations that I've used.

▲ Poncho Ridge Line Lean-To

▲ Poncho Tent

▲ Poncho Diagonal Lean-To

itchy base layers allowed. For this reason, wool is a not a recommended base layer fabric. These garments should also be form fitting—not loose and baggy.

COLD WEATHER ACCESSORIES
Wool or Fleece Hat

Up to 30 percent of your body heat can be lost through your head. Warm head protection is critical. In extreme conditions, a balaclava is an excellent alternative that provides face and neck protection.

Cold Weather Gloves

Don't risk frostbite to your extremities. A pair of cold-weather gloves should be in your pack or on your person if Bugging Out during the winter season. In a survival situation, the ability to use your fingers and hands is imperative. Almost every survival function requires good hand dexterity—using a knife, lighting a fire, tying knots, preparing food, administering first aid, etc. Nothing will cripple your hands like cold weather—pack gloves! The pair I pack is a very simple set of 100 percent wool gloves I bought at an Army/Navy surplus store for $5.99.

SHEMAGH

Pronounced schmahhg, the shemagh is a large square scarf worn primarily in the desert regions of the world to protect one's face from sun, wind, and sand. It's an item widely used by American and British troops serving in the Middle East. The shemagh is much more than just a head and face wrap. It's probably the most multifunctional survival item I have ever owned with literally hundreds of uses. It makes an excellent BOB addition. It can be purchased at many Army/Navy surplus stores and we also carry several different colorways at www.willowhavenoutdoor.com.

RAIN PONCHO

A light-weight military-style poncho will prove to be one of your most valuable Bug Out items. I would probably put this on my top ten list of Bug-Out items. While there are many different makes and models of ponchos, the most popular are constructed from sealed rip-stop nylon. This makes them very light-weight and crushable—perfect for a BOB. They come with a drawstring hood and also with metal grommets in key points around the edge.

The grommets add versatility and multifunctional uses. Using these grommets, some cordage, and a little creativity, you can use the military poncho as a quick and effective survival shelter.

Thoughtful preparation and planning is absolutely necessary if you expect to survive the extreme elements. Use common sense when choosing clothing for your immediate environment. If you have distinct seasons where you live, be sure to change out the clothing in your BOB at least once a year.

Find more survival clothing packing instructions in *Build the Perfect Bug Out Bag* by Creek Stewart, available at store.livingreadyonline.com.

Be a Turncoat

HOW REVERSIBLE JACKETS CAN SAVE YOUR NECK

BY JAMES CARD

A hunter wearing camouflage disappears into the woods never to be seen again. Later when his body is found, searchers would say they walked right by him. Another hunter wearing camouflage disappears into the woods. He breaks his leg, becomes hypothermic and before he grows any weaker, he takes off his coat, and flips it inside out. The new outer shell is blaze orange and the searchers quickly find him.

One evening, a woman gets her car stuck in a blizzard. She gets out wearing a dark wool overcoat and steps into the road to inspect the scene and is hit by a passing truck. Another woman gets stuck in a blizzard on a dark night. She removes her coat and turns it inside out. The outer shell is bright yellow with reflective tape stitched into the fabric. As she walks around the car and figures out how to get out of the jam, the headlights of oncoming motorists bounce off the reflective strips of her coat and they have time to ease into the other lane.

Makes sense, doesn't it? Reversible jackets (and vests, coats or overalls) have been around for a long time but are often overlooked as a simple yet effective way to be seen or spotted when you really need people to see you. The blaze orange and camouflage combination used by hunters is the most common and great for when exploring the outdoors. The reversible jackets with reflective strips are best for when you expect to be working around lights (usually headlights) in an urban environment. Also, the jackets with reflective strips looks similar to those used by emergency personnel and by wearing one of those, you're unlikely to be mistaken for a looter in the aftermath of a natural disaster.

Although marketed to law enforcement officers, the Reversible High Vis Duty Jacket by 5.11 Tactical is a useful jacket for anyone. It has a wind and water repellent outer shell, hand warmer pockets, cargo pockets and the high-visibility yellow shell is stitched with strips of 3M Scotchlite tape. $140. www.511tactical.com

Bug-Out Bag
Shelter Options

BY JAMES D. NOWKA

Exposure can kill you in less than three hours, so having a survival shelter plan is vital. Shelter, just like every other piece of preparation, starts with listening to that strong voice of common sense that developed through all of our experiences. Each of us has a pretty firm understanding of "hot." Many of us know a pretty good thing or two about "cold." Simply living is enough to give most people some sense of the dangers at hand as it pertains to shelter needs.

Problems most often grow from minor and manageable to severe and dangerous when people, for whatever reason, decide to ignore that "gut feeling" that something just isn't right. You should always take advantage of what the body has to say and with full urgency when it comes to shelter. The clock is already ticking toward that three-hour mark when the gut feeling starts talking to the mind. In a bug-out situation, when you are away from home or any adequate cool or warmth, you can't afford to waste a minute. Try to imagine the growing stress and the racing thoughts that would come should troubles grow from bad to worse when there's limited time and no adequate relief in sight.

Your bug-out bag should account for shelter in several different ways. Keep several shelter contingencies in an easy to reach place so you don't have to root through the entire bag to locate those items of most immediate need.

TENTS

Preparation calls for the right tools to meet the right situations. There is not one perfect tent to carry a family through all of its potential needs. Any family should look at a couple of tents with the aims of fulfilling short-term survival situations (a bug out bag situation) and the potential need for longer-term housing (see the sidebar).

TENTS AS TEMPORARY HOMES

Those purchasing a tent that could serve as home after disaster might go for something substantial. A number of tents could offer a touch of comfort in a difficult spot. You might set up camp right at the remnants of the house to allow for prompt and efficient work. Montana Canvas, for instance, makes a 10-by-12 wedge tent that feels more like a room inside. You could put a wood stove in there. If it's 20 degrees below zero beyond the canvas walls, you could easily bring it to a comfortable 60 degrees inside.

Some of the cabin tents out there are pretty incredible and good options to consider. There are a number of durable, canvas models on the market. Some people actually put floors inside and use them as vacation homes.

Those preparing for the destructive events that might require alternative shelter on their properties might consider stepping beyond what most typically think of as tents. The portable garages out there are typically 10-by-20 feet. It's a lot of space. One or two of those shelters would allow a family to set up some kitchen and dining room space as well as a couple bedrooms. You might put some air conditioners in there. It wouldn't be the house. It might still feel like home.

When choosing a tent for a bug-out bag, go for something that's small and light. The tent is only one part of a bigger package, and the entire pack has to be carried. That tent will be less about usual comforts than it is a means of keeping out of the elements. Backpacking tents work well for those sleeping one or two. Those who are bugging out as a family could find some pretty large dome tents that pack up fairly small and can sleep four to eight people.

In each case, think about durability and ease in set-up. A survival situation isn't the time to fumble with instructions. For that matter, you wouldn't want to compromise your efforts by snapping off one of those flimsy fiberglass poles. In the longer term, durability is an obvious consideration. Ease also has an important place. A disaster is going to mean there are a variety of tasks to accomplish, and you would do well for yourself in getting that shelter up as a base of operations as quickly as possible.

Choose according to the family's needs. There isn't a tent that's going to feel as comfortable as the house. In the midst of crisis, the closer you can get, the easier the recovery process will be to manage.

TARP

A tarp is another essential shelter item. You can place it under your tent to keep the bottom of your shelter dry, and you can also rig it with some paracord to create a block to the wind, sun or rain.

PONCHO AND CLOTHES

Always include a high-quality, military-style poncho in your bag. It will keep you dry (an important step to preventing hypothermia), but with a little paracord and secure knots, you can turn it into a makeshift tent. Also include an extra change of clothes in a waterproof bag, if possible.

Buyer's Guide to Tents

Manufacturer/Model: Oware/CatTarp 1 (tarp)
Price: $
Weight: 8 oz.
Dimensions: 5' 6" × 8' 9"
Pack Size: n/a
No. of people: 1
Seasons: 3

Manufacturer/Model: Crazy Creek Products/Crazy Crib (hammock)
Price: $$
Weight: 23 oz.
Dimensions: 3' 8" × 7' 10"
Pack Size: 1' 4" × 7' × 2"
No. of people: 1
Seasons: 3

Manufacturer/Model: Integral Designs/ Element Solo
Price: $$
Weight: 11 oz.
Dimensions: 3' 3.4" × 7' 2.6"
Pack Size: 7.9" × 3.1"
No. of people: 1
Seasons: 3

Manufacturer/Model: Eureka!/Solitare
Price: $$
Weight: 41 oz.
Dimensions: 2' 8" × 8'
Pack Size: 4" × 17.5"
No. of people: 1
Seasons: 3

Manufacturer/Model: Brooks-Range/ Ultralite Solo Tarp
Price: $$
Weight: 6.7 oz.
Dimensions: 5' × 8'
Pack Size: n/a
No. of people: 1
Seasons: 3

Manufacturer/Model: Easton Mountain Products/Sundial S
Price: $$-$$$$ (two sizes)
Weight: 32 oz.; 72 oz.
Dimensions: 9' 4" × 7' × 7'; 10' 8" × 7' 4" × 7'
Pack Size: 1' 3" × 7"; 1' 11" × 9"
No. of people: 1-3
Seasons: 3

Manufacturer/Model: The Coleman Company, Inc./Avior ×1
Price: $$$
Weight: 56 oz.
Dimensions: 7' 9" × 2' 8"
Pack Size: n/a
No. of people: 1
Seasons: 3

Manufacturer/Model: L.L. Bean/Micro-light Solo Tent
Price: $$$
Weight: 47 oz.
Dimensions: 7' 7" × 3' 1" × 3' 1"
Pack Size: 6" × 1' 4"
No. of people: 1
Seasons: 3

Manufacturer/Model: Sierra Designs/ Light Year I
Price: $$$
Weight: 43 oz.
Dimensions: 20 sq. ft., height of 3' 2"
Pack Size: 1'10" × 6"
No. of people: 1
Seasons: 3

Manufacturer/Model: Terra Nova Equipment/Wild Country Zephyros 1
Price: $$$
Weight: 55 oz.
Dimensions: 7' 3" × 4' 9"
Pack Size: 1' 8.4" × 5.5" × 3' 1"
No. of people: 1
Seasons: 3

Pricing key (based on manufacturer's suggested retail price):

$ = under $75
$$ = $76–$100
$$$ = $101–$125
$$$$ = $126–$150
$$$$$ = $151–$200
$$$$$$ = $201–$250
$$$$$$$ = over $251

Manufacturer/Model: Equinox Ltd/ Myotis Ultralite Sculpted Tarp
Price: $$$-$$$$$ (2 sizes)
Weight: 14.5; 21 oz.
Dimensions: 8' × 8'; 10' × 10'
Pack Size: n/a
No. of people: 1-2
Seasons: 3

Manufacturer/Model: Recreational Equipment, Inc. (REI)/Passage 1
Price: $$$$
Weight: 59 oz.
Dimensions: 7' 6" × 3' × 3'
Pack Size: 7.5" × 1' 9"
No. of people: 1
Seasons: 3

Manufacturer/Model: Six Moon Designs/Gatewood Cape
Price: $$$$
Weight: 11 oz.
Dimensions: 35 sq. ft. (360 degrees of protection. Doubles as shelter and rain gear)
Pack Size: 10" × 8" × 1.5"
No. of people: 1
Seasons: 3

Manufacturer/Model: Snow Peak/Penta Ease Tarp
Price: $$$$
Weight: 32 oz.

Dimensions: Contact manufacturer
Pack Size: n/a
No. of people: 1
Seasons: 3

Manufacturer/Model: ALPS Mountaineering/Mystique 1
Price: $$$$$
Weight: 52 oz.
Dimensions: 3' 6" × 7' 10" × 3'
Pack Size: 6" × 1' 4"
No. of people: 1
Seasons: 3

Manufacturer/Model: Mountain Laurel Designs/Monk Spectralite.60 (tarp)
Price: $$$$$
Weight: 48 oz.
Dimensions: 3' × 4'
Pack Size: n/a
No. of people: 1
Seasons: 3

Manufacturer/Model: Big Agnes/Seedhouse SL 1
Price: $$$$$
Weight: 41 oz.
Dimensions: 9' 5" × 3' 9"
Pack Size: 4" × 1' 5"
No. of people: 1
Seasons: 3

Manufacturer/Model: Lawson Hammock Company/Blue Ridge Camping Hammock
Price: $$$$$
Weight: 68 oz.
Dimensions: 7' 6" × 3'
Pack Size: 1'10" × 6"
No. of people: 1
Seasons: 3

Manufacturer/Model: Recreational Equipment, Inc. (REI)/ Quarter Dome T1
Price: $$$$$
Weight: 55 oz.
Dimensions: 7' 1" × 3' 3" × 3' 1"
Pack Size: 6.5" × 1' 7.5"
No. of people: 1
Seasons: 3

Manufacturer/Model: Six Moon Designs/Wild Oasis (tarp)
Price: $$$$$
Weight: 13 oz.
Dimensions: 35 sq. ft.
Pack Size: 1' 3" × 6"
No. of people: 1
Seasons: 3

Manufacturer/Model: Kelty/Gunnison 1.2
Price: $$$$$
Weight: 67 oz.
Dimensions: 7' 7" × 1' 5" × 3' 2"
Pack Size: 1' 8" × 6"
No. of people: 1
Seasons: 3

Manufacturer/Model: Eureka!/Backcountry 1
Price: $$$$$
Weight: 52 oz.
Dimensions: 8' × 3' × 3' 2"
Pack Size: 1' 3.5" × 6"
No. of people: 1
Seasons: 3

Manufacturer/Model: Mountain Hardwear/Sprite 1
Price: $$$$$
Weight: 52 oz.
Dimensions: 18 sq. ft., height of 3'1"
Pack Size: 1' 7" × 6"
No. of people: 1
Seasons: 3

Manufacturer/Model: Crazy Creek Products/Crazy Crib LE× W/ Tarp (hammock)
Price: $$$$$
Weight: 70 oz.
Dimensions: Crib: 3' 8" × 8' 2" Tarp: 6' 5 × 8' 8"
Pack Size: 1'6" × 8" × 3"
No. of people: 1
Seasons: 3

Manufacturer/Model: Montbell North America/Chronos Dome 1
Price: $$$$$
Weight: 69 oz.

Dimensions: 7' 3" × 3' 4" × 3' 6"
Pack Size: Contact manufacturer
No. of people: 1
Seasons: 3

Manufacturer/Model: Big Sky International/Mirage 1P 1D
Price: $$$$$
Weight: 24 oz.
Dimensions: 8' 7" × 3' 5" × 3' 3"
Pack Size: 1' 6" × 5"
No. of people: 1
Seasons: 3

Manufacturer/Model: Catoma Outdoor/ Raider
Price: $$$$$
Weight: 34.88 oz.
Dimensions: 6' 8" × 3' 4" × 2'
Pack Size: 1' 1" × 5" × 5"
No. of people: 1
Seasons: 3

Manufacturer/Model: The North Face/ Solo 12
Price: $$$$$$
Weight: 42 oz.
Dimensions: 24.5 sq. ft.
Pack Size: 1' 8" × 5"
No. of people: 1
Seasons: 3

Manufacturer/Model: Tarptent/Sublite
Price: $$$$$$
Weight: 19.5 oz.
Dimensions: 7' 2" × 3' 6" × 3' 6"
Pack Size: 1' 2" × 4"
No. of people: 1
Seasons: 3

Manufacturer/Model: Easton Mountain Products/Rimrock 1P

Price: $$$$$$

Weight: 57 oz.

Dimensions: 7' 1" × 3' 4" × 3'

Pack Size: 1' 3" × 6"

No. of people: 1

Seasons: 3

Manufacturer/Model: Paha Que Wilderness, Inc./Bear Creek Solo Tent

Price: $$$$$$

Weight: 49 oz.

Dimensions: 7' × 3' 4" × 3'

Pack Size: 1' 2" × 4"

No. of people: 1

Seasons: 3

Manufacturer/Model: Tarptent/Moment

Price: $$$$$$

Weight: 35 oz.

Dimensions: 7' × 3' 6"

Pack Size: 1' 8" × 4"

No. of people: 1

Seasons: 3

Manufacturer/Model: Catoma Outdoor/ Limbo 1

Price: $$$$$$

Weight: 54 oz.

Dimensions: 8' × 3' × 2' 6"

Pack Size: 1' 9" × 6"

No. of people: 1

Seasons: 3

Manufacturer/Model: LightHeart Gear/ LightHeart Solo

Price: $$$$$$

Weight: 27 oz.

Dimensions: 11' 1" × 5' 5" × 3' 7"

Pack Size: Contact manufacturer

No. of people: 1

Seasons: 3

Manufacturer/Model: L.L. Bean/Microlight Tent FS 1

Price: $$$$$$$

Weight: 43 oz.

Dimensions: 7' 6" × 3'

Pack Size: Contact manufacturer

No. of people: 1

Seasons: 3

Manufacturer/Model: MSR/ Hubba 1P

Price: $$$$$$$

Weight: 52 oz.

Dimensions: 8' 2" × 2' 2" × 3' 4"

Pack Size: 1' 8" × 6"

No. of people: 1

Seasons: 3

Manufacturer/Model: Macpac/Microlight

Price: $$$$$$$

Weight: 56 oz.

Dimensions: 8' 2" × 2' 2" × 3' 4"

Pack Size: 1' 8" × 6"
No. of people: 1
Seasons: 3

TWO-PERSON TENTS

Manufacturer/Model: Eagles Nest Out-
    fitters/Dry Fly Rain Tarp
Price: $$
Weight: 22 oz.
Dimensions: 10' 6" × 5' 2"
Pack Size: n/a
No. of people: 2
Seasons: 3

Manufacturer/Model: Integral Designs/
    Siltarp 2
Price: $$$
Weight: 14 oz.
Dimensions: 8' × 10'
Pack Size: 7.9" × 3.9"
No. of people: 2-3
Seasons: 3

Manufacturer/Model: Integral Designs/
    Guides Siltarp2
Price: $$$
Weight: 16 oz.
Dimensions: 8' × 10'
Pack Size: 7.9" × 3.9"
No. of people: 2-4
Seasons: 3

Manufacturer/Model: Easton Mountain
    Products/Sundial S
Price: $$$
Weight: 32 oz.; 72 oz.
Dimensions: 9' 4" × 7' × 7';
    10' 8" × 7' 4" × 7'

Pricing key (based on manufacturer's suggested retail price):

$ = under $75
$$ = $76–$100
$$$ = $101–$125
$$$$ = $126–$150
$$$$$ = $151–$200
$$$$$$ = $201–$250
$$$$$$$ = over $251

Pack Size: 1' 3" × 7"; 1' 11" × 9"
No. of people: 1-3
Seasons: 3

Manufacturer/Model: Equinox Ltd/
    Myotis Ultralite Sculpted Tarp
Price: $$$$
Weight: 14.5; 21 oz.
Dimensions: 8' × 8'; 10' × 10'
Pack Size: n/a
No. of people: 1-2
Seasons: 3

Manufacturer/Model: MSR/E-Wing
    (open shelter)
Price: $$$$$
Weight: 16 oz.
Dimensions: 11' 2" × 7' 4"
Pack Size: 4' 5" × 9"
No. of people: 2
Seasons: 3

Manufacturer/Model: MSR/ Fast Stash
    2P
Price: $$$$$
Weight: 65 oz.
Dimensions: 7' 6" × 5' 6"
Pack Size: 1' 8" × 6"
No. of people: 2 +gear
Seasons: 3

Manufacturer/Model: Mountain Laurel
    Designs/SuperTarp
Price: $$$$$$
Weight: 25 oz.
Dimensions: 10' 6" × 10' 6"
Pack Size: n/a
No. of people: 2
Seasons: 3

Manufacturer/Model: Gossamer Gear/
    Q-Twinn Tarp
Price: $$$$$$$
Weight: 7.2 oz.
Dimensions: 8' 5" × [5' 7" (front entrance
    width) 5' 2" (rear entrance width)] ×
    3' 8"
Pack Size: n/a
No. of people: 2
Seasons: 3

THREE-PERSON TENTS

Manufacturer/Model: Integral Designs/
    Siltarp 2
Price: $$$
Weight: 14 oz.
Dimensions: 8' × 10'
Pack Size: 7.9" × 3.9"
No. of people: 2-3
Seasons: 3

Manufacturer/Model: Integral Designs/
    Guides Siltarp2
Price: $$$
Weight: 16 oz.
Dimensions: 8' × 10'
Pack Size: 7.9" × 3.9"
No. of people: 2-4
Seasons: 3

Manufacturer/Model: Easton Mountain
    Products/Sundial S
Price: $$$
Weight: 32 oz.; 72 oz.
Dimensions: 9' 4" × 7' × 7'; 10' 8" × 7' 4"
    × 7'
Pack Size: 1' 3" × 7"; 1' 11" × 9"
No. of people: 1-3
Seasons: 3

Manufacturer/Model: Integral Designs/
    Siltarp 3
Price: $$$$$
Weight: 21 oz.
Dimensions: 10' × 12' × 7'
Pack Size: 7.9" × 4.7"
No. of people: 3-5
Seasons: 3

Manufacturer/Model: Granite Gear/
    White Lightnin' 10×12 (tarp)
Price: $$$$$$
Weight: 23 oz.
Dimensions: 10' × 12'
Pack Size: n/a
No. of people: 3-4
Seasons: 3

Manufacturer/Model: ALPS Mountain-
    eering/Aries 3
Price: $$$$$$

Weight: 6 lbs. 11 oz.

Dimensions: 6' 9" × 7' 4" × 4' 2"

Pack Size: 1' 9" × 7.5"

No. of people: 3

Seasons: 3

Manufacturer/Model: Cabela's/ ×PG

Price: $$$$$$

Weight: 78 oz.

Dimensions: 7' 9" × 5' 7" × 4'

Pack Size: 1' 7" × 6"

No. of people: 3

Seasons: 3

Manufacturer/Model: Sierra Designs/
Flash 3 UL

Price: $$$$$$

Weight: 89 oz.

Dimensions: 7' 2" × 5' 9" × 3' 8"

Pack Size: 1' 6" × 7"

No. of people: 3

Seasons: 3

FOUR-PERSON TENTS

Manufacturer/Model: Integral Designs/
Guides Siltarp2

Price: $$$

Weight: 16 oz.

Dimensions: 8' × 10'

Pack Size: 7.9" × 3.9"

No. of people: 2-4

Seasons: 3

Manufacturer/Model: Eastern Mountain
Sports/Big Easy 4

Price: $$$$

Weight: 9 lbs. 6 oz.

Dimensions: 7' 7" × 7' 10" × 4' 9"

Pack Size: 2' 2" × 10"

No. of people: 4

Seasons: 3

Manufacturer/Model: Integral Designs/
Siltarp 3

Price: $$$$$

Weight: 21 oz.

Dimensions: 10' × 12' × 7'

Pack Size: 7.9" × 4.7"

No. of people: 3-5

Seasons: 3

Manufacturer/Model: Eureka!/Copper
Canyon 4

Price: $$$$$

Weight: 19 lbs. 4 oz.

Dimensions: 8' × 8' × 7'

Pack Size: 2' 2" × 7"

No. of people: 4

Seasons: 3

Manufacturer/Model: Mountainsmith/
Genesee 4

Price: $$$$$

Weight: 6 lbs. 14.5 oz.

Dimensions: 8' × 7' × 4' 4"

Pack Size: 1' 7.5" × 8"

No. of people: 4

Seasons: 3

Manufacturer/Model: NEMO Equip-
ment, Inc./Bugout 9' × 9'

Price: $$$$$

Weight: 76 oz.

Dimensions: 9' × 9' × 6'

Pack Size: 1' 4" × 8"

No. of people: 4

Seasons: 3

Manufacturer/Model: Recreational
Equipment, Inc. (REI)/ Camp Dome 4

Price: $$$$$

Weight: 10 lbs.

Dimensions: 8' 4" × 7' 6" × 5' 2"

Pack Size: 2' 1" × 8.5"

No. of people: 4

Seasons: 3

Manufacturer/Model: Oware/Pyramid
Tarp 10' × 10'

Price: $$$$$

Weight: 32 oz.

Dimensions: 10' × 10' × 5' 10"

Pack Size: n/a

No. of people: 4

Seasons: 3

Manufacturer/Model: East Mountain
Sports/Big Easy 4

Price: $$$$$

Weight: 9 lbs. 6 oz.

Dimensions: 7' 7" × 7' 10" × 4' 9"

Pack Size: 2' 2" × 10"

No. of people: 4

Seasons: 3

Manufacturer/Model: Recreational
Equipment, Inc. (REI)/Half Dome 4
HC

Price: $$$$$

Weight: 8 lbs. 3 oz.

Dimensions: 7' 10" × 7' 2" × 4' 3"

Pack Size: 1' 10" × 8"

No. of people: 4

Seasons: 3

Manufacturer/Model: Big Agnes/Rabbit
Ears 4

Price: $$$$$

Weight: 9 lbs.

Dimensions: 7' 6" × 8' × 5'

Pack Size: 1' 2" × 1' 11" × 7"

No. of people: 4

Seasons: 3

Manufacturer/Model: Granite Gear/
White Lightnin' 10×12 (tarp)

Price: $$$$$

Weight: 23 oz.

Dimensions: 10' × 12'

Pack Size: n/a

No. of people: 3-4

Seasons: 3

Manufacturer/Model: Kelty/Salida 4

Price: $$$$$

Weight: 7 lbs. 3 oz.

Dimensions: 10' 2" × 6' 8" × 4' 9"

Pack Size: 2' 2" × 8"

No. of people: 4

Seasons: 3

Manufacturer/Model: ALPS Mountain-
eering/Lyn× 4

Price: $$$$$

Weight: 7 lbs. 9 oz.

Dimensions: 7' 6" × 8' 6" × 4' 4"

Pack Size: 1' 11.5" × 7"

No. of people: 4

Seasons: 3

Manufacturer/Model: Mountain Hard-
wear/Hoop Dreams 4

Price: $$$$$

Weight: 52 oz.

Dimensions: 9' 7" × 9' 7" × 4' 2"

Pack Size: 1' 7" × 5"

No. of people: 4

Seasons: 3

Manufacturer/Model: Mountain Equipment Co-op (MEC)/Camper 4

Price: $$$$$$$

Weight: 7 lbs. 11 oz.

Dimensions: 7' 5.5" × 6' 4" × 4' 6.5"

Pack Size: 1' 8.5" × 7.8" × 7.8"

No. of people: 4

Seasons: 3

Manufacturer/Model: Black Diamond/ Mega Light (tarp shelter)

Price: $$$$$$$

Weight: 45 oz.

Dimensions: 7' 2" × 7' 2" × 4' 9"

Pack Size: 5" × 10"

No. of people: 4

Seasons: 4

Manufacturer/Model: Hilleberg the Tentmaker Tarp 20 ×P

Price: $$$$$$$

Weight: 67 oz.

Dimensions: 14' 4.8" × 14' 4.8"

Pack Size: n/a

No. of people: 4

Seasons: 3

Manufacturer/Model: Kelty/Gunnison 4.2

Price: $$$$$$$

Weight: 8 lbs. 15 oz.

Dimensions: 8' 5" × 6' 11" × 4' 5"

Pack Size: 2' × 8"

Pricing key (based on manufacturer's suggested retail price):

$ = under $75
$$ = $76–$100
$$$ = $101–$125
$$$$ = $126–$150
$$$$$ = $151–$200
$$$$$$ = $201–$250
$$$$$$$ = over $251

No. of people: 4

Seasons: 3

Manufacturer/Model: Marmot/Limestone 4P

Price: $$$$$$$

Weight: 11 lbs. 11 oz.

Dimensions: 8' 4" × 7' 2" × 5' 1"

Pack Size: 2' 3.5" × 10"

No. of people: 4

Seasons: 3

Manufacturer/Model: Big Agnes/Mad House 4

Price: $$$$$$$

Weight: 11 lbs. 3 oz.

Dimensions: 7' 8" × 7' 1" × 5' 3"

Pack Size: 2' × 9"

No. of people: 4

Seasons: 3

Manufacturer/Model: The North Face/ Bedrock 4 B×

Price: $$$$$$$

Weight: 11 lbs. 6 oz.

Dimensions: 7' 8" × 7' 2" × 5'

Pack Size: 2' × 9"

No. of people: 4

Seasons: 3

Manufacturer/Model: Bergans of Norway/Compact 4P

Price: $$$$$$$

Weight: 8 lbs. 9 oz.

Dimensions: 7' 5" × 6' 7" × 3' 3"

Pack Size: Contact manufacturer

No. of people: 4

Seasons: 3

Manufacturer/Model: Tarptent/Hogback

Price: $$$$$$$

Weight: 65 oz.

Dimensions: 7' 2" × 7' 2" × 4' 1"

Pack Size: 1' 6" × 5"

No. of people: 4

Seasons: 3

Manufacturer/Model: Sierra Designs/ Yahi 4

Price: $$$$$$$

Weight: 10 lbs. 14 oz.

Dimensions: 7' 8" × 7' 11" × 5' 7"

Pack Size: 2' 2" × 10"

No. of people: 4

Seasons: 3

Manufacturer/Model: Big Sky International/Revolution 4P

Price: $$$$$$$

Weight: 4 lbs. 8 oz.

Dimensions: 8' 6" × 8' × 4'

Pack Size: 1' 7" × 7"

No. of people: 4

Seasons: 3

Manufacturer/Model: MSR/Twin Brothers

Price: $$$$$$$

Weight: 5 lbs.

Dimensions: 14' × 7' 6" × 5' 8"

Pack Size: 1' 8" × 7"

No. of people: 4-6

Seasons: 3

Manufacturer/Model: Exped LLC/ Pegasus

Price: $$$$$$$

Weight: 14 lbs. 9.6 oz.

Dimensions: 7' 7" × 6' 3" × 4' 5"

Pack Size: 2' × 10"

No. of people: 4

Seasons: 3

FIVE-PERSON TENTS

Manufacturer/Model: Oware/FlatTarp5 9.5×13.5'

Price: $$$$

Weight: 26 oz.

Dimensions: 9' 6" × 13' 6"

Pack Size: n/a

No. of people: 5

Seasons: 3

Manufacturer/Model: Integral Designs/ Siltarp 3

Price: $$$$$

Weight: 21 oz.

Dimensions: 10' × 12' × 7'

Pack Size: 7.9" × 4.7"

No. of people: 3-5

Seasons: 3

ELZBIETA SEKOESKA /SHUTTERSTOCK.COM

Manufacturer/Model: Brooks-Range
  Mountaineering/Stubai
Price: $$$$$$$
Weight: 51 oz.
Dimensions: 7' × 11' 5" × 5' 6"
Pack Size: 1' 8" × 10"
No. of people: 5+
Seasons: 3

Manufacturer/Model: Mountainsmith/
  Conifer 5+
Price: $$$$$$$
Weight: 14 lbs. 10 oz.
Dimensions: 10' × 10' × 6' 2"
Pack Size: 2' 2.5" × 10.5"
No. of people: 5+
Seasons: 3

Manufacturer/Model: MSR/Twin Broth-
  ers
Price: $$$$$$$
Weight: 5 lbs.
Dimensions: 14' × 7' 6" × 5' 8"
Pack Size: 1' 8" × 7"
No. of people: 4-6
Seasons: 3

SIX-PERSON TENT

Manufacturer/Model: MSR/Twin Broth-
  ers
Price: $$$$$$$
Weight: 5 lbs.
Dimensions: 14' × 7' 6" × 5' 8"
Pack Size: 1' 8" × 7"
No. of people: 4-6
Seasons: 3

EIGHT-PERSON TENT

Manufacturer/Model: Eureka!/Tetragon
  8
Price: $$$$$$$
Weight: 20 lbs. 2 oz.
Dimensions: 10' × 12' × 6' 4"
Pack Size: 1' 6" × 8"
No. of people: 8
Seasons: 3

Sleeping Bag vs. Space Blanket

IN AN EMERGENCY, WHICH WILL SERVE YOU BEST?

Five minutes ago: Your vehicle careened off the road in icy conditions. You're OK, but the vehicle is damaged.

Four minutes ago: You tried to drive out of the ditch, but it's no use. Walking to help is out of the question. You're miles from anything.

Three minutes ago: The engine shut off. It makes awful noises when you try to restart it.

Two minutes ago: Phone calls for help went unanswered. Tow trucks are busy helping others. Friends and family aren't available.

One minute ago: The sun dipped below the horizon. The warm interior of your vehicle dissipated as the cold crept inside.

Right now: You're reaching for the winter survival kit in the trunk. Are you equipped to stay warm until help arrives?

BY BEN SOBIECK

Here in the Upper Midwest, winter car survival kits are common. And some have either a sleeping bag or a Mylar space blanket and I wanted to see how they compared. Which is the better choice: a sleeping bag or a space blanket?

I spent a chilly night in my car and tested both.

THE SET-UP

My experiment took place on a 30-degree Minnesota night in November. That's not extreme cold by Minnesota standards, but it's enough to conjure hypothermia. My family wouldn't want me outside in 10 degrees anyway. I hit the hay in my 1999 Honda Civic coupe. It stayed parked in the driveway. The keys never touched the ignition. I did not warm the vehicle before or during my experiment.

My attire reflected the average not-concerned-about-winter-survival Joe. I wore a baseball hat, a hooded sweatshirt, jeans with plenty of tears, socks that were more hole than cloth and a dilapidated pair of sneakers.

I used a single 4 foot by 6 foot Mylar space blanket from Lifeline. For those unfamiliar, a space blanket is the glorified tinfoil you see at outdoors shops. It's packed into a square the size of a deck of cards. This particular model claimed to reflect 90 percent of body heat. Mylar is a brand name owned by Dupont Teijin Films. Its generic name is biaxially-oriented polyethylene terephthalate (BoPET). But since Mylar is easier to say, it's become like Kleenex or Xerox.

The sleeping bag employed was one I've had for years. It's a cloth Coleman rated for sub-freezing temperatures.

THE LIGHT BULB

After sawing logs in both options, a light went off in my head. What if I combined the two? I wrapped the space blanket over my sleeping bag.

The combination was hardly a gamble, but even I was surprised by the results. I didn't become warmer, but I didn't lose

SPACE BLANKET PROS & CONS

PROS

Yes, it's actually warm. I wrapped the space blanket tight against my body and kicked the driver's seat back. Despite feeling like a well-placed sneeze would turn it to shreds, the "glorified tinfoil" was remarkably warm. It radiated heat in an almost electric way. For such an unassuming product, this warmth caught me by surprise. It shrugged off the 30-degree night.

Portability. At about the size of a deck of cards, there was no questioning the portability of the lightweight space blanket. This continued beyond the first use. I folded it back into a square and stuffed it into a plastic bag. It's ready for when I need it again.

It lights up like a Christmas tree. Along with heat, the space blanket reflected light. Whenever a car drove by, the headlights triggered an explosion of light across the blanket. It would be ideal for signaling help.

Mobility. I adjusted my sleeping arrangements with ease. The space blanket didn't get caught on the steering wheel or stick shift. Had I some tape and more blankets, I could've lined the interior in Mylar. Keep that tip in mind when designing your own winter car survival kits.

Transparency. Mylar is a strange material. It's reflective in lit conditions. Turning out the lights has the opposite effect. With my head above the space blanket and my mobile phone beneath, I was able to work the dimly lit touch screen with total clarity. This isn't so much an advantage as an observation. There could be a benefit. I just don't see it.

CONS

Zero comfort. If comfort equals morale in survival situations, then the space blanket is downright depressing. Other than the warmth, nothing about the space blanket added to my comfort. The average person will want a degree of comfort. On that note, go add a pillow to your winter car survival kit. My neck sorely missed it during the experiment.

Coverage gaps. It was difficult to get a tight seal around my body. Tape would've solved this problem. I didn't think that far ahead. If space blankets are part of your survival kit, be sure to include tape. You don't want warmth escaping.

Punctures. Snuggling up the space blanket brought on a couple punctures. These could've quickly grown into large tears. Surprisingly, the intact Mylar resisted my attempts to rip it outright.

Breathability. The Mylar material wasn't breathable. Tucking my head under the blanket felt downright suffocating. This meant I had to keep my face uncovered. Not ideal in cold conditions. This was par for the course, though. The packaging contained a suffocation warning.

heat, either. Adding the space blanket prevented the usual cooling of a frigid overnight in a sleeping bag.

CONCLUSION

If I had to pick just one, I'd go with the sleeping bag. The comfort factor went a long way with me.

But in the real world, I'm going with both. Tossing a few space blankets next to my sleeping bag isn't going to eat up much trunk room.

That's a few space blankets, not just one. They're small and inexpensive. Why not keep a pile? While you're at it, pick up some tape.

The overnight experience made me realize how many ways space blankets could be used. Line tent walls with them to keep in warmth. Or put them on the outside to reflect heat in the summer.

Wrap a bottle in them to keep contents warm or cool. Signal rescuers. Side your water heater with them for better efficiency.

However you use them, space blankets are an essential for winter car survival kits. So is a sleeping bag. Use both, but don't stop at that. Include tools, food, fire-making items, a snow-melting tin, clothes and a phone charger. You'll be at your best when things are at their winter worst.

SLEEPING BAG PROS & CONS

PROS

Warm. No surprises here, the sleeping bag felt warm as ever. The 30-degree night didn't faze me.

Comfortable. The soft, flannel lining was far more comfortable than the austere space blanket. The stuffing padded me against the car seat. Sleep came easy.

No coverage gaps. Unlike the space blanket, there were no coverage gaps. I slid in, zipped up and felt warm all over. Its shape contoured to mine.

Breathability. No risk of suffocation here. I could've crawled to the bottom of the sleeping bag without a problem.

Durability. Mice rented the sleeping bag a couple years back. Even with the damage, the sleeping bag should hold up for years to come. I'm not sure I could say the same about the space blanket. Those punctures could have compromised future reliability.

CONS

Bulky. The padding is a great feature, but it also takes up more space. That means it's more of a challenge to make everything fit. Had there been other people with sleeping bags, it would've been a tight fit. The space blanket provides warmth using a far smaller area.

Portability. My sleeping bag takes a good amount of space in the trunk. Storing sleeping bags for a family of four would leave little room for anything else. That doesn't seem practical. Since I'm the only one who ever occupies that car, I can worry about myself. Others might choose the space blankets for their portability advantage.

No reflectivity. Whereas the space blanket could double as a reflective signal, my forehead could reflect more light than the sleeping bag.

Buyer's Guide to Sleeping Bags

Manufacturer/Model: ALPS Mountaineering/Desert Pine
Price: $$$
Weight: 3 lbs. 12 oz.
Lengths: 72", 80", 84", 86"
Girth: 64"
Shape: Mummy
Temperature Rating (F): 20°
Shell Material: Ripstop
Fill Material: Proprietary synthetic
Hood: yes

Manufacturer/Model: Marmot/Trestles 15
Price: $$$
Weight: 3 lbs. 14 oz.
Lengths: 72"; 78"
Girth: 62"; 64"; 70"
Shape: Mummy
Temperature Rating (F): 12°
Shell Material: Polyester
Fill Material: Proprietary synthetic
Hood: yes

Manufacturer/Model: Eureka!/Dual-Temp 20/40
Price: $$$
Weight: 3 lbs. 6 oz.
Lengths: 72"
Girth: 66"
Shape: Semi-rectangular
Temperature Rating (F): 20°
Shell Material: Ripstop, taffeta
Fill Material: Proprietary synthetic
Hood: no

Manufacturer/Model: Kelty/Mistral -20
Price: $$$
Weight: 6 lbs. 3 oz.; 6lbs. 11 oz.
Lengths: 80"; 86"
Girth: 64"; 66"
Shape: Mummy
Temperature Rating (F): -4°
Shell Material: Ripstop

Fill Material: Proprietary synthetic
Hood: yes

Manufacturer/Model: Mountain Hardwear/Petaluma 20
Price: $$$$
Weight: 3 lbs. 1 oz.
Lengths: 70", 76"
Girth: 56", 58"
Shape: Mummy
Temperature Rating (F): 20°
Shell Material: Taffeta
Fill Material: Proprietary synthetic
Hood: yes

Manufacturer/Model: Mountain Equipment Co-op (MEC)/Aquila -7C
Price: $$$$$$
Weight: 43 oz.
Lengths: 72"; 78"
Girth: 57"
Shape: Mummy
Temperature Rating (F): 19°
Shell Material: Polyester
Fill Material: Down
Hood: yes

Manufacturer/Model: Recreational Equipment, Inc. (REI)/Radiant (with wide option)
Price: $$$$$$
Weight: 40oz.; 43 oz.; 3 lbs. 2 oz.
Lengths: 72"; 78"
Girth: 62"; 70"
Shape: Mummy
Temperature Rating (F): 19°
Shell Material: Ripstop
Fill Material: Down
Hood: yes

Manufacturer/Model: Mountain Equipment Co-op (MEC)/Phoenix Hybrid -20C
Price: $$$$$$
Weight: 4 lbs. 12 oz.
Lengths: 66"; 72"; 78"

Pricing key (based on manufacturer's suggested retail price):

$ = under $75
$$ = $76–$100
$$$ = $101–$125
$$$$ = $126–$150
$$$$$ = $151–$200
$$$$$$ = $201–$250
$$$$$$$ = over $251

Girth: 54"
Shape: Mummy
Temperature Rating (F): -4°
Shell Material: Polyester with water-shedding treatment
Fill Material: Down and Proprietary synthetic
Hood: yes

Manufacturer/Model: Big Agnes/Hog Park 20
Price: $$$$$
Weight: 5 lbs. 11 oz.
Lengths: 78"
Girth: 80.5"
Shape: Rectangular
Temperature Rating (F): 20°
Shell Material: Ripstop
Fill Material: Proprietary synthetic
Hood: yes

Manufacturer/Model: Brooks-Range/Elephant Foot Sleeping Bag
Price: $$$$$
Weight: 16 oz.
Lengths: 61"
Girth: 60"
Shape: Mummy
Temperature Rating (F): 15°
Shell Material: Proprietary synthetic
Fill Material: Down
Hood: no

Manufacturer/Model: Marmot/Women's Angel Fire
Price: $$$$$
Weight: 44 oz.
Lengths: 66"; 70"
Girth: 58"
Shape: Mummy
Temperature Rating (F): 20°
Shell Material: Ripstop
Fill Material: Down
Hood: yes

Manufacturer/Model: Sea to Summit/ Traverse XT1
Price: $$$$$$$
Weight: 36 oz.; 38 oz.; 43 oz.
Lengths: 72"; 78"
Girth: 59"; 61"
Shape: Mummy
Temperature Rating (F): 5°
Shell Material: Proprietary synthetic
Fill Material: Down
Hood: yes

Manufacturer/Model: Big Agnes/Roxy Ann 15 (2013)
Price: $$$$$$$
Weight: 42 oz.; 47 oz.
Lengths: 66"; 70"
Girth: 68"; 70"
Shape: Semi-rectangular
Temperature Rating (F): 15°
Shell Material: Water-resistant microfiber ripstop
Fill Material: Down
Hood: yes

Manufacturer/Model: Therm-a-Rest/ Haven Top Bag
Price: $$$$$$$
Weight: 31 oz.; 34 oz.
Lengths: 72"; 78"
Girth: 62"; 64"
Shape: Mummy
Temperature Rating (F): 15°
Shell Material: Ripstop
Fill Material: Down
Hood: yes

Manufacturer/Model: Sierra Designs/ Mobile Mummy 800 3-Season
Price: $$$$$$$
Weight: 36 oz.
Length: 72"; 78"
Girth: 64"; 68"
Shape: Mummy
Temperature Rating (F): 16°
Shell Material: Ripstop
Fill Material: Down
Hood: yes

Manufacturer/Model: Sierra Designs/ Zissou 12
Price: $$$$$$$
Weight: 39 oz.
Lengths: 72"; 78"
Girth: 62"; 64"
Shape: Mummy
Temperature Rating (F): 12°
Shell Material: Ripstop
Fill Material: Down
Hood: yes

Manufacturer/Model: Marmot/Women's Ouray
Price: $$$$$$$
Weight: 3 lbs. 10 oz.
Lengths: 66"; 70"
Girth: 58"; 60"
Shape: Mummy
Temperature Rating (F): 15°
Shell Material: Ripstop
Fill Material: Down
Hood: yes

SLEEPING BAGS RATED 21–32°F

Manufacturer/Model: Kelty/Tumbler 30/50
Price: $$
Weight: 3 lbs. 13 oz.
Lengths: 78"
Girth: 68"
Shape: Rectangular
Temperature Rating (F): 30°
Shell Material: Ripstop
Fill Material: Proprietary synthetic
Hood: no

Manufacturer/Model: REI/Polar Pod
Price: $$
Weight 3 lbs. 4 oz.; 3 lbs. 8 oz.
Lengths: 66"; 72"; 78"
Girth: 68"
Shape: Mummy
Temperature Rating (F): 30°
Shell Material: Taffeta
Fill Material: Polyester
Hood: yes

Manufacturer/Model: L.L. Bean/Adventure Sleeping Bag, Rectangular 30°
Price: $$$
Weight: 3 lbs. 13 oz.; 4 lbs. 2 oz.
Lengths: 72"; 78"
Girth: 69"
Shape: Rectangular
Temperature Rating (F): 30°
Shell Material: Ripstop
Fill Material: Proprietary synthetic
Hood: no

Manufacturer/Model: Mountain Equipment Co-op (MEC)/Mirage -5C
Price: $$$
Weight: 3 lbs. 9 oz.
Lengths: 66"; 72"; 78"
Girth: 63"
Shape: Barrel
Temperature Rating (F): 23°
Shell Material: Water-repellent ripstop
Fill Material: Proprietary synthetic
Hood: no

Manufacturer/Model: Marmot/Cloudbreak 30
Price: $$$$$

Pricing key (based on manufacturer's suggested retail price):

$ = under $75
$$ = $76–$100
$$$ = $101–$125
$$$$ = $126–$150
$$$$$ = $151–$200
$$$$$$ = $201–$250
$$$$$$$ = over $251

Weight: 32 oz.; 36 oz.
Lengths: 72"; 78"
Girth: 60"
Shape: Mummy
Temperature Rating (F): 30°
Shell Material: Ripstop
Fill Material: Proprietary synthetic
Hood: yes

Manufacturer/Model: Recreational Equipment, Inc. (REI)/Lumen
Price: $$$$$
Weight: 43 oz. 47 oz.
Lengths: 72"; 78"
Girth: 62"
Shape: Mummy
Temperature Rating (F): 27°
Shell Material: Ripstop
Fill Material: Proprietary synthetic
Hood: yes

Manufacturer/Model: Therm-a-Rest/ Saros
Price: $$$$$
Weight: 47 oz.; 3 lbs. 3 oz.
Lengths: 72"; 78"
Girth: 62"; 64"
Shape: Mummy
Temperature Rating (F): 23°
Shell Material: Water-repellant polyester
Fill Material: Proprietary synthetic
Hood: yes

Manufacturer/Model: Sierra Designs/ Backcountry Bed 600 2-Season
Price: $$$$$
Weight: 40 oz.
Lengths: 72"; 78"
Girth: 61"; 65"
Shape: Mummy bed
Temperature Rating (F): 27°
Shell Material: Ripstop
Fill Material: Down
Hood: yes

Manufacturer/Model: Mammut/Kompakt 3-Season
Price: $$$$$
Weight: 3 lbs. 3 oz.
Lengths: 71"; 77"
Girth: 33"

Shape: Mummy
Temperature Rating (F): 23°
Shell Material: Proprietary synthetic
Fill Material: Proprietary synthetic
Hood: yes

Manufacturer/Model: Mountain Laurel Designs/Spirit Quilts 28-38-48
Price: $$$$$
Weight: 19oz.; 21 oz.; 23 oz.; 26 oz.
Lengths: 66"; 70"; 74"; 78"
Girth: 46"; 48"; 50"; 52"
Shape: Mummy
Temperature Rating (F): 28°
Shell Material: Proprietary water-resistant ripstop
Fill Material: ClimaShield Apex
Hood: no

Manufacturer/Model: Western Mountaineering/Tamarack
Price: $$$$$$$
Weight: 19 oz.
Lengths: 60"
Girth: 58"
Shape: Semi-rectangular
Temperature Rating (F): 30°
Shell Material: Proprietary synthetic
Fill Material: Down
Hood: no

Manufacturer/Model: Montbell North America/Down Hugger 900 #2
Price: $$$$$$$
Weight: 24 oz.
Lengths: 72"; 78"
Girth: 53"-75"; 57"-81"
Shape: Mummy
Temperature Rating (F): 23°
Shell Material: Ballistic Airlight with proprietary water-repellent treatment
Fill Material: Down
Hood: yes

Manufacturer/Model: Western Mountaineering/Sycamore MF
Price: $$$$$$$
Weight: 32 oz.; 34 oz.
Lengths: 72"; 78"
Girth: 62"
Shape: Semi-rectangular

Temperature Rating (F): 25°
Shell Material: Proprietary synthetic
Fill Material: Down
Hood: yes

Manufacturer/Model: Mountain Equipment Co-op (MEC)/Megalite -2C
Price: $$$$$$$
Weight: 21 oz.
Lengths: 66"; 72"; 78"
Girth: 64"
Shape: Mummy
Temperature Rating (F): 28°
Shell Material: Ripstop
Fill Material: Down
Hood: yes

Manufacturer/Model: Recreational Equipment, Inc. (REI)/Flash
Price: $$$$$$$
Weight: 26 oz.; 28 oz.
Lengths: 72"; 78"
Girth: 60"
Shape: Mummy
Temperature Rating (F): 29°
Shell Material: Ripstop
Fill Material: Down (top), PrimaLoft Sport (bottom)
Hood: yes

Manufacturer/Model: GoLite/Men's Z30 Two-Season
Price: $$$$$$$
Weight: 25 oz.; 27 oz.
Lengths: 72"; 78"
Girth: 60"; 62"
Shape: Mummy
Temperature Rating (F): 30°
Shell Material: Proprietary water-repellent synthetic
Fill Material: Down
Hood: yes

Manufacturer/Model: Western Mountaineering/Alder MF
Price: $$$$$$$
Weight: 31 oz.; 33 oz.
Lengths: 72"; 78"
Girth: 62"
Shape: Semi-rectangular
Temperature Rating (F): 25°

Shell Material: Proprietary synthetic microfiber
Fill Material: Down
Hood: no

SLEEPING BAGS RATED 32–44°F

Manufacturer/Model: Columbia Sportswear/Radiator 40 Semi-Rec
Price: $
Weight: 43 oz.
Lengths: 72"; 78"
Girth: 63"
Shape: Semi-rectangular
Temperature Rating (F): 40°
Shell Material: Proprietary synthetic ripstop
Fill Material: Proprietary synthetic
Hood: no

Manufacturer/Model: Kelty/Mistral 40
Price: $$
Weight: 3 lbs. 8 oz.; 3 lbs. 12 oz.; 3 lbs. 15 oz.
Lengths: 72"; 78"
Girth: 64"; 66"; 72"
Shape: Mummy
Temperature Rating (F): 40°
Shell Material: Ripstop
Fill Material: Proprietary synthetic
Hood: yes

Manufacturer/Model: Marmot/Mavericks 40 Semi Rec
Price: $$
Weight: 35 oz.; 44 oz.
Lengths: 72"; 78"
Girth: 60"; 62"
Shape: Semi-rectangular
Temperature Rating (F): 40°
Shell Material: Water-repellant treated polyester
Fill Material: Proprietary synthetic
Hood: no

Manufacturer/Model: Marmot/Rockaway 35
Price: $$$
Weight: 3 lbs. 6 oz.; 3 lbs. 9 oz.
Lengths: 72"; 78"
Girth: 58"; 60"

Shape: Semi-rectangular
Temperature Rating (F): 33°
Shell Material: Water-repellant polyester and taffeta
Fill Material: Proprietary synthetic
Hood: yes

Manufacturer/Model: Millet/Baikal 1100
Price: $$$
Weight: 41 oz.; 43 oz.
Lengths: 73"; 79"
Girth: 63"; 65"
Shape: Mummy
Temperature Rating (F): 32°
Shell Material: Ripstop
Fill Material: Proprietary synthetic
Hood: yes

Manufacturer/Model: Mountain Hardwear/Flip 35/50
Price: $$$$
Weight: 44 oz.
Lengths: 72"
Girth: 62"
Shape: Semi-rectangular
Temperature Rating (F): 40°
Shell Material: Taffeta
Fill Material: Proprietary synthetic
Hood: no

Manufacturer/Model: Montbell North America/Burrow Bag #5
Price: $$$$
Weight: 34 oz.; 35 oz.
Lengths: 72"; 78"
Girth: 53"-75"; 57"-81"
Shape: Mummy
Temperature Rating (F): 39°
Shell Material: Nylon
Fill Material: Water-repellant treated proprietary synthetic
Hood: yes

Manufacturer/Model: Mountain Equipment Co-op (MEC)/Aquila 0C
Price: $$$$$
Weight: 34 oz.
Lengths: 72"; 78"
Girth: 59"
Shape: Mummy
Temperature Rating (F): 32°

Shell Material: Water-repellent polyester
Fill Material: Down
Hood: yes

Manufacturer/Model: L.L. Bean/L.L. Bean Ultralight Sleeping Bag 35°
Price: $$$$$
Weight: 32 oz.; 36 oz.
Lengths: 72"; 78"
Girth: 60"
Shape: Semi-rectangular
Temperature Rating (F): 35°
Shell Material: Ripstop
Fill Material: PrimaLoft Sport
Hood: yes

Manufacturer/Model: GoLite/Unisex Adventure 40 One-Season Semi-Rec
Price: $$$$$
Weight: 32 oz.; 35 oz.; 37 oz.
Lengths: 66"; 72"; 78"
Girth: 62"; 64"
Shape: Semi-rectangular
Temperature Rating (F): 40°
Shell Material: Proprietary water-repellent synthetic
Fill Material: Down
Hood: no

Manufacturer/Model: The North Face/Basalt 40/4
Price: $$$$$
Weight: 39 oz.; 43 oz.
Lengths: 77"; 83"
Girth: 66"; 68"
Shape: Mummy
Temperature Rating (F): 40°
Shell Material: Polyester taffeta

Fill Material: Water-resistant down
Hood: no

Manufacturer/Model: Mountain Hardwear/Laminina 35
Price: $$$$$
Weight: 38 oz.
Lengths: 66"; 72"; 78"
Girth: 62"; 64"
Shape: Mummy
Temperature Rating (F): 32°
Shell Material: Ripstop
Fill Material: Proprietary synthetic
Hood: yes

Manufacturer/Model: MusucBag/Classic
Price: $$$$$
Weight: 3 lbs. 12 oz.; 4 lbs. 2 oz.; 4 lbs. 10 oz.
Lengths: 61"-66"; 67"-72"; 73"-80"
Girth: 47"; 50"; 53"
Shape: Mummy suit with arms and legs
Temperature Rating (F): 39°
Shell Material: Ripstop
Fill Material: Polyester
Hood: yes

Manufacturer/Model: NEMO Equipment, Inc./W'S Harmony™ 40 PrimaLoft
Price: $$$$$
Weight: 33 oz.
Lengths: 66"
Girth: 62"
Shape: Spoon
Temperature Rating (F): 40°
Shell Material: Water-repellant ripstop
Fill Material: Proprietary sythetic
Hood: yes

Manufacturer/Model: Marmot/Always Summer
Price: $$$$$
Weight: 29 oz.; 32 oz.
Lengths: 72"; 78"
Girth: 63"; 65"
Shape: Mummy
Temperature Rating (F): 40°
Shell Material: Ripstop
Fill Material: Down
Hood: yes

Manufacturer/Model: Big Agnes/Big Creek 30
Price: $$$$$$
Weight: 5 lbs. 8 oz.
Lengths: 74"
Girth: 110"
Shape: Rectangular
Temperature Rating (F): 30°
Shell Material: Ripstop
Fill Material: Proprietary synthetic
Hood: yes

Manufacturer/Model: Feathered Friends/Vireo Nano
Price: $$$$$
Weight: 8 oz.; 8.7 oz.; 9.4 oz.
Lengths: 62"; 68"; 74"
Girth: 64"
Shape: Mummy
Temperature Rating (F): 35°
Shell Material: Proprietary synthetic
Fill Material: Down
Hood: no

Manufacturer/Model: Millet/Dreamer Composite 1000
Price: $$$$$
Weight: 39 oz.
Lengths: 73"
Girth: 63"
Shape: Mummy
Temperature Rating (F): 34°
Shell Material: Polyester
Fill Material: Proprietary synthetic and down
Hood: yes

Manufacturer/Model: Eagles Nest Outfitters/Ignitor Topquilt
Price: $$$$$
Weight: 23 oz.
Lengths: 73"
Girth: 4' wide
Shape: Semi-rectangular; rectangular
Temperature Rating (F): 35°
Shell Material: Water-repellent ripstop and taffeta
Fill Material: Down
Hood: no

Manufacturer/Model: Mammut/Sphere UL Spring
Price: $$$$$$
Weight: 18 oz.
Lengths: 73"; 77"
Girth: 56"
Shape: Mummy
Temperature Rating (F): 39°
Shell Material: Proprietary water-repellent synthetic
Fill Material: Down
Hood: yes

Manufacturer/Model: Exped/Ultralite 300
Price: $$$$$$
Weight: 20 oz.
Lengths: 71"
Girth: 57"
Shape: Trim fit mummy
Temperature Rating (F): 41°
Shell Material: Ripstop
Fill Material: Down
Hood: yes

Manufacturer/Model: Therm-a-Rest/ Auriga 35F Down Blanket
Price: $$$$$$
Weight: 21 oz.; 24 oz.
Lengths: 70"; 76"
Girth: 48"; 52"
Shape: Semi-rectangular/ rectangular
Temperature Rating (F): 35°
Shell Material: Polyester
Fill Material: Down
Hood: no

Manufacturer/Model: Nunatak Gear LLC/Arc AT 3/4 Quilt
Price: $$$$$$
Weight: 8 oz.
Lengths: 64"; 72"; 78"
Girth: 42"
Shape: Mummy
Temperature Rating (F): 40°
Shell Material: Epic by Nextec, pertex microlight, pertex quantum
Fill Material: Down
Hood: no

Manufacturer/Model: MusucBag/Patagon
Price: $$$$$$$
Weight: 36 oz.
Lengths: 61"-66"; 67"-72"; 73"-78"
Girth: 47"; 50"; 53"
Shape: Mummy suit with arms and legs
Temperature Rating (F): 36°
Shell Material: Ripstop
Fill Material: Polyester
Hood: yes

Manufacturer/Model: Eastern Mountain Sports/Mountain Light 35°
Price: $$$$$$
Weight: 24 oz.
Lengths: 72"; 78"
Girth: 60"
Shape: Mummy
Temperature Rating (F): 35°
Shell Material: Pertex water-repellant ripstop
Fill Material: Down
Hood: yes

Manufacturer/Model: Sea to Summit/Trek I
Price: $$$$$$
Weight: 29 oz.; 32 oz.
Lengths: 72"; 78"
Girth: 60"; 61"
Shape: Semi-rectangular
Temperature Rating (F): 32°
Shell Material: Proprietary water-resistant synthetic
Fill Material: Down
Hood: yes

Pricing key (based on manufacturer's suggested retail price):

$ = under $75
$$ = $76–$100
$$$ = $101–$125
$$$$ = $126–$150
$$$$$ = $151–$200
$$$$$$ = $201–$250
$$$$$$$ = over $251

Manufacturer/Model: Feathered Friends/Vireo UL
Price: $$$$$$$
Weight: 8 oz.; 8.7 oz.; 9.4 oz.
Lengths: 62"; 68"; 74"
Girth: 64"
Shape: Mummy
Temperature Rating (F): 35°
Shell Material: Proprietary sythetic
Fill Material: Down
Hood: no

Manufacturer/Model: Nunatak Gear LLC/Arc Edge
Price: $$$$$$$
Weight: 11 oz.; 12 oz.; 13 oz.
Lengths: 64"; 70"; 76"
Girth: 43"; 46"
Shape: Mummy
Temperature Rating (F): 40°
Shell Material: Epic by Nextec, pertex quantum
Fill Material: Down
Hood: no

Manufacturer/Model: Kelty/SB 35
Price: $$$$$$
Weight: 25 oz.; 28 oz.
Lengths: 72"; 78"
Girth: 62"; 64"
Shape: Mummy
Temperature Rating (F): 35°
Shell Material: Ripstop
Fill Material: Down
Hood: yes

SLEEPING BAGS RATED OVER 45°F

Manufacturer/Model: Recreational Equipment, Inc. (REI)/Travel Sack
Price: $
Weight: 19 oz.
Lengths: 78"
Girth: 60"
Shape: Mummy
Temperature Rating (F): 55°
Shell Material: Polyester taffeta
Fill Material: Synthetic
Hood: yes

Manufacturer/Model: Eureka!/Minnow
Price: $
Weight: 37 oz.
Lengths: 60"
Girth: 52"
Shape: Rectangular
Temperature Rating (F): 45°
Shell Material: Polyester taffeta
Fill Material: ThermaShield™
Hood: no

Manufacturer/Model: Kelty/Tumbler 50/70
Price: $
Weight: 28 oz.
Lengths: 78"
Girth: 68"
Shape: Rectangular
Temperature Rating (F): 50°
Shell Material: Polyester ripstop
Fill Material: Proprietary synthetic
Hood: no

Manufacturer/Model: Marmot/NanoWave55
Price: $
Weight: 8 oz.
Lengths: 72"; 78"
Girth: 60"; 62"
Shape: Mummy
Temperature Rating (F): 55°
Shell Material: Water-repellent polyester taffeta
Fill Material: Proprietary synthetic
Hood: yes

Manufacturer/Model: Marmot/NanoWave 50
Price: $$
Weight: 30 oz.
Lengths: 72"; 78"
Girth: 60"; 62"
Shape: Semi-rectangular
Temperature Rating (F): 50°
Shell Material: Water-repellent polyester taffeta
Fill Material: Proprietary synthetic
Hood: yes

Manufacturer/Model: MusucBag/Lite
Price: $$
Weight: 46 oz.; 56 oz.; 63 oz.
Lengths: 61"-66"; 67"-72"; 73"-80"
Girth: 47"; 50"; 53"
Shape: Mummy suit with arms and legs
Temperature Rating (F): 46°
Shell Material: Polyester taffeta
Fill Material: Polyester
Hood: yes

Manufacturer/Model: Recreational Equipment, Inc. (REI)/ Travel Down
Price: $$$$
Weight: 29 oz.
Lengths: 78"
Girth: 60"
Shape: Mummy
Temperature Rating (F): 45°
Shell Material: Polyester taffeta
Fill Material: Down
Hood: yes

Manufacturer/Model: Montbell North America/Alpine Down Hugger 800 Thermal Sheet
Price: $$$$$
Weight: 15 oz.
Lengths: 72"
Girth: 57"-68"
Shape: Semi-rectangular
Temperature Rating (F): 50°
Shell Material: Water-repellent proprietary ripstop
Fill Material: Down
Hood: no

Manufacturer/Model: Brooks-Range Mountaineering Equipment/Cloak 45
Price: $$$$$
Weight: 13 oz.
Lengths: 74"
Girth: 40"
Shape: Rectangular
Temperature Rating (F): 45°
Shell Material: Water-repellent nylon
Fill Material: Down
Hood: no

Manufacturer/Model: Sea to Summit/ Traveller TR1
Price: $$$$$
Weight: 14 oz.; 17 oz.
Lengths: 72"; 79"
Girth: 57"; 60"
Shape: Tapered rectangular
Temperature Rating (F): 50°
Shell Material: Ripstop
Fill Material: Down
Hood: no

Manufacturer/Model: Sea to Summit/ Spark Sp 1
Price: $$$$$$$
Weight: 12 oz.; 14 oz.
Lengths: 72"; 79"
Girth: 57"
Shape: Mummy
Temperature Rating (F): 46°
Shell Material: Proprietary synthetic
Fill Material: Down
Hood: yes

WOMEN'S SLEEPING BAGS RATED BELOW 20°F

Manufacturer/Model: The North Face/ Aleutian 20/-7
Price: $$$
Weight: 3 lbs. 10 oz. 4 lbs.; 4 lbs. 6 oz.
Lengths: 72"; 78"
Girth: 63"; 64"
Shape: Mummy
Temperature Rating (F): 20°
Shell Material: Water-resistant polyester taffeta
Fill Material: Proprietary synthetic
Hood: yes

Manufacturer/Model: Big Agnes/Lulu
Price: $$$$$
Weight: 3 lbs. 5 oz.; 3 lbs. 10 oz.
Lengths: 66"; 70"
Girth: 68"; 70"
Shape: Semi-rectangular
Temperature Rating (F): 15°
Shell Material: Water-repellent ripstop
Fill Material: Proprietary synthetic
Hood: yes

Manufacturer/Model: Eastern Mountain Sports/Women's Boreal 20
Price: $$$$$
Weight: 22 oz.
Lengths: 66"
Girth: 59"
Shape: Mummy
Temperature Rating (F): 20°
Shell Material: Ripstop
Fill Material: Proprietary synthetic
Hood: yes

Manufacturer/Model: The North Face/W Cat's Meow
Price: $$$$$
Weight: 3 lbs. 7 oz.; 3 lbs. 12 oz.
Lengths: 66"; 72"
Girth: 61"
Shape: Mummy
Temperature Rating (F): 20°
Shell Material: Polyester
Fill Material: Proprietary synthetic
Hood: yes

Manufacturer/Model: Recreational Equipment, Inc. (REI)/Serrana
Price: $$$$$$
Weight: 3 lbs. 2 oz.; 3 lbs. 6 oz.
Lengths: 66"; 72"
Girth: 60"
Shape: Mummy
Temperature Rating (F): 19°
Shell Material: Ripstop
Fill Material: Down
Hood: yes

Manufacturer/Model: Eastern Mountain Sports/Women's Mountain Light 15°
Price: $$$$$$$
Weight: 32 oz.
Lengths: 66"
Girth: 59"
Shape: Mummy
Temperature Rating (F): 15°
Shell Material: Water-repellent Pertex
Fill Material: Down
Hood: yes

Manufacturer/Model: Mountain Hard-
wear/Heratia 15 Women's
Price: $$$$$$$
Weight: 39 oz.; 41 oz.
Lengths: 68"; 70"
Girth: 56"; 58"
Shape: Mummy
Temperature Rating (F): 15°
Shell Material: Nylon
Fill Material: Down
Hood: yes

WOMEN'S SLEEPING BAGS RATED 21–32°F

Manufacturer/Model: Marmot/Women's
Trestles 30
Price: $$$
Weight: 3 lbs. 4 oz.; 3 lbs. 8 oz.
Lengths: 66"; 70"
Girth: 58"; 60"
Shape: Mummy
Temperature Rating (F): 30°
Shell Material: Water-repellent polyester
taffeta
Fill Material: Proprietary synthetic
Hood: yes

Manufacturer/Model: Mountain Equip-
ment Co-op (MEC)/Aquilina 0C
(Women's)
Price: $$$$$
Weight: 34 oz.
Lengths: 64"; 70"
Girth: 59"
Shape: Mummy
Temperature Rating (F): 32°
Shell Material: Water-repellent polyester
Fill Material: Down
Hood: yes

Manufacturer/Model: Big Agnes/Wom-
en's Moon Hill 26
Price: $$$$$
Weight: 30 oz.; 34 oz.
Lengths: 66"; 70"
Girth: 54"; 56"
Shape: Mummy
Temperature Rating (F): 26°
Shell Material: Ripstop

Fill Material: Proprietary synthetic
Hood: yes

Manufacturer/Model: Big Agnes/Wom-
en's Mirror Lake 22
Price: $$$$$
Weight: 39 oz.; 42 oz.
Lengths: 66"; 70"
Girth: 54"; 56"
Shape: Mummy
Temperature Rating (F): 22°
Shell Material: Ripstop
Fill Material: Down
Hood: yes

Manufacturer/Model: GoLite/Women's
Z30 Three-Season
Price: $$$$$$$
Weight: 20 oz.; 22 oz.
Lengths: 66"; 72"
Girth: 54"; 56"
Shape: Mummy
Temperature Rating (F): 30°
Shell Material: Water-repellent Pertex
Quantum
Fill Material: Down
Hood: yes

Manufacturer/Model: Recreational
Equipment, Inc. (REI)/Joule
Price: $$$$$$$
Weight: 34 oz.; 36 oz.
Lengths: 66"; 72"
Girth: 58"
Shape: Mummy
Temperature Rating (F): 23°
Shell Material: Nylon taffeta
Fill Material: Down
Hood: yes

WOMEN'S SLEEPING BAGS RATED 33–44°F

Manufacturer/Model: Mountainsmith/
Boreas 40F Synthetic
Price: $$
Weight: 3 lbs. 5 oz.
Lengths: 78"
Girth: 68"
Shape: Rectangular
Temperature Rating (F): 40°

Shell Material: Ripstop
Fill Material: Proprietary synthetic
Hood: yes

Manufacturer/Model: Recreational
Equipment, Inc. (REI)/Halo +40
Price: $$$
Weight: 26 oz.
Lengths: 66"; 72"
Girth: 58"
Shape: Mummy
Temperature Rating (F): 40°
Shell Material: Ripstop
Fill Material: Down
Hood: yes

Manufacturer/Model: Kelty/Women's
SB 35
Price: $$$$$
Weight: 40 oz.
Lengths: 68"
Girth: 58"
Shape: Mummy
Temperature Rating (F): 35°
Shell Material: Ripstop
Fill Material: Water-resistant down
Hood: yes

CHILDREN'S SLEEPING BAGS RATED BELOW 20°F

Manufacturer/Model: Eureka!/Cypress
Price: $
Weight: 3 lbs. 7 oz.
Lengths: 66"
Girth: 60"
Shape: Mummy
Temperature Rating (F): 15°
Shell Material: Polyester Taffeta

Pricing key (based on manufacturer's suggested retail price):

$ = under $50
$$ = $51-$75
$$$ = $76–$100
$$$$ = $101–$125
$$$$$ = $126–$150
$$$$$$ = $151–$200
$$$$$$$ = $201–$250

Fill Material: ThermaShield
Hood: yes

Manufacturer/Model: Kelty/Little Tree
  20
Price: $
Weight: 41 oz.
Lengths: 64"
Girth: 56"
Shape: Mummy
Temperature Rating (F): 20°
Shell Material: Polyester taffeta
Fill Material: Proprietary synthetic
Hood: yes

Manufacturer/Model: The North Face/
  Youth Aleutian 20/-7
Price: $$
Weight: 46 oz.
Lengths: 60"
Girth: 56"
Shape: Mummy
Temperature Rating (F): 20°
Shell Material: Polyester
Fill Material: Proprietary synthetic
Hood: yes

CHILDREN'S SLEEPING BAGS RATED 21°F–40°F

Manufacturer/Model: Mountainsmith/
  Boreas Jr. 40
Price: $
Weight: 35 oz.
Lengths: 61"
Girth: 56"
Shape: Rectangular
Temperature Rating (F): 40°
Shell Material: Ripstop
Fill Material: Proprietary synthetic
Hood: yes

Manufacturer/Model: Marmot/Kid's
  Maverricks 40 Semi Rec
Price: $$
Weight: 30 oz.
Lengths: 60"
Girth: 56"
Shape: Semi-rectangular
Temperature Rating (F): 40°
Shell Material: Water-repellent polyester

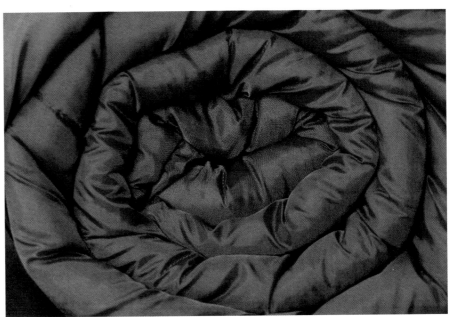

ZOUZOUBABY / SHUTTERSTOCK.COM

Fill Material: Proprietary synthetic
Hood: no

Manufacturer/Model: Recreational
  Equipment, Inc. (REI)/Nodder
Price: $$
Weight: 40 oz.
Lengths: 60"
Girth: 52"
Shape: Mummy
Temperature Rating (F): 25°
Shell Material: Ripstop
Fill Material: Polyester
Hood: yes

Manufacturer/Model: Kelty/Big Dipper
  30
Price: $$
Weight: 3 lbs. 1 oz.
Lengths: 60"
Girth: 56"
Shape: Mummy
Temperature Rating (F): 30°
Shell Material: Polyester taffeta
Fill Material: Proprietary synthetic
Hood: yes

Buyer's Guide to Sleeping Pads

Pricing key (based on manufacturer's suggested retail price):

$ = under $50
$$ = $51-$75
$$$ = $76–$100
$$$$ = $101–$125
$$$$$ = $126–$150
$$$$$$ = over $151

LENGTH OF 48" AND UNDER

Manufacturer/Model: Oware/Foam ³⁄₁₆" Thick Sleeping Pad
Price: $
Pad Type: Foam
Weight: 2.75 oz.
Shape: Rectangular
Length: 40"
Width: 19"
Thickness: ³⁄₁₆"
Packed Size: 40" × 5"
Inflatable: No

Manufacturer/Model: Therm-a-Rest/ Trail Scout
Price: $
Pad Type: Self-inflating
Weight: 14 oz.
Shape: Semi-rectangular
Length: 47"
Width: 20"
Thickness: 1"
Packed Size: 11" × 4.6"
Inflatable: Yes

Manufacturer/Model: Montbell North America/Extension Pad 30
Price: $
Pad Type: Closed cell foam
Weight: 2.5 oz.
Shape: Rectangular
Length: 20"
Width: 11.8"
Thickness: ¹⁄₂₅"

Packed Size: 11.8" × 1.6" × 4.7"
Inflatable: No

Manufacturer/Model: Therm-a-Rest/ RidgeRest SOLite (Small)
Price: $
Pad Type: Molded closed cell foam
Weight: 9 oz.
Shape: Rectangular
Length: 48"
Width: 20"
Thickness: ⅝"
Packed Size: 20" × 6.5"
Inflatable: No

Manufacturer/Model: Big Agnes/ Air Core
Price: $
Pad Type: Inflatable
Weight: 14 oz.
Shape: Rectangular
Length: 48"
Width: 20"
Thickness: 3.25"
Packed Size: 3" × 9.5"
Inflatable: Yes

Manufacturer/Model: ALPS Mountaineering/Lightweight Air Pad Short
Price: $
Pad Type: Self-inflating
Weight: 6 oz.
Shape: Rectangular
Length: 20"
Width: 48"
Thickness: 1.5"
Packed Size: 4" × 21"
Inflatable: Yes

Manufacturer/Model: Gossamer Gear/ Nightlight Sleeping Pad (torso length)
Price: $
Pad Type: "Egg crate" pattern foam
Weight: 4.55 – 4.90 oz.
Shape: Rectangular
Length: 29"

Width: 19"
Thickness: ¾"
Packed Size: 18" × 10.75" × 2.25"
Inflatable: No

Manufacturer/Model: Big Agnes/ Air Core
Price: $
Pad Type: Inflatable
Weight: 14 oz.
Shape: Rectangular
Length: 48"
Width: 20"
Thickness: 3.25"
Packed Size: 3" × 9.5"
Inflatable: Yes

Manufacturer/Model: NEMO Equipment, Inc./Ora 20S Sleeping Pad
Price: $$
Pad Type: Self-inflating
Weight: 13.5 oz.
Shape: Mummy
Length: 48"
Width: 20"
Thickness: 1"
Packed Size: 8" × 4"
Inflatable: Yes

Manufacturer/Model: Kelty/PDSI 3/4
Price: $$
Pad Type: Self-inflating
Weight: 16.5 oz.
Shape: Bio-mummy ¾
Length: 48"
Width: 20"
Thickness: 1"
Packed Size: 6.5" × 10" × 3.5"
Inflatable: Yes

Manufacturer/Model: Hyalite Equipment/Adventurer AC
Price: $$
Pad Type: Self-inflating
Weight: 16 oz.
Shape: Rectangular

Length: 48"

Width: 20"

Thickness: 2.5

Packed Size: 4" × 12"

Inflatable: Yes

Manufacturer/Model: L.L. Bean/Path-finder Sleeping Pad Short

Price: $$

Pad Type: Self-inflating

Weight: 22 oz.

Shape: Rectangular

Length: 48"

Width: 20"

Thickness: 2"

Packed Size: 21" × 6"

Inflatable: Yes

Manufacturer/Model: Montbell North America/UL Comfort System Pad 120

Price: $$

Pad Type: Self-inflating

Weight: 14.6 oz.

Shape: Rectangular

Length: 47"

Width: 20"

Thickness: 1"

Packed Size: 3.9" × 10"

Inflatable: Yes

Manufacturer/Model: Hyalite Equipment/Peak Elite AC

Price: $$

Pad Type: Inflatable

Weight: 11 oz.

Shape: Rectangular

Length: 48"

Width: 20"

Thickness: 2.5"

Packed Size: 4" × 12"

Inflatable: Yes

Manufacturer/Model: Klymit/Intertia X Wave

Price: $$$

Pad Type: Inflating

Weight: 10.5 oz.

Shape: Semi-rectangular

Length: 48"

Width: 25"

Thickness: 1.5"

Packed Size: 3" × 7"

Inflatable: Yes

Manufacturer/Model: NEMO Equipment, Inc./Zor™ 20S Sleeping Pad

Price: $$$

Pad Type: Self-inflating

Weight: 14 oz.

Shape: Mummy

Length: 48"

Width: 20"

Thickness: 1"

Packed Size: 7" × 3.5"

Inflatable: Yes

Manufacturer/Model: Gossamer Gear/ Air Beam Sleeper

Price: $$$

Pad Type: Inflatable

Weight: 9.9 oz.

Shape: Rectangular

Length: 48"

Width: 21"

Thickness: 1.5"

Packed Size: 3" × 4"

Inflatable: Yes

Manufacturer/Model: Therm-a-Rest/ ProLite Plus

Price: $$$

Pad Type: Self-inflating

Weight: 15 oz.

Shape: Mummy

Length: 47"

Width: 20"

Thickness: 1.5"

Packed Size: 11" × 4"

Inflatable: Yes

Manufacturer/Model: Hyalite Equipment/Adventurer AC

Price: $$$

Pad Type: Inflatable

Weight: 13.4 oz.

Shape: Mummy

Length: 48"

Width: 20"

Thickness: 2.5"

Packed Size: 4" × 12"

Inflatable: Yes

Manufacturer/Model: Big Agnes/Insulated Air Core

Price: $$$

Pad Type: Inflatable

Weight: 15 oz.

Shape: Rectangular

Length: 48"

Width: 20"

Thickness: 3.25"

Packed Size: 5" × 7.5"

Inflatable: Yes

Manufacturer/Model: Klymit/Inertia X-Lite

Price: $$$

Pad Type: Inflatable

Weight: 6.1 oz.

Shape: Semi-rectangular

Length: 42"

Width: 18"

Thickness: 1.5"

Packed Size: 2.5" × 5.5"

Inflatable: Yes

Manufacturer/Model: Hyalite Equipment/Peak Oyl Mtn (Uber)

Price: $$$

Pad Type: Self-inflating

Weight: 13 oz.

Shape: Mummy

Length: 45"

Width: 94"

Thickness: 3.8"

Packed Size: 5" × 11"

Inflatable: Yes

Manufacturer/Model: Therm-a-Rest/ NeoAir Trekker (Large Torso)

Price: $$$$

Pad Type: Inflating

Weight: 15 oz.

Shape: Rectangular

Length: 47"

Width: 25"

Thickness: 2.5"

Packed Size: 11" × 3.7"

Inflatable: Yes

Manufacturer/Model: Therm-a-Rest/ NeoAir XTherm (Small)

Price: $$$$$

Pad Type: Inflatable
Weight: 11 oz.
Shape: Semi-rectangular
Length: 47"
Width: 20"
Thickness: 2.5"
Packed Size: 9" × 3.3"
Inflatable: Yes

Manufacturer/Model: Exped/DownMat UL 7 XS
Price: $$$$$$
Pad Type: Inflatable
Weight: 14 oz.
Shape: Rectangular
Length: 47"
Width: 21"
Thickness: 2.8"
Packed Size: 4" × 9"
flatable: Yes

LENGTH OF 49"–72"

Manufacturer/Model: Gossamer Gear/ Thinlight Insulation Pad
Price: $
Pad Type: Foam
Weight: 2.4 – 2.8 oz.
Shape: Rectangular
Length: 59 1/8"
Width: 19 3/8"
Thickness: 1/8"
Packed Size: 19 3/8" × 4"
Inflatable: No

Manufacturer/Model: ALPS Mountaineering/Foam Mat Regular 375
Price: $
Pad Type: Foam
Weight: 9 oz.
Shape: Rectangular
Length: 72"
Width: 20"
Thickness: 3/8"
Packed Size: 20" × 6"
Inflatable: No

Manufacturer/Model: Therm-a-Rest/ RidgeRest Classic
Price: $
Pad Type: Foam

Weight: 14 oz.
Shape: Rectangular
Length: 72"
Width: 20"
Thickness: 5/8"
Packed Size: 20" × 8"
Inflatable: No

Manufacturer/Model: Hyalite Equipment/Classic AC
Price: $
Pad Type: Inflatable
Weight: 22 oz.
Shape: Rectangular
Length: 72"
Width: 20"
Thickness: 2.5"
Packed Size: 4" × 12"
Inflatable: Yes

Manufacturer/Model: Eastern Mountain Sports/Hobo Sleeping Pad
Price: $
Pad Type: Self-inflating
Weight: 28 oz.
Shape: Rectangular
Length: 72"
Width: 20"
Thickness: 1"
Packed Size: Contact manufacturer
Inflatable: Yes

Manufacturer/Model: Oware/Foam 1/2" Thick, Winter Sleeping Pad
Price: $
Pad Type: Foam
Weight: 7.5 oz.
Shape: Rectangular
Length: 60"
Width: 20"
Thickness: 1/2"
Packed Size: 20" × 7"
Inflatable: No

Manufacturer/Model: Slumberjack/ Denali Composite
Price: $
Pad Type: Foam
Weight: 28 oz.
Shape: Mummy
Length: 50"

Width: 20"
Thickness: 1.25"
Packed Size: 20" × 6"
Inflatable: No

Manufacturer/Model: Hyalite Equipment/Classic SI
Price: $
Pad Type: Self-inflating
Weight: 32 oz.
Shape: Rectangular
Length: 72"
Width: 20"
Thickness: 1"
Packed Size: 6" × 13"
Inflatable: Yes

Manufacturer/Model: Eastern Mountain Sports/Siesta Sleeping Pad
Price: $$
Pad Type: Self-inflating
Weight: 21.5 oz.
Shape: Semi-rectangular
Length: 72"
Width: 20"
Thickness: 1"
Packed Size: 6" × 20"
Inflatable: Yes

Manufacturer/Model: Exped/AirMat Lite 5 M
Price: $$
Pad Type: Inflatable
Weight: 18 oz.
Shape: Rectangular
Length: 72"
Width: 21"
Thickness: 2"
Packed Size: 9" × 4"
Inflatable: Yes

Pricing key (based on manufacturer's suggested retail price):

$ = under $50
$$ = $51-$75
$$$ = $76–$100
$$$$ = $101–$125
$$$$$ = $126–$150
$$$$$$ = over $151

Manufacturer/Model: Mountain Equipment Co-op (MEC)/Reactor 2.5 Sleeping Pad
Price: $$
Pad Type: Self-inflating
Weight: 21 oz.
Shape: Rectangular
Length: 71"
Width: 20"
Thickness: 1"
Packed Size: 11.4" × 6"
Inflatable: Yes

Manufacturer/Model: Klymit/Static V
Price: $$
Pad Type: Inflatable
Weight: 18.1 oz.
Shape: Semi-rectangular
Length: 72"
Width: 23"
Thickness: 2.5"
Packed Size: 5" × 9"
Inflatable: Yes

Manufacturer/Model: Montbell North America/UL Comfort System Air Pad 180
Price: $$
Pad Type: Self-inflating
Weight: 18.69 oz.
Shape: Rectangular
Length: 71"
Width: 20"
Thickness: 3"
Packed Size: 4.3" × 8.2"
Inflatable: Yes

Manufacturer/Model: Eureka!/Singlis ST
Price: $$
Pad Type: Inflatable
Weight: 15 oz.
Shape: Rectangular
Length: 72"
Width: 20"
Thickness: 2.8"
Packed Size: 3" × 10"
Inflatable: Yes

Manufacturer/Model: Vaude/Air Mattress
Price: $$
Pad Type: Inflatable

Weight: 14 oz.
Shape: Rectangular
Length: 71"
Width: 20"
Thickness: 2"
Packed Size: 6" × 4"
Inflatable: Yes

Manufacturer/Model: Montbell North America/UL Comfort System Pad 180
Price: $$
Pad Type: Self-inflating
Weight: 22.2 oz.
Shape: Rectangular
Length: 71"
Width: 20"
Thickness: 1"
Packed Size: 4.7" × 10"
Inflatable: Yes

Manufacturer/Model: Vaude/Sove
Price: $$
Pad Type: Self-inflating
Weight: 28 oz.
Shape: Rectangular
Length: 72"
Width: 20"
Thickness: 1"
Packed Size: 10.5" × 8"
Inflatable: Yes

Manufacurer/Model: High Peak USA/Eco Lite
Price: $$
Pad Type: Self-inflating
Weight: 25 oz.
Shape: Rectangular
Length: 72"
Width: 20"
Thickness: 1"
Packed Size: 11" × 5"
Inflatable: Yes

Manufacturer/Model: Mountain Equipment Co-op (MEC)/Reactor 3.8 Sleeping Pad
Price: $$
Pad Type: Self-inflating
Weight: 26 oz.
Shape: Rectangle
Length: 72"

Width: 21"
Thickness: 1.5"
Packed Size: 11.5" × 6.5"
Inflatable: Yes

Manufacturer/Model: Kelty/PDa
Price: $$
Pad Type: Inflatable
Weight: 14.5 oz.
Shape: Mummy
Length: 72"
Width: 20"
Thickness: 2"
Packed Size: 8" × 6" × 1.5"
Inflatable: Yes

Manufacturer/Model: Therm-a-Rest/NeoAir XLite
Price: $$
Pad Type: Inflatable
Weight: 12 oz.
Shape: Semi-rectangular
Length: 72"
Width: 20"
Thickness: 2.5"
Packed Size: 9" × 4"
Inflatable: Yes

Manufacturer/Model: Crazy Creek Products/HEX 2.0 PowerLounger
Price: $$
Pad Type: Doubles as chair
Weight: 29.8 oz.
Shape: Rectangular
Length: 53.5"
Width: 17.5"
Thickness: ½"
Packed Size: 17.5" × 5.5"
Inflatable: No

Manufacturer/Model: REI/REI AirRail 1.5 Self-Inflating Sleeping Pad
Price: $$
Pad Type: Self-inflating
Weight: 26 oz.
Shape: Mummy
Length: 72"
Width: 23"
Thickness: 1.5"
Packed Size: 9" × 6.5"
Inflatable: Yes

Manufacturer/Model: Eureka!/Dualis ST
Price: $$$
Pad Type: Self-inflating
Weight: 47 oz.
Shape: Rectangular
Length: 72"
Width: 20"
Thickness: 1.25"
Packed Size: 5" × 23"
Inflatable: Yes

Manufacturer/Model: Therm-a-Rest/ProLite
Price: $$$
Pad Type: Self-inflating
Weight: 16 oz.
Shape: Mummy
Length: 72"
Width: 20"
Thickness: 1"
Packed Size: 11" × 4.1"
Inflatable: Yes

Manufacturer/Model: Cabela's/XPG Sleeping Pad
Price: $$$
Pad Type: Inflatable
Weight: 20.25 oz.
Shape: Rectangular
Length: 72"
Width: 23.5"
Thickness: 2.5"
Packed Size: 7.5" × 3"
Inflatable: Yes

Manufacturer/Model: ALPS Mountaineering/Ultra-Light Series Regular
Price: $$$
Pad Type: Self-inflating
Weight: 24 oz.

Pricing key (based on manufacturer's suggested retail price):

$ = under $50
$$ = $51-$75
$$$ = $76–$100
$$$$ = $101–$125
$$$$$ = $126–$150
$$$$$$ = over $151

Shape: Semi-rectangular
Length: 72"
Width: 20"
Thickness: 1.5"
Packed Size: 5" × 20"
Inflatable: Yes

Manufacturer/Model: Hyalite Equipment/Adventurer SI
Price: $$$
Pad Type: Self-inflating
Weight: 30 oz.
Shape: Mummy
Length: 72"
Width: 20"
Thickness: 1.5"
Packed Size: 7.5" × 13"
Inflatable: Yes

Manufacturer/Model: Therm-a-Rest/NeoAir Camper
Price: $$$
Pad Type: Inflatable
Weight: 24 oz.
Shape: Rectangular
Length: 72"
Width: 20"
Thickness: 3"
Packed Size: 4" × 12"
Inflatable: Yes

Manufacturer/Model: NEMO Equipment, Inc./Tuo 20R Sleeping Pad
Price: $$$
Pad Type: Inflatable
Weight: 36 oz.
Shape: Mummy
Length: 72"
Width: 20"
Thickness: 1.6"
Packed Size: 9.5" × 6"
Inflatable: Yes

Manufacturer/Model: REI/REI Stratus Insulated Air – Regular
Price: $$$
Pad Type: Inflatable
Weight: 20 oz.
Shape: Rectangular
Length: 72"
Width: 20"

Thickness: 2.5"
Packed Size: 5.25" × 7"
Inflatable: Yes

Manufacturer/Model: Big Agnes/Sleeping Giant
Price: $$$
Pad Type: Memory Foam
Weight: 39 oz.
Shape: Rectangular
Length: 66"
Width: 20"
Thickness: 1"
Packed Size: 5" × 20"
Inflatable: No

Manufacturer/Model: Kelty/PDsi
Price: $$$
Pad Type: Self-inflating
Weight: 23.5 oz.
Shape: Bio-mummy
Length: 72"
Width: 20"
Thickness: 1"
Packed Size: 5" × 8" × 10"
Inflatable: Yes

Manufacturer/Model: Kelty/Recluse 2.5ni
Price: $$$
Pad Type: Inflatable
Weight: 24 oz.
Shape: Mummy
Length: 72"
Width: 20"
Thickness: 2.5"
Packed Size: 11" × 6"
Inflatable: Yes

Manufacturer/Model: Klymit/Inertia X-Frame
Price: $$$
Pad Type: Inflatable
Weight: 9.1 oz.
Shape: Semi-rectangular
Length: 72"
Width: 18"
Thickness: 1.5"
Packed Size: 3" × 6"
Inflatable: Yes

Manufacturer/Model: Vaude/Venus
Price: $$$
Pad Type: Self-inflating
Weight: 27 oz.
Shape: Rectangular
Length: 72"
Width: 21.6"
Thickness: 1.25"
Packed Size: 10" × 8"
Inflatable: Yes

Manufacturer/Model: Therm-a-Rest/ LuxuryMAP (Regular)
Price: $$$
Pad Type: Self-inflating
Weight: 3lbs. 4oz.
Shape: Rectangular
Length: 72"
Width: 20"
Thickness: 3"
Packed Size: 6.2" × 21"
Inflatable: Yes

Manufacturer/Model: Big Agnes/Q-Core
Price: $$$$
Pad Type: Inflatable
Weight: 25 oz.
Shape: Rectangular
Length: 66"
Width: 20"
Thickness: 3.5"
Packed Size: 5" × 9.5"
Inflatable: Yes

Manufacturer/Model: Vaude/Norrsken
Price: $$$$
Pad Type: Inflatable
Weight: 21 oz.
Shape: Rectangular
Length: 72"
Width: 21"
Thickness: 2"
Packed Size: 10" × 6"
Inflatable: Yes

Manufacturer/Model: Crazy Creek Products/Air Chair Plus
Price: $$$$
Pad Type: Inflatable
Weight: 45 oz.

Shape: Rectangular
Length: 70"
Width: 20"
Thickness: 2.5"
Packed Size: 20" × 4"
Inflatable: Yes

Manufacturer/Model: REI/ REI Camp Bed 3.5 Self-Inflating Sleeping Pad
Price: $$$$
Pad Type: Self-inflating
Weight: 4 lbs. 9 oz.
Shape: Rectangular
Length: 72"
Width: 25"
Thickness: 3.5"
Packed Size: 6.25" × 26"
Inflatable: Yes

Manufacturer/Model: Big Agnes/Box Canyon Bedroll
Price: $$$$
Pad Type: Air mesh
Weight: 28 oz.
Shape: Rectangular
Length: 66"
Width: 20"
Thickness: ¾"
Packed Size: 5" × 22"
Inflatable: No

Manufacturer/Model: REI/REI Camp Bed 3.5 Regular
Price: $$$$
Pad Type: Self-inflating
Weight: 4lbs. 9oz.
Shape: Rectangular
Length: 72"
Width: 25"
Thickness: 3.5"
Packed Size: 6.25" × 26"
Inflatable: Yes

Manufacturer/Model: Hyalite Equipment/Peak Oyl Lite
Price: $$$$
Pad Type: Self-inflating
Weight: 19 oz.
Shape: Mummy
Length: 72"
Width: 20"

Thickness: 1"
Packed Size: 6" × 13"
Inflatable: Yes

Manufacturer/Model: Mammut/Slide-stop Mat
Price: $$$$
Pad Type: Self-inflating
Weight: 26 oz.
Shape: Body fit
Length: 72"
Width: 20"
Thickness: 1.3"
Packed Size: 10.2" × 5.1"
Inflatable: Yes

Manufacturer/Model: Hyalite Equipment/Peak Oyl Elite (POE)
Price: $$$$$
Pad Type: Self-inflating
Weight: 26 oz.
Shape: Mummy
Length: 72"
Width: 20"
Thickness: 1.5"
Packed Size: 7.5" × 13"
Inflatable: Yes

Manufacturer/Model: NEMO Equipment, Inc./Astro Insulated Lite
Price: $$$$$
Pad Type: Inflatable
Weight: 19 oz.
Shape: Rectangular
Length: 72"
Width: 20"
Thickness: 3"
Packed Size: 8" × 4"
Inflatable: Yes

Manufacturer/Model: Therm-a-Rest/ NeoAir Trekker (Regular)
Price: $$$$$
Pad Type: Inflatable
Weight: 17 oz.
Shape: Rectangular
Length: 72"
Width: 20"
Thickness: 2.5"
Packed Size: 9" × 4.5"
Inflatable: Yes

Manufacturer/Model: Warmlite/D.A.M. 56
Price: $$$$$
Pad Type: Inflatable
Weight: 20 oz.
Shape: Semi-rectangular
Length: 65"
Width: 22"
Thickness: ½"
Packed Size: Contact manufacturer
Inflatable: Yes

Manufacturer/Model: Big Agnes/Triple Core
Price: $$$$$
Pad Type: Inflatable
Weight: 34 oz.
Shape: Rectangular
Length: 66"
Width: 20"
Thickness: 4.25"
Packed Size: 6" × 23"
Inflatable: Yes

Manufacturer/Model: Exped/SynMat UL 7 S
Price: $$$$$$
Pad Type: Inflatable
Weight: 14 oz.
Shape: Rectangular
Length: 64"
Width: 21"
Thickness: 2.8"
Packed Size: 9" × 4"
Inflatable: Yes

Manufacturer/Model: Big Agnes/Q-Core SL
Price: $$$$$$
Pad Type: Inflatable
Weight: 16 oz.
Shape: Rectangular
Length: 72"
Width: 20"
Thickness: 3.5"
Packed Size: 3.5" × 8.5"
Inflatable: Yes

Manufacturer/Model: Mammut/Light Pump Mat UL
Price: $$$$$$
Pad Type: Inflatable
Weight: 19.7 oz.
Shape: Alipine
Length: 72"
Width: 20"
Thickness: 3"
Packed Size: 7.5" × 4.7"
Inflatable: Yes

Manufacturer/Model: Exped/SynMat UL 7 M
Price: $$$$$$
Pad Type: Inflatable
Weight: 16oz.
Shape: Rectangular
Length: 72"
Width: 21"
Thickness: 2.8"
Packed Size: 9" × 4"
Inflatable: Yes

Manufacturer/Model: Mammut/Light Pump Mat EXP
Price: $$$$$$
Pad Type: Inflatable
Weight: 27.8 oz.
Shape: Alpine
Length: 72"
Width: 20"
Thickness: 3"
Packed Size: 17" × 5"
Inflatable: Yes

Manufacturer/Model: Exped/DownMat 9 M
Price: $$$$$$
Pad Type: Inflatable
Weight: 35 oz.
Shape: Rectangular
Length: 72"
Width: 21"
Thickness: 3.5"
Packed Size: 9" × 6"
Inflatable: Yes

Manufacturer/Model: Exped/Synmat UL 9 S
Price: $$$$$$
Pad Type: Inflatable
Weight: 21 oz.
Shape: Rectangular
Length: 72"

Width: 21"
Thickness: 3.5"
Packed Size: 9" × 5"
Inflatable: Yes

Manufacturer/Model: Exped/DownMat 7 M
Price: $$$$$$
Pad Type: Inflatable
Weight: 20 oz.
Shape: Rectangular
Length: 72"
Width: 21"
Thickness: 2.8"
Packed Size: 9" × 4"
Inflatable: Yes

Manufacturer/Model: Exped/DownMat UL 7 M
Price: $$$$$$
Pad Type: Inflatable
Weight: 20 oz.
Shape: Rectangular
Length: 72"
Width: 21"
Thickness: 2.8"
Packed Size: 9" × 4"
Inflatable: Yes

Manufacturer/Model: Exped/DownMat XP 9 M
Price: $$$$$$
Pad Type: Inflatable
Weight: 34 oz.
Shape: Rectangular
Length: 72"
Width: 21"
Thickness: 3.5"
Packed Size: 9" × 6"
Inflatable: Yes

Pricing key (based on manufacturer's suggested retail price):

$ = under $50
$$ = $51-$75
$$$ = $76–$100
$$$$ = $101–$125
$$$$$ = $126–$150
$$$$$$ = over $151

Manufacturer/Model: Therm-a-Rest/
NeoAir XTherm (Regular)
Price: $$$$$$
Pad Type: Inflatable
Weight: 15 oz.
Shape: Mummy
Length: 72"
Width: 20"
Thickness: 2.5"
Packed Size: 9" × 4"
Inflatable: Yes

LENGTH OVER 73"

Manufacturer/Model: NEMO Equipment, Inc./Ora 25L Sleeping Pad
Price: $$$
Pad Type: Self-inflating
Weight: 31 oz.
Shape: Rectangular
Length: 76"
Width: 25"
Thickness: 1.5"
Packed Size: 8.5" × 6"
Inflatable: Yes

Manufacturer/Model: Big Agnes/Hinman
Price: $$$
Pad Type: Self-inflating
Weight: 39 oz.
Shape: Rectangular
Length: 78"
Width: 20"
Thickness: 1.5"
Packed Size: 5.5" × 21"
Inflatable: Yes

Manufacturer/Model: Mountain Equipment Co-op (MEC)/Reactor 6.5 Sleeping Pad
Price: $$$$
Pad Type: Self-inflating
Weight: 3lbs. 10 oz.
Shape: Rectangular
Length: 78"
Width: 26"
Thickness: 2.5"
Packed Size: 27" × 8"
Inflatable: Yes

Manufacturer/Model: Therm-a-Rest/
Trail Pro (Large)
Price: $$$$
Pad Type: Self-inflating
Weight: 40 oz.
Shape: Mummy
Length: 77"
Width: 25"
Thickness: 2"
Packed Size: 13" × 6.7"
Inflatable: Yes

Manufacturer/Model: Klymit/Inertia XL
Price: $$$$
Pad Type: Inflatable
Weight: 16.8 oz.
Shape: Mummy
Length: 77"
Width: 25"
Thickness: 1.5"
Packed Size: 4" × 9"
Inflatable: Yes

Manufacturer/Model: NEMO Equipment, Inc./Cosmo Air
Price: $$$$$
Pad Type: Inflatable
Weight: 29 oz.
Shape: Rectangular
Length: 76"
Width: 25"
Thickness: 4"
Packed Size: 9" × 4.5"
Inflatable: Yes

Manufacturer/Model: Hyalite Equipment/Peak Oyl Mtn (Long)
Price: $$$$$
Pad Type: Inflatable
Weight: 27 oz.
Shape: Mummy
Length: 78"
Width: 20"
Thickness: 1.5"
Packed Size: 6" × 11"
Inflatable: Yes

Manufacturer/Model: Warmlite/D.A.M. 64
Price: $$$$$
Pad Type: Inflatable

Weight: 24 oz.
Shape: Semi-rectangular
Length: 74"
Width: 26"
Thickness: ½"
Packed Size: Contact manufacturer
Inflatable: Yes

Manufacturer/Model: Warmlite/D.A.M. 70
Price: $$$$$$
Pad Type: Inflatable
Weight: 26 oz.
Shape: Semi-rectangular
Length: 80"
Width: 28"
Thickness: ½"
Packed Size: Contact manufacturer
Inflatable: Yes

Manufacturer/Model: Vaude/Dream
Price: $$$$$$
Pad Type: Self-inflating
Weight: 4 lbs. 10 oz.
Shape: Rectangular
Length: 78"
Width: 26"
Thickness: 4"
Packed Size: 27.5" × 6"
Inflatable: Yes

Manufacturer/Model: Vaude/Norrsken Large
Price: $$$$$$
Pad Type: Inflatable
Weight: 30.5 oz.
Shape: Rectangular
Length: 78"
Width: 24"
Thickness: 2"
Packed Size: 10" × 7"
Inflatable: Yes

CHAPTER THREE

Hydration and Water Purification Gear

The first survival rule of threes involves shelter. The second involves water: You can survive for three days without water. Water is essential to life and following a disaster, water may be difficult to come by. Water service may be cut off entirely, and if not, the water supply likely will be contaminated. A solid preparedness plan makes many contingencies for water.

This chapter details everything you need to meet your hydration needs in an emergency. From best practices for storing emergency stockpiles of water to selecting the right emergency water containers to having multiple ways to filter and purify contaminated water. The Buyer's Guides in this chapter cover microfilters, water bottles with built-in filters, water filter straws and UV light water purifiers.

Your Personal Clean Water Act

THE U.S. ENVIRONMENTAL PROTECTION AGENCY DECLARED THAT 55 PERCENT OF AMERICAN RIVERS AND STREAMS ARE UNFIT TO SUSTAIN AQUATIC LIFE. THEIR STUDY FOUND POLLUTION FROM MERCURY, NITROGEN, AND BACTERIA IN VITAL SOURCES OF DRINKING WATER. EMPOWER YOURSELF AND LEARN HOW TO GET CLEAN WATER AT THE MOST BASIC LEVEL.

IAKOV FILIMONOV / SHUTTERSTOCK.COM

BY JOHN D. MCCANN

CONTAIN AND CARRY

All survival kits should provide a container, or some means, to hold water. The container should allow you to purify water in it, and hold water in it for transfer if possible. A recommendation often made is the carrying of a non-lubricated con-

dom. It is small (can even be carried in a mini kit), and can hold a considerable amount of water if it is supported in a sock, sleeve, or trouser leg. I carried one or more in my kits for years.

I have found a small soft water container that folds up flat enough to fit in a mini kit. It is called the Emergency Water Bag and has a gusseted bottom. It is sold

at Survival Resources (survivalresources.com) with a one-quart water line marked on it for use with water purification tablets. They can be folded up very small, yet allow you to carry a quart of water with you. It is sterile as there is a tear off tab on the top to open the bag for the first time. It has a roll down top, which is secured shut with wire tabs specially designed so the ends are covered to prevent puncturing the bag. You simply roll the top down three times, curve the ends together and twist the tabs to secure. The bag is tall and small around, so it is not very stable when setting on the gusseted bottom, but it is a great alternative, specifically for mini kits because of its ability to fold down very small. They are packaged three per bag.

For many years I tried to find a small water container that could be rolled or folded up and kept in a small survival kit. I also wanted it to provide a one-quart line so I could add one water purification tablet, knowing I had the proper amount of water for the tablet. I also wanted it to be free standing and yet have the option of attaching it to a pack or carrying it with the addition of a piece of cordage. Having failed in my search I decided I would design and build one of my own. After many attempts, I finally succeeded and called it the Aqua-Pouch. It is now available from Survival Resources.

As required in my prerequisites, the one-liter Aqua-Pouch is a free standing, zip-closure, water storage container designed for use with water purification tablets. The pouch has a line marked for one liter of water for easy measuring when using water purification tablets. The Aqua-Pouch is extremely sturdy, FDA-approved food grade pouch, which has a gusseted bottom and measures 6.5" wide x 10" high. It can be rolled or folded for easy storage, yet its freestanding ability allows for easy filling and pouring. This pouch will hold boiling water and it can be frozen and then thawed. Because of the large top opening, you can also place snow in it and carry it between your clothing layers for melting. The Aqua-Pouch also has grommets at the top that allow you to attach cordage so you can have a means of transporting the pouch, or attaching it to a pack.

HYDRATION SYSTEMS

Another type of water container that was introduced quite a few years ago, and has become very popular with the military and hikers, is the hydration system. It is basically a flexible water reservoir (or bladder) that is contained a protective carrying case. It has a long tube that hangs out with a drinking valve. Most have to be bitten when drinking so the water does not run out when not in use, but some new styles have an on and off valve as well. Many backpacks today offer a hydration bladder included and often have a separate cavity between the pack and the back for the bladder to be inserted. Many are also being offered in mini backpacks or fanny packs, which could be used to build your survival kit directly into. Various companies, such as Camelbak and Blackhawk's HydraStorm line, are manufacturing these types of hydration systems.

PRE-FILTER

If you use chemicals to purify water, the length of time the chemicals take to properly purify the water can be affected by the turbidity of water. Therefore, you always want to start out with the clearest water possible. If you are using a mechanical filtering device, sediment and other debris in muddy or cloudy water can easily clog the filters. My suggestion

HARD-SIDE CANTEENS

The Nalgene bottles, which are BPA free, are heavy-duty bottles that have wide mouths. I prefer wide mouths, especially when you are trying to fill them from a source of water in the field. My preferred bottle is the 32-ounce Guyot stainless steel single wall bottle, now made for Nalgene. This bottle allows me to boil water while in the bottle which is very handy in a survival situation. It also allows you to melt water that freezes in it when in a cold climate. You can also place hot water in it and use it as a foot warmer in a sleeping bag, after placing it into a sock.

The military style canteen does not have a wide mouth but fits inside the old-style military canteen cup, which is one of my favorites for boiling water or cooking, and being metal (stainless steel) provides the options listed for the Guyot bottle. These bottles can be carried in various sized, medium to large kits. The old military stainless steel canteens are no longer available (except at some military surplus shops), but are what I carry during winter months. Like the Guyot bottle above, they can be placed into a fire if your water freezes, and also double as a foot warmer in a sleeping bag. If you can find one of these old stainless steel military canteens, I highly recommend you buy it.

▲ Check out the scorch marks: metal containers allow for boiling the water.

FLEXIBLE CANTEENS

These are manufactured by various companies such as Nalgene and Platypus. They are made from a clear flexible plastic laminate which allow them to be folded or rolled up when not in use. They come in various sizes, even one that is designed to fit in the cargo pocket of trousers. They can be carried rolled or folded in a kit for use when needed, or carried filled and then rolled or folded for storage to reduce size. They have leak-proof caps, and some have gusseted bottoms, so they will stand up when filled. Also, most can be frozen, and some can even be boiled. These flexible canteens are available with small mouth and large mouth openings. This is often a trade-off, as the small mouth packs are better, but the wide mouth is easier to fill.

▲ Flexible canteens save enormous space in backpacks or bug-out bags.

The Aqua-Pouch in action with a sling-strap for easy carrying.

Blackhawk's HydraStorm and the Frontier Filter and the Frontier Pro.

Removing sediment by pre-filtering.

is to pre-filter water before attempting to purify or filter it.

When water is located in the field, it is not always clear and often contains a lot of debris or sediment. Pre-filtering reduces the turbidity. Keep in mind, this does not purify water, it only removes solid particles from the water. Pre-filtering can be as simple as straining the water through a bandana or T-shirt to eliminate as much debris or sediment as possible. I noticed that various companies included cone coffee filters in their survival kits for pre-filtering water. What they don't tell you is that a "cone" coffee filter will not hold water unless it is supported. My wife, Denise, and I experimented with a multitude of cone coffee filters with the corrugated seams and none of them would hold water without being supported. We experimented with various ways to support the filter during use and finally came up with a solution that is effective, yet folds up very flat. It is called the Pre-Filter Support Sheath, made from poly material, and it works very well. The pre-filter is inserted completely into the sheath. The sheath is then placed on top of your water container. You then simply pour water into the filter to filter out debris, sediment, bugs, etc. The water flows through holes on the side, which are placed above the seam of the filter, and down into your

water container. Again, this does not purify the water, it only pre-filters it.

FILTER

Most water filters only filter water, not purify it. And, although there are some units that both filter and purify water, most do not. Depending on the size of the filter, a filter will eliminate protozoa (such as giardia and cryptosporidium), and most bacteria. They will not eliminate viruses, such a hepatitis A, or bacteria smaller than the size listed on the filter (normally 0.2—0.3 microns).

One thing I have learned about filters: if they are ceramic filter-based systems, they remove waterborne enteric pathogens down to 0.2 microns and pleated glassfiber media filters only remove down to 0.3 microns. I have also found that the ceramic systems get clogged easier and normally pump slower. The smaller the holes in the filter media require more effort to force water through it.

A small handheld filter is the Frontier Filter by Aquamira Technologies, Inc. Basically it is a small filter (3-⅞" × 1" in diameter). A small plastic straw (included) attaches to the filter, and the filter body is inserted directly into water, with care taken not to submerge or otherwise contaminate the straw. You then drink directly from the straw. It is small

enough to be carried in a small kit. The Frontier Filter is certified to remove 99.9 percent of giardia and cryptosporidium, but is not certified to remove bacteria or viruses. Therefore, for maximum protection, use the Frontier Filter in conjunction with some form of water purification tablets.

A new filter being offered by Aquamira Technologies is the Frontier Pro. Though larger than the original Frontier Filter (It measures 6 ⅞" × 1 ¼" in diameter) it provides a lot more versatility. It has an adapter for water bladder systems, can be attached to most commercial water bottles, and something I really like, can be converted to a gravity flow system. Again, even though this device is certified to remove 99.9 percent of giardia and cryptosporidium, it is not certified to remove bacteria or viruses. Therefore, for maximum protection, use the Frontier Pro in conjunction with some form of water purification tablets.

CHEMICAL TREATMENT

The first option is Iodine tablets, which makes questionable water safe to drink. A major brand of Iodine tablets is Potable Aqua, which is manufactured by WPC Brands, Inc. There are 50 tablets in a small glass bottle (2" × 1"). If this is too big for you, Survival Resources sells a small glass

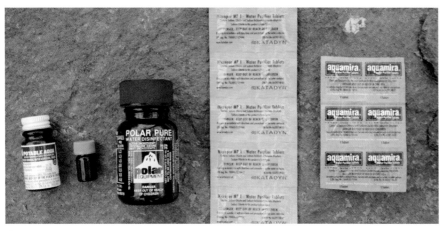

Chemical water purifers have the advantage of being small for mini kits.

The SteriPen zapping some iffy tapwater.

vial with a Teflon screw cap (necessary for re-packaging iodine tablets) which measures only 1 ⅜" × ⅝" diameter. It only holds half as much, but is great for mini kits. Two tablets treat one quart or one liter of water. Directions are printed on the label. It should be noted that iodine treatment makes water taste like iodine and leaves it colored. Potable Aqua also offers P.A. Plus neutralizing tablets to remove the iodine taste and color.

My preferred method of chemical treatment in the field is chlorine dioxide, which is effective against, viruses, bacteria, and cysts, including both giardia lamblia and cryptosporidium. There are various chlorine dioxide-based products available, and I prefer the tablet form. The other thing I like about chlorine dioxide is that the water has no after taste.

The first to offer chlorine dioxide tablets as a means for purification was Katadyn with a product called Micropur MP1. This system uses one tablet per liter of water. Each tablet is in a foil capsule with ten capsules per sheet. They are available in 20 packs (two sheets per package) or 30 packs (three sheets per package). Many other companies are now also offering chlorine dioxide-based tablets including Aquamira and Potable Aqua.

Aquamira also offers a two-part liquid purification system, that when mixed, produces chlorine dioxide. One of the two bottles also has a mixing cap on top.

Place seven drops from each bottle in the mixing cap and let stand for five minutes. You then fill a container with one quart or one liter of water and add the mixture from the cap. Then shake or stir and let stand for 15 minutes (30 minutes if the water is very cold or turbid).

PURIFY

A water purifier actually purifies water by inactivating all water-borne enteric pathogens, to include viruses, bacteria, and protozoa cysts (or at least 99.9 percent). Unlike filters, purifiers actually make water safe to drink, no matter what the pathogens are.

One water purifier that is available is called the SteriPEN. They have various different models, but the one I thought might be best for a survival kit is the SteriPEN Adventure Opti. This is a small unit that can be carried in a small provided belt sheath, or carried in a case, that doubles as a solar charging unit. The SteriPEN creates ultraviolet (UV) light that disrupts the DNA of microbes in seconds. Without functional DNA, microbes can't reproduce or make you sick. The SteriPEN exceeds the U.S. EPA Guide Standard and Protocol for Testing Microbiological Water Purifiers, destroying over 99.9999 percent of bacteria, 99.99 percent of viruses, 99.9 percent of all protozoan cysts, including giardia and cryptosporidium. It has a patent-pending Optical

Water Sensing System that turns the unit on only when it is correctly submerged in water. It purifies 0.5 liters of water in 48 seconds, and one liter of water in 90 seconds. I liked the idea of the unit having the option of being carried in a belt sheath, or inside the solar charging case. Even when carried in the sheath, the extra batteries can be charging in the solar charging case, which has a clip on it to attach to the back of your pack while on the move.

The SteriPEN directions also indicate that the water you are going to purify must be above 32 degrees F (0 degrees C), and if it is not, you should bring it up to that temperature before purifying. The directions also indicate that the unit is intended for use, and is most effective, in clear water. If clear water is not available, you should first try to filter the water. If it is necessary to treat turbid, murky or cloudy water in an emergency situation, then they provide further instruction, including using two treatments.

The other thing that I am always concerned with in a survival situation is depending on anything that runs on batteries, or can be broken. Even though this device is getting a lot of positive reviews, I would recommend carrying an alternative, like chemicals, in the event the unit is lost, broken, or the batteries go dead and there is no sun to help recharge them.

3 Must-Have Water Containers
for Your Bug-Out Bag

BY CREEK STEWART

Because a Bug-Out Bag (BOB) is a 72-hour kit, I suggest you pack a minimum of approximately three liters of fresh drinking water per person.

Even with three full liters, there is little margin for error. Certain weather climates increase the amount of water a person needs to survive. You'll consume more water if your journey is especially rigorous.

Personal hygiene can also tap into your water supply. The water you carry will constitute a large percentage of the overall weight of your Bug-Out Bag.

The good news is that the weight will decrease as you hydrate. In a survival situation, a good emergency water storage container can be invaluable.

Divide your supply up among three different emergency water storage containers. I never suggest carrying all three liters in a single emergency water storage container for two reasons:

1. If you have only one emergency water storage container and you lose or break it, you no longer have a viable way to carry and store water. This can present a very serious threat. Natural water-tight containers are not easy to find or make.

2. It's easier to distribute weight in your Bug-Out Bag when it is divided into two or three smaller emergency water storage containers. I suggest dividing your water into the following three different containers:
   - a wide-mouth hard bottle
   - a metal water bottle
   - a collapsible soft bottle

WIDE-MOUTH HARD BOTTLE

Nalgene bottles are durable and crush resistant. Although "Nalgene" is actu-

ally a brand, the word has been adopted generically to describe any hardened plastic bottle (sort of like Kleenex and Xerox).

I have used Nalgenes in countless adventures and never has one failed me. I've even dropped one from 50 feet while rock climbing and it came out unscathed. Get the wide mouth version. They are easier to fill and they can double as a dish to eat from if necessary.

On their sides are printed measuring units, which is convenient for preparing dehydrated meals. I've also never had one leak. You can trust it in your pack.

METAL WATER BOTTLE

These canteens weigh about the same as any Nalgene bottle. Rather than just carrying two Nalgene bottles, I suggest opting for a metal alternative.

A metal emergency water storage container can be used to boil and purify drinking water collected "in the field" should your immediate supply run dry.

COLLAPSIBLE SOFT BOTTLE

Packing a collapsible, soft emergency water storage container allows you to reduce bulk as water is used. Consume the contents of this emergency water storage container first.

When empty, they take up virtually no space and weigh just a few ounces.

They are not as durable, but with the two other containers listed above, you can afford to sacrifice durability for weight and space with this option.

8 Water Storage Options for Your Home

BY ANGELA PASKETT

It is easy to take water for granted. We turn on the tap, and it comes pouring out, fresh and clean and ready to use in any way we need. But what if it didn't come out? Or what if your water source was contaminated? Either of those scenarios could happen as a result of a major disaster or breakdown in the water treatment or delivery system.

In a disaster, before you need any food, you will need clean water. Contaminated water can carry a whole host of different bacteria (E. coli, Giardia) protozoa, and parasites and cause diseases including cholera. Drinking contaminated water can lead to serious illness and even death.

In most cases, it is impractical, if not impossible, to store a large amount of water. Because of this, FEMA recommends storing one gallon (4L) per person per day for two weeks. That is 14 gallons (53L) of water for each member of your family. In theory, this amount will be adequate for drinking and sanitation, however, most of us can easily use more than one gallon (4L) per day.

Try turning off your water for the day and you'll quickly realize just how many ways you use water. Calculate the water you use in a day and you'll find how fast washing, drinking, cooking, and more add up. The easiest solution to having clean water in an emergency is to have a supply of water stored in your home. Here are eight containers you can use for water storage.

STORE-BOUGHT GALLONS OF WATER

You can purchase jugs of drinking water that look like milk jugs, commonly found in most grocery and variety stores.

Pros
- inexpensive, usually less than a dollar per gallon
- readily available at most stores
- manageable weight

Cons
- thin jug plastic has a short shelf life and frequently develops leaks
- cannot be stacked

WATER BOTTLES

The single-serving kind can be purchased individually or by the case.

Pros
- readily available at many stores
- inexpensive if purchased by the case
- portable, single serve, and resealable
- cases can be stacked

Cons
- small, so you need many to get your 1-gallon-per-person-per-day quota, especially for a large family
- make a lot of waste

REUSED PETE BOTTLES

Two-liter soda bottles are inexpensive examples of PETE (polyethylene terephthalate) bottles. Empty soda bottles offer an almost free water storage option that you would otherwise be throwing away. Offer to help clean up after a party and you can go home with a bunch of them! Wash them with dish soap and sanitize by rinsing with a mixture of ten parts water to one part bleach (e.g., 10 cups water to 1 cup bleach) before filling.

Pros
- practically free
- good size to fit in little unused spaces in your house like behind the couch or in a closet
- easy to carry—they weigh only about 4½ pounds (2kg) when full

Cons
- difficult to stack
- need to be thoroughly cleaned before filling with water
- water should be rotated every six to twelve months, more frequently than commercially filled bottles

WATERBRICKS

Waterbricks are plastic, cube-shaped containers that hold 3½ gallons (13L) of water and can stack like building blocks.

WATER STORED AROUND THE HOME

Don't forget that there are places in your home where you already have clean water that you could use in an emergency:

- water heater
- pipes
- ice cube trays

Water that isn't safe to drink but could be used for other purposes during an emergency:

- toilet tank
- water bed
- swimming pool

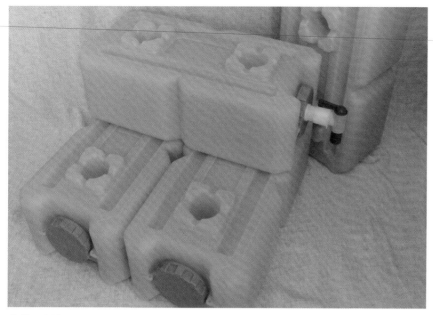

▲ Waterbricks

Pros

- weigh only 28 pounds (13kg) full and come with carrying handles
- wide mouth opening makes for easy cleaning
- stable when stacked
- low profile—can fit under a bed
- available spout makes dispensing water easy

Cons

- expensive—cost about seventeen dollars each, plus more for the spout

FIVE-GALLON HARD PLASTIC JUGS

Five-gallon jugs come in a variety of shapes and colors and can be found in most stores that sell camping equipment, as well as in many emergency supply retailers.

Pros

- sturdy construction
- available spout attachments dispense water easily
- hold approximately one day's worth of water for a family of four or five

Cons

- slightly more expensive than other options

- moderately heavy, about 40 pounds (18kg) each when full
- some are designed to stack, but others aren't, so they can use up a lot of floor space

BATHTUB WATER BLADDER

In an emergency situation, you can fill your bathtub with water to create a reserve of water. Before you fill the tub, fit it with a bathtub water bladder such as the AquaPod to keep the water clean and contained.

Pros

- holds as much water as your bathtub
- packs small when not in use

Cons

- most are designed for one-time use
- designed to be filled right before an emergency
- sharp-clawed indoor pets can damage the bladder
- tub is unavailable for anything else when the water bladder is in use

30- TO 55-GALLON DRUM

Large plastic barrels that can hold 30 to 55 gallons (114 to 208L) of water are available at most emergency supply retailers.

Pros

- large volume
- small footprint for the amount of water they hold

Cons

- cost
- very heavy, so very difficult to move when full
- need a pump or siphon system to get water out
- bulky—it might be tough to find a place for one of these in a small home
- round shape can leave wasted space in corners where it is stored

WATER STORAGE TANK

A few manufacturers have created water storage tanks that can hold between 160 and 320 gallons (606L and 1,121L).

Pros

- very large volume
- some are rectangular-shaped, so there is no wasted corner space
- easy-to-dispense water when using the attached spouts
- most have vents that let air in, allowing water to flow out smoothly

Cons

- cost
- weight
- require a large space for storage—again maybe not a good fit for a small home

Find more survival water information in *Food Storage for Self-Sufficiency and Survival* by Angela Paskett, available at store.livingreadyonline.com.

Ready-to-Drink
Natural Water Sources

BY CREEK STEWART

In a survival situation, gathering water that doesn't need to be purified is certainly preferred. It saves time, fuel, and energy. Finding fresh drinking water is certainly not a guarantee, but sure is nice.

Keeping in the theme of energy conservation, here's a list of the most practical methods for gathering water that does not need to be purified, starting with the easiest.

RAIN

Rain can be collected and consumed without treatment or purification. However, you need to collect it in your own container. As soon as rainwater comes in contact with the earth or another water source (e.g., puddle, pond, stream), it needs to be purified. So what's the best way to collect the rainwater without having it touch the ground? If you set your container out in the rain and just waited for it fill, it would take a very long time to fill up (if it ever does).

The most effective way to gather rainwater is to build a rain-catch system. If possible, use a tarp, plastic sheet, garbage bag, or rain jacket to capture and funnel rain water into one or more containers. Lining a hole in the ground or depression is an excellent makeshift survival container and can often hold more water than smaller containers.

You can also use natural materials from nonpoisonous trees and plants to collect rainwater. Bark is excellent for funneling and directing water towards larger collection areas. Large leaves can also be used to increase collection surface area and to direct water into containers. Every square inch of surface area is important when you might need every last drop of water to stay alive.

No survival scenario is the same. The only constants that remain the same from situation to situation are the principles behind the skills that work. As long as you understand basic survival principles, you will be able to improvise a working solution. With rain collection, the survival principle you need to understand is *increased surface area*.

SNOW

The old survival adage of "Don't eat snow!" is true. Eating snow can sap valuable energy through your digestive system. In a cold-weather environment, you need to hang on to every last calorie. If possible, melt snow before you consume it and use only snow that is fresh and white. The chances that snow is contaminated increase the longer the snow sits on whatever surface it has landed on.

Four proven ways to effectively melt snow for drinking are:

1.Metal Container

Melting snow in a metal container over heat (fire) is the fastest way to melt snow for drinking. Many metal containers will work, including baking pans, makeshift tin foil cups, wheel hubcaps, coffee cans, or even soda cans.

2. Drip 'n Sip

Place snow in a cloth bag, bandana, or sock and hang it next to a fire. Position a container so that the melting snow drips into it. The cloth wrap also acts as a crude filter.

3. Snow-Kabob

Skewer a snowball onto a spiked stick positioned next to a fire. Allow the melting snow to drip into a container.

4. Snow Buddy

If no heat source is available, pack a container with snow and place it under your clothes close to your body. Your body heat will slowly melt the snow. This will also suck away your body heat and should be considered a last resort.

DEW

At night when temperatures drop, moisture in the air condenses and collects on exposed surfaces. This is what we commonly refer to as dew. Dew accumulates in surprisingly large amounts each morning, even on blistering hot days. The dew that collects on grass and vegetation is considered perfectly fine to drink. The trick is gathering it. Have you ever walked through dew-soaked grass? What happens? Your shoes and pants get soaked, right? Collecting dew is surprisingly simple and incredibly effective. I've collected a gallon of dew in less than one hour. The process is simple: Walk through as much dewy grass as possible and ring out the dew into a container. Tie off as many items as you can to your lower legs—

bandanas, T-shirts, towels, etc. The more dew you can soak up, the faster you can gather it. Hurry, though; dew evaporates quickly, and then you have to wait another twenty-four hours.

Find more survival water information in *The Unofficial Hunger Games Wilderness Survival Guide* by Creek Stewart, available at store.livingreadyonline.com.

Buyer's Guide to Microfilters

Pricing key (based on manufacturer's suggested retail price):

$ = under $75
$$ = $76–$100
$$$ = $101–$150
$$$$ = $151–$200
$$$$$ = over $200

GRAVITY FED

Manufacturer/Model: Vapur/MicroFilter
Price: $
Weight: 2.7 oz.
Dimensions: 5.75" × 10"
Filter Power source: Gravity
Filtration type: Hollow Fiber
Capacity: Holds 1 L; filter life-500 L
Output: ½ L / minute

Manufacturer/Model: Katadyn/Base Camp
Price: $$
Weight: 11 oz.
Dimensions: 3" × 6.5" × 2.4"
Filter Power source: Gravity
Filtration type: Glassfiber, activated carbon granulate
Capacity: 750 L
Output: ½ L / minute

Manufacturer/Model: Platypus/Gravity-Works 4 L Water Filter
Price: $$$
Weight: 10.75 oz.
Dimensions: 3.25" × 9.5"
Filter Power source:: Gravity fed
Filtration type: Hollow fiber
Capacity: 8 L; filter life-1,500 L
Output: 4 L / 2.5 minutes

HAND PUMP

Manufacturer/Model: Katadyn/Hiker Microfilter
Price: $
Weight: 11 oz.
Dimensions: 3" × 6.5" × 2.4"
Filter Power source: Hand-pump
Filtration type: Glassfiber, activated carbon granulate
Capacity: 750 L
Output: 1 L / minute

Manufacturer/Model: Miniwell/Portable Water Filter L610
Price: $$
Weight: 8.6 oz.
Dimensions: 6.5" × 2" × 3.1"
Filter Power source: Hand-pump
Filtration type: Abs, carbon fiber, UF
Capacity: 1,000 L
Output: ½ L / minute

Manufacturer/Model: Katadyn/Hiker Pro Microfilter
Price: $$
Weight: 11 oz.
Dimensions: 3" × 6.5" × 2.4"
Filter Power source: Hand-pump
Filtration type: Glass fiber, activated carbon granulate
Capacity: 1,150 L
Output: 1 L / minute

Manufacturer/Model: Katadyn/Vario
Price: $$
Weight: 15 oz.
Dimensions: 7.5" × 4"
Filter Power source: Hand-pump
Filtration type: Glass fiber filter, ceramic pre-filter, active charcoal
Capacity : 2,000 L (glassfiber) / 400 L (carbon)
Output: Up to 2 L / minute

Manufacturer/Model: Katadyn/Mini
Price: $$$
Weight: 8 oz.
Dimensions: 3.2" × 7" × 2"
Filter Power source: Hand-pump
Filtration type: Ceramic depth filter
Capacity: 7,000 L
Output: ½ L / minute

Manufacturer/Model: MSR/MiniWorks EX Water Filter
Price: $$$$
Weight: 16 oz.
Dimensions: Contact manufacturer
Filter Power source: Hand-pump
Filtration type: Ceramic carbon
Capacity: Contact manufacturer
Output: 1 L / 1.5 minutes

Manufacturer/Model: Diercon/Expedition Water Filter KP02-04
Price: $$$$$
Weight: 14.4 oz.
Dimensions: 1.8" × 8.6"
Filter Power source: Gravity fed
Filtration type: Ceramic filter
Capacity: 5,000 L
Output: 1 L / minute

Manufacturer/Model: Katadyn/Combi
Price: $$$$$
Weight: 21 oz.
Dimensions: 12" × 2.4"
Filter Power source: Hand-pump
Filtration type: Ceramic depth filter, activated carbon granulite
Capacity: 50,000 (ceramic) / 400 (carbon)
Output: 1 L / minute

Manufacturer/Model: MSR/HyperFlow Microfilter
Price: $$$$
Weight: 7.8 oz.

Dimensions: 3.5" × 7"
Filter Power source: Hand-pump
Filtration type: Hollow Fiber
Capacity: 1,000 L
Output: 3 L / minute

Manufacturer/Model: Diercon/Expedition Water Filter KP01-04
Price: $$$$$
Weight: 16 oz.
Dimensions: 1.8" × 8.6"
Filter Power source: Hand-pump

Filtration type: Ceramic filter
Capacity: 5,000 L
Output: 1 L / minute

Manufacturer/Model: Katadyn/Pocket
Price: $$$$$
Weight: 20 oz.
Dimensions: 10" × 2.4"
Filter Power source: Hand-pump
Filtration type:: Ceramic depth filter
Capacity: 50,000 L
Output: 1 L / minute

Manufacturer/Model: Katadyn/Expedition
Price: $$$$$
Weight: 11 lbs. 7.4 oz.
Dimensions: 23" × 8"
Filter Power source: Hand-pump
Filtration type: Ceramic depth filter
Capacity: 100,000 L
Output: 4 L / minute

Buyer's Guide to Water Bottles with Built-In Filters

Manufacturer/Model: Brita/Soft Squeeze Sport Bottle
Price: $
Container size: 20 oz.
Filter Power source: Drop-in bottle filter
Filtration type: Activated carbon and ion exchange resin
Capacity: 40 gallons

Manufacturer/Model: Nalgene/24 Ounce "On The Go" Filter for Good
Price: $ (This price does not include filter which is sold separately)
Container size: 24 oz.
Filter Power source: Drop-in bottle filter
Filtration type: for use with Brita filters
Capacity: n/a

Manufacturer/Model: Cool Gear/ez-freeze pure
Price: $$
Container size: 24 oz.
Filter Power source: Drop-in freezer stick bottle filter
Filtration type: Patented filter and freezer stick technology
Capacity: 100 gallons

Manufacturer/Model: Aquamira/Frontier Sport Filter
Price: $$
Container size: This product is for use with water bottles that use straws; product does not include a water bottle
Filter Power source: Drop-in bottle filter
Filtration type: Polypropylene fiber and plastic carbon
Capacity: 100 gallons

Manufacturer/Model: ZeroWater/Travel Bottle
Price: $$$
Container size: 28 oz.
Filter Power source: Drop-in bottle filter
Filtration type: 5-Stage Ion Exchange filter
Capacity: Filter changes color when replacement needed

Manufacturer/Model: Brita/Hard Sided Bottle Persimmon
Price: $$$
Container size: 23.7 oz.
Filter Power source: Drop-in bottle filter
Filtration type: Activated carbon and ion exchange resin
Capacity: 40 gallons

Pricing key (based on manufacturer's suggested retail price):

$ = under $10
$$ = $11–$15
$$$ = $16–$20
$$$$ = $21–$25
$$$$$ = over $25

Manufacturer/Model: CamelBak/Groove .6L
Price: $$$
Container size: 20 oz.
Filter Power source: Drop-in bottle filter
Filtration type: Plant-based activated carbon
Capacity: 48 gallons

Manufacturer/Model: Brita/34-Ounce Big Water Bottle
Price: $$$$
Container size: 34 oz.
Filter Power source: Drop-in bottle filter
Filtration type: Activated carbon and ion exchange resin
Capacity: 40 gallons

Manufacturer/Model: ÖKO/Original Filtration Bottle 650 ml
Price: $$$$
Container size: 22 oz.
Filter Power source: Drop-in bottle filter
Filtration type: ÖKO level-2 filtration-positively charged electro-adsorption
Capacity: 50 gallons

Manufacturer/Model: Aquamira/Water Bottle with Filter
Price: $$$$$

Container size: 20 oz.
Filter Power source: Drop-in bottle filter
Filtration type: Activated coconut shell carbon, plastic and other proprietary filter aids
Capacity: 100 gallons

Manufacturer/Model: Clearbrook/Survival High Performance Water Filter Bottle
Price: $$$$$
Container size: 32 oz.

Filter Power source: Drop-in bottle filter
Filtration type: Ionic adsorption micron water filter technology
Capacity: 100 gallons

Manufacturer/Model: Sawyer/Personal Water Bottle with Filter
Price: $$$$$
Container size: 34 oz.
Filter Power source: Drip-in bottle filter
Filtration type: Hollow fiber filter
Capacity: 1 million gallons

Buyer's Guide to Water Filter Straws

Manufacturer/Model: Aquamira/Frontier Emergency Water Filter System
Price: $
Filter Power source: Expandable, drink-through straw
Filtration type: Proprietary carbon impregnated filter block
Capacity: 20 gallons

Manufacturer/Model: WATERisLIFE Straw
Price: $
Filter Power source: Drink-through straw filter
Filtration type: Iodine filtration system
Capacity: 211 gallons

Manufacturer/Model: Vestergaard/LifeStraw
Price: $$
Filter Power source: Drink-through filter straw
Filtration type: Hollow fiber microfiltration technology
Capacity: 264 gallons

Manufacturer/Model: Miller ProSource/H20 Survival Straw
Price: $$$
Filter Power source: Drink-through straw filter
Filtration type: 2-stage Multi-layer Hierarchical filtration system—antibacterial activated Carbon with silver ions
Capacity: 400 gallons

Manufacturer/Model: Aquamira/Frontier Pro Portable Water Filter
Price: $$$
Filter Power source: Drink-through straw filter; bottle filter; gravity-fed filter
Filtration type: Coconut shell carbon, plastic and other proprietary filter aids
Capacity: 50 gallons

Manufacturer/Model: aquagear/aquagear Advanced Water Filtration Straw
Price: $$$
Filter Power source: Drink-through straw filter
Filtration type: Iodinated resin filtration system
Capacity: 25 gallons

Pricing key (based on manufacturer's suggested retail price):

$ = under $15
$$ = $16–$20
$$$ = $21–$25
$$$$ = $26–$30

Buyer's Guide to UV Light Water Purifiers

Treatment capacity is for ½L

Manufacturer/Model: SteriPEN/Emergency
Price: $
Weight: 5.5 oz.
Filtration type: UV light
Power source: AA Lithium batteries (not included)
Capacity: 3,000 (lamp life)
Treatment capacity in 1 charge: 200

Manufacturer/Model: SteriPEN/Traveler
Price: $
Weight: 5.5 oz.
Filtration type: UV light
Power source: AA Lithium batteries (not included)
Capacity: 3,000 treatments (lamp life)
Treatment capacity in 1 charge: 200

Manufacturer/Model: Aqua Ultraviolet/ Drinking Water 15 Watt
Price: $$
Weight: 11 lbs.
Filtration type: UV light
Power source: Lamp
Capacity: Contact manufacturer
Treatment capacity in 1 charge: 2-4 gallons / minute

Manufacturer/Model: SteriPEN Classic with Pre-Filter
Price: $$
Weight: 5.5 oz.
Filtration type: UV light
Power source: AA Lithium batteries (not included)
Capacity: 8,000 treatments (lamp life)
Treatment capacity in 1 charge: 200

Manufacturer/Model: SteriPEN/Adventurer Opti
Price: $$$
Weight: 3.8 oz.
Filtration type: UV light
Power source: CR123 (included) or RCR123
Capacity: 8,000 treatments (lamp life)
Treatment capacity in 1 charge: 80-100 depending on battery

Manufacturer/Model: CamelBak/All Clear Bottle
Price: $$$
Weight: 14 oz.
Filtration type: UV light
Power source: 2 3.7V lithium ion batteries; can be charged with most USB compatible power sources
Capacity: 25 oz.
Treatment capacity in 1 charge: 80 cycles or 16 gallons

Manufacturer/Model: SteriPEN/Sidewinder
Price: $$$
Weight: 16.6 oz.
Filtration type: UV light
Power source: hand crank
Filtration type: UV light
Capacity: 8,000 treatments (lamp life)
Treatment capacity in 1 charge: 1 L / 1.5 min

Manufacturer/Model: SteriPEN/Ultra
Price: $$$
Weight: 4.94 oz.
Filtration type: UV light
Power source: Internal Lithium-Ion battery
Capacity: 8,000 treatments (lamp life)
Treatment capacity in 1 charge: 100

Manufacturer/Model: SteriPEN/Freedom
Price: $$$$
Weight: 2.6 oz.
Filtration type: UV light
Power source: Internal Lithium-Ion battery
Capacity: 8,000 treatments (lamp life)
Treatment capacity in 1 charge: 40

Manufacturer/Model: SteriPEN/ Defender
Price: $$$$
Weight: 5.5 oz.
Filtration type: UV light
Power source: AA Lithium batteries (not included)
Capacity: 8,000 treatments (lamp life)
Treatment capacity in 1 charge: 200

Manufacturer/Model: SteriPEN/Protector Opti
Price: $$$$
Weight: 3.6 oz.
Filtration type: UV light
Power source: CR123 (included) or RCR123
Capacity: 8,000 treatments (lamp life)
Treatment capacity in 1 charge: 100

Manufacturer/Model: eSpring®/UV Water Purifier Above Counter Unit with Existing Faucet
Price: $$$$$
Weight: 10.8 lbs.
Filtration type: UV light
Power source: Wall outlet
Capacity: 1,320 gallons
Treatment capacity in 1 charge: Contact manufacturer

CHAPTER FOUR

Emergency Food and Cooking Gear

While you can survive for three weeks without food, those three weeks wouldn't look like successful survival; they would be three weeks of slow starvation with your body painfully shutting down in stages.

Food is essential for both physical and psychological survival needs. A warm meal of familiar foods can create a sense of wellbeing and stability in the midst of a disaster.

This chapter outlines the principles of long-term food storage in your home and includes a food storage checklist to help you start your food stockpile. It also includes an overview of pre-packaged survival foods. And because disasters often disrupt electric and gas service, this chapter includes alternative cooking methods and camp stoves to help you prepare hot meals in any condition.

Emergency Food Storage Basics

BY JAMES D. NOWKA

Some view preparedness as some kind of new trend. Honestly, there's nothing new about it. So many of the things preppers need to consider to assure family safety after a disaster, whether it's food or otherwise, are more a matter of remembering life as it used to be. The idea of having a strong food supply in the home never lost importance. Most, however, simply failed to recognize it.

GETTING STARTED

Getting a good start on food planning requires some thought on the length of time the family would want to be able to meet from a place of self-reliance. Some are comfortable with an emergency food supply that would feed the family for a month. Others will assemble and stock a food locker that accounts for three months of meals. Smaller numbers aren't comfortable in taking any chances and have an emergency supply that would sustain the family for a year or more.

There isn't an overall right or wrong answer. Risks vary across the country. Even those living in the same region would have varying degrees of comfort. You might hold lesser confidence than another in the ability of society-at-large to restore food supplies with certain haste. A few out there want to be ready for doomsday. Everyone is different.

The frequency of short- to mid-term emergencies suggests real risk in having any less than several weeks of food ready to go at any given time. After meeting that minimum, you should build your storage locker according to your own concerns. It's a process that should be undertaken with some reason. You shouldn't have to overextend the family finances to reach your desired threshold.

Many preppers would suggest that having a food locker that would cover a few months is pretty reasonable. Major disasters have certainly impacted community food supplies for extended periods. The family with the food locker built for a month or less could run the risk of depleting supplies too quickly after highly destructive events.

On the other end, some would argue food plans that extend beyond a year serve only to delay the inevitable if something should happen that would require use of that full supply. If stores are gone for that long, you might surmise they aren't coming back. At and before that point, you would want to look to planting and hunting or potentially raising animals for sustenance just as people did in the old days.

HOW MUCH FOOD DO YOU NEED?

The next big question to ponder is how much food you would need for the family to eat. Those prepping should take note of what the family is eating in the day-to-day when planning their stock to meet their chosen timeframes. Pay attention to typical consumption and then purchase enough that would allow family members to ratchet up caloric intake as needed during a period of recovery. Your typical diet might not be sufficient based on the stresses and physical requirements bound to accompany a disaster aftermath.

The U.S. Department of Agriculture's recommendations for caloric intake differ not only by age and sex but also by one's level of activity. An average, sedentary 40-year-old man, for instance, would need 2,400 calories to balance his intake with the energy his body would burn as a matter of living. The same man, if active, would need 2,800 calories to meet the needs of body function and that added exertion.

Women typically require less food than men to account for what their bodies burn. The average, sedentary 40-year-old woman would need 1,800 calories,

according to the USDA. Her active counterpart would require 2,200 to maintain a healthy balance. Caloric needs tend to peak for men and women as they move through their late teens and early 20s. Active men in their 20s to mid-30s typically require 3,000 calories a day while their female counterparts would need about 2,400.

Those planning for food storage to account for a disaster should aim for the higher end of the calorie charts for several reasons. It'll take more than light meals — salads wouldn't suffice — to properly fuel

the body when putting forth some heavy labor that isn't part of your normal routine. Recovery takes real work. Even the in-shape prepper who spends 40 minutes a day at the gym would likely encounter some pretty big demands on the body depending on the extent of any damage left behind in a disaster event.

Following a disaster, you'd have to deal not only with exertion but also with working the body in ways in which it isn't accustomed. You might be stressing muscles that don't get much work on the average day. There might be trees to chop

VITAMINS: ARE THEY WORTH THE TROUBLE?

It seems the jury is still out when it comes to the value of vitamin supplements. Reading three different articles about vitamins and other nutritional products on the market will likely provide three different expert opinions on their value or lack thereof in terms of improving your health. Some swear by them. Others don't bother.

Those who aren't convinced in their value have some valid arguments. If people eat proper diets that provide them with all the vitamins and minerals needed, it's safe to say they can get by without the hassle and additional expense. Certainly, generation after generation got by before those little, white bottles with childproof caps started showing up on the store shelves.

With that said, I take a multivitamin and other supplements tailored to some specific health considerations. Though a proper diet would indeed be sufficient to meet my needs, I consider a multivitamin an insurance policy should I leave a few blanks to fill in on any given day. Beyond the multivitamin, I take niacin based on the reports of its success for some in building good cholesterol while lowering the bad. I take a selenium supplement knowing the soil in my region largely lacks that beneficial element.

In terms of preparation for a disaster recovery, multivitamins might well provide the right insurance policy should you lose the ability to provide the typical variety and balance available with a normal and typical diet. On the average day, vitamins would never be construed as a replacement for a proper diet. They're called supplements for a reason. A healthy day-to-day diet needs to be the first step.

Those who follow the directions on the bottles aren't going to experience harm by the common, well-established products on the market. Again, there are all sorts of debates on how much those products will benefit someone. A good prepper might want to read both sides of the debate on any given supplement before heading out to make the purchase.

If nothing else, there is something to be said for the placebo effect. Those who believe they're helping their bodies might actually do so regardless of the contents of that tablet. Your body might well respond to the mind's view of nutrition offered by the vitamins taken.

Every prepper will find his own best answers, whether it's vitamins or any other part of the plan. The experts might not agree on how much or whether a multivitamin will help. I tend to think it can't hurt.

ANTHONY BERENYI / SHUTTERSTOCK.COM

and wood to haul. It's possible you'd tackle some of your own roofing work or repair on other damages left to the family home.

Your energy output might well extend beyond muscular considerations depending on circumstances. Winter emergencies could put families in situations of limited heat. If the furnace went out, it might well mean hunkering down in 50-degree temperatures rather than the more comfortable 70 degrees. In that circumstance, the body would burn some additional calories in its own efforts to maintain sufficient warmth.

MREs, a common pack-away for preppers, tend to suggest that calorie intake for the common day and the average man or woman wouldn't suffice for the highly active. The meals are designed for soldiers and used by the military but are readily available to the civilian community. Each comes at more than 1,200 calories. It goes without saying that the sedentary man or woman wouldn't want to have three per day for any length of time if he or she is looking to maintain a slender waistline.

PLANNING A BALANCED DIET
Remember that while preparing for a disaster is about survival, it's also about comfort. Devise food plans that'll contribute to your family's wellbeing from both standpoints. Those who don't enjoy Spam shouldn't pack it away regardless of

its endless shelf life. Build a food plan that matches with how your family would eat when it isn't dealing with all of those added stresses and emotions of emergency.

Those planning their food stock should just as much rely on logic and good sense in planning out amounts that go beyond the usual. The very point of storage is to make it through any period that would present an inability to replenish the shelves. It's a far better position to recognize you might have over-prepared than it is to watch food supplies dwindle when the community still hasn't recovered.

Thoughts would turn from how much food is sufficient to what types of foods would best leave the family ready for whatever a disaster might bring. Assembling your food for the long-term has some elements that aren't all that different from how you go about your grocery shopping on a week in and week out basis. Whether you are planning for next week or for food to last for an entire year, you're still going to think about how to provide for some variety and decent, balanced meals and snacks. The body's need for good nutrition doesn't halt when a disaster happens. Good plans will include fruits, vegetables, grains and protein sources.

There's one key difference when buying for the long term. You have to pay attention to how long those foods would survive on the shelf. Your potential food

selections become far narrower. The deli, produce and bakery sections of the store aren't going to do much for the long-term shopper. "Use by" dates take on a far greater level of importance. It requires some good strategy.

It's vital to have enough food. It's just as vital to have the right food. Many people have chest freezers in the basement. They're great appliances from the perspective of extending the family's food supplies. You shouldn't, however, consider those frozen food items as part of your long-term emergency provisions.

The basement freezer would certainly stand to provide for the family's needs pretty well in the very shortest of terms. In a case of electricity loss, the freezer would become the immediate priority of your meal planning. The family would have to get through as much as possible before its contents thawed and became spoiled.

FOOD FOR LONG-TERM STORAGE
Preppers buying for the long-term have to think differently, but there are nonetheless many options available that would allow a person to eat pretty well. You wouldn't have to survive only on rice and water. The numbers of foods that'll hold up for the long term are becoming more plentiful all the time.

Many foods that a family would typically purchase for their day-to-day living would hold up perfectly well for several years. Canned goods are a great example. The canning process entails the use of high heat to kill off bacteria in food and establishing a vacuum seal to prevent new bacteria from getting in. The bacteria are what cause food to spoil.

Many commercially canned goods remain viable for lengthy periods of time. A prepper might take note of the "best by" and "use by" dates and keep a keen eye out for dates that stretch out for lengthy periods. It's also helpful to recognize the difference between the terms.

Many folks don't take chances and they make sure to get through their food before the stamped-on deadline regardless of how it's presented. The dates, in either category, aren't required by government. "Use by" or "sell by" designations generally refer to the potential for spoilage. They're estimates and don't provide any set-in-stone guarantees. The "best by" designation, meanwhile, is indicative of flavor, texture or other factors that wouldn't bear on product safety.

Canned items produced by Hormel Foods, for instance, boast an indefinite shelf life. As surreal as it sounds, those foods would be safe for consumption long after we're gone. One could buy a can of Spam today and fry it up in 40 years. The company's offerings, which include Spam, its chili, corned beef hash and beef stew, carry "best by" dates on the packages. The company, however, indicates those dates might apply to flavor but have no bearing on food safety as long as the seal remains intact and uncompromised.

A little bit of research might reveal a number of canned options that would do well in storage, particularly if it's a commonly used good that could go into a rotation. Del Monte Foods, for instance, indicates its canned goods have a shelf life, as it pertains to quality, of two to three years. It's a good amount of time on its own. Though the foods would be best by the dates printed on the cans, they remain safe for consumption beyond that time so long as the container isn't dented or damaged, the company says.

Dried and freeze-dried foods offer years and sometimes decades of storage life. Powdered milk and eggs would provide for long storage life and also the nutrition and comfort of having those staple foods at hand regardless of whether they're available in fresh form. Dried beans will last forever as long as they're properly stored. They'd provide families with another source of protein to draw from.

Dried grains would provide for your carbohydrates and also store wonderfully. Rice will be just as good 20 years from now as it is today so long as it's properly kept. Quinoa, though pricey, might make for a good addition to the food locker.

It's a dried, grain-like South American plant that'll carry a good, long shelf life. It's noted for high nutritional value that includes pretty high protein content for a plant-based food.

A number of foods people often go to for everyday nutrition and comfort could have some long-term potential. Wax-coated hard cheeses are known to last for significant periods without the need for refrigeration. Canned and pouched tuna and other seafoods typically have a shelf life of several years. Manufacturers generally recommend use within a year or two for taste, but again, the family that packs tuna salad sandwiches in the family's lunches on a fairly regular basis will be able to keep the stock on the fresh side by rotating.

Technology is lengthening the shelf lives of more foods all the time. Consumers are more regularly able to purchase irradiated food products. It's a process that utilizes radiation to kill of the bacteria that would contribute to food spoilage. Advances in aseptic processing are contributing to more shelf-stable food products. It's a process that's based in part around the use of sterile packaging.

In recent years, dairy companies have introduced shelf-stable milk that can sit unrefrigerated on a shelf for six months without going bad. The products rely on aseptic packaging after pasteurizing milk at higher than typical temperatures to assure that bacteria are killed off. A six-month shelf life isn't optimal for long-term food planning, but it's an interesting example of where technology is heading. It wasn't so long ago when people would've thought

it a joke to have milk that doesn't require refrigeration.

Shelf-stable milk might be an option beyond powdered milk for the family that's planning for just a few months of contingency and depends upon their typical glasses of milk with breakfast and dinner. The families that find having regular, ready to drink milk important to their lives might switch to shelf-stable products, have a few months of supply at hand and keep the products stored away for emergency use in a rotation so it's used before expiration.

STORING YOUR FOOD

Having sufficient supplies of long stable foods is vital, though it's also important to assure it is stored properly. Preppers should have a cool and dry place to serve as the storage locker as a means of prolonging shelf life. The family with no other suitable options might put up some shelves in a spare bedroom.

Proper storage also means keeping food in a manner that wouldn't attract rodents that are always looking for that next big meal. No matter how well the home is sealed, it's no match for hungry mice that get a sense that food awaits. Five-gallon pails with sturdy lids — snap or screw-on — serve well for storing grains and other loose dried goods.

You should think through all the little details that could provide challenges should the time come to put your food planning to emergency use. For instance, you wouldn't have much luck with an electric can opener if the power is out. It makes sense to keep a manual model in your drawer full of kitchen gadgets.

You might consider methods to warm food if the power is out. It might mean a camp stove. You might keep a good supply of propane or charcoal at the ready for the backyard grill. Some of the MREs on the market are self-heating.

PURCHASING EXTRA FOOD ON A BUDGET

There are many different ways to tackle a suitable food plan. Those looking for the ultimate in convenience could achieve everything needed to feed the family for an entire year without stepping off of their properties. It could be as simple as pulling out the credit card, spending 10 min-

utes on the Internet and waiting for the delivery truck to arrive.

A variety of companies offer annual packs of freeze-dried and canned foods with shelf lives of 25 years or more. They're specifically assembled to offer some variety and take away the guesswork in building a preparedness plan. It's a viable option for some people, though it isn't difficult to imagine the price factor would drive many toward other options.

GVICTORIA /SHUTTERSTOCK.COM

The packages start at about $1,000 and can go to $3,000 or beyond. The packages, meanwhile, are usually put together on a per-person basis. Many of the packages out on the market aren't unreasonable from a cost perspective when broken down to a per-meal basis. Some are comparable to how much people would spend on food for the family from week to week.

What becomes unreasonable for many is the idea of building a full year of additional food that'll be stashed away, lying in wait and paid for in one, big, lone transaction. It wouldn't work for a lot of people's budgets. Whether it's planning a home

improvement or saving for the next car, the average family of four wouldn't likely have $4,000 to $12,000 in rainy day money to spend on that kind of insurance regardless of how important they find it.

A family could build a good degree of security with methods that are a little bit friendlier to the pocketbook. Food plans, like so many areas of preparation, can be developed gradually. The family that doesn't have a lot of expendable cash can still set a solid plan into action bit by bit. A food plan might not stretch to a year or even several months of contingency right from the get-go. A new prepper might recognize that simply beginning your plan puts your family in a far stronger position than most.

Your family might start by doubling up on the typical grocery bill when a little extra money becomes available. You could load up a second cartload and get the pantry stocked sufficiently to meet a couple of weeks' worth of meals instead of just one. You might then build on that by adding a few additional shelf-stable, long-viable products to the cart during each subsequent shopping trip.

Much of your plans wouldn't necessarily require any firm line of separation between your preps and your family's everyday eating. The important part of preparation is getting that solid foundation laid so your family's food availability

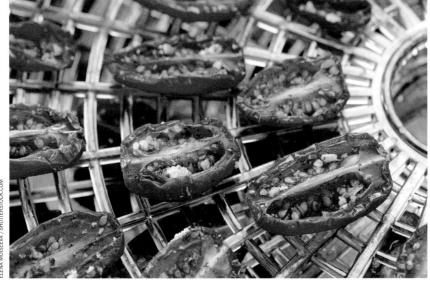

ELENA MOISEEVA /SHUTTERSTOCK.COM

stretches beyond the immediate. A number of items — based on shelf life — might rotate from the emergency food locker to the everyday pantry when you shop and bring home some replacements.

After that foundation is in place and your family has a sizable cache of food, you might grab a new can of sweet corn from the grocery store based on Sunday's recipe. You could then swap it out for the can that's been in the locker for six months or a year and is still well beneath its "best by" date. That Sunday meal wouldn't taste a bit different. The family, meanwhile, could maintain an emergency locker of fairly recent goods.

PREPACKAGED SURVIVAL FOOD

Families might not go to a website and order a full year of shelf-stable food contingencies. They might, however, rely on some of those products as part of a more varied food plan. Starting at about $100, a prepper could buy a 5-gallon pail filled with a variety of individually packaged, freeze-dried vegetable servings.

A few cases of MREs might make up a significant portion of your meal planning if you're looking for ease and are only stretching out the plan for a few weeks of self-reliance. Those developing longer plans might still purchase a few cases to extend variety and flexibility. They're pre-packaged complete meals and come as varied as the selections in the grocery store's TV dinner case. They'll last on a shelf for five or more years if kept cool and dry.

SUSTAINABLE FOOD SOURCES

Those who begin to understand preparedness as a lifestyle will come to recognize readiness means more than packing away supplies. The notion of living a self-reliant lifestyle during the average day applies well to food and diet. Families might gain from a diet that goes beyond the offerings at the nearby supermarket.

Many would be able to take their emergency food plans beyond shelf-stable goods. Those who live in rural areas might

SEED STOCK

Gardening is a common sense use of your land that provides a great deal to any household. It's a great hobby that gets you outdoors. It's enjoyable to very literally watch your efforts take root and grow into something valuable. Come harvest, there's something richly satisfying about meals that are made of your own time and work. You shouldn't discount another important quality of homegrown food: the prepper knows exactly where it came from and precisely what went into its creation.

Knowing what makes up your food takes on just a bit more nuance in today's era. Preppers who understand that gardening could move from a hobby to a necessity might think deeper and consider the very seeds they're putting into the ground. Those who are planting for richer flavors and those worried about long-term needs would ultimately come to the same conclusion. It makes the best sense to rely on heirloom varieties.

We've come to an era in which a few big corporations did some interesting work, came up with some interesting products and, as result, hold patents on many of the seeds available in those small packets down at the hardware store. They're engineered in a way that would benefit the simple gardener. They're also engineered in a way that would benefit the company's ultimate goals.

The hybrid products on the market promote ease, better yield and resistance to disease. It's appealing to many for obvious reasons. The companies selling them fail to promote that there is limited to no ability to collect seeds from those plants that would allow gardeners to grow anew in the next season without another trip to the hardware store for yet another packet.

A wise prepper would recognize the value of having enough seeds to go one year in advance of the growing period to come. Collecting seeds and allowing a garden to rebuild itself from year to year is the ultimate exercise in self-reliance. Hybrid seeds are typically a one-year-and-done option. Those who gather seeds from non-heirloom plants and sow them in spring are bound to be disappointed by the next yield.

The real differences between heirloom and hybrid varieties go beyond planting. Those who are old enough and carry a good memory would recognize that produce today doesn't taste quite the same as that from the gardens of our grandparents. Taste is important. The seed companies aimed for a gardener's simplicity and their own bottom line. They were bound to lose something in the process.

Many like it easy, but easy rarely means better. It's worth looking around at seed options before planting. It's worth spending the additional time and care on plants that might not be as disease resistant as the modern hybrids. We get what we give. It could mean a tastier garden this year. It could mean reliable seeds for the next.

approach their neighbors to talk about planning and get a sense of what they might be able to accomplish together if needs ever required. Those outside of the cities would very likely be able to maintain a strong sense of normalcy through teamwork if a disaster were to impact food supplies.

Those in rural areas would often have the capability to establish an economy on the smallest of scales. Bartering techniques might put everyone in better position. One neighbor might have some chickens and eggs while another raises beef or goats. One might have fruit trees while another is growing a large garden with 15 or more different vegetables. Some might have canned goods. Hunters and fishermen would have some commodities to offer. You would want to develop those relationships and have those conversations well before push comes to shove.

Those in urban and suburban areas, and even those with small properties, shouldn't discount gardening as a potential food source. Even those on properties with space for only a small garden tucked along the back fence might be surprised by how much food they'd be able to produce through spring and summer. Gardening requires some time investment each day, but it's as economical as it gets from the place of dollars and cents. It gives you a stronger appreciation of food, which can't be discounted in today's era.

There's nothing better than fresh vegetables from the garden. Even a few tomato plants, for instance, might yield more fruit than a family could reasonably eat. You could stew some and make soups and sauces to can for later use.

With a garden, you can make long-term, shelf-stable foods of your own. Food dehydrators are fairly inexpensive and tremendous tools. With a few hours, you can take the garden-fresh vegetable that would normally decay in a week and turn it into a food that would be just as viable 10 years down the road.

Some are comfortable in giving a 30-year shelf life to some foods that have had their moisture removed. Those looking to prep inexpensively could find a dehydrator for $50 or less. You could vac-uum seal dehydrated foods for an even better likelihood of long-term viability.

There's no way around it. Food planning will take some spending at the front end. Though when considering the importance of food to comfort and survival, it's an investment that can't be overlooked or under planned. When considered over the long term, planning provides preppers with a certain degree of economy. Even beyond gardening and hunting, preppers might well be able to eat cheaper.

Those who utilize chest freezers return to mind and offer an example of how storage and planning provides benefits that go even beyond readiness. Many have those freezers to provide the ability to buy meats in larger quantities after they go on a deep sale. They can freeze them and have plenty to eat over extended periods at lower costs. You could extend that to shelf-stable goods and build up on stock whether through in-store deals, coupons or bulk stores.

Shifting your mindset on food to the long term might well contribute to health. People are creatures of habit, and food marks an area where many could benefit from developing good ones. Modern society's relationship with food has, by many measures, fallen into a pretty unhealthy territory as a result of our convenience culture. The bad stuff is everywhere. Nourishing, balanced meals are too often supplanted by those quick and easy foods that come packed with fat, sodium, bad carbs and any number of unnatural ingredients carrying names most couldn't pronounce.

Too many are willing to sacrifice the healthy and wholesome for the easier items, particularly if it tastes good. It goes further to explain why appropriate planning is such a foreign concept to so many. Those who rely so heavily on unhealthy foods are demonstrating their lack of concern for what might sit around the next corner.

Efforts spent on preparing, whether for food or otherwise, mean doing better for your family. Our meals are important components of our lives, and with a little effort, preparing could mean better eating now and months ahead. Those approaching preparedness with the idea of having more comfort and confidence amid all of our world's uncertainties can't overlook the importance of food. It's tough to imagine much more taxing on our bodies or spirits than lacking variety, quality or simply enough on the daily dinner plate.

Food Storage Purchasing Checklist

BY ANGELA PASKETT

GRAINS (APPROX. 25 POUNDS [11KG] PER PERSON PER MONTH)

- six-grain cereal
- nine-grain cereal
- amaranth
- barley
- corn meal
- farina/germade
- flour
- oat groats, whole
- oats, instant
- pancake mix
- pasta: egg noodles
- pasta: spaghetti
- pasta: macaroni
- pasta: other
- quinoa
- rice, brown
- rice, white
- rice, instant
- spelt
- wheat, white
- wheat, red

DAIRY (APPROX. 6 POUNDS [3KG] PER PERSON PER MONTH)

- instant milk
- non-instant milk
- cheese powder
- cheese, canned
- cheese, freeze-dried
- buttermilk powder
- sour cream powder
- yogurt, dry culture
- yogurt, freeze-dried

LEGUMES (APPROX. 5 POUNDS [2KG] PER PERSON PER MONTH)

- black beans
- kidney beans
- lentils
- lima beans
- mung beans
- navy beans
- pink beans
- pinto beans
- red beans
- split peas

OTHER PROTEIN (AS DESIRED)

- canned meat: tuna
- canned meat: wild game
- canned meat: other
- freeze-dried meat: beef
- freeze-dried meat: chicken
- freeze-dried meat: ham
- freeze-dried meat: other
- textured vegetable protein (TVP)
- powdered eggs
- peanut butter

FRUITS (APPROX. 15 POUNDS [7KG] PER PERSON PER MONTH)

- canned peaches
- canned pears
- canned mandarin oranges
- canned pineapple
- canned mixed fruit
- freeze-dried apples

SOURCES FOR FOOD STORAGE

Augason Farms
1911 South 3850 West
Salt Lake City, UT 84104
800-878-0099
augasonfarms.com

Honeyville Grain
1080 North Main Suite 101
Brigham City, UT 84302
888-810-3212
honeyville.com

Emergency Essentials
653 North 1500 West
Orem, UT 84057
800-999-1863
beprepared.com

Food Insurance
695 North Kay's Drive Suite 7b
Kaysville, UT 84037
866-946-8366
foodinsurance.com

Nitro-Pak Preparedness Center
375 West 910 South
Heber City, UT 84032
800-866-4876
nitro-pak.com

Ready Made Resources
239 Cagle Road
Tellico Plains, TN 37385
800-627-3809
readymaderesources.com

The Ready Store
14015 S Minuteman Drive
Draper, UT 84020
800-773-5331
www.thereadystore.com

Thrive Life
691 S Auto Mall Dr.
American Fork, UT 84003
877-743-5373
thrivelife.com

- freeze-dried berries
- freeze-dried pineapple
- freeze-dried peaches
- dehydrated apples
- raisins
- other dried fruits

VEGETABLES (APPROX. 15 POUNDS [7KG] PER PERSON PER MONTH)

- canned beans
- canned corn
- canned mixed vegetables
- canned peas
- canned spinach
- canned tomato products
- other canned vegetables
- dehydrated beans
- dehydrated broccoli
- dehydrated carrots
- dehydrated corn
- dehydrated onions
- dehydrated potatoes (flakes, dices, powdered)
- other dehydrated vegetables
- freeze-dried beans
- freeze-dried corn
- freeze-dried peas
- freeze-dried peppers
- other freeze-dried vegetables
- tomato powder

FATS (APPROX. 2 POUNDS [907G] PER PERSON PER MONTH)

- coconut oil
- olive or vegetable oil
- shortening
- other oil
- butter powder
- shortening powder
- Sugars (approx. 5 pounds [2kg]
- per person per month)
- brown sugar
- powdered sugar
- white sugar
- honey
- corn syrup
- maple syrup
- molasses
- jam and jelly
- drink mixes

FOOD STORAGE BLOGS

Food Storage and Survival: foodstorageandsurvival.com
Chef Tess Bakeresse: cheftessbakeresse.blogspot.com
Dehydrate 2 Store: dehydrate2store.com
Everyday Food Storage: everydayfoodstorage.net
Food Storage Made Easy: foodstoragemadeeasy.net
Food Storage Moms: www.foodstoragemoms.com
Game & Garden: gameandgarden.com
My Food Storage Cookbook: myfoodstoragecookbook.com
Ready Nutrition: readynutrition.com
Simply Canning: simplycanning.com

BAKING NEEDS (AS DESIRED)

- baking powder
- baking soda
- cocoa powder
- cornstarch
- unflavored gelatin
- yeast

SPICES AND FLAVORINGS (AS DESIRED)

- basil
- bouillon: beef
- bouillon: chicken
- chili powder
- cilantro
- cinnamon
- cumin
- dill seed
- extract: almond
- extract: mint
- extract: vanilla
- garlic powder
- ginger
- Italian seasoning
- lemon pepper
- mustard: dry
- onion powder
- oregano
- paprika
- parsley flakes
- pepper
- sage
- salt: canning
- salt: iodized
- seasoned salt
- thyme

- vinegar
- other spices and flavorings

CONDIMENTS (AS DESIRED)

- barbecue sauce
- ketchup
- mayonnaise
- mustard
- olives
- peppers: banana
- peppers: hot
- pickles
- relish
- salad dressing
- salsa
- soy sauce
- teriyaki sauce

CONVENIENCE MEALS

- canned soups
- canned pasta
- canned chili
- boxed pasta or rice meals
- freeze-dried or dehydrated meals
- MREs

GARDEN SEEDS

- non-hybrid (also called open-pollinated or heirloom) seeds suited to your region's growing conditions

Find complete survival food storage information in *Food Storage for Self-Sufficiency and Survival* by Angela Paskett, available at store.livingreadyonline.com.

Porkchops Unlimited

HOW I TRAPPED FERAL HOGS, GAINED A YEAR'S WORTH OF BACON AND SAVED THE ECOSYSTEM

BY JILL J. EASTON

The hog was tearing uncontrollably around the catch circle, the snare cable closed securely (we hoped) around its snout and one ear. The hog was fast — faster than I would have believed possible—snorting and champing its jaws. Foam-slobber flew from its mouth as it charged. The only thing that kept it from tearing into us was the puny looking snare cable fastened to a large tree.

"That thing is evil incarnate, and he's going to break the cable if we wait," said Jim, my husband. "No time to take pictures. I'm going to shoot it."

Amazingly, the hog went down with Jim's first shot. It wasn't until it was dead on the ground that the reason this pig had been spending so much time in our food plot became clear. The hog had three trotters on the ground. One of its front legs was missing halfway up, evidently destroyed by a misplaced bullet. This boar had a huge frame, but it weighed only 168 pounds. The power of a healthy hog with all four hooves on the ground would be unimaginable.

Whether they are called razorbacks, Russian boars or just plain hogs, wild swine aren't fine. They destroy natural areas, outcompete native species, obliterate crops and pass on diseases to wild and farm animals. The only people who have anything good to say about pigs on the lam are the outlaw hunters and outfitters who turn them out for hunting.

SPREADING PIGS

Hogs cheat. They have incredible reproduction rates and few predators other than man. One pregnant sow can become the great-great grandpig of more than 800 offspring in two years under optimum conditions. All they need is adequate water, thick cover to hide in during the day and relief from constant deep snow. In many areas, they become completely nocturnal, so hunters without dogs have little effect on hog populations.

Swine aren't native to North America. They escaped from the early Spanish explorers and pilgrim colonies. But there is a broad swath of the United States where feral pigs can prosper. The hog line, north of which they don't thrive, runs north of New Hampshire to the east, through mid-Wisconsin and South Dakota to the north and the Rocky Mountains to the west.

There are also feral hogs in Hawaii and in several Canadian provinces.

It's estimated that there are more than 2 million wild pigs in Texas alone and more than 6 million in the U.S., mostly in the midsection and Southern states.

"The introduction of feral hogs throughout Arkansas (and the U.S.) is the most successful large-mammal stocking program in history," said Thurman Booth, United States Department of Agriculture Animal and Plant Health Inspection Service State director for Arkansas. "Those persons responsible were once thought to be providing additional hunting opportunities. Now, they are beginning to be viewed as villains."

After you have seen thriving bottomland plowed up better than a cultivator could do it, a field of nearly ripe corn torn to shreds, turkey nests emptied of eggs or duck marshes turned into mud baths, it becomes clear why farmers, ranchers and lands managers hate pigs.

"Feral hogs cause serious damage in Arkansas and throughout the Southeast," Booth said. "Illegal translocation of live feral hogs must be stopped before control measures have a chance of success."

WILD HOG BASICS

Hogs are omnivores, meaning they eat almost everything. The long list includes acorns, carrion, grain, grasses, fruit, water plants, reptiles, bird eggs, and roots. Pretty much anything that they can get in their mouths is food to a pig.

Female hogs live in groups called sounders or drifts, made up of one or more sows, their grown offspring and current young. Boar hogs tend to travel alone except when a female is ready to breed. Sows mate and piglets are born during all months of the year. Breeding is more dependent on weather than season. Young pigs are isolated in a protected area for about 10 days, and begin traveling with the packs in about 6 weeks.

Feral hogs have a shield of cartilage that covers their shoulders and tapers back over the ribs. In males, the shield hardens and thickens with each injury, and boar hogs fight a lot. Shooting one in the heart or the head with a small-caliber bullet might not work.

Male hogs grow tusks on either side of their snouts. The upper-jaw tusks are called whetters and the lower jaw holds the cutters, which are long outward-projecting tusks that are constantly sharpened to a razor-like edge. A big bore's tusk can cut through a 3-inch root, a dog or a hand as easily as we bite an apple.

Pig hoof prints are rounded and the two sides of the print are usually more spread out than a deer's. Dewclaws behind the hoof might show up as smaller circles on wet ground.

One other useful bit of information is that hogs can't turn their necks from side to side. When a hog is grabbed by the back legs, it can't turn around enough to get its tusks into you. Since many people bring some of their pork-on-the-hoof home to fatten before slaughter, this is a good way to keep control of an animal until it can be caged.

CONTROLLING PIG POPULATIONS

Trappers, with their knowledge of sign-reading and snaring techniques, are in a good position to help control feral hogs. It's easy to become a quick hero and get trapping access to new land if you have the equipment and know-how to take hogs.

There are many ways to control hogs, but two of the most successful are traps and snares. Both require specialized equipment. A big boar hog can generate an incredible amount of power and torque. So any equipment you use needs to be built for 400 pounds of angry muscle slamming into it. Ordinary gauges of snare wire, or hog wire on a trap probably won't be good enough. Build heavy or buy heavy duty with good welds to trap hogs.

SNARING

To hold hogs, it is important to have thick enough cable to do the job. The other essential part of hog snaring is to have the snare fastened to something strong enough to withstand serious stress. Find a tree thick enough to take a lot of damage, or cross-stake your snare with long, heavy-weight rods. The snare cable and any fasteners or links should also be extra heavy to withstand the power of these strong animals.

"The $3/32$- and $7/64$-size snares are popular in the Midwest," said Thad Davis of Thompson Snares. "The $3/32$ snares should be at least -feet long with a tree-lock anchor for pigs that weigh 100 pounds or less. If I was going after bigger pigs, I would step up to $7/64$ at least 8 feet long and make sure whatever I anchor to can stand a tussle. For pigs in Hawaii, they use $1/8$ stainless steel and they regularly catch 200 pounders."

Snares for average-size hogs, the ones on either side of 100 pounds, should be about 7 inches off the ground and the loop should be at least 1 foot across. If a hog isn't snared after three or four nights, but they are still coming through your pinch point, lower the loop a few inches. Snares work best if they are placed along frequently used trails with brush piles on either side of the path to prevent detours.

Trapping with a single cable restraint will catch one pig out of a sounder, but its thrashing will probably drive the rest of the group away. To catch more of them, gang setting is the key. Set half-a-dozen or more snares at different heights.

CONTAINMENT TRAPS

"Putting the trap in the right place is everything when catching hogs," said Patrick Thompson, who traps on his family's extensive cattle holdings in the Ozark mountains. Thompson traps hogs using home-built traps made of cow fencing and steel bars and he keeps them moving from pond areas to travelways to the fields where cows and young calves are kept. Catching three or four mid-sized sows and young is a regular occurrence for him.

Thompson usually takes the hogs he traps to a holding pen and feeds them pig grower for several weeks. This cleans out any carrion or other nasty things they might have eaten. Then he moves them into the freezer. Wild hog is excellent table fare, usually leaner than domestic pork. But fall hogs that eat a lot of acorns or peanuts might taste unusual.

A cage trap in the right place can put a mighty dent in a local hog population, since one trap can hold a passel of hogs. Most traps have either a guillotine-style door, or one that is spring loaded to slam shut and lock. Either way, the door shuts when hogs step on a plate connected to the door-firing mechanism.

NEW GROUND

Do you want to get permission to trap new ground? Want to fill up your freezer with delicious pork? Want to match wits with one of the smartest animals in the forest? Want to extend your trapping season? Just go to local landowners and offer your services to control one of the most destructive aliens on our land, the feral pig.

The Buyer's Guide to Pre-Packaged Food

BY CHARLEY HOGWOOD

Arguably, storing food for the long haul should be the top priority for those of us aiming toward a prepared way of life. There are tons of articles, blog posts, and YouTube videos on hunting, canning and preserving food for your family and there are various pros and cons to each method. Recently, there's been an increase in marketers of pre-packaged food for long-term survival, and even a year's worth of food can be purchased from your local big box store. As with all trends, popularity breeds an increase in competition and sometimes a decrease in quality. If you're going to purchase pre-packaged food for long-term survival, here are four key points to keep in mind.

FREEZE-DRIED VS. DEHYDRATED FOOD

Both processes do significantly increase shelf life and portability, as the food is much lighter in weight. Dehydrating will not extend the shelf life nearly as long as freeze-drying. You can expect a dehydrated item to store well for months rather than multiple years depending on how much moisture was removed. The more a food item is dried, the more brittle the texture becomes and the longer it can be stored.

Why is this important? This is important because over the last several years, lesser companies have been using the two terms interchangeably. If they can't explain how they make it, don't buy it. Freeze-dried foods will have a longer shelf life but keep in mind that storage conditions vary widely. Temperature and moisture are two of the five most common enemies of storage with contamination, light and insects rounding out the list. Additionally, regular rotation is the key to proper storage. Keep a record system detailing the age of all of your supplies.

APPETITE FATIGUE

We've all been there, standing in front of the fridge, staring at that Tupperware container of leftovers wondering if it's possible to enjoy meatloaf for the third day in a row. Why the hesitation? We call that appetite fatigue, the concept that our bodies need variety. In a stressful environment, you're more likely to run into this, and much quicker, than you would in your everyday life.

Why is this important? Because one of the greatest survival attributes is a positive attitude and high morale. Nothing makes people more miserable than hunger, and then they feel angry at what's for dinner. We call that "hangry," a combination of the words 'hungry' and 'angry'. How is this going to affect the way you communicate with your family? Try to look for a long-term food solution that offers both quality and a variety of choices so you can keep your family healthy and happy. One of the great things about commercial competition is the sheer volume in the variety of choices for long-term food solutions.

MEAL PLANNING

Not all meals are created equal. Take a good look at the package labeling, and you might be surprised to learn that there is no standard, with serving sizes ranging from ¼ cup to 1-½ cups. Also, look at the entrées—do they consider mashed potatoes a meal?

Remember that these pre-packaged meals sold by the bucket are supposed to be used for emergency meals during lean times. You'll need protein and calories. The average male, between the ages of 30-40, doing moderate work, should have between 2,400-2,600 calories a day, as a conservative estimate. How many calories are in your half a cup of spaghetti?

FOOD FOR SURVIVAL KITS

BY JOHN MCCANN

Some of the best emergency preparedness items are from backpacking companies. After all, backpackers are obsessed with reducing the weight of their packs and manufactures have responded to serve their needs. Besides lightweight tents and titanium tent stakes, innovations in food preparation have been going on for years. Emergency food should be carried in every survival kit, except for maybe the smallest. However, if you carry a larger kit, such as a pack or vehicle kit, you will want to include emergency rations. These will provide you with more calories and will sustain you for a longer period of time without having to collect food.

M.R.E.s Military or civilian M.R.E. (Meal, Ready to Eat) is a complete food package that provides an entrée (such as beef stew, chicken & rice pilaf, chili w/ macaroni, etc.), a side dish, a dessert, a cracker pack with a spread, a beverage base and condiment pack. The entrée can be eaten right out of the pouch without preparation, but they taste better if heated. The military version provides a heating device that you place in a separate pouch and add water and the entrée pouch. It automatically heats the entrée pouch. This perk is not included in any of the civilian versions. These rations have a shelf life of 3 to 5 years. M.R.E.s can be obtained from Brigade Quartermasters and other military suppliers, but only the civilian version is available. The heaters can still be obtained from Cheaper Than Dirt. These rations are suitable for large kits but are rather bulky. I find that if you carry only the entrée, they take up much less room (of course, this also means fewer calories).

Freeze-dried meals Another type of emergency rations is the freeze-dried meal. Everyone's opinion is different, but I find that these taste the best (but they are bulky). They can be folded down to take up less space, but care should be taken to not break the seal. The biggest drawback is the need for water to rehydrate them. I don't find this a problem because I usually can boil all the water I need. However, in a survival situation where water is scarce, they are not the best choice.

When comparing prices be sure to take into account the protein-per-day of servings. In order to keep costs down, a food manufacturer may reduce the amount of protein. Sometimes they avoid meats altogether, choosing instead to add TVP or texturized vegetable protein. Real protein is needed to maintain health and muscle mass for the long term.

TASTE REALLY DOES MATTER

We hear this all the time, "Well in a survival situation, you'll eat whatever's on your plate!" That may be true from a functional perspective, but how is this going to affect your ability to work as a team? Plus, if you could prevent this from happening now, pre-disaster, wouldn't that be a better plan?

Thankfully, most of the major players in the long-term food game offer free samples so that you can try their food before purchasing a large quantity. This should be something that you share with your family, and get their input on as well. Make it a tasting competition so even the kids think it's fun.

Overall, be a conscientious shopper, ask questions before you purchase, and always read the label. Remember, you're planning for your health, and that's a very important decision that shouldn't be taken lightly.

Seal the Deal

VACUUM SEALERS AREN'T JUST FOR FOOD ANYMORE

BY COREY GRAFF

When things get interesting, freshness is survival. And while they're commonly employed to seal in the freshness on perishable goods, vacuum sealers — those nifty air-sucking devices that spit out Star Trek-looking plastic food packages from the future — can be employed for other practical uses, too.

Grandpa was a turn-of-the-century trout angler and woodsman who wisely advised that there was one piece of gear you never went into the outdoors without: your bum wad. That's toilet paper, Jack. Arse wipe. But even, in your moment of greatest need, is your dunny roll dry? Nothing can cast a dark cloud of unhappy feelings over your day like wet potty paper. And nothing can protect your wipes from the elements like a vacuum sealer can. An added benefit is that the sealer will compress the roll, making it easier to store mass amounts of it at home or in your backpack. It'll simply take up less space. And, by golly, it'll be dry when you need it.

The same tip can be employed with clothing (which, coincidentally, may end up being your toilet paper if you don't follow the tip above). Every bug-out bag needs at least one change of clothes in the event of soak-through. A vacuum-sealed package containing long underwear and socks, shirts and pants will not only be bone dry but will be shrunk down to backpack sized portions for ready use. Compactness is key when backpacking. In fact, dozens of uses for backpackers can be imagined — sealing medicine, important papers, fire-starting stuff, electronics, first aid supplies or snacks (which can attract bears if they get a whiff of your trail mix).

Think about it. A vacuum sealer does three things: It keeps oxygen out, preventing bacteria and mold from attacking

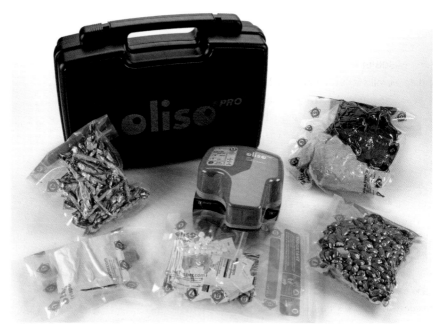

With the Oliso PRO Outdoors Series vacuum sealer, the LIVING READY staff tested it on anchovies, almonds, toilet paper, a first aid kit, a pair of wool socks, boxer shorts and a t-shirt.

food; it keeps good moisture in (foods) and unwanted moisture out; and it seals in flavor. Flavorful food is not just a novelty. In times of crises, sinking your teeth into a tasty piece of meat—as opposed to gnawing on a freakish-looking unidentified piece of musty leather—is a real pick-me-up. You need happy thoughts when bad things happen. Fresh, good-tasting food is a critical morale booster.

Be creative about what you can seal. Your backpack and vehicle should contain photos of close loved ones. These pictures can be an important motivator to survive and keep your spirits up if you get lost or stuck. By sealing them, you have a makeshift lamination — maybe not archival quality, but a good basic level of protection from moisture.

Numerous shooters have been vacuum sealing ammunition to prevent corrosion

and as an alternative storage solution. There are even a few YouTube videos about this. I own a few bricks of .22 ammo that have so badly oxidized that my semi-auto .22 rifle won't feed the greenish little rounds at all. Some seal ammo in bulk or by the box but another way to look at it is to seal 25 rounds or so and tuck these mini-sealed ammo packs into your backpack or gun room. No matter where you are, you'll have some ammo that will feed, extract and fire no matter what. In addition, the sealed ammo won't clang around like traditional .22 ammo containers that sound like Mexican maracas in the squirrel woods. Oxygen. Moisture. Mold. Keep the bad things out. Seal the good things in. And, like Grandpa used to say, do it now, while you still can.

The Ultimate
Survival Cooler

ICEY-TEK CAN KEEP THINGS COOL WHEN THE POWER IS OUT

BY BEN SOBIECK

When the folks at our sister brand, *Deer & Deer Hunting*, first brought over this Icey-Tek 55-quart cooler for the Living Ready staff to check out, I couldn't believe it. Not the cooler. The price tag.

"You paid $295 for a cooler?" I said. "In that case, I'd like to tell you about the ocean front property I'm looking to sell cheap."

But it soon became clear why the *Deer & Deer Hunting* crew had the cooler. It's not just a cooler. It's a time machine.

Which is to say, time ceases to exist inside it. That makes it the ultimate emergency food storage container.

THE ULTIMATE EMERGENCY FOOD STORAGE CONTAINER

Here's what I mean. An average $50 or so cooler off the shelf at the local superstore will keep things cold for about 12 hours. After that, the ice melts and you're left with cooler soup.

The *Deer & Deer Hunting* crew had no use for cooler soup. What they needed was something like a portable, non-electric refrigerator for keeping game fresh for long periods of time.

They got it with the Icey-Tek coolers. It's almost magical how ice doesn't melt inside the cooler. The super-insulated cooler will keep ice solid for days, not hours. Adding wild game and other food doesn't change that performance.

Stack that against the typical survival food buckets and survival food storage containers out there, and suddenly $50 doesn't look like such a great deal.

NOT JUST FOR EMERGENCY FOOD STORAGE

While it's clear how the Icey-Tek coolers could help hunters, campers and others in the outdoors, the preparedness community might still need help seeing the benefits. After all, $295 is just one of the price points. They go up from there, too. That's money that could be spent on other preps.

Look at it this way. Icey-Tek coolers aren't just for survival food storage. They could be used for...

- Keeping medicine, such as insulin, cold during extended blackouts
- Storing food from the fridge and freezer when the power is out
- Bugging out
- Bugging in
- Keeping heirloom seeds fresh at a stable temperature (remember that coolers don't make things hot or cold, they just retain the temperature inside)
- Storing ammunition in a cool, dark, dry place

Coolers can seem like an afterthought. But a cooler isn't just a cooler. There are good ones and bad ones. Your preparedness is only as good as its weakest link.

The cooler is available in a variety of sizes:

- 25-quart
- 40-quart
- 55-quart
- 70-quart

Build Your Own
Earthen Oven

WITH AN EARTHEN OVEN, YOU GET PEACE OF MIND BY HAVING AN ALTERNATIVE COOKING SOURCE.

BY STACY HARRIS

Ever since I can remember I have wanted to make and cook in an earthen oven. I have always studied the subject of history through the eyes of food and have noticed that every culture has cooked in some form of an earthen oven. Wood-fired earthen ovens have been one of the most natural cooking structures used by people throughout the world for thousands of years and continue to be made and cooked in by novices and professionals today.

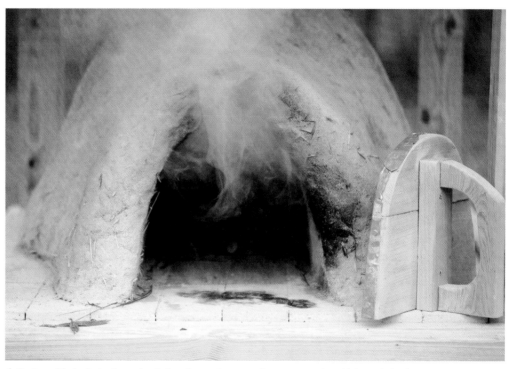

The incredible heat retention and radiation of an earthen oven allows you to cook multiple meals for days.

Building an earthen oven is not difficult and basically consists of natural resources such as clay, sand, and straw that have hardened sufficiently enough to hold heat. This type of oven does not have a fire burning in it continuously, as in most forms of cooking, but instead is fired for a few hours, the coals are scraped out, and then the cooking begins. The thick walls sufficiently give heat lasting for up to twenty hours allowing time to cook many meals from the one fire.

Anything that can be cooked in a conventional oven can be cooked in an earthen oven. For centuries the earthen oven has fed our ancestors with the best of cuisine. These ovens, made from basic elements, allowed town bakers of the early colonies to make their livelihood preparing bread for the townsfolk. Cooks in the colonies were allowed access to the baker's oven at the end of a long day of baking. The bakers allowed the cooks to put large kettle of beans in the cooling ovens and baked them overnight for the next day's meals.

Today, chefs are beginning to see the advantages of cooking in earthen ovens. Many upscale pizzerias and bakeries are using them to prepare extraordinary works of "art" for consumers to eat. Unlike conventional ovens that have a cycling of temperatures, the earthen oven's heat is steady and cooks food much more evenly.

I particularly love using my earthen oven for preparing a week's worth of meals in advance. The high temperatures can begin anywhere from 550 degrees to 800 degrees and slowly decrease over the next 20 hours. A typical lineup of a day of cooking begins with pizza and bread, then a few pies, a casserole, and lastly soups and beans. I love the fact that I can use no electricity and produce an abundance of delicious food.

Aside from the amazing food the oven produces, the oven also serves survival needs. The oven consists of rudimentary ingredients that are found almost anywhere. A crude form of the oven can be quickly assembled at nearly any location.

There are no gadgets to break and if the "furnace" cracks you can simply patch it with a little mud. With an oven requiring few tools and no electricity, a hungry man is soon able to prepare delicious meals from scratch.

CONSTRUCTING YOUR EARTHEN OVEN

WHAT YOU NEED

The components to the earthen oven are simple, and for the most part, easy to find. You will need firebrick, sand, clay, newspaper, and straw. If you do not have newspaper, large leaves will also work. They will be removed before you cook in your oven. You can find the firebrick and clay at your local masonry. The clay from the riverbank will work fine but is harder to carry and difficult to get the proportions right when mixing with the sand.

- 40 Firebricks
- 700 pounds all-purpose sand
- (approx. 290 pounds for the form, 400 pounds for the oven, and 10 pounds to finish the mouth).
- 200 pounds (dry weight) fireclay
- one or two days of newspaper
- about a quarter bale of straw
- a tarp to mix the materials

HOW TO BUILD IT

Build the Base

Form a firm base for the oven. Flatten out a spot of ground or build a sturdy foundation. Lay the firebrick out on the working surface. Try to get the surface as flat as possible because this will be the floor of your oven. I had enough thin firebricks to make a second layer. This helps retain more heat in my oven. The oven I built is 32" × 45" which equals out to eight bricks wide by five bricks deep.

Sketch Out the Form

After the base is set, the next step is to build the form. Start by drawing out the general shape of the oven with chalk on

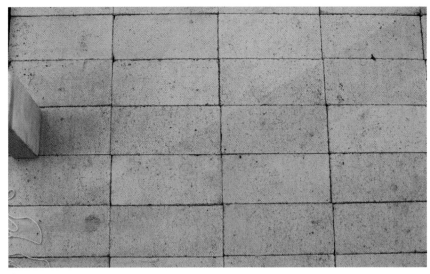

Sketch out the design on the foundation using children's sidewalk chalk.

The oven takes shape during the sand castle stage. Keep the sand moist for easier molding.

Wet newspaper makes the sand form easier to remove later on.

the brick. Tie a piece of string to the chalk and pivot it around the base, making three circles. The first circle should touch both of the outer edges and back of the floor of bricks. Follow it by drawing another circle 3 inches closer in toward the middle and then a final one another 3 inches closer in toward the middle. This will be your template for the dome and the two layers involved. Draw a mouth to your template by centering two lines 4 inches from the edge with chalk. Then draw another pair of lines, each coming four inches closer to the center. Stop each line about 7 inches from the front edge. You will need that space later. So, the inside circle for your

oven should be 20 inches and the mouth approximately 12 inches.

Work the Sand

And now for the fun part, the building of the form with sand. This is where the shape of the oven takes place. You will need to do this the same day you build the first layer of your oven or the sand will start to dry and blow away. Add water to the sand until just wet and form a mound in the shape of the oven. Basically, the dome can be any height, but follow this one absolutely necessary rule: the height of the dome-to-mouth ratio must be between 60 to 65 percent. If the mouth is too high, the oven will not carry heat properly, and if the mouth is too low, the smoke will not draw and the fire will not burn well. I built the dome and mouth around 16 inches and 10 inches respectively. It is a good idea to place a board at the mouth of the oven to keep the front straight and square. Cover the form in strips of wet newspaper. This will make it easy to remove the sand later.

Get Muddy

Now it is time to play in the mud! Spread out a tarp or canvas and place sand and clay in the middle. It should be two parts sand to one part clay. Add water and start incorporating the mix with your feet. Get the kids out to do this; they will love it. The

▲ Get the kids involved in the project and give the clay mixture a good stomping.

▲ After the first layer of clay is applied, let it sit for a couple days.

▲ Remove the sand from inside bit by bit over the course of several days as the oven settles.

consistency you are looking for is something very workable, not too wet and not crumbly.

Start piling the mud on the sand form. Bring the mud to nearly the "second" chalk line, anticipating settling as you build up. Treat the mud like bricks, keeping the mud square and stacking it. After you complete the first layer, let it set for a day or two.

Add the Second Layer
Scratch the surface of the first layer so this next layer will adhere well. I did this with a fork making scrape marks all over the outside layer of the clay. Mix the mud as before, but now add some hay or straw to the mix. This will act as rebar and strengthen the mud. Layer the same way as the first layer. After completion, again let set overnight before finishing the mouth of the oven.

Final Steps
Remove the board from the front of the oven. Mound the remaining sand to continue out another couple of inches. Place newspaper as before and then create a nice round mouth to your oven with some more mud mix.

After the oven has stiffened some (about a week) dig out some of the sand

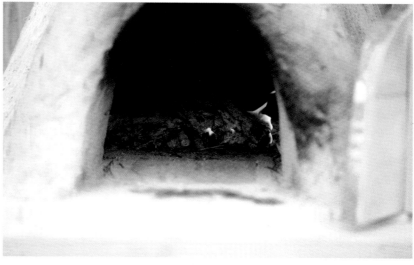

Season the oven with a test fire to find cracks that need patching up.

from inside. Watch for cracking. Wait a couple more days if any cracks form. Continue to remove sand a little over several days until the dome is empty. After the sand is completely out of the oven, the oven should start drying more rapidly.

Let the oven dry before using it. This will probably take four to six weeks, depending on the weather.

While waiting for it to dry, make a door for it by cutting out a piece of wood in the shape of the entrance. Making a cardboard template helps a lot for getting the right shape.

Make a Test Fire
Before you bake your first loaf of bread, start a fire in the oven to get rid of any remaining moisture. Do not be tempted to bake a loaf of bread in it. Until the oven is completely dry it will simply not hold enough heat. After the first fire, cracks will appear on the oven. Simply rub some of the mud mix into the cracks.

You are done making the oven and it is ready for use. The oven, as durable as it feels, will need to be covered from the rain by a tarp or some other material.

COOKING IN THE EARTHEN OVEN

Light the oven like you would a campfire. On the mouth of the oven, bring ablaze pieces of hardwood split into two-inch diameter. Once burning, push the mass into the center of the oven. A rooker, made specifically for the job, makes this easy, but a hoe will work also. The oven will have to heat for a few hours to reach high temperatures. Prepare your desired meal in the meantime.

Keep an eye on the oven as the wood burns down. For a long while the wood will smoke and turn the inside all sooty. Let it keep burning. After an hour or two, the smoke will dissipate and the soot will burn off. This is when the oven is ready. Remove the ash.

Wash the oven floor with a wet mop. This will clean the ash off and help remove hotspots from the oven.

Now you're ready to bake. You can place a thermometer in the oven to check for the correct temperature or if you are making bread or pizza you can use the old method of using cornmeal to test the temperature. Throw a handful of cornmeal in the center of the oven and if it catches fire, wait or wash the oven out again to further cool it. What you are looking for is the cornmeal to turn brown. Using a peel, place the bread dough directly on the firebrick floor. Close the door and let bake three to five minutes for a pizza and ten minutes for the bread. Of course every pizza oven will differ.

Stacy Harris is the author of *Recipes & Tips for Sustainable Living*. Watch a video about making an earthen oven on her website at gameandgarden.com.

8 Powerless Cooking Methods

BY ANGELA PASKETT

Many emergency situations will result in the loss of electricity. The majority of your food storage still needs to be cooked. Making a plan for cooking without electricity will help ensure you're not eating all your food storage cold and raw. So here are some options for cooking when there is no electricity.

FIRE

Build a fire in a fire pit, barrel, or other enclosure so you don't add an uncontrolled fire to your emergency! Do not cook your food over fuel that produces toxic fumes as it burns like tires or carpet. Roast your food on a stick, or use a metal grate or tripod over your fire and cook in sturdy pots and pans.

WOOD OR COAL STOVE

The flat top of a wood or coal stove can be used to cook like a range. An antique wood-burning kitchen stove would be ideal, but a stove built to heat a home with a flat top would work as well. Cooking on a wood stove will serve the dual purpose of heating your home as well—perfect for a winter emergency.

ROCKET STOVE

Rocket stoves are designed to burn biomass fuel like sticks, but use less of it than an open fire. You can make your own rocket stove, or purchase one like the EcoZoom stove. Volcano Stoves use a similar fuel-conserving design as a rocket stove and are also available with a propane adaptor for an additional fuel option.

BARBECUE GRILL

An outdoor grill, either gas or charcoal, is a simple powerless cooking option many of us already use regularly. But it's not just for steaks and burgers. Any food small enough to fall through the grate can be cooked in foil or a pan over the heat source.

CAMPING STOVE

With styles ranging from pocket-sized backpacking stoves to briefcase-style double burner stoves, there's surely one of these portable stoves that will fit your needs for preparedness and maybe even make itself a regular participant on your camping trips as well. Larger camping stoves, like those built by Camp Chef, use the same propane tanks as a gas grill, increasing your cooking options with the same fuel you may already have on hand. Each of these camping stoves uses a specific fuel, so be sure you have sufficient fuel stored to be able to use your stove when you need it.

GAS RANGE

If you have a gas range in your kitchen and the gas lines are not damaged, you can use that range in your home for cooking. Just bypass the electronic ignition and light it with a match or other fire starter. A gas oven will not work without power, only the stove top.

SOLAR OVEN

Make a solar oven or purchase one like the All American Sun Oven. Solar ovens magnify the heat from the sun and work on sunny days in any season. In winter months, your best cooking time is between 10 A.M. and 2 P.M., so plan your meals accordingly. A solar oven can cook anything you'd put in your normal oven and can also be used to dehydrate foods and pasteurize water.

WONDERBOX OR HAYBOX

After food has reach the correct temperature or water has been brought to a boil with one of the previous cooking methods, placing the pot into one of these insulated containers allows the food to continue cooking without using additional fuel.

Having alternate methods of cooking the food you have stored will give you the ability to have a hot meal even when the power is out. And I don't know about you, but for me a hot meal beats cold soup in a can any day.

Find complete survival food storage information in *Food Storage for Self-Sufficiency and Survival* by Angela Paskett, available at store.livingreadyonline.com.

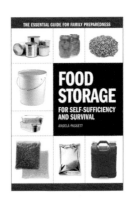

Product Review

EcoZoom Versa Rocket Stove

BY CHARLEY HOGWOOD

The folks at EcoZoom asked us if we were interested in trying out their Versa stove and writing an unflinching review of our findings. That takes nerve and you better be ready to take a punch if your product is lacking in any way. Of course we said yes, always happy to discover a worthy survival solution or to thin the herd of junk products where needed.

We first saw their stoves at a survival expo out in Colorado a couple years ago and were intrigued. Rocket stoves come in various designs and many people have tried to create their own version. Some even make them from debris lying around. There are usually a couple of problems with rocket stoves. They are either made in pieces from debris and not easy to transport, or they are made of some kind of structural steel/concrete and could double as a ship anchor. Some designs are even dangerously hot to the exterior touch due to lack of insulation, which is a fire hazard in itself. One thing is for sure though; they work great if you can get your muddy hands on a good one.

We found that there actually is a solid solution to this problem. In the Versa model we found that EcoZoom has created a good combination of strength, weight, portability and safety. Here's what we found as we put the stove through some paces.

PROS

- Much easier than making a full campfire
- Much easier to contain/extinguish than a campfire
- Can be moved while hot, unlike a typical fire
- Has convenient handles for transport
- Stable footprint, just find and clear a small level spot anywhere
- Works well in windy conditions
- Potentially works well in rainy conditions due to the fire being shielded
- Multi-fuel (biomass, charcoal or anything that burns)
- As opposed to a typical charcoal fire, you can adjust the temperature and not have to carry charcoal with you unless you want to. The stove does come standard with a nice heavy-duty cast iron charcoal grate that allows you to get every last bit of heat from briquettes before they fall through to the lower ash chamber.
- Great instructions using pictures that are easy to understand
- Their charity program will send a stove to a needful family for every unit they sell through their Z+ Program

> **ECOZOOM VERSA ROCKET STOVE SPECS**
> Weight: 14.25 lbs.
> Dimensions: 11.5" × 9.5"
> Fuel Type: wood, charcoal, or solid biomass fuel
> Pot included: no
> Boil Time: 4 min. for 1 L
> Pot base: 9.5"

CONS

The well insulated structure and refractory brick makes it a heavy piece of equipment, so it's not a convenient trail stove. This stout little rocket is best suited as an off-grid cooking option in case of disaster, or a base camp stove, but you won't be throwing this in a backpack anytime soon. For hiking, I'll rely on either a bush craft stove or a portable cooking system.

THE VERDICT

In the end, we love this thing and consider it to be one of those things you will only need to buy once and keep using for many years to come. Its amazing ability to be useful in almost any environment, using almost any combustible solid material is a big plus for us as we are hard on equipment and go to some rough places.

Product Review
The Kelly Kettle

Runs on twigs: scrap up some burnable debris, torch it up and the heat flowing up the inside chimney gets the water inside the Kelly Kettle boiling hot in no time.

BY CHAD LOVE

When you're cold, wet, tired and in the elements, hot water for tea, coffee or cooking is good. But hot water quickly is much, much better. And there's not much out there that boils water in the field more quickly or efficiently than the Kelly Kettle

So what exactly is a Kelly Kettle? This clever little bit of camping/preparedness kit is an import from Ireland that was originally used to heat water for Irish boatmen and fishing guides. It's simply a double-walled kettle with a big hole in the middle of it. That's it. You fill the kettle with water, place it on its base, place a few twigs (or anything, really) in the base, light it, feed it a few more twigs, and in just a few minutes you have boiling water. It's that simple.

The Kelly Kettle is what's known in bushcraft/preparedness circles as a "volcano" kettle, which doesn't mean it spews hot magma, rather the name comes from the basic design of its center fire hole. Due to the kettle's extremely large surface area, when a fire is lit in its center, the water heats up very quickly. What's more, the Kelly Kettle is very effective in windy condition, as the fire is protected from the wind. In fact, the fire burns hotter as it gets windier because the kettle's stand acts like a bellows that draws air into the fire chamber. The final effect, with flames shooting out from the top of the kettle's chimney and hot steam piping into the air, is, well, volcano-like.

I first discovered the Kelly Kettle while researching alternatives to propane stoves. Like many outdoorsmen, when I'm on hunting or fishing trip I usually take a little one-burner propane stove for heating up water for tea, coffee, etc. It works well enough when the wind's calm, but not so much when the wind blows. Since I live in Oklahoma, where the wind blows pretty much non-stop, I had been looking for a wind-proof alternative to my propane stove, something I can take on a fishing or hunting trip and use to boil water quickly and easily right on the tailgate or ground. But the Kelly Kettle is equally useful as an emergency/backup source of hot water for homeowners, campers, picnickers or anyone who needs hot water quickly, reliably, and with minimal fuel.

Thinking the Kelly Kettle might be the ticket, I ordered one. And on first use, I was, quite frankly, shocked at how quickly this thing boils water with such little fuel. Soon after receiving mine, I decided to test it in a cold, wet and howling mid-winter wind. With just a little grass tinder and twigs scrounged from my yard and placed in the stainless steel base, it took less than four minutes from striking a ferro rod to the grass and feeding twigs into the fire, to boiling water ready for the French press.

The Kelly Kettle has since become a permanent and valued part of my camping/preparedness kit. It's rugged, simple, efficient, and works well with virtually any combustible material you feed it. With a price range from $59.95 for the aluminum "Trekker" model that holds 17 ounces of water all the way, to $84.99 for the stainless steel base camp model that holds 50 ounces of water, the Kelly Kettle is not inexpensive. But then, good gear rarely is.

Buyer's Guide to Backpacking Stoves

ALCOHOL STOVES

Manufacturer/Model: Trangia / Spirit Stove
Price: $
Weight: 10.2 oz.
Dimensions: 3.75" × 2.5"
Fuel Type: Alcohol
Pot included: No
Burn Time: 25 minutes
Boil Time: 8 minutes for 1L

Manufacturer/Model: Trail Designs / Caldera Cone System
Price: $
Weight: Varies (each cone handcrafted to fit your pot)
Dimensions: Contact manufacturer
Fuel Type: Alcohol
Pot included: No
Burn Time: Contact manufacturer
Boil Time: 6-7 minutes for 2 cups

Manufacturer/Model: Trail Designs / Caldera Sidewinder Stove System
Price: $$
Weight: 9.9 oz.
Dimensions: 6" × 4.25"
Fuel Type: Alcohol
Pot included: Yes
Burn Time: Contact manufacturer
Boil Time: 6-7 minutes for 2 cups

Manufacturer/Model: Vargo / Decagon Stove
Price: $$
Weight: 1.2 oz.
Dimensions: 2.25" × 1.25"
Fuel Type: Alcohol
Pot included: No
Burn Time: 20 minutes
Boil Time: 5-6 minutes for 2 cups

Manufacturer/Model: Trangia / 27-2 UL (Kit)
Price: $$$
Weight: 30.3 oz.
Dimensions: 7" × 4"
Fuel Type: Alcohol
Pot included: Yes
Burn Time: 25 minutes
Boil Time: 8 minutes for 1L

CANISTER STOVES

Manufacturer/Mode: Primus / ClassicTrail
Price: $
Weight: 8 oz.
Dimensions: 4.9" × 4.9" × 2.2"
Fuel Type: Canister
Pot included: No
Burn Time: Contact manufacturer
Boil Time: 3 minutes

Manufacturer/Model: Vargo / Triad XE Multi-Fuel Stove
Price: $
Weight: 1.5 oz.
Dimensions: 3.9" × 1.2"
Fuel Type: Canister (alcohol, fuel tabs or fuel gels)
Pot included: No
Burn Time: 15 minutes (alcohol); 13 minutes (fuel tab); 20 minutes (fuel gel)
Boil Time: 5-6 minutes for 2 cups (alcohol); 8 minutes for 2 cups (fuel tab and gel)

Manufacturer/Model: The Coleman Company, Inc. / PerfectFlow 1-Burner Propane Stove
Price: $
Weight: 16.4 oz.

Dimensions: 7.7" × 7.8" × 6.63"
Fuel Type: Canister
Pot included: No
Burn Time: 132 minutes (high)-9 hours (low)
Boil Time: Contact manufacturer

Manufacturer/Model: Optimus / Crux Lite
Price: $
Weight: 2.5 oz
Dimensions: 2.8" × 2.2" × 2.2"
Fuel Type: Canister (butane/propane)
Pot included: No
Burn Time: 90 minutes at maximum output per 230g canister
Boil Time: 3 minutes to boil 1L

Manufacturer/Model: The Coleman Company, Inc. / PowerPack 1-Burner Stove
Price: $
Weight: 4 lbs.
Dimensions: 13.38" × 12.5" × 4"
Fuel Type: Canister (propane)
Pot included: No
Burn Time: 132 minutes (high)-9 hours (low) per 494g canister
Boil Time: Contact manufacturer

Pricing key (based on manufacturer's suggested retail price):

$ = under $50
$$ = $51–$75
$$$ = $76–$100
$$$$ = $101–$150
$$$$$ = $151–$200
$$$$$$ = $201+

Pricing key (based on manufacturer's suggested retail price):

$ = under $50
$$ = $51–$75
$$$ = $76–$100
$$$$ = $101–$150
$$$$$ = $151–$200
$$$$$$ = $201+

Manufacturer/Model: Optimus/Crux
Price: $
Weight: 2.9 oz.
Dimensions: 1.3" × 3.3" × 2.2"
Fuel Type: Canister (butane/propane)
Pot included: No
Burn Time: 90 minutes at maximum output per 230g canister
Boil Time: 3 minutes for 1L

Manufacturer/Model: Camp Chef / Butane One Burner Stove
Price: $
Weight: 5 lbs.
Dimensions: 12.5" × 14.5" × 3.75"
Fuel Type: Canister (butane)
Pot included: No
Burn Time: 120 minutes (high)-4 hours (low)
Boil Time: 10 minutes

Manufacturer/Model: The Coleman Company, Inc. / Micro Backpack Stove
Price: $$
Weight: 6 lbs.
Dimensions: 4.5" × 4" × 2.4"
Fuel Type: Canister (butane/propane)
Pot included: No
Burn Time: 60 minutes (high)
Boil Time: 3.25 minutes for 1L

Manufacturer/Model: MSR / Pocket Rocket
Price: $$$
Weight: 4.2 oz.
Dimensions: 4" × 2" × 2"
Fuel Type: Canister
Pot included: No

Burn Time: 60 minutes per 227g canister
Boil Time: 3.5 minutes for 1L

Manufacturer/Model: Optimus / Crux Weekend HE Cook System
Price: $$$
Weight: 9.7 oz.
Dimensions: 4.9" × 6.5"
Fuel Type: Canister
Pot included: Yes
Burn Time: 90 minutes at maximum output per 230 g canister
Boil Time: 3 minutes for 1L

Manufacturer/Model: Primus / Profile
Price: $$$$
Weight: 11 lbs. 11.2 oz.
Dimensions: 23.2" × 3.9" × 12.6"
Fuel Type: Canister
Pot included: No
Burn Time: Contact manufacturer
Boil Time: 3 minutes

Manufacturer/Model: Primus / Eta Express
Price: $$$$
Weight: 15.8 oz.
Dimensions: 5.9" × 3.9"
Fuel Type: Canister
Pot included: Yes
Burn Time: 85 minutes per 230g canister
Boil Time: 2.6 minutes

Manufacturer/Model: Primus / Profile Dual
Price: $$$$$
Weight: 10 oz.
Dimensions: 21.5" × 12.25" × 3.25"
Fuel Type: Canister (Propane/butane)
Pot included: No
Burn Time: Contact manufacurer
Boil Time: 3 minutes

Manufacturer/Model: MSR / WindPro II
Price: $$$$$
Weight: 11 lbs. 14.4 oz.
Dimensions: 6.5" × 5" × 4"
Fuel Type: Canister
Pot included: No
Burn Time: 60 minutes per 8 oz.
Boil Time: 3 minutes

Manufacturer/Model: MSR / SuperFly
Price: $$$$$
Weight: 6.2 oz.
Dimensions: Contact manufacturer
Fuel Type: Canister
Pot included: No
Burn Time: 60 minutes per 227g canister
Boil Time: 3 minutes for 1L

LIQUID FUEL STOVES

Manufacturer/Model: Primus / Eta Power Multi Fuel Kit
Price: $$$
Weight: 14.2 oz.
Dimensions: 3.9" × 5.9"
Fuel Type: Naphtha fuel, lead-free petrol and kerosene
Pot included: No
Burn Time: Contact manufacturer
Boil Time: 3.5 minutes

Manufacturer/Model: The Coleman Company, Inc. / Sportster II Dual Fuel™ 1-Burner Stove
Price: $$$
Weight: 3 lbs. 1.3 oz.
Dimensions: 7.38" × 7.8" × 6.55
Fuel Type: Unleaded gasoline
Pot included: No
Burn Time: 105 minutes at maximum output
Boil Time: 4 minutes for 1 qt.

Manufacturer/Model: The Coleman Company, Inc. / Dual Fuel™ 2-Burner Stove
Price: $$$$
Weight: 12 lbs.
Dimensions: 20.13" × 12.88" × 6.63"
Fuel Type: Unleaded gasoline
Pot included: No
Burn Time: 120 minutes with both burners at maximum output
Boil Time: 4 minutes

Manufacturer/Model: Optimus / Nova
Price: $$$$
Weight: 15.3 oz.
Dimensions: 5.5" × 3.1" × 2.5"

Fuel Type: Optimus Arctic fuel, white gas, kerosene, diesel and jet fuel
Pot included: No
Burn Time: 150 minutes at maximum output per 450 ml fuel
Boil Time: 3.5 minutes for 1L

Manufacturer/Model: The Coleman Company, Inc. / Classic 2-Burner Stove
Price: $$$$
Weight: 11 lbs. 1.6 oz.
Dimensions: 19.6" × 6" × 5.38"
Fuel Type: Liquid Fuel
Pot included: No
Burn Time: 120 minutes with both burners at maximum output
Boil Time: Contact manufacturer

Manufacturer/Model: Primus / Omni-Fuel
Price: $$$$$
Weight: 15.6 oz.
Dimensions: 5.6" × 3.5" × 2.6"
Fuel Type: Gas, gasoline/petrol, diesel, kerosene/paraffin and aviation fuel
Pot included: No

Burn Time: 70 minutes per 230g
Boil Time: 3.1 minutes

Manufacturer/Model: MSR / DragonFly Multifuel Stove
Price: $$$$$
Weight: 18 oz.
Dimensions: 6.3" × 5" × 3.5"
Fuel Type: White gas, kerosene, unleaded auto fuel, diesel and jet fuel
Pot included: No
Burn Time: 66 minutes/white gas; 153 minutes/kerosene; 136 minutes/diesel
Boil Time: 3.5 minutes for 1L/white gas; 3.9 minutes for 1L/kerosene; 3.5 minues for 1L/diesel

Manufacturer/Model: Optimus / Hiker+
Price: $$$$$
Weight: 3 lbs. 8 oz.
Dimensions: 7.1" × 7.1" × 4.3"
Fuel Type: Optimus Arctic Fuel, white gas, kerosene, diesel and jet fuel
Pot included: No
Burn Time: 120 minutes at maximum output per 350ml
Boil Time: 3.5 minutes for 1L

Manufacturer/Model: MSR / XGK EX Expedition Stove
Price: $$$$$
Weight: 17.2 oz.
Dimensions: 5" × 3.9" × 3.5"
Fuel Type: White gas, kerosene, diesel
Pot included: No
Burn Time: 109 minutes/white gas; 98 minutes/kerosene; 170 minutes/diesel
Boil Time: 3.5 minutes/white gas; 2.8 minutes/kerosene; 4.5 minutes/diesel

Manufacturer/Model: MSR / Whisper-Lite International Stove
Price: $$$$$
Weight: 15.5 oz.
Dimensions: 6.5" × 5" × 4"
Fuel Type: White gas, kerosene and unleaded auto fuel
Pot included: No
Burn Time: 110 minutes/white gas; 155 minutes/kerosene
Boil Time: 3.5 minutes for 1L/white gas; 4.4 minutes for 1L/kerosene

CHAPTER FIVE

Lighting and Power Sources

Emergency lighting is a practical part of any preparedness plan. Power outages are all too common following even relatively minor weather events. This chapter is full of products that will help you keep some lights on even when the power is off—from lanterns to headlamps to flashlights to emergency glow sticks. You will also learn how to make emergency candles from common household items. It also covers generators, solar generators, solar power packs and solar panels.

JENS OTTOSON / SHUTTERSTOCK.COM

13 Emergency Lighting Options

SOLUTIONS THAT KEEP LIGHTS ON WHEN THE POWER IS OFF

BY BRETT ORTLER

Power outages happen all the time. As the East Coast Blackout of 2003 showed, the U.S. power grid is unreliable under normal circumstances. Extreme weather—be it strong winds, ice or excessive heat—make outages, blackout and brown outs even more likely, and depending on the extent of the damage, you could be without power for days if not weeks. The good news is there are a number of emergency lighting products available that can brighten even in the darkest of power outages.

ADJUST YOUR EXPECTATIONS

As you explore emergency lighting options, it's important to note that emergency lighting is just that—a sufficient light source to help you survive in an emergency, whether it's a long-term one or short-term one. To be sure, a hurricane lamp or a battery-powered flashlight hardly produces the ambiance of a suburban house full of recessed lights and incandescent bulbs. This becomes clear enough when you see your child's face haloed by the battery-powered flashlight as you hustle him to the basement as the storm sirens wail.

TRADITIONAL BATTERY-POWERED FLASHLIGHTS

From the 4,100-lumen Torchlight to the venerable Maglite, there is a baffling array of flashlights on the market, which is a good thing. While cheap, poorly made products have proliferated, with a little research, it's not hard to find reliable, well-made flashlights by well-known brands (Jet Beam, Fenix, Pelican).

Cost: Ranges wildly; most flashlights are quite cheap, but higher-end models can be hundreds of dollars.

Pros: Safe, reliable and easy enough for a child to use, flashlights are the first line of defense in a power outage. Thanks to advances in LED bulbs, they can also be surprisingly bright and efficient. There are also dozens of different types for a variety of uses, including high-powered searchlights.

Cons: Battery life and light output/performance differs a great deal between models and manufacturers. In addition, while flashlights are great for finding your way through the dark, as anyone who's tried to read by flashlight can tell you, flashlights are by no means an ideal light source for long-term use. Other light sources (headlamps, lanterns) are often better in sedentary situations or when you need to illuminate the entire room, not just a swathe of it.

Advice:

- When you buy multiple flashlights, make sure they all run on the same type of battery (AA for example). You'll only need to stock one type of battery, making the stock easier to maintain and ensuring all your flashlights will be in working order when needed because you'll have the right type of battery on hand.
- Don't assume that a more expensive flashlight is the best option.

On the contrary, it's often better to have a number of cheaper options. (In a real respect, the more flashlights, the merrier.)

- A flashlight isn't any good if you don't know where it is; keep your flashlights in a single designated place and always return it when there when not it use.

RECHARGEABLE FLASHLIGHTS

Powered by a simple hand-crank mechanism or small solar cells, rechargeable flashlights are just what you'd expect—a flashlight with a renewable power source instead of a battery. For hand-crank flashlights, the amount of work that you'll have to put in varies—usually five minutes of cranking will get you a decent amount of light. Solar flashlights usually need to be recharged for the better part of a day, in order to produce several hours' worth of light.

Most of these flashlights use LED bulbs, which are quite bright and energy-efficient. Better yet, many variants include a radio, a cell phone charger, even USB ports, making them unique and versatile lighting options.

Cost: Flashlight-only products are quite cheap; combination radio/flashlight/cellphone charger options are more expensive.

Pros: For the hand-crank flashlights, if you've got the time and energy to power them up, they aren't a bad short-term lighting option. They also provide a half-decent workout. Solar power flashlights are good options, especially if you're in the boondocks and short on batteries.

Cons: Given that they need to be powered up before use, hand-crank flashlights aren't a great option if you need immediate illumination. (Solar flashlights—if the weather has been sunny—avoid this problem.) Quality varies wildly, and there is a myriad of manufacturers, so choose a manufacturer you trust. (Freeplay Energy's products have been well-reviewed by preparedness-minded folks.)

Advice: While they are hardly a comprehensive lighting solution, they're

always handy to have, especially given the versatility of the more expensive models.

KEYCHAIN LIGHTS

Perhaps the simplest lighting solution, keychain flashlights are also one of the cheapest and most portable. I've used the keychain light on my keys dozens and dozens of times without replacing the battery.

Cost: Inexpensive

Pros: Simple, easy, and discrete, their LED bulbs produce more light than you'd expect.

Cons: As you might expect, they only produce a small amount of light, and their batteries can be harder to find than your average AA and AAA varieties.

Advice: Perfect for when you're on the move, they are a handy addition in almost any situation and especially useful in Bug-Out bags.

HEADLAMPS

If you're like me, when you think of headlamps, you immediately think of old-timey miners, but headlamps aren't what they used to be. Today's headlamps are often inexpensive, easy to use, and bright thanks to LED bulbs. Better yet, if you shop around you can often find headlamps with red/green LED bulbs so you don't lose your night vision when using them. And while wearing a headlamp might look a little strange at first, headlamps are one of the only hands-free lighting solutions.

Cost: Pretty cheap; even "expensive" models are only around $50.

▲ Headlamp

Pros: Easy to come by and can produce a good amount of light (anywhere from 50-150) lumens. Perhaps the biggest advantage is the most obvious—you don't need to lug around a lantern or a flashlight, which makes working (or reading) in the dark a cinch.

Cons: As they are battery-operated, they can be somewhat short-lived, and some take more esoteric battery varieties.

Advice: A great option for when you're on the go, they are simple, but quite useful. (This is true in non-emergency situations, too; they are incredibly popular among amateur astronomers.)

CHEMICAL GLOW STICKS

While certainly not anything more than a temporary lighting solution, chemical glow sticks are simple and easy to come by. With that said, they might be a fun novelty option for a camping trip or a rave, chemical glow sticks aren't much of a lighting solution if you need to light your home for a few days.

Cost: Inexpensive but you can't reuse them.

Pros: Other than candles, they are probably the cheapest lighting option, at least in terms of a one-off purchase.

Cons: Probably the worst lighting option, in terms of light output and overall usefulness. Most are not reusable, and there's also no way to turn them off, which could prove problematic in an emergency situation where you want to stay incognito.

Advice: I avoid them. Their output is too weak and there are simply other glow stick options out there that are better. (See below.)

BATTERY-POWERED GLOW STICKS AND REUSABLE GLOW STICKS

While chemical glow sticks aren't an ideal emergency lighting solution, battery-powered glow sticks (including Lifegear's LED model) provide a decent amount of light. (As a perk, Lifegear will even replace the batteries in its LED model over its lifetime—not including shipping and handling).

UV Paqlite has a line of reusable glow sticks that contain crystals that absorb light during the day and then glow all night long thanks to some clever chemistry.

Cost: While more expensive than traditional chemical glow sticks, they aren't all that spendy. The UV Paqlite is somewhere around twenty dollars and the LED glow sticks are only a few dollars.

Pros: Both varieties of non-traditional glow sticks produce a halfway decent amount of light—certainly enough to get by in a camp at night. They are hardly spotlights, however. While the Lifegear light is dependent on batteries, the UV Paqlite is certain to produce light no matter what.

Cons: The Lifegear LED light's appeal is in part based on the free batteries, which could prove problematic in an extended disaster.

Advice: The UV Paqlite is the rare lighting option that is renewable, and for that reason, it's not a bad item to try out, especially if you're interested in longer-term lighting solutions. (It might not light up your living room, but it's better than nothing.) The LED flashlights, on the other hand, are a good short-term solution or for when you're on the go.

CELL PHONE APPLICATIONS

When cell phones first became really popular, everyone used the cell phone-screen-as-a-flashlight trick. Soon after that, legitimate cell phone flashlight applications were released, and today, they are wildly popular—I have three on my phone. They usually use the phone's camera flash as a light source and provide a number of unique lighting options.

Cost: Many of these apps are free or cost under five dollars. However, you must have a call phone with both a camera flash and the ability to download and run apps.

Pros: Because they are essentially computer programs, cell phone flashlights are more than simple flashlights. They can also serve as makeshift emergency beacons, as many feature an SOS command or even a full-fledged Morse Code translator.

SAFETY NOTE

All combustion-based lanterns and lamps produce carbon monoxide, which can quickly lead to carbon monoxide poisoning and death. These types of lamps are for use only in the outdoors or in areas with sufficient ventilation. Indoor use is not recommended. When burning any combustion-based lamp, be sure to have a functioning carbon monoxide detector near your, just in case. And whatever light source you choose, be sure to read your owner's manual first.

△ Aladdin Lamp

△ LED Lantern

Cons: They positively drain your phone's battery, and in a survival situation, a working cell phone is probably a lot more important than a flashlight. (Given how useful a cell phone can be, this is even true if you don't have service.)

Advice: While flashlight apps are handy in a pinch, I wouldn't rely on them long-term in a survival situation. Even if you have a solar panel, they are so power-hungry that other lighting sources outclass them simply based on efficiency.

BATTERY-POWERED CAMPING LANTERNS

In the time before LED bulbs, camping lanterns were bulky, heavy, power-hungry devices. Thanks to LEDs and improvements in materials technology, these battery-powered lanterns are lighter and brighter than ever, and a great choice for use in any emergency situation.

Cost: Inexpensive.

Pros: They provide a bright, consistent light and are very easy to use. It's also quite easy to find older models for almost nothing at thrift stores and the like. Unlike fuel-burning lamps, battery-powered lanterns don't produce carbon monoxide gas.

Cons: Even with LED technology, battery-powered lanterns are often fairly bulky, so they aren't well suited for Bug-

Out bags. Older models use the relatively clunky six-volt batteries—and sometimes even two—and these aren't always easy to find, at least at your traditional department stores. Even when you find them, they are often rather expensive when compared to more traditional battery types.

Advice: A necessity for any base camp, camping lanterns are reliable, simple and bright, and perfect for use indoors or out. When purchasing one, be sure its battery type is common and that you've got an ample supply.

ALADDIN LAMPS

A famous name in lighting and once one of the most popular light sources in the country, the Aladdin Lamp is famous for the soothing glow it gives off. This glow is the result of its wick, which consists of rare-earth metals (cerium and thorium) that become incandescent when heated by kerosene.

Cost: New lamps are expensive (over a hundred dollars), and used lamps are something of a hot commodity on the antiques market.

Pros: Aladdin lamps were marketed as the "magic" light, thanks to their bright, comforting output, and that's no exaggeration; the light they produce is gorgeous. They also put out a good deal of heat, and

can serve as de facto heaters in the winter. (Note: they emit carbon monoxide, so be sure to see the safety note sidebar.)

Cons: Given the ascendancy of propane, kerosene isn't always easy to come by, especially if you're in a rural area, and it's also somewhat expensive, about the price of diesel. Also, if you've never used an Aladdin, the process of lighting one and maintaining it isn't exactly intuitive, and neither is replacing the wick. In addition, many users complain that these lamps can be sooty and produce less-than-pleasant odors if lower-grade fuel is used. Given that these lamps burn at a high temperature, there is also a fire/burn risk, especially if handled by small children.

Advice: If you already have an Aladdin Lamp and have experience using it, it's not a bad lighting option, as long as you're aware of the carbon monoxide risk. If you don't already have one, their cost is somewhat prohibitive; for the same money, you could buy a number of other emergency lighting options.

OTHER KEROSENE-BASED LAMP OPTIONS

Of course, Aladdin lamps aren't the only kerosene lamps out there. There are many lamp options, and they range from ten-dollar kerosene lamps from a discount department store to somewhat more expensive (but well-known) lamps like Dietz hurricane lamps.

Cost: Relatively inexpensive.

Pros: Simple and easy to set up, they are cheap and easy to transport. Some lamps don't require kerosene and can instead use citronella oil as a fuel.

Cons: The lamp's light output isn't particularly bright, and they can produce sooty, black smoke; over time, the wick also needs to be maintained. In addition, because they emit carbon monoxide, they need to be used outdoors.

Advice: While decidedly low-tech—in many respects, a kerosene lamp is essentially a higher-powered candle—they are handy, simple to use in an emergency and

141

▲ Candle

inexpensive. All in all, not a bad option to have in one's stable of lighting options.

DOUBLE-MANTLE PROPANE LANTERNS

In many double-mantle propane lanterns, a screw-in propane tank serves as part of the lantern body itself. This "plug-and-play" approach makes it simple to swap out used tanks, and many such lanterns are pressure-regulated, so the fuel flow (and resulting light) is consistent.

Cost: More expensive than kerosene lanterns, but still not terribly expensive. In addition, propane is cheaper and easier to find than kerosene

Pros: Simple to use, the twin mantles produce a bright light, and there is little smoke or soot. Limiting your usage and using a lower setting can extend the burn time you'll get out of a canister—sometimes extending it by more than 12 hours.

Cons: When you first purchase a lantern, you need to literally tie the mantles onto the burners. While not difficult, it's not entirely foolproof. Mantles also eventually need to be replaced.

Advice: Given how ubiquitous propane is, its low cost, and how simple many of the double-mantle lanterns are, these are a great option.

CANDLES

Alongside the oil lamp, the candle was among the first artificial lighting sources, and even in an age of high technology, they are still useful today. (In fact, they are useful in part because they are so low-tech; no matter what happens, a flame, a wick and wax will always get you light when you need it.) There are a number of different candle options—everything from votive candles (the candles you remember from church) to dedicated survival candles, and either variety is handy to have.

Cost: Incredibly inexpensive.

Pros: Candles are dirt cheap, and if you shop the clearance section, you can often get them for next to nothing. They're also easy to transport, making them an easy emergency lighting solution. A single survival candle can also last a long time—more than thirty hours in some cases—making them quite cost-effective, and if you stock up on them, you can be assured of light when you need it for months to come.

Cons: A serious fire risk, candles should be used with caution indoors, especially around children. In addition, they don't provide a great deal of light, so don't expect to light up your whole house while using them. Candles are also essentially useless if you're on the go.

Advice: Candles are among the most useful—and ubiquitous—emergency lighting sources. Be sure to have a stash for when the lights go out.

12-VOLT SOLAR SETUP

While renewable resources like wind and solar power are enticing power options, setting up a reliable renewable system isn't simple. When it comes down to it, you have to do your homework and run the numbers; thankfully, a few all-in-one solar lighting kits that have done most of the legwork for you do exist. One example is the LEDTronics Solar Panel 3-Bulb system, which consists of a solar panel, a controller box and four outlets—three of which are dedicated to LED bulbs and one that can be used to charge a cell phone. With a full charge, the lights will operate for the better part of a day (and sometimes longer).

Cost: By far the most expensive option on this list—at about two hundred dollars—it also offers perhaps the largest upside in a long-term disaster.

Pros: While there are many other do-it-yourself solar options, the LEDTronics Solar Panel 3-Bulb system takes the guesswork out of things, a major benefit if you've ever attempted to tackle (the somewhat tricky) world of solar power.

Cons: The lights must be used indoors only, as the equipment is not rated for the outdoors.

Advice: If you've got the money, this seems like a great emergency lighting source.

Make Emergency Candles
from 5 Everyday Items

BY CREEK STEWART

A survival situation is one in which we don't have everything we need. Suddenly, we must use what we have—the resources on hand and our wits—to meet basic human survival needs. This often involves creative solutions to common problems. I've always said that the ability to improvise is one of the most important survival skills.

These five makeshift lighting and small-scale heating solutions can be deployed as a last resort if you find yourself in a sudden and unexpected survival scenario. You just never know when one of these innovative ideas might shed some light into your darkness one day. Even candle-sized flames can provide lifesaving heat in a well-designed survival shelter. It is common practice for arctic adventurers to use candles to raise the inside temperature of makeshift snow caves. These tiny heat sources also make suitable stoves to heat single cup meals.

1. SHINING SARDINES

Sardines are an excellent survival food. They have a long shelf life and are full of protein and fats. Maybe you have some sardines packed in your emergency food storage. If not, consider them. With that in mind, oil lamps have been used for hundreds of years. From rendered whale blubber to modern kerosene lanterns, oil lamps are excellent off-grid lighting solutions. What do sardines and oil lamps have to do with each other? Quite a lot actually, if your sardines are packed in olive oil.

After eating the fish, place a natural fiber wick into the remaining oil and slightly over the edge of the sardine container. The wick, in this case a cotton string from a mop head, will absorb the oil. Once the wick is fully soaked, simply light the end. A sardine lamp with just a little bit of oil will burn for many hours and put off steady heat. Yes, it will smell like fish but you can also top it off with some more olive oil or any cooking oil for that matter.

CAUTION! DANGER!

Candles are notorious causes for house fires. Makeshift improvised candles are even more dangerous. Use only as a last resort, burn only on a noncombustible surface and keep close watch on any makeshift candle. A house fire can turn a bug-in scenario into a bug-out scenario in the blink of an eye!

2. GLOWING CRAYOLAS

If you have small children, games and toys are excellent items to pack in an emergency kit. Simple toys such as crayons and coloring books can help keep their mind off of the misfortune that caused the lights to go out in the first place. But if you've focused only on toys and no essentials, like candles, flashlights or space heaters,

⚠ Double-bonus: sardines have a long shelf-life as a survival food and the leftover oil can fuel a candle.

⚠ Like a mini-flare, crayons can provide temporary lighting in a pinch. Just don't tell your kids.

The cool glow of a water jug lantern cuts the glare of a headlamp.

A makeshift bacon-wrap candle gives your home the smell of a never-ending breakfast.

Use a forked stick to jam the wick to the bottom of the Crisco tub. Grease the tip of the wick to help get the candle started.

then you may have to sacrifice some of their least favorite crayon colors and make some Crayndles (Okay, I made that word up). Crayons are basically colored wax. If you're in a hurry, just break the point off and light the paper label at the end of the crayon. As the wax melts, the paper becomes a wick and one crayndle will last about 30 minutes. Not too bad.

You can also get a little more creative and sandwich a natural fiber wick (like a shred of t-shirt material) between three crayons that have been stripped of their labels. Bind everything together with two short pieces of wire. Paper clips work well. Then, simply light the wick. I got one of these to burn for about an hour. Not too bad for a 10-second makeshift Crayndle.

3. BLAZING BOTTLES

If you've remembered anything I wrote in *Build the Perfect Bug Out Bag*, then I know you have a headlamp packed in your 72-hour disaster kit. Yet as nice as headlamps are, they aren't always the perfect lighting solution. Ever tried having dinner or playing cards across the table with someone who's wearing a headlamp flashlight? It's really annoying and gets really old, really fast. You get blinded every time they look at you.

Instead, set a relaxing mood perfect for cards and a sardine dinner using a

headlamp and a water-filled clear plastic milk jug (or any clear container filled with water). Invert the headlamp around the bottle so that the light shines toward the center of the bottle. The water diffuses and diverts the light, making a nice, mellow, glowing lamp that will help set a perfect mood during any disaster bug-in.

4. BEACONING BACON

If you're like my mom, then you have a jar in the cupboard where you pour and keep excess bacon grease. This grease makes the perfect improvised survival candle. Jam in a natural fiber wick and light. It'll burn as long as any comparable sized candle. The second best thing to the taste of bacon is the smell of bacon.

No bacon grease? No problem. If the electricity is out, then the bacon in the fridge is going to go bad anyway, so you might as well use it for something. Tear off the fatty pieces and jam them in a jar around a natural fiber wick, and this will burn like a candle as well. The fatty bacon pieces will melt just like wax. Mmmmm, smells like bacon. Tip: smear the wick with bacon fat first.

5. KINDLING CRISCO

But what if the electricity is off for more than 30 days straight and you need a light source (or small-scale heat source) that

will shine for at least a month? No problem, Crisco's got your back.

Press a natural fiber wick (like a cotton T-shirt shred or a mop strand) using a forked stick to the bottom of a can of Crisco, smear the tip of the wick with Crisco to get it to burn better, and you've got one of the longest- burning emergency candles on the planet. Yum, doesn't that make you hungry? Fried chicken anyone? I have tested this and I've heard reports of these burning for more than 30 days straight.

THE TAKEAWAY KNOWLEDGE

What's the lesson here? Make sure you have non-electric lighting solutions, heating solutions and cooking solutions in place just in case the grid goes down. If your solutions are battery powered, you will also need extra batteries as well. Oil lamps, flashlights, candles and glow sticks are great emergency light sources. Don't resort to smashing bacon fat into a jar with your bare hands unless you absolutely have to.

The Golden Age of
Illumination

BY JAMES CARD

Flashlights, lanterns and other illumination products have come a long way in the last few years. Some companies specialize in tiny lights that wash out a room in brilliant glow. Others make flashlights that are nearly indestructible. There are spotlights that can light up football fields and some manufactures have figured out how to increase the shine time of lights through innovations in battery technology. What is very interesting are advances in Light Emitting Diode (LED) applications as inventors have figured out many uses for this versatile illumination technology.

1. POINT AND SHOOT

It's a small flashlight that slightly looks like a gun and feels like a gun when you get it into your hand. The forward-facing push button to light it up is like a trigger and feels natural. Besides being a handy flashlight, the CL-43 can be used as a companion with your handgun and it works like this: draw and point your handgun while at the same time drawing and pointing the CL-43. As both hands merge together to form a two-handed grip on the gun, the CL-43 will end up parallel to the slide (depending on your gun and hand size) and pointing its beam towards the direction the gun is aimed. It kicks out 420 lumens, takes three CR123 lithium batteries and there is an adapter for it to use AA batteries. ($140. www.keltecweapons.com)

2. LIKE A FLASHING POST-IT NOTE

APALS (All Purpose Adhesive Light Strips) are small disposable strips that have an embedded LED light that can be seen up to a quarter mile away. By pressing the button, it lights up to a fast or slow-blinking strobe or a light that is constantly on. It can run up to 80 hours and is waterproof and shockproof. It was designed for war: soldiers slap them on each other's backs so they don't shoot each other during night operations. For civilians, it is useful for hikers, bikers and boaters that do not want to get run over in the dark. (10 pack for $44. www.brite-strike.com)

3. EVERYDAY EXECUTIVE CARRY

The EPLI (Executive Precision Lighting Instrument) is for people that have enough crap on their keychain and do not want to add a tiny penlight to the jangling blob of keys, bottle openers and mini-Swiss Army knives. The EPLI is for those that value a sleek flashlight and prefer to carry a light in a shirt or coat pocket like they would a handsome pen. It runs on two AAA batteries and kicks out 220 lumens that can be also set on a strobe and a low-light setting. ($80. www.brite-strike. com)

4. MORE LIGHT, LESS FIRE

The Lumenyte Emergency Signaling Device makes setting out road flares look like a primitive practice, like a caveman fooling around with a fiery stick. About the size and feel of a hockey puck, set out this blinking strobe during roadside trouble. It can run up to 400 hours without changing the battery—doing the job equal to 700 incendiary flares. With two holes in the hard plastic case, it can be attached in various ways as needed. ($20 per device. www.lumenytesecurity.com)

5. NIGHT BLASTER POWER PACK

Match the Tracer Sport Light 170 VP with their 12v 10Ah lithium polymer battery pack and you have a combo for a night of fun. The spotlight will shine across a football field (over 650 yards) and with the variable power, the 75W halogen bulb can be dimmed or brightened with the touch of a knob and the beam tightened or brightened. Extremely lightweight, it has a weatherproof polycarbonate body and can be run on a 12v cigar plug or the battery pack.

The battery pack weighs just 25.9 ounces and can easily fit in a cargo pocket. The battery has a built-in fuel gauge that shows the remaining juice and it discharges the energy on a very flat curve, meaning it provides power until the very end rather than trickling down and out. The Tracer battery packs can be recharged from a wall socket or on a car lighter. Besides firing up the spotlight, it can be used to charge phones, DVD players and other 12v electronic gadgets. (Spotlight $130, battery $210. www.tracerpower. com)

Product Review

Maxxeon Pocket Floodlight

BY JIM COBB

While I can't say I'm a true flashlight nut, I do appreciate having something reliable to light up the night. I've owned several Maglites of various sizes, as well as several other name brand and off brand lights.

The Maxxeon WorkStar 330 Hunter's Pocket Floodlight leaves them all in the dark.

FIRST IMPRESSIONS

The light has a rubberized RealTree camo print coating. While the camo pattern is nice and all, the coating itself immediately grabs your attention, as well as your fingers. It has an almost-but-not-quite sticky feeling. From the first time you hold it, you have no worries about dropping it, even if your hands are wet.

The Maxxeon Pocket Floodlight takes three AAA batteries, which are included. What is really nice is these batteries are Energizers, not some no name brand. You unscrew either end of the light to insert the batteries and the battery placement diagram is right on the package. If you miss seeing it and put the batteries in wrong, it is a simple matter to reverse them so the light turns on properly.

At 6.5 inches, it is a bit longer than other flashlights of this general size. This isn't necessarily a bad thing, just an observation.

The on/off button is at the butt end of the light. You have two options, either press it lightly and hold or press it firmly until it clicks on. The button is a little stiff but I like that as it will help prevent the light from being turned on in your pocket or pack.

There is a pen clip on the side of the light, so you can keep it secured in a shirt pocket or attach it to the brim of a ball cap.

The threaded joints as well as the glass lens have embedded O rings, making the light water resistant. The on/off button is also covered in rubber, completely sealing the inner workings of the light. The cap on the button is also glow-in-the-dark, though it didn't glow all that brightly for me. But, really, if you need a glow-in-the-dark button to tell you which end is which on this light, you have some serious issues.

USING THE MAXXEON POCKET FLOODLIGHT

Information provided by Maxxeon states the Pocket Floodlight puts out about 140 lumens. I have no real way to test whether it is truly 140 lumens, but I can tell you this: If you accidentally shine it into your eyes, your reaction is going to be along the lines of OH MY GOD, TURN IT OFF! followed by rapid blinking as you try to get rid of this floating ball of light that seems to now be permanently part of your vision. This is an extremely bright light.

What is really cool about this light is that there are no "hot spots" or shadows. With most pen lights and other flashlights, you'll get a bright spot in the center, then it sort of fades out around that. With the special reflector Maxxeon has devised, here you get a bright light that is consistent from side to side. It also shines at sort of a 1:1 ratio, meaning the circle of shining light is roughly the same diameter as the distance between the light and the object. In other words, holding the light 12 inches from a wall gives you roughly a 12-inch diameter circle of light.

For comparison purposes, I took both the Maxxeon Pocket Floodlight and one of my Mini Maglites outside at night. Standing about seven feet away from my grill.

There are few downsides to this light, in my opinion. With other pen lights, you can twist the lens and the light adjusts narrow or wide. There is no such adjustment here. I don't know that it is truly needed, though.

This light also isn't great for distance. It is a flood light, meaning it, well, floods the area with light. This is as opposed to a spotlight, that allows you to focus the beam onto a specific area. Again, not a bad thing as long as you understand that going in.

Information from Maxxeon states the battery life is about 2 hours to half-life and 4 hours total of useable light. Admittedly, I've not used a stopwatch every time I've turned the light on but I can say I've spent a LOT of time playing with this thing outside at night and it has yet to even noticeably dim.

With the batteries installed, the Maxxeon Pocket Floodlight weighs in at about an ounce. Heavy enough to where you'll know it is in your hand, yet light enough to carry in your pack or pocket without concern.

THE VERDICT

The Maxxeon Pocket Floodlight retails for about $45, plus shipping. This product would make for an excellent addition to any survival kit, particularly one stored in a vehicle so as to not only provide light for repairs but also to signal for help.

Buyer's Guide to Lanterns

Pricing key (based on manufacturer's suggested retail price):

$ = under $20
$$ = $21–$40
$$$ = $41–$60
$$$$ = $61–$85

BATTERY POWERED LANTERNS

Manufacture/model: Telebrands Corp./ Olde Brookyln Lantern
Price: $
Dimensions: 6.5" × 4.5" × 9.5" (14" high when using swing-up handle)
Weight: 1.24 lbs.
Lantern type: Battery powered
Average run time: LED shines for 100,000 hours
Batteries: 2 D (not included)
Battery life: Contact manufacturer
Beam Type: Built-in dimmer to adjust brightness
Bulb Type: LED
Light Output: Contact manufacturer
Strobe: No
Waterproof: Contact manufacturer

Manufacture/model: Black Diamond/ Orbit Lantern
Price: $$
Dimensions: Collapsed height – 4"; extended height – 5.5"
Weight: 3 oz. (with batteries)
Lantern type: Battery powered lantern
Average run time: 13 hours (hight); 100 hours (low)
Batteries: 4 AAA
Battery life: Contact manufacturer
Beam Type: Dimmer for adjustable brightness; dual reflectors
Bulb Type: DoublePower LED
Light Output: 60 lumens
Strobe: No
Waterproof: Water resistant

Manufacture/model: Blackfire/Blackfire Clamplight Lantern
Price: $$$
Dimensions: 9" × 3 ⅞"
Weight: 37.92 oz.
Lantern type: Battery powered
Average run time (hours): Contact manufacturer
Batteries: 3 AA (not included)
Battery life: Contact manufacturer
Beam Type: Hi/low/strobe
Bulb Type: LED (2CREE® brilliant white LED)
Light Output: 230 lumens on high; 95 lumens on low; 100 lumens as flashlight
Strobe: Yes
Waterproof: Contact manufacturer

Manufacture/model: Black Diamond/ Apollo Lantern
Price: $$$
Dimensions: Open – 3" × 9.5" / closed – 3" × 5.2"
Weight: 7.8 oz. (with batteries)
Lantern type: Battery powered lantern
Average run time (hours): High 15 / low 60
Batteries: 4 AA (not included) NRG compatible
Battery life: 60 hours
Beam Type: Dual reflector system; dimming switch to adjust illumination
Bulb Type: DoublePower LED
Light Output: 80 Lumens
Strobe: No
Waterproof: Water resistant

Manufacture/model: Coast/EAL20
Price: $$$
Dimensions: 8.25" H
Weight: 32 oz.
Lantern type: Battery powered
Average run time : Contact manufacturer
Batteries: 4 D (not included)
Battery life: 100 hours

Beam Type: built-in dimmer
Bulb Type: LED
Light Output: 375 lumens
Strobe: Has a "lashing red" mode

Manufacture/model: Black Diamond/ Titan Lantern
Price: $$$$
Dimensions: Collapsed height – 7.9"; extended height – 9.8
Weight: 24 oz.
Lantern type: Battery powered mini lantern/flashlight
Average run time: 168 hours
Batteries: 4 D batteries
Battery life: 11 hours continuous use
Beam Type: Dimmer for adjustable brightness; dual reflectors
Bulb Type: QuadPower LED
Light Output: 25 lumens
Strobe: Yes
Waterproof: Water resistant

ALEXANDER ERDBEER / SHUTTERSTOCK.COM

PROPANE

Manufacture/model: Stansport/Propane Lantern-Double Mantle w/ Amber Globe

Price: $$

Dimensions: 12" × 8" × 8"

Weight: 3lbs. 4.8 oz.

Lantern type: Propane

Average run time 600 candle power

Batteries: N/a

Battery life: N/a

Beam Type: Amber glass globe (attracts fewer bugs) with a dimmer to adjust illumination

Bulb Type: 2 silk mantles

Light Output: 600 candle power

Strobe: No

Waterproof: No

Manufacture/model: Coleman/Perfect-Flow InstaStart Propane Lantern

Price: $$$$

Dimensions: 12.9" × 8.5" × 6.5"

Weight: 4 lbs.

Lantern type: Propane – InstaStart™ ignition—matchless lighting

Average run time 4 hours 18 minutes (high); 9 hours 15 minutes (low)

Batteries: N/a

Battery life: N/a

Beam Type: Adjustable dimmer knob

Bulb Type: Insta-Clip® tube mantles

Light Output: 1540 lumens

Strobe: No

Waterproof: No

CANDLE

Manufacture/model: Peregrine UCO/ Original Candle Lantern

Price: $$

Dimensions: Collapsed – 4.25" × 2"; open – 6.5" × 2"

Weight: 6.4 oz.

Lantern type: Candle lit lantern

Average run time 9 hours

Batteries: N/A

Battery life: One candle – 9 hours of light

Beam Type: 360 degree illumination

Bulb Type: Spring loaded candle tube

Light Output: Constant Flame –9h per candle

Strobe: No

Waterproof: No

ELECTRIC

Manufacture/model: Primus/Polaris Lantern-XL

Price: $$$$

Dimensions: 3.7" × 9.8"

Weight: 17.3 oz.

Lantern type: Electric

Average run time : 17-300 hours

Batteries: 3 D

Battery life: Contact manufacturer

Beam Type: Adjustable –5 different levels

Bulb Type: LED

Light Output: 110 lumens

Strobe: No

Waterproof: Water resistant (IPX4)

Buyer's Guide to Headlamps

Pricing key (based on manufacturer's suggested retail price):

$ = under $25
$$ = $26–$50
$$$ = $51–$100
$$$$ = $101–$150
$$$$$ = $151–$200

Manufacture/model: Coleman /T 4
Price: $
Dimensions: Contact manufacturer
Weight: Contact manufacturer
Head lamp type: Battery powered
Average run time 20 hours (high); 35 hours (low)
Batteries: 2 AAA
Battery life: 35h on low
Beam Type: contact manufacturer
Bulb Type: Lifetime LED
Light Output: 40 lumens
Strobe: No
Waterproof: Water resistant

Manufacture/model: Black Diamond/ Storm Headlamp
Price: $$
Dimensions: Contact manufacturer
Weight: 3.9 oz. (with batteries)
Head lamp type: Battery powered
Average run time 200 hours
Batteries: 4 AAA
Battery life: Contact manufacturer
Beam Type: contact manufacturer
Bulb Type: 1 QuadPower, 2 SinglePower LED
Light Output: 160 lumens
Strobe: Yes
Waterproof: Yes

Manufacture/model: LED Lenser/H5
Price: $$
Dimensions: Contact manufacturer
Weight: 4.09 oz.
Head lamp type: Battery operated
Average run time 20 hours
Batteries: 3 AAA
Battery life: N/A
Beam Type: bright, long-distance beam, or circular low beam
Bulb Type: LED
Light Output: 25 lumens
Strobe: No
Waterproof: No

Manufacture/model: Cabela's/Alaskan Guide X White Headlamp by Princeton Tec
Price: $$
Dimensions: contact manufacturer
Weight: 8 oz.
Head lamp type: Battery operated
Average run time (hours): 90 hours
Batteries: 3 AAA
Battery life: n/a
Beam Type: contact manufacturer
Bulb Type: LED
Light Output: 78 lumens
Strobe: No
Waterproof: No

Manufacture/model: Snow Peak/Mola Headlamp
Price: $$
Dimensions: 1" × 2.3" × 1.9"
Weight: 2.4 oz.
Head lamp type: Battery operated
Average run time 80 hours (low) 45 hours (high) 160 hours (strobe
Batteries: 2 AAA
Battery life:
Beam Type: contact manufacturer
Bulb Type: LED
Light Output: 110 lumens
Strobe: Yes
Waterproof: Water resistant (IPX4)

Manufacture/model: Black Diamond/ Icon Headlamp
Price: $$$
Dimensions: Contact manufacturer
Weight: 7.8 oz. (with batteries)
Headlamp type: Battery operated headlamp
Average run time (hours): High 75 / low 175
Batteries: 4 AA
Battery life: 80-75 hours
Beam Type: Flood / spot
Bulb Type: LED
Light Output: 200 lumens
Strobe: Yes
Waterproof: Yes

Manufacture/model: Mammut/X-Shot
Price: $$$
Dimensions: Contact manufacturer
Weight: 3.3 oz.
Head lamp type:
Average run time (hours): Flood-light: High 80h / Low 200h; Dual-Light 30h; Spot-Light: 15h
Batteries: 3 AA
Battery life: 200h max
Beam Type: Spot / Flood
Bulb Type: 1HiFlux LED, 2 Definition LED
Light Output: 200 lumens
Strobe: no
Waterproof: Water resistant (IPX6)

Manufacture/model: Princeton Tec/ Apex Headlamp

Price: $$$

Dimensions: Contact manufacturer

Weight: 9.8 oz.

Head lamp type: Battery powered head-lamp

Average run time 200 hours

Batteries: 4 AA (or Lithium or NiHM Rechargeable)

Battery life: Contact manufacturer

Beam Type: Flood / Spot

Bulb Type: LED

Light Output: 275 lumens

Strobe: No

Waterproof: Yes

Manufacture/model: Light & Motion/ Solite 250

Price: $$$$

Dimensions: 1" × 1" × 1.25"

Weight: 5.25 oz.

Head lamp type: Battery operated

Average run time 2.5-20 hours

Batteries: Rechargeable

Battery life: Contact manufacturer

Beam Type: Flood / Spot

Bulb Type: LED

Light Output: 250 lumens

Strobe: No

Waterproof: Water resistant (Fl-1 Certi-fication)

Manufacture/model: Surefire/Minimus LED Headlamp

Price: $$$$

Dimensions: Contact manufacturer

Weight: 3.3 oz (with batteries)

Head lamp type: Battery powered

Average run time: High 1.5 / low 50 hours

Batteries: 1 123A

Battery life: 10 year shelf-life

Beam Type: Contact manufacturer

Bulb Type: LED

Light Output: 100 lumens

Strobe: No

Waterproof: No

Generator Basics

BY JAMES NOWKA

Buying a generator could be a daunting task for those who aren't sure about what they'll need. Those purchasing for emergency purposes wouldn't have to go as far as getting a generator that is able to power their entire home.

For emergencies, I suggest a 5,000-watt generator. They typically fall in the $500 to $700 range.It will provide enough power to run the water pump, keep the refrigerator running and put a chill on the freezer when needed. It would still have enough capacity to power up a few lights. It's enough to meet basic needs during a short- to mid-term stretch without electricity. The 5,000-watt unit might not account for wants, but if the power is down, those bits of comfort might not be available anyhow.

Those thinking about a unit that would also power up a television might consider the fact that access to cable or satellite systems would also likely be compromised. Those concerned about having enough light could light up a few Coleman lanterns or Aladdin lamps to complement what they're able to achieve from the generator.

Using the outlets isn't necessary. Get a model that includes wheels and purchase some lengthy, heavy-duty extension cords. It might not be as convenient, but it's a good solution if you are only focusing on needs.

Keep the generator outside to avoid the risk of carbon monoxide poisoning. An owner should spend due time with the manual to assure comfort and proper usage.

Don't overload it. You should pay close attention to what you're powering. Remember Ohm's law: volts multiplied by amps provides wattage.

For maintenance, it's smart to start up the generator once a month and let it run for an hour with a couple light bulbs turned on. You wouldn't want to have an engine that doesn't start when a moment of need finally arrives. As for preparedness, those with generators should make sure to have enough gas on hand to meet their preparedness goals. I keep about 15 gallons handy, but remember to use it and replenish. Gas isn't good forever.

Product Review
PowerPot Portable Generator

BY BEN SOBIECK

The PowerPot is a portable generator that converts heat from hot water into electricity for charging cell phones and other gadgets.

The PowerPot works like this. First, fill the 46-ounce pot up ⅔ of the way with water. Attach a USB 2.0 plug into the side of the pot. Connect your cell phone or other gadget to the USB 2.0 plug. It cranks out electricity as soon as the water warms up. That's it. No moving parts. No degree in thermodynamics required. All you need are a heat source and some water. Phones will charge in 1-2 hours.

MORE THAN JUST A PORTABLE GENERATOR

In addition to being able to charge gadgets, the PowerPot does a lot more.

For starters, it's a pot that can boil water inside, and the ability to boil water is a major advantage in a survival situation.

There's nothing special about the way it needs to be used. Heat water with it just like you would any other pot. The only exception is that the water doesn't need to be boiling for it to work.

That means you can use the PowerPot on or near a fire, on a portable stove, inside a solar oven, on the hood of a hot car or any other method that heats water. The stove in the Living Ready kitchen was used for this review out of convenience, but field tests have shown how responsive this device is to any heat source. Charging times may vary depending on heat intensity, but who cares? It works. That's what matters.

Second, the PowerPot comes with an LED attachment that's painfully bright. It could easily light up a room in the dark or a camp. This might seem redundant considering a heat source may also be producing light (fires, for example), but remember that illumination at night can equal safety. And it's just not possible to be too safe.

Third, the PowerPot comes with a small bowl for cooking. The bowl sits on top of the larger pot, creating a double-boiler for food. It can't heat a lot of food, but this added functionality really adds to the versatility of the overall product.

However, PowerPot stresses that the pot with the water should not be used to also cook food. Only water should be used. Food goes in the separate bowl.

THE CONS

None of the PowerPot cons are bad enough to make this product not worth the money. But there are some that are worth noting anyway.

The PowerPot can't be run through the dishwasher. I know that's not a big deal for most prepared folks, including me, but it should be mentioned.

POWERPOT SPECS

Voltage: 5 volts
Regulator Current: 1 amp max
Power: 5 watts max
Weight: 18.2 ounces
Dimensions: 4.5" × 5.5" without bowl/lid or 4.5" × 8" with bowl/lid
Volume: 46 oz.

In the words of the instructions, "the bottom of the PowerPot becomes much hotter than a typical cooking pot during operation." This isn't a product for kids or people with butterfingers.

It's not a large item, which is both good and bad. It's built for portability, so rely on something else if a large amount of water or food is needed.

Finally, there's an inherent risk any time electricity, heat and water are put into close quarters. I wouldn't rate that as a high risk, but it's worth considering.

The PowerPot floored Living Ready staff, and it couldn't be recommended higher. It should be a required item for any emergency kit, from rural to urban. I even personally have one.

3 Tips for Choosing a
Portable Solar Panel

BY BEN SOBIECK

Few pieces of techie survival gear pack the cool factor punch of portable solar panels. But before you fall under the spell of any portable solar generator, there are some things to keep in mind.

HOW MUCH ENERGY DO YOU NEED?

Remember that prepper rule of thumb that says too much is never enough? It's still a good rule, but it does not apply nearly as much with portable solar panels. Overkill means you'll be wasting money and space.

For example, this Goal Zero Guardian 12V Solar Recharging Kit will juice a car battery. At $200, that's too much if you're only looking to keep your $100 cell phone charged.

A better option for small gadgets would be the Goal Zero Switch 8 Recharging Kit. It offers a smaller panel and a sleek, rechargeable battery to take anywhere.

Aim for the Goldilocks zone. Not too much. Not too little. Then go ahead and buy multiples of that particular model.

HOW MUCH ABUSE WILL YOU PUT IT THROUGH?

"This is cool" or "this is good" isn't enough of a qualifier when it comes to portable solar panels. "It didn't fall apart when it fell out of my truck and got mauled by a bear"

is better. If it can't stand up to conditions, it's not worth your money.

This is another Goldilocks scenario. There are portable solar panels with reinforced shells, such as this Goal Zero Escape, that can take a beating and then some.

However, if your portable solar panel never leaves the backyard, all that armor is just going to cost you extra. Go with something more efficient for your dollar, like the Goal Zero Nomad.

IS IT EASY TO USE?

Simplicity equals versatility with all survival gear, and that's especially true with

portable solar panels. If you can't tell how to use it without opening the box, it's probably not worth the time.

On that note, check to see if the portable solar panel comes with the adapters you need (USB, cigarette lighter) before you buy it. It can be a big headache to mess around with scores of cords, plugs and wires just to get you the point of actually using the portable solar panel.

Don't forget that those adapters and cords need to be on-hand. If they don't fit in the carrying case for the portable solar panel, chances are they could wind up lost.

Product Review

Bushnell PowerSync SolarWrap

BY BEN SOBIECK

The Bushnell PowerSync SolarWrap is making a lot of buzz in the outdoors and survival markets. The SolarWrap's roll-out design comes in three versions: the mini, the 250 and the 400. This review will use the 400.

The 10.1-ounce SolarWrap 400 comes in a case that sports handles for straps and other carrying methods. It's compact, less than the size of an average hammer.

The product also includes a cord with micro and standard USB ends, as well as an adapter for charging the SolarWrap from an outlet. Opening the case, the actual SolarWrap itself comes with USB attachments at either end that open with a flip. One is for mini USB, one is for standard USB.

USING THE DEVICE

The SolarWrap must be turned on to work. Blinking lights indicate how much charge is in the internal battery.

The SolarWrap rolls out to 29.25 inches. Once deployed, it can be positioned just about anywhere there is sunlight —a tree, the hood of a car, a sidewalk, a post. Just be sure to have some kind of anchor so the roll doesn't curl up, a problem flat solar panels don't have.

Hooking up a device is simple. Just plug it into the USB port. Slip the device under the roll to protect it from the sun

and you're done. The SolarWrap charged this iPod in about an hour.

While in the sun, the SolarWrap simultaneously charges its internal battery. That's an innovative feature. It means the SolarWrap's battery can be used when the sun isn't shining. The SolarWrap can also be charged using a wall outlet. Setting that up requires just a couple quick steps with the included adapter.

DRAWBACKS

All of this adds up to a portable, versatile product that works great. Still, there were some drawbacks. The USB tabs kept popping open throughout the review of this product. This could cause those USB connections to become dirty. Since this review was first written, Bushnell informed Living Ready the tabs are being addressed.

The included accessories don't fit inside the carry case. It'd be nice if they did so they won't become lost.

The rollout feature is slick, but I'm concerned that it may become torn. If that did happen, Paul Ahnold at Bushnell informs me that a break in one solar cell will not affect the rest. I can appreciate the foresight of that design element.

IS IT RIGHT FOR YOU?

So should you buy the Bushnell PowerSync SolarWrap? It depends on how much

> **TIP**
>
> Pair any solar charging device with the PowerPot. The PowerPot uses heat and water to produce electricity.
>
> Between solar and heat power generation, you'll stay juiced in just about any scenario.

power you actually need. For charging phones and gadgets, it's a winner.

For heavy uses, such as running lights at night or charging a car battery, you're better off with a larger panel, like this Goal Zero Guardian.

Along those same lines, the SolarWrap may not stand up to exceptionally hard, rugged use. Go with something with a tough shell instead, like the Bushnell SolarBook or this Goal Zero Escape.

Still, sportsmen, hikers, campers, preppers, and even commuters will find a lot to appreciate in the Bushnell PowerSync SolarWrap.

Buyer's Guide to Solar Power

SOLAR GENERATORS

Solar generators pricing key (based on manufacturer's suggested retail price):

$$$ = under $200
$$$$ = $201–$500
$$$$$ = $501–$1000
$$$$$$ = $1,001–$15,000

Manufacture/model: Goal Zero / Yeti 150 Solar Generator
Price: $$$
Dimensions: 7.75" × 5.75" × 6.75"
Weight: 12 lbs.
Recharged by: AC, 12V, Solar
Charge time (if applicable): Varies. Wall: 6h; Car: 8h; Nomad 13 Solar Panel: 26-52 hours; Nomad 20 Solar Panel: 17-34h; Boulder 15 Solar Panel: 22-44h; Boulder 30 Solar Panel: 11-22h; Escape 30 Briefcase: 11-22h
Power Output: USB, 12V, AC
What it will power: USB devices, 12V devices, AV inverters
Voltage: Contact manufacturer

Manufacture/model: Goal Zero / Yeti 400 Solar Generator
Price: $$$$
Dimensions: 10.25" × 8" × 8"
Weight: 29 lbs.
Recharged by: AC, 12V, Solar
Charge time (if applicable): Varies; Wall: 5h; car: 13h; Nomad 20: 40-80h; Boulder 15: 53-106; Boulder 30: 26-52; Escape 30: 26-52
Power Output: USB, 12V, AC
What it will power: USB devices, 12V devices, AC Inverters
Voltage: Contact manufacturer

Manufacture/model: Goal Zero / Yeti 1250 Solar Generator
Price: $$$$$$
Dimensions: 11" × 16" × 14.5"
Weight: 103 lbs.
Recharged by: AC, 12V, Solar
Charge time (if applicable): Varies; Wall: 16-20h; Car: 40+h; Nomad 20: 125-250h; Boulder 30: 80-160h; Escape 30: 80-160h
Power Output: USB, 12V, AC, Anderson Power Pole
What it will power: Large and/or multiple USB devices, 12V devices, AC inverters
Voltage: Contact manufacturer

POWER PACKS

Power packs pricing key (based on manufacturer's suggested retail price):

$ = $50–$75
$$ = $76–$100
$$$$ = $101–$200
$$$$$ = $201–$350

Manufacture/model: Brunton/Ember
Price: $
Dimensions: 3.5" × 2.5" × ¾"
Weight: 5 oz.
Recharged by: pc, solar
Charge time (if applicable): Contact manufacturer
Power Output: USB, 5V
What it will power: handheld electronics
Voltage: Contact manufacturer

Manufacture/model: Brunton / Restore 2200
Price: $$
Dimensions: 3" × ⁷/₁₀"
Weight: 8.14 oz.
Recharged by: Wall, Car and USB, Solar
Charge time (if applicable): USB: 2-3h; ac/usb: 2-3h; solar panel: 10h
Power Output: USB-Micro, Mini
What it will power: USB devices, Apple
Voltage: Contact manufacturer

Manufacture/model: RND/Solar Powered External Battery Pack
Price: $$
Dimensions: Contact manufacturer
Weight: Contact manufacturer
Recharged by: Solar, battery pack
Charge time (if applicable): Contact manufacturer
Power Output: USB 5000mAh
What it will power: USB powered devices
Voltage: Contact manufacturer

Manufacture/model: Brunton/Freedom Solar 2200
Price: $$
Dimensions: 5.4" × 3" × ⁷/₁₀"
Weight: 6.3 oz.
Recharged by: Solar
Charge time (if applicable): USB: 2-3h; AC/USB: 2-3h; Integrated solar panel: 20h
Power Output: USB
What it will power: USB devices
Voltage:

Manufacture/model: Goal Zero / Sherpa 50 Power Pack
Price: $$$$
Dimensions: 4.5" × 1.5" × 5.25"
Weight: 18 oz.
Recharged by: AC, 12V, Solar
Charge time (if applicable): Varies; Wall: 3h; Car: 3h; Nomad 13: 8-16h; Nomad 20: 6-12h; Boulder 15: 8-16h; Boulder 30: 4-8h; Escape 30: 4-8;
Power Output: USB, 12V, AC (sold separately)

What it will power: All medium USB devices, Laptops, AC inverters

Voltage: Contact manufacturer

Manufacture/model: Goal Zero / Sherpa 100 Power Pack

Price: $$$$$

Dimensions: 5.8" ×1.5" × 5.25"

Weight: 25 oz.

Recharged by: AC, 12V, Solar

Charge time (if applicable): Varies; Wall: 3h, Car: 4h; Nomad 13: 15-30h; Nomad 20: 10-20h; Boulder 15: 13-26h; Boulder 30: 7-14h; Escape 30: 7-14h

Power Output: USB, 12V, AC (sold separately)

What it will power: All medium USB devices, Laptops, AC inverters

Voltage: Contact manufacturer

SOLAR PANELS

Solar panel pricing key (based on manufacturer's suggested retail price):

$ = $50–$75
$$ = $76–$100
$$$ = $101–$125
$$$$ = $126–$150
$$$$$ = $151–$200

Manufacture/model: Brunton/Explorer 5 Watts

Price: $

Dimensions: 4.5" × 9" × 1"

Weight: 14.8 oz.

Recharged by: Solar

Charge time (if applicable): Contact manufacturer

Power Output: 5v, 1000mA USB

What it will power: USB devices

Voltage: 5V

Manufacture/model: Goal Zero / Nomad 7 Solar Panel

Price: $$

Dimensions: Folded – 9" × 1.5" × 6.5" / Unfolded – 9" × 1.5" × 17"

Weight: 12.8 oz.

Recharged by: Solar

Charge time (if applicable): Vary by product; Guide 10 Plus: 3-6 hours; Goal Zero Switch 8: 3-6 hours

Power Output: USB, 12V

What it will power: Most USB and 12V devices (not tablets); most handheld USB devices—including: cell phones (and smart phones), GPS, MP3 players

Voltage: Open circuit – 8-9V

Manufacture/model: Bushnell/Power-Sync SolarWrap Mini

Price: $$

Dimensions: 4.3" × 1.25"

Weight: 3.1 oz.

Recharged by: solar, wall

Charge time (if applicable): From wall: 4h; from solar: 10h

Power Output: 5v 1a, USB

What it will power: USB devices

Voltage:

Manufacture/model: Voltaic/Fuse 4W Solar Charger

Price: $$$

Dimensions: 11.5" × 7" × ½"

Weight: 19 oz. (including battery, bag, solar panels)

Recharged by: Solar

Charge time (if applicable): Solar: 5h

Power Output: USB (optional AC/DC chargers)

What it will power: USB devices

Voltage: panels: 6-12V

Manufacture/model: Goal Zero / Boulder 30 Solar Panel

Price: $$$

Dimensions: 21" × 18" × 1"

Weight: 6.5 lbs.

Recharged by: Solar

Charge time (if applicable): Vary by product; Sherpa 50: 4-8h; Sherpa 100: 7-14h; Escape 150: 11-22h; Yeti 150: 11-22h; Yeti 400: 26-52h; Yeti 1250: 80-160h

Power Output: None

What it will power: Any Goal Zero recharger

Voltage: Open circuit: 18-20V

Manufacture/model: Sierra Wave/10-Watt Solar Collector

Price: $$$

Dimensions: 29" × 11.5" (unfolded) / 8.25 × 11.5" (folded)

Weight: 28 oz.

Recharged by: Solar

Charge time (if applicable): Contact manufacturer

Power Output: 5V, 6V, USB, and 15V

What it will power: USB devices , 12V DC vehicle chargers

Voltage: 5v, 6v, 15v

Manufacture/model: Goal Zero / Boulder 15 Solar Panel

Price: $$$

Dimensions: 11" × 28" × 1"

Weight: 3.5 lbs.

Recharged by: Solar

Charge time (if applicable): Vary by product; Sherpa 50: 8-16h; Sherpa 100: 13-26h; Escape 150: 22-44h; Yeti 150: 22-44h; Yeti 400: 53-106h

Power Output: Solar port

What it will power: Any Goal Zero recharger

Voltage: Open circuit: 18-20V

Manufacture/model: Goal Zero / Nomad 13 Solar Panel

Price: $$$$$

Dimensions: (folded) 10.5" × 9" × 1"

Weight: 22 oz.

Recharged by: Solar

Charge time (if applicable): Vary by product; Guide 10 Plus 2.5 – 5h; Switch 8: 4h; Sherpa 50: 8-16h; Sherpa 100: 15-30h; Escape 150: 26-52h; Yeti 150: 26-52h

Power Output: USB

What it will power: Most USB and 12V devices (include: cell phone, smart phone, GPS, MP3 player)

Voltage: Open circuit – 18-22V

Manufacture/model: Goal Zero / Nomad 20 Solar Panel

Price: $$$$$

Dimensions: (unfolded) 30.5" × 13" × 1"

Weight: 21 oz.

Recharged by: Solar

Charge time (if applicable): Vary by product; Switch 8: 4h; Guide 10 Plus: 2.5-5h; Sherpa 50: 6-12h; Sherpa 100: 10-20h; Escape 150: 17-34h; Yeti 150: 17-34h; Yeti 400: 40-80h

Power Output: USB

What it will power: Any Goal Zero Recharger

Voltage: Open circuit: 18-22V

Manufacture/model: Brunton / Solar Marine 7 Watts

Price: $$$$$

Dimensions: $7/10$" × $1/2$" × $3/50$"

Weight: Contact manufacturer

Recharged by: Solar

Charge time (if applicable): Contact manufacturer

Power Output: 7 watts, 400 mA, 12V

What it will power: cell phones, iPads, iPhones (USB devices)

Voltage: 12V

SOLAR CHARGERS

Solar panel pricing key (based on manufacturer's suggested retail price):

$ = under $50
$$ = $50–$100
$$$ = $101–$150
$$$$ = $151–$200
$$$$$ = over $200

Manufacture/model: C Crane/Universal Solar Powered Battery Charger

Price: $

Dimensions: 6.8" × 4.5" × 2.3"

Weight: 11.8 oz.

Recharged by: Solar

Charge time (if applicable): Contact manufacturer

Power Output: 5v 150mA

What it will power: batteries (D, C, AA, AAA)

Voltage: 5v

Manufacture/model: Brunton/Solarflat 2(6V) Watts

Price: $

Dimensions: 6" × 10" × $9/10$"

Weight: 30.8 oz.

Recharged by: Solar

Charge time (if applicable): Contact manufacturer

Power Output: 6V

What it will power: Link multibple units together

Voltage: 6V

Manufacture/model: Rothco/Cell phone/iPhone Solar Charger

Price: $

Dimensions: Contact manufacturer

Weight: Contact manufacturer

Recharged by: Solar, pc

Charge time (if applicable): pc: 2h; Solar: 11-13h

Power Output: USB

What it will power: cell phones, USB devices, touch players

Voltage: Contact manufacturer

Manufacture/model: Rothco/Deluxe Cell phone/iPhone Solar charger

Price: $$

Dimensions: Contact manufacturer

Weight: Contact manufacturer

Recharged by: Solar, pc

Charge time (if applicable): Solar: 4-5h; pc: 2h

Power Output: USB

What it will power: USB devices- cell phones, touch players

Voltage: Contact manufacturer

Manufacture/model: Voltaic/Amp Solar Charger

Price: $$

Dimensions: 6.5" × 5.5" × 1.5"

Weight: 17 oz. (including battery and solar panel)

Recharged by: Solar, USB, AC/DC chargers

Charge time (if applicable): Solar: 9h

Power Output: USB, 6V, 5V, 12V

What it will power: cellphones, game consoles, MP3 players, cameras, etc.

Voltage: 6v, 12v

Manufacture/model: Solio/BOLT battery Pack + Solar Charger

Price: $$

Dimensions: 3.5" × 3.5" × 1"

Weight: 5.3 oz.

Recharged by: Solar, USB, wall outlet

Charge time (if applicable): USB: 4.5h; solar: 8-10h

Power Output: USB, 5-5.5V

What it will power: USB devices

Voltage: 5-5.5V

Manufacture/model: Powertraveller Ltd./Powermonkey Explorer

Price: $$

Dimensions: (Battery) 3.5" × 1.3" × 1"

Weight: 2.9 oz.

Recharged by: Solar, USB, included universal mains charger

Charge time (if applicable):

Power Output: 5v, USB,

What it will power: Majority of smart phones, cell phones, iPods, MP3 / MP4, PDAs and portable game consoles; 5v devices

Voltage: 5v

Manufacture/model: Eton/BoostSolar

Price: $$

Dimensions: $3/4$" × 6" × 6"

Weight: 11.7oz.

Recharged by: Solar, USB

Charge time (if applicable): Contact manufacturer

Power Output: USB, 5v

What it will power: Most USB devices

Voltage: Contact manufacturer

Manufacture/model: Powertraveller Ltd./Solarmonkey Adventurer

Price: $$$

Dimensions: 6.7" × 3.7" × $9/10$"

Weight: 9 oz.

Recharged by: Solar, USB, internal mains charger (sold separately)
Charge time (if applicable): Solar: 8-12h
Power Output: USB, 5v
What it will power: 5v devices—Apple products, mobile phones, GPS, e-readers, etc.
Voltage: 5V

Manufacture/model: Berkey/MP Solar Charger
Price: $$$
Dimensions: 7" × 9" × 1.5"
Weight: Contact manufacturer
Recharged by: Solar, Aux-backup
Charge time (if applicable): Contact manufacturer
Power Output: 6V, 7.2V, 12V
What it will power: batteries, phones, disc players, digital cameras, PDA's, radios, etc.
Voltage: 6V, 7.2V 12V

Manufacture/model: Bushnell/Power-Sync SolarWrap 250
Price: $$$$
Dimensions: 9.125" × 2.4"
Weight: 9.2 oz.
Recharged by: wall outlet; solar

Charge time (if applicable): Wall: 4h; Solar: 6h
Power Output: USB, 5v, 1a
What it will power: USB devices
Voltage: 5v

Manufacture/model: Powertraveller Ltd./Powermonkey Extreme 12V
Price: $$$$
Dimensions: 5.9" × 2.33" × 1.1"
Weight: 16 oz.
Recharged by: Solar, USB, included universal mains charger
Charge time (if applicable): 18-22h
Power Output: USB, 5V, 12V, DC
What it will power: Most 5V devices, 12V devices, USB devices, car chargers
Voltage: 5V, 12V

Manufacture/model: Power Film Solar/ F15-600
Price: $$$$$
Dimensions: 23.7" × 21"
Weight: 11.68 oz.
Recharged by: Solar, 12V charger
Charge time (if applicable): Contact manufacturer
Power Output: 12V

What it will power: USB (conversion plug) 12v batteries (cellphones, cameras, camp lighting, MP3 players, GPS)
Voltage: 15.4V

Manufacture/model: JOOS/Orange Portable Solar Charger
Price: $$$$$
Dimensions: 8.5" × 5.75" × ⅖"
Weight: 24 oz.
Recharged by: Sun, USB
Charge time (if applicable): Solar: 12h; USB: 4-5h
Power Output: 5v, 100mA USB
What it will power: Any USB device
Voltage: 5v

Manufacture/model: Bushnell/Power-Sync SolarBook 850
Price: $$$$$
Dimensions: 9.25" × 8.3" × 1.3"
Weight: 24 oz.
Recharged by: Solar, wall charger
Charge time (if applicable): Wall: 6h; solar: 3.5h
Power Output: 5v, 1a
What it will power: USB devices
Voltage: 5v

CHAPTER SIX

Multipurpose Tools, First Aid & Hygiene

The right tool makes any job easier. This chapter is full of practical survival tools that you will find essential in any emergency. From prybars and axes to zip ties and duct tape, this gear will help you clear the path back to everyday life.

This chapter also covers essential first aid tools and will help you assemble a first-rate survival first aid kit. Debris combined with dangerous conditions is a recipe for injuries both during and following a disaster, when emergency services are often overwhelmed. Help might not be on the way for quite some time. A good first aid kit and certified first aid training can help you stand in the gap and keep a bad situation from getting worse.

Medicine Cabinet for the Real World

COMPOUNDS, MATERIALS, GADGETS, GELS AND GOOP TO PATCH UP LIFE'S INEVITABLE BREAKDOWNS

BY JAMES CARD

GREAT STUFF
For filling all of the gaping holes in your life (or your drafty cabin).

PARACORD
A survival kit classic, its uses are endless around the house or camp.

ZIP TIES
Get a variety of sizes and colors and keep them stashed everywhere.

WD-40
The workshop standard. Also doubles as a fire starter.

TARP TAPE
Tarp is one of the most useful materials around but it takes a beating. This patches it up.

GORILLA TAPE
Kind of like duct tape on steroids.

PIPE STRAP
With a few nails or screws, this metal tape can hobble together anything.

BAG BALM
An old-time ointment for chapped skin, rashes, and burns. Soldiers in WWII used it on rifles to prevent rust.

RATCHET TIE DOWN
Our ancestors developed leverage and the ratchet for a reason. Use it.

AMAZING GOOP
It bonds to everything, stays flexible and is UV resistant. Good for sealing out water leaks.

LIQUID WRENCH
Ever try to change a car tire with rusted lug nuts? Remember how you cursed and kicked? Use this.

NRA GUN CARE SYSTEM
A combo of oil, solvent and cleaner to keep the shooting irons in good shape.

EYE AND EAR PROTECTION
There's enough damage in this world. Protect the important parts.

TRAIL MARKING TACKS
Save time and avoid getting lost in the dark by tagging trees along your trail.

TEAR AID
It's like a Band-Aid for fabrics.

RIG RUST-INHIBITING GREASE
Grease—not just for guns but anything metal.

LOCKTITE STIK 'N SEAL
An all-purpose adhesive for wood, metal, glass, rubber, you-name-it.

CITRONELLA CANDLE
The small hockey puck-shaped candle throws enough light to illuminate a workbench and annoys mosquitoes.

SNO SEAL
Because waterproof leather boots equal happy feet.

TEAR MENDER
The quick fix for patching tears in fabrics since 1932.

MASTER LOCK
For the times when some things shouldn't be left alone.

GORILLA GLUE
Like the saying, "use enough gun," the same goes for glue.

KRAZY GLUE
For fixing the tiny stuff, and it stops bleeding, too.

LAVA SOAP
Your father and grandfather used it for a reason. So should you.

DR. BRONNER'S 18-IN-1 SOAP
Use it to wash yourself, your dog, your dishes, or about anything.

Tools for Ground Zero

BY JAMES CARD

A storm just destroyed your community. Wreckage is everywhere and you hear cries for help. Be sure you have the tools you need to get to work.

SLEDGEHAMMER

Concrete makes up a large part of a home, along with lumber. Mixed together in a snarled mass, sometimes brute force is the only way to go until other tools can be used to pry, cut or hack your way in. (Rockforge, homedepot.com)

PRYBARS

Use the power of leverage to your advantage when cracking apart nailed beams or lifting some tangled rubble. Keep a large crowbar handy along with smaller ones for tight spaces. The 14-inch FuBar Demolition Bar can hack, pry, pull nails and has a strikeable surface. (stanleytools.com)

GLOVES

After a disaster, it's all about helping hands. Keep lots of leather work gloves to pass out so people can pitch in without worry of splinters, abrasions, muck and dirt.

ILLUMINATION

There is a good chance you will be working in the dark after a natural disaster and even if there is daylight, you might find yourself peering into a dark hole under a collapsed home looking for survivors. Headlamps are the way to go as they keep your hands free to work efficiently. Princeton Tec's Vizz has three distinct beam profiles: a powerful spotting beam, a dim flood beam for close-up work and a red beam that protects night vision. (princetontec.com)

SAFETY-TOE WORK BOOTS

A ravaged community recovering after a storm is the opposite of a construction site: it's deconstruction but the same dangers exist. Body parts can be smashed, hacked or punctured. To keep helping with the rescue effort you have to stay on your feet. The leather 4216 Red Wing Safety boot has a non-metallic toe protector and is waterproof. The BOA lacing system tightens up the boot with a dial for a tight fit and without the worry of laces unraveling or getting snagged and tripping you up. (redwingshoes.com)

CLEATS

For working on slippery surfaces such as an oil spill or on an incline like a sagging roof, use some snow cleats for extra purchase. The Diamond Grip Ice Trekkers were designed for snow and ice but will work in a pinch to save you from slipping and breaking your neck. (icetrekkers.com)

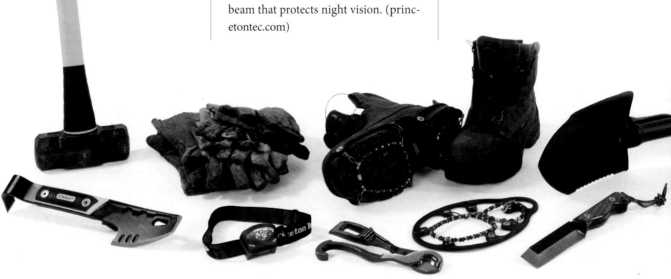

WIRE CUTTERS

Think of all the hidden wires inside of a building and then the building is turned inside out. You'll need to cut through tangles of wires of all sizes. The Rescue Tool does that and has a spanner wrench for loosening hose couplings, a pry bar and a slot for shutting off gas safety valves. (channellock.com)

SHOVELS

Shovels of all shapes and sizes are useful after a disaster; even snow shovels for scooping out mud and sludge and garden spades can be used to fill sandbags. For tight spaces, like digging near the foundation of a collapsed house, folding camp shovels will get the job done. The Gerber E-Tool is a military-grade digging tool for trenches and holes. It folds up to about the size of a dinner plate and also has a serrated blade edge for sawing roots and a pick for hacking at rock. (gerbergear.com)

CLOSE-QUARTER WORK

For prying apart small stuff, most knives are not up to the task and the blade could easily crack or bend. The Pro Tool Chisel Utility Knife is a combination knife, chisel and pry tool. It can take hammer blows for deeper gouging and it can rip apart a wooden pallet like nothing. The hardwood ash handle gives this beast of a tool a classy appearance. (protoolindustries.net)

TWO-WAY RADIOS

With cell phone service disrupted after a disaster, more chaos is added to the equation. Give a two-way radio to your partner and you can scout blocked roads; report the damage and dangers, and round up people for help where it is most needed. The Motorola Talkabout MS355R is a key communication tool for this scenario. It is waterproof, it floats, has a built in flashlight, receives weather alerts and has dual power. It ranges up to 35 miles depending on various conditions. (motorola.com)

TREE WORK

With downed trees everywhere, their huge canopies can transform a neighborhood into an instant jungle. A chainsaw will get the job done but if there is a gas shortage, you will want to use it sparingly and save it for the big stuff. Fiskars axes, hatchets and loppers are three key tools for taking down limbs and branches. It's a lot of muscle work but the tools are lightweight, well balanced and very sharp which make your clearing efforts much more efficient. (fiskars.com)

DEPENDABLE CHAINSAW

Other than a dead boat motor, nothing will make a person swear more than a chainsaw that will not start. It's a lot worse in an emergency situation. Talk to people that cut a lot of firewood and ask professional tree trimmers on what brands they like. The Stihl pictured has been running strong for 15 years (stihlusa.com). For clearing trees after a disaster, an 18-inch bar will serve you well and it is an all-around choice for work around the house or farm. Shooting glasses and earmuffs can serve double duty as eye and ear protection when working with power tools. (radians.com)

EXTRA GAS

Keep an extra gas can full, along with the proper oil mix. Talk with some of your friends and neighbors that will be helping out in the event of a disaster. See what kind of oil/gas mix their chainsaws use so the oil/gas ratio can be mixed and easily shared if gas supplies are low.

50 Items that Disappear Before a Disaster

BY TOM SCIACCA

Have you ever noticed how, whenever a big storm is predicted, people start rushing to stores to clean them out of every food item and supplies they have on the shelves? In one sense, it's probably good that they are trying to anticipate the emergency, despite being last-minute about it. It sure beats those people who don't bother to prepare at all, then complain when emergency services are overwhelmed by requests for assistance.

But why panic in the first place? Why not have a stash of necessary items always ready for such an emergency? Even if there isn't a storm approaching, it's nice to know that you don't have to rush out to the store every time you run out of toilet paper.

With this in mind, I crowdsourced CampingSurvival.com's Facebook fans to find out what they felt were the emergency supplies that stores were most likely to run out of when people start to panic. Then I compiled the top comments in various categories. Some of the items (canned meat, for instance) may not be the absolute first things for a store to run out of, but are still items that you should consider having among your supplies nonetheless. Take this list and compare it to what you have stocked up. Check to see what you may be missing or what you need more of.

FOOD

1. Bread
2. Butter
3. Cereal
4. Coffee
5. Eggs
6. Flour
7. Fruit, canned and fresh
8. Honey
9. Meats, canned
10. Milk
11. Peanut butter
12. Pet food
13. Salt
14. Sugar
15. Vegetables (canned and root)
16. Water

POWER & LIGHT

17. Batteries
18. Candles
19. Charcoal
20. Coolers
21. Flashlights
22. Gasoline
23. Generators
24. Glow sticks
25. Ice
26. Lamp oil and oil lanterns
27. Lighter fluid
28. Matches
29. Propane, propane stoves

FUN

30. Alcohol, drinking
31. Beer
32. Cigarettes
33. Condoms

FIRST AID

34. Alcohol, rubbing
35. Antiseptic
36. Aspirin/pain relievers
37. Cold medicine
38. First aid kits

HYGIENE

39. Feminine hygiene products
40. Paper plates/napkins
41. Shampoo
42. Soap
43. Toilet paper

BABIES

44. Baby food/formula
45. Diapers

HARDWARE

46. Duct tape
47. Plastic bags
48. Plywood
49. Radios
50. Rope

8 Overlooked Survival Items You Already Own

IMPROVISED EMERGENCY GEAR FROM THE GARAGE

BY JAMES CARD

LANTERN

When the power is out candles are cozy in the house but useless in windy conditions. Coleman lanterns (which can run on a variety of fuels) throw out enough light to illuminate a work area or a makeshift kitchen. Save the flashlight and their declining batteries for more specific tasks.

PRUNING LOPPERS

In natural disasters, trees are always part of the problem: they crush houses, block roads, and create all sorts of mayhem. When dealing with a large-canopied tree you need to clear some limbs away before the real chainsaw work begins and loppers will do the job faster and safer than an axe or hand saw.

FIVE-GALLON BUCKET

You can use it to haul anything, store anything, or wash anything including giving yourself a sponge bath. Top it off with a swivel seat and it doubles as a handy stool. The uses are nearly limitless. Choose ones that have never held toxic materials.

HARD-PLASTIC WATER BOTTLES

Besides water, the bottles are useful for storing anything that needs to be airtight, waterproof and have hard-case protection. Another bonus is that they are transparent so you can quickly note what's inside. Keep first aid and repair kits inside and nuts and bolts and nails in another. It's useful for storing food items since critters cannot chew through the hard plastic.

SUPER-SIZED GARBAGE BAGS

One garbage bag, many uses: impromptu rain poncho, ground tarp, or primitive

shelter. Use them as waterproof covers for backpacks, sleeping bags and anything else. Filled with soft materials, they can be used as a sleeping mattress. In a disaster situation with debris and rubbish everywhere, garbage bags will always be in demand.

FENCE PLIERS

A standby tool of farmers everywhere. It's a hammer, staple puller, wire cutter, and pliers all in one. They are an incredible bargain as most cost around $8 to $16.

BREATHABLE FISHING WADERS

Waders become an improvised biohazard suit when working in flooded areas. In times of extreme flooding, fecal coliform concentrations can go through the roof. Sewage systems overflow and people are basically waist deep in a bacterial cocktail of wastewater and dung.

KNEE PADS

In an emergency or disaster situation, you will be crawling, kneeling, and working on things close to the ground. Surplus military kneepads such as those in the photo can be picked up for as little as $5 a pair.

Build the Perfect First Aid Kit

BY JAMES HUBBARD M.D., M.P.H.

This article contains suggestions for general medical supplies everyone should have on hand. The suggested quantities are for the minimum amounts you will need. You can increase these quantities depending on your storage area, family size and if you're planning on treating others.

FIRST AID SUPPLIES FOR A LONG-TERM STORAGE AREA

This supply list is ideal for first aid kits you keep in your home and your bug-out location.

Elastic Bandages

Minimum: two per family member. The 3-inch (8cm) or 4-inch (10cm) widths are the most versatile.

Notes: Also known as ACE bandages, these bandages will last for several wrappings before the elastic wears out. Wash them if they get dirty. Washing tends to damage the elastic, but they are still usable.

Alternative: Any cloth will do. Tear or fold the cloth into strips that are 3 to 6 inches (8 to 15cm) wide.

Adhesive Bandages

Minimum: at least 100 of the regular size and 25 of the larger ones

Notes: They're also known by the brand name Band-Aids. They make excellent sterile dressings for small wounds.

Alternative: gauze or cloth placed in the middle of the sticky side of a strip of tape

Cotton Balls

Minimum: one package

Notes: Use for small dressings. Great for packing a nosebleed. Add petroleum jelly or antibiotic ointment to make the packing easier to insert and remove. Petroleum-jelly-coated cotton balls also can take the place of kindling to start a fire.

Alternatives: tampons or strips of cloth for nasal packing

Tampons

Minimum: one box

Notes: Use for packing nosebleeds and bullet wounds in addition to feminine hygiene. Can also be used as fire tinder.

Alternative: cloth or gauze

Cotton Tip Applicators, Long Stems

Minimum: box of 100

Notes: Good for applying ointment to small wounds or in nostrils. (Don't use to clean out ears. Doing so irritates the ear canals and tends to pack some wax next to the eardrum, making it difficult to remove.)

Alternative: short-stem cotton tip applicators

Gauze Sponges, Sterile

Minimum: two packs

Notes: Sterile gauze sponges are especially useful for burns because burns are prone to infection, even if you keep them clean.

Alternative: Boil cloth or gauze for 20 minutes. Let it dry and use, or keep the dried material in a resealable plastic bag until needed.

Gauze Sponges, Nonsterile

Minimum: two packs (200 per pack)

Notes: The most versatile are the 3" × 3" (8cm × 8cm) and 4" × 4" (10cm × 10cm) sizes.

Alternative: clean cloth or gauze rolls

Gauze Rolls

Minimum: one roll per person, minimum of four rolls

Notes: Also called Kerlix gauze rolls, these are very versatile: Make a gauze pad by cutting a roll to size and folding to make it thicker. Wrap around a dressing before taping to keep the tape off your skin, or use it as a wrap to secure a splint.

Alternative: gauze sponges or a clean cloth

Nonstick or Nonadherent Dressing Pads

Minimum: one box

Alternative: Coat one side of regular cloth or gauze with antibiotic ointment or honey, or use regular gauze or cloth.

QuikClot or Celox Clotting Bandages

Minimum: two packs of the gauze type

Notes: Use only on heavily bleeding wounds that won't stop with direct pressure. Use the gauze style because the granule style is harder to clean from the wound.

Alternative: Apply direct pressure to the wound or a tourniquet or both.

Bandage Scissors

Minimum: two pairs

Notes: Good quality scissors will cut better and last longer.

Alternative: any scissors or knife

Vet Wrap

Minimum: one roll per person

Notes: Also know as Coban, vet wrap is thin, stretchable, self-adherent material that comes in a roll. It can be used in place of tape to hold a bandage in place, to cover large bandages or to wrap around a splint.

Alternative: cloth and tape

Duct Tape

Minimum: two rolls

Notes: Use it to tape bandages and close cuts—and that's just a start. Duct tape has numerous uses in an emergency situation.

Alternative: any type of tape

Paper Tape

Minimum: two rolls

Notes: This is ideal for sensitive skin.

Alternative: wrapping and pinning the dressing in place

Super Glue

Minimum: two tubes

Notes: Use it to cover small nicks, close cuts and help tape stick.

Alternative: any glue

Safety Pins

Minimum: Keep ten to 20 in a small box or pinned to each other.

Notes: Pin bandages or pin a shirttail around an arm for a makeshift sling. Use to pick out splinters, to punch just the right size holes for pinhole glasses or to stick a hole in a plastic bag or bottle for pressure irrigation.

Alternative: straight pins

SAM Splints

Minimum: two regular size ones, plus one per extra family member; purchase smaller sizes for children

Notes: These are some of the most versatile splints on the market. They're light, and you can cut them to almost any size and bend them into just about any shape you need.

Alternative: Sticks, paint stirrers or newspapers secured with wraparound cloth will work. Even a pillow, a coat or any thick material is better than nothing.

Slings

Minimum: one per family member and smaller sizes for children

Notes: They're cheap and lightweight.

Alternative: Wrap and pin some strong cloth around your arm and neck. A belt can work, or wrap your shirttail around your arm and pin the tail to your shirt.

Tongue Depressors

Minimum: box of 100

Notes: Also called tongue blades; use for looking in throats, applying ointment to wounds and making finger splints.

Alternative: Popsicle sticks

Petroleum Jelly

Minimum: one large container or three smaller ones

Notes: Vaseline is the most common brand name. It can be used to seal chest wounds, keep bandages from sticking, relieve chapped lips and face, and help remove tar or glue from the skin.

Disposable Gloves, Nonsterile

Minimum: four boxes of 100 each

Notes: They reduce the amount of germs getting in a wound and protect the caregiver from any germs in bodily fluids. Consider the vinyl type to avoid latex allergies. Go for one-size-fits-all or the large size. Gloves that are too large are bulky but usable, whereas gloves that are too small are unusable. The cheaper ones work well but may be more likely to tear, in which case just slip a second pair over the first.

Alternative: a pair of dishwashing gloves

Disposable Gloves, Sterile

Minimum: one box of ten pairs

Notes: Save sterile gloves for use on the initial treatment of wounds. These gloves are especially important when tending to wounds that involve broken bones or burns because of the higher risk of infection. It's better to get a size too large than too small.

Syringes

Minimum: five

Notes: The 10ml syringes are handy for irrigating wounds, cleaning out ears and measuring liquid dosages. If you get ones without needles, match them with a box of 1-inch (3cm), 22- or 23-gauge needles for injections, picking out splinters, lancing abscesses, etc. If you get ones with needles, be sure the needles can be removed so you can use only the syringe for irrigation and measuring. Save the needle for future use.

Bulb Syringes

Minimum: one adult size and one child size

Notes: good for irrigating wounds and ears

14-gauge, two-inch (5cm) long Hollow Needles

Minimum: two

Notes: Use to treat someone who has a tension pneumothorax and needs air pressure released from the chest. Use with a syringe to drain fluid from the abdomen or chest.

Intravenous (IV) Catheters

Minimum: two 14- or 16-gauge; several smaller ones (18- to 22-gauge) if you plan to start IVs

Notes: Use these in many of the same ways you use a hollow needle. You can pull the needle out and keep the flexible plastic catheter in place. Angiocath is a popular brand.

Blankets

Minimum: one per person

Notes: Thermal reflective blankets are lighter for travel. Blankets are a must to prevent hypothermia, to which trauma victims are especially susceptible.

Paracord

Minimum: 16 feet (5m) of 550-lb. (250kg) paracord

Notes: Use to secure a splint or make a spine board for neck and back injuries or a makeshift stretcher. Unravel the finer threads and you have some strong string. You can purchase survival bracelets/straps woven out of one continuous length (typically several feet) of Paracord. I recommend having a minimum of two survival bracelets on hand.

Matches and Lighters

Minimum: two matchboxes or more in a waterproof container, along with several lighters

Notes: These may be needed to sterilize instruments or to start a fire to boil water.

Alternative: commercial flint and steel firestarter sets

Thermometers

Minimum: two

Notes: Any oral type (digital, non-mercury, etc.) will do.

Tweezers

Minimum: one regular size and one with thin tips (needle nose)

Notes: The needle nose, especially, is great for removing ticks. Grab the tick by its head and pull steadily and firmly.

Headlamp

Minimum: one, with extra batteries

Notes: This provides an excellent hands-free light source.

Thick Plastic Jar with Lid

Minimum: one

Notes: Use it to store any used sharp items that have been contaminated with blood or pus until you can properly dispose of them. You'll need to take the jar to a place that disposes of medical waste or, if that's not available, burn the jar.

DISINFECTANTS
Peroxide

Minimum: two pints

Bleach

Minimum: one gallon

Notes: Warning: Bleach is highly corrosive in the concentrated form. Protect your eyes and skin when handling it.

To sanitize instruments, counters, etc., add 1 tablespoon (15ml) of bleach to a gallon (3.7L) of water, and allow the instruments to soak at least ten minutes.

Alternative: Calcium hypochlorite. To use as a disinfectant for counters or instruments, make a bleach solution from the calcium hypochlorite, then mix it with water. To make the bleach solution, mix one heaping teaspoon (5g) of the calcium hypochlorite granules into two gallons (7.6L) of water. Allow it to sit at least 30 minutes. (The solution stays good for a couple of weeks.) Mix one part of the solution to nine parts water. For example, add 1½ ounces (9 teaspoons; 45ml) to each quart (liter) of water. Use in a spray bottle if available.

Rubbing (Isopropyl) Alcohol

Minimum: two pints

Alternative: alcohol pads, one box

Betadine (Povidone-Iodine) 10 Percent Solution

Minimum: one pint to one gallon (½L to 7.6L)

Notes: You can use Betadine to protect your thyroid in place of potassium iodine tablets if radioactive iodide becomes a threat from something such as a nearby nuclear reactor leak. In this case, paint 1½ teaspoons (7ml) on the chest or abdomen daily.

Alternative: Betadine (povidone-iodine) pads

OVER-THE-COUNTER MEDICINES

Before using any of these medications, carefully read the precautions, interactions and dosages. Always keep the packaging and instructions with the medication. Have liquid or chewable versions for children.

- **ibuprofen** (Advil, Aleve) or **acetaminophen** (Tylenol) for pain and fever relief
- **diphenhydramine** (Benadryl) for allergies or to use as a sleep aid
- **ranitidine** (Zantac), famotidine (Pepcid) or your favorite antacid for heartburn and acid reflux
- **loperamide** (Imodium) for diarrhea
- **potassium iodide tablets** to protect the thyroid from radioactive iodine
- **pyrantel pamoate** for pinworms

Topicals (For the Skin)
- **lidocaine gel** for numbing
- **hydrocortisone** 1 percent cream for itchy, noninfectious rashes
- **aloe vera** (bottle or live plant) for soothing burns and irritated skin
- **antibacterial ointment** (Neosporin, triple antibiotic or bacitracin)
- **tea tree oil** for poison ivy, lice and scabies, along with antifungal and antibacterial use
- **clove oil** for toothaches
- **permethrin** 1 percent, or pyrethrin plus piperonyl butoxide, for head lice
- **permethrin** 5 percent for scabies

Nasal Inhalers

Minimum: one

Notes: A nasal decongestant can constrict blood vessels and help control nosebleeds. A brand name example is Afrin.

Find detailed step-by-step first aid instruction for common medical emergencies in *Living Ready Pocket Manual First Aid* by James Hubbard, M.D., M.P.H., available at store.livingreadyonline.com.

Survival
Hygiene Aids

BY JAMES D. NOWKA

Hygiene is an area of preparation you can't afford to overlook. Biological functions aren't going to take a furlough for reasons of inconvenience. Having the means to get the grime off of your body is a morale and confidence builder, and both are important in times of challenge. Further, it's a health issue.

Alcohol-based hand sanitizers have been a big trend of recent years. The sanitizers are everywhere, and they're better than nothing. Still, you shouldn't rely on them as the overriding hygiene prep. From the place of practicality, sanitizers might kill some germs, but they aren't going to remove the filth. Bath-in-a-bag kits are handy and work well, though many do not have to take on that additional expense.

There's really nothing better than the regular soap and water. A family might not have showers available if a storm knocks the community off the municipal water system or inhibits the ability to draw from the well. Some might have adequate water storage to dedicate a portion for hygiene. Those who don't can still most often

meet needs. With the exception of those living in the desert, most people have fairly close access to water. Though you wouldn't drink directly from a lake, river or stream, that water might just suffice for washing up.

Use some forethought, common sense and good judgment. If the only nearby water source is the filthy, contaminated harbor, you might think better of collecting from it for hygiene purposes. In that case, have those bath kits ready. Those using untreated water for washing would want to take greater care. While working in New Orleans after Hurricane Katrina, we had access to our showers, but had untreated water flowing through the pipes. I felt comfortable in using that water for showering from the shoulders down. I wouldn't, however, use it to brush my teeth as some did. I relied on bottled water to cleanse my face and ears. I didn't want to risk giving contaminants any easy entry point that could lead to illness.

Toilet access would become an issue should a family lose typical water access. One solution might be a five-gallon pail and commode seat. Preppers might include waste alleviation and gelling bags, which are also referred to as WAG bags.

BORIS BULYCHEV / SHUTTERSTOCK.COM

The bags contain a material that neutralizes odors and speeds the decay process. They're sealable and can be deposited in the trash. Depending on the length of time before water is restored, it could be a somewhat pricey option. They typically sell for a few dollars apiece.

There are a variety of chemical camping toilets on the market at a wide range of prices. They're basically smaller, personal versions of the portable bathrooms you would see at festivals or on construction sites. Of course, those with fewer hangups with their daily functions could get by with a shovel.

Consider personal comfort and that of the family members. It'll provide the best guide to most adequate solutions.

HYGIENE AIDS CHECKLIST

- ☐ hand sanitizer
- ☐ Bath-in-a-bag kit
- ☐ soap
- ☐ five-gallon pail
- ☐ commode seat
- ☐ WAG bags
- ☐ camping-sized chemical toilet

7 Items for Survival First Aid Kits

BY BRENDAN MICHAELS

A lightweight trauma first aid kit, carried in the pockets of pants or survival kit, ensures you have the equipment to help you prevail in an unexpected emergency situation.

The items in the lightweight first aid kit detailed in this article were chosen for effectiveness and portability. The equipment is small enough that you don't notice you are carrying it. Use these first aid tips to create your own personalized version. Use it on its own or add it to your survival kit.

1: BLACKHAWK TACTICAL PANTS

The carrying platform of the lightweight first aid kit starts with Blackhawk tactical pants that have two large-capacity cargo pockets with elastic webbing inside of them to secure the items in the kit for fast access and comfortable wear. There are two front pockets on your upper thigh and a hidden side pocket that provides needed storage for extra medical supplies with fast access.

2: HEMOSTATIC AGENT TO STOP ARTERIAL BLEEDING

Dr. Maurizio A. Miglietta writes in his article "Trauma and Gunshot Wounds: What you need to know to save a life" that the five areas where people can bleed enough to cause shock are the chest, abdomen, pelvis, long bones (e.g. femur) and bleeding out at the scene of injury.

Applying a gauze bandage on the wound along with pressure can stop the bleeding in many cases. Direct pressure on the wound constricts the blood vessels manually, helping to stem blood flow.

When direct pressure does not stop the bleeding or when it is difficult to apply direct pressure to the source of internal bleeding, a hemostatic agent like Qui-kClot should be used on the wound. Qui-kClot is a mineral material that absorbs the water in the blood, speeding up the natural blood clotting process by highly concentrating platelet and clotting factor molecules in the blood that remains in the wound.

Clotting is the body's natural blood-loss mechanism and it works well. Clotting has a tampening effect on the blood flow through the veins. This is important especially when a tourniquet cannot be used or a pressure dressing cannot apply enough pressure to an internal chest or pelvis wound.

3: TRAUMA/PRESSURE BANDAGE

A typical trauma bandage has a wound pad designed to keep the injury clean of debris and help stop bleeding with an elastic wrap that holds the bandage in place with pressure. The wound pad helps stop the flow of blood, which starts the clotting process. The pressure feature of a trauma bandage uses an elastic wrap to apply pressure on the wound site to help stop severe bleeding by constricting the damaged blood vessels manually.

Ross Johnson, a combat-experienced 18D Special Forces medic, was taught in his medical training that the magic combo for treating a gunshot wound is packing it with Kerlix gauze and wrapping it with an Ace bandage. In combat, Ross once lost control of an Ace bandage that got away from him and wasted precious time in treating a wounded solider. So he created a new trauma bandage called the Olaes modular bandage to improve upon existing trauma bandage designs.

Ross named his advanced bandage design after the junior Special Forces medic on his team, Staff Sergeant Tony B. Olaes. Olaes was killed in action while supporting Operation Enduring Freedom on Sept. 20, 2004, during a combat patrol near the town of Shkin in Afghanistan's Paktika Province when his vehicle came under fire from enemy forces.

The Olaes modular bandage combines gauze and elastic wrap so in an emergency you only have to pull one item out of your aid bag instead of two. The Olaes modular bandage has three meters of gauze, an elastic wrap, a 5 × 7-inch piece of plastic, and a plastic cup to apply direct pressure to the wound area. The gauze is designed to stay in the dressing pocket or be removed from the dressing pocket depending on the treatment of the wound needed.

The 5 × 7-inch plastic sheet included inside the bandage is important to treat a wound where the bowels are exposed. The plastic can also be used on a chest wound that is feeding air into the chest cavity and collapsing the lung. To treat this, the plastic is tapped down on three sides, with the fourth side open to allow air to escape when the patient breathes. Carry 24 inches of rolled up medical tape in your pocket to secure the plastic on three sides of the chest.

The Olaes bandage uses a plastic cup that places a focused direct pressure on the wound area to help stop bleeding by closing damaged vessels. The plastic cup can also be used to protect a wounded eye against the pressure of a bandage placed over the head. One 4-inch Olaes modular bandage is about the size of a large dinner roll and it is carried comfortably in the right cargo pocket.

4: TOURNIQUET

A tourniquet can help stop bleeding in an arm or a leg when a pressure dressing and QuikClot sponge does not stop it. The tourniquet cuts off blood flow that steals oxygen from getting to the limb and prevents toxins from leaving the limb.

This is not good for an extended period of time but if it prevents death through blood loss, the complications can be dealt with at a hospital.

The SOF Tactical Tourniquet was designed by Ross. The tourniquet is made out of a wide heavy duty nylon strap that relies on a metal clip to hold the strap in place to avoid slippage that can occur with tourniquets that use a Velcro fastener. The tourniquet has a handle machined from a solid piece of aircraft aluminum with a dual locking mechanism once the handle is twisted to the desired tightness.

The right cargo pocket of the Blackhawk tactical pants holds the SOF Tactical Tourniquet, folded in a ready-to-use configuration.

5: TRAUMA SHEARS

Trauma shears are an important tool for self aid in order to quickly and safely cut away clothing from bleeding areas so you can assess the wound and treat it before losing too much blood.

Trauma shears are designed to cut through clothing of all types like denim and leather. They can also cut through seat belts and the side of boots.

Paul Howe, a combat Special Forces veteran, believes in self treating wounds to free up fellow team members to secure the target. Once the area is secure the team will come back to help. In Paul's book *Leadership and Training for the Fight* he reviews how this medical self-treatment is part of a "fight through" mentality where you do not dwell on dying but instead focus on what you are doing to ensure your survival.

The left cargo pocket of the Blackhawk tactical pants hold a pair of 7.5-inch or smaller stainless steel trauma shears held in place by the elastic which ensures the shears do not restrict your leg movement and can be comfortably carried throughout the day without noticing them.

6: MEDICAL GLOVES

Gloves are needed to safeguard yourself against HIV or other blood-borne pathogens and to protect your patient from infection. In an extreme emergency the gloves can be cut open and taped down as a chest seal.

Nitrile gloves are made of durable synthetic latex that is three times more puncture resistant than rubber. Nitrile has a low resistance to friction making it easy to slide on the gloves. Two pairs of extra large Nitrile gloves are carried securely in the right cargo pocket in an elastic band inside the pocket.

7: LAERDAL FACE SHIELD TO PERFORM CPR

The Laerdal Face shield is a non-latex plastic sheet and hydrophobic filter that helps protects you from possible contact with the victim's face, saliva or blood when performing mouth-to-mouth resuscitation.

The Laerdal Face shield comes in a package the size of a teabag. It is carried securely in the right cargo pocket in an elastic band inside the pocket.

CONCLUSION

These first aid tips are by no means a comprehensive first aid guide. They offer a good place to start. Before you go out and buy first aid items, become educated in their use first. Applying first aid incorrectly is sometimes worse than doing nothing at all.

CHAPTER SEVEN

Communication and Navigation

Communication is critical during an emergency but can be difficult if the grid goes down or is overwhelmed. This chapter explains how the U.S. national grid system works so you can better understand its function and limitations. It also covers essential survival apps for your smartphone. (Worried your phone won't have enough juice to get you through a disaster? Select one of the alternative-power-source chargers detailed in chapter 5.) Plus, there are Buyer's Guides to GPS devices and weather radios.

But what if everything goes dark? We've got you covered with a guide for how to get from point A to point B without batteries (a skill humans mastered centuries prior to GPS).

One Grid to Rule Them All

HOW THE U.S. NATIONAL GRID SYSTEM WORKS TO DELIVER PINPOINT ACCURACY FOR LATITUDE AND LONGITUDE COORDINATES

BY BRETT ORTLER

In a country with global positioning satellite (GPS) software on every smartphone, we often take GPS technology for granted, and with it comes a dependence on longitude and latitude. But longitude and latitude has a dark side.

A mapping system is only as useful as it is universal, and when used in disaster relief or in an emergency response situation, longitude and latitude coordinates have serious limitations. Much of the problem has to do with notation—there are three different ways to record a position's longitude and latitude, but they aren't easily interchangeable. Converting between notations is time-consuming, especially in a widespread disaster, where several notations are likely being used simultaneously and many different coordinates need to be translated quickly.

This leads to a variety of problems. Converting coordinates wastes resources and manpower and can even lead to outright errors, causing assistance to be sent to the wrong locations entirely. More than anything, relying on longitude and latitude wastes time, and in an emergency situation, delays can cost lives.

This isn't just a problem for officials involved in search-and-rescue or disaster response. This is something that should concern every citizen interested in being prepared for a disaster: whether you're lost in the woods or trying to find your way amid the ruins of a ravaged city, you need a mapping system that is universal, simple, and precise. Thankfully, that system already exists: it's called the U.S. National Grid.

PROBLEMS IN THE FIELD

The problems of longitude and latitude aren't obvious until you've seen them crumble in an emergency situation. No one recognizes this more than Steve Swazee, a 31-year veteran of the U.S. Navy and U.S. Marine Corps, and a vocal proponent of the U.S. National Grid. He helped coordinate the Pentagon's response to Hurricane Katrina, and he has seen the perils of relying on latitude and longitude in an emergency situation. "If you have a disaster, you need a grid," says Swazee. He notes that the strongest supporters of the National Grid System are people who have first-hand experience where an emergency response effort was unduly complicated because of a lack of a universal system.

Swazee cites the case of the crash of the Maryland State Police rescue helicopter known as Trooper 2 as a textbook example of the perils involved in depending on longitude and latitude. In that case, a state police helicopter went down in a heavily wooded area while transporting medical patients.

Emergency responders were given a set of longitude and latitude coordinates,

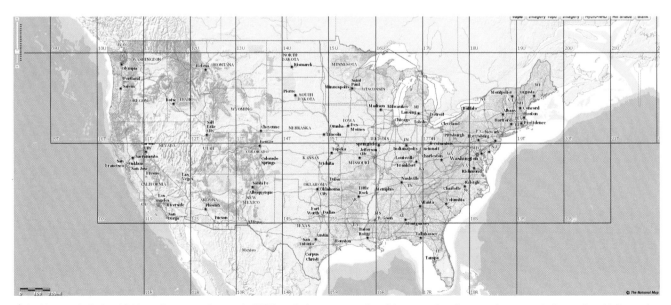

▲ In this example National Grid coordinate map, the areas in 15T. Zones in the western portion of the country have lower numbers; areas in the east have higher numbers.

but they were not informed that the coordinates were in the "degrees, minutes and seconds" notation. Instead, the responders plotted the coordinates using a different notation, and they directed emergency crews to a location that was 30 miles away from the actual crash site. Meanwhile, a seriously injured survivor was waiting for rescue and wasn't attended to for two hours.

Given the complexity of referring to longitude and latitude, this is an easy mistake to make, especially in a pressure situation. Even the National Transportation Safety Board's Accident Report inadvertently confused two different longitude and latitude notations; the report was later amended with an errata sheet to correct the error.

THE SPACE SHUTTLE COLUMBIA AND THE I-ET BRIDGE COLLAPSE

When the space shuttle Columbia disintegrated over a wide swath of the southern U.S., the recovery effort was slowed because of the inherent complexities of longitude and latitude. There were thousands of people involved in locating wreckage and the astronauts' remains, but many had little to no training on the different latitude or longitude notations. This

led to confusion and delays—a serious problem since many shuttle components presented public health hazards. To make matters worse, the various local, state and federal agencies each had their own mapping standards.

A similar incident occurred during the recovery effort for the I-35 bridge collapse in Minneapolis. While on a much smaller scale than the Columbia disaster, Swazee notes that the grid system used to coordinate search and rescue was redrawn four times.

AN OUTDATED SYSTEM

According to Swazee, the problem with longitude and latitude is much more than a notation issue. The system is essentially a relic of sea-faring navigation and was originally created to assist in navigation over long distances. When it's used on this scale, it's fairly straightforward, but most everyday uses are much more specific. More often than not, we're interested in knowing about a destination that is meters wide, not miles wide.

On a small scale, longitude and latitude become ever more difficult to use, largely because its coordinates consist of a base-60 system. Each degree of longitude or latitude can be broken into 60 minutes,

which are further divisible into 60 seconds. Simply put, a base-60 system isn't intuitive.

ABOUT THE GRID

To avoid the problems inherent with the use of longitude and latitude, we need a new system altogether. Military planners realized this after World War II, so they created the Military Grid Reference System (MGRS), which covers the entire globe and provides users with a consistent system for obtaining a unique spatial address, with absolute precision, no matter the scenario. The U.S. National Grid is an offshoot of this system and covers only U.S. territories.

HOW IT WORKS

All National Grid coordinates consist of three simple parts: a grid zone designation, a regional code, and local area coordinates.

Consider the following National Grid coordinate: 15TVK919779.

The first part is a grid zone designation, which is a combination of a number (10-19) and a single letter (R-U). In all, there are about 35 grid zones in the contiguous U.S. Once you know your location's grid zone, you've got a pretty good idea of its geographic context nationwide.

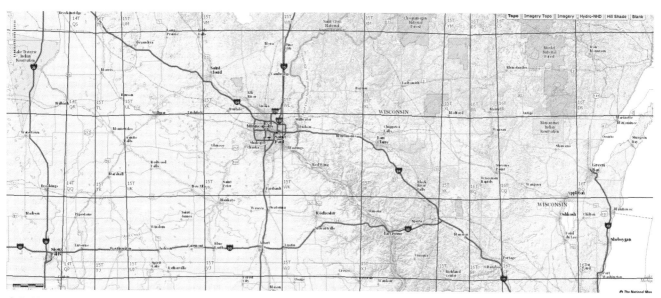

In this example, the regional code is VK and taking a quick look at the National Grid map gives us a pretty good idea of where our site is located—somewhere near the Twin Cities metropolitan area in Minnesota.

Local coordinates can have four, six, eight or ten digits. The more coordinates you have, the more precise your measurement.

In the example National Grid coordinate on page 176, the grid zone is 15T. Zones in the western portion of the country have lower numbers; areas in the east have higher numbers. Similarly, the further south an area is, the closer its letter is to the beginning of the alphabet; areas further north are closer to the end of the alphabet.

REGIONAL CODES

Grid designations give you a rough idea of where you are; a regional code gets you a lot closer. It locates a position within an area of 100,000 square meters. Regional codes consist of a combination of two letters; these combinations were ordered and labeled carefully to avoid repetition as much as possible. (Regional codes only repeat every 1,000 miles or so, making it highly unlikely that responders will mistake one nearby region code for another.)

In our example on page 177, the regional code is VK. Taking a quick look at the National Grid map gives us a pretty good idea of where our site is located— somewhere near the Twin Cities metropolitan area in Minnesota.

ABSOLUTE PRECISION

The real power of the National Grid System comes from its local coordinates, which make up the last portion of a national grid coordinate and consist of a number with an even number of digits. Local coordinates can have four, six, eight or ten digits. The more coordinates you have, the more precise your measurement. Each subsequent grid square is divided into ever smaller—and more precise—squares.

A coordinate with four digits places you within a 1,000-meter square. Six digits place you within an area the size of a football field (100 meters). Eight digits locate you within a ten-meter square (the size of an average house). And if you use ten digits, it'll place you within one square meter—the size of a manhole cover.

That's the real power of the National Grid System: With a number that's only one digit longer than a phone number (sans area code) you can locate a site within a 10-meter square.

READING THE MAP

In our example on the opposite page, the local coordinates read: 919779. Our coordinates are six digits long, so we'll be locating a site within 100 meters. It's helpful to think of these coordinates as two halves; there is an eastern component (919) and a northern component (779).

In a digital map-viewing program, like the free National Map software produced by the United States Geological Survey, one can simply zoom in from level to level. In our case, we start by looking for VK 97. Then we can zoom in even closer by zooming to VK 9177.

Finally, we simply need to zoom in even closer and find VK 919 779. (Note that going from one level to the next simply involves taking one digit from each half of the area coordinate.)

When we do, we find our destination: the Minnesota State Capitol Building

NOT JUST DIGITAL

Of course, in an emergency situation, we won't always have access to digital maps. Thankfully, National Grid coordinates are easy to use on paper maps that incorporate a Universal Transverse Mercator projection. This map projection style is quite common and is used by the U.S. armed services, and on many other maps.

Using the National Grid Coordinates on a paper map is simple. The first rule is important: When reading a local area map you always read right (east) first, then up (north). When reading on a local map, it's often helpful to think of the coordinates as decimals. So in our example, the numbers would read 91.9 and 77.9. The first numbers of each half are very important; they are referred to as principal digits, and

The local coordinates read: 919779. Our coordinates are six digits long, so we'll be locating a site within 100 meters. When we do, we find our destination: the Minnesota State Capitol Building.

they tell you the specific grid line to look for on the local map. So we need to read right (east) first, and we need to look for the eastern gridline 91. Then we simply have to look 90 meters further east. From there, we read up to northern gridline 77. Then we read 90 meters further north. This is fairly easy to do with just a map alone, but the National Grid folks have also produced specific rulers to make things even easier.

WHY USE THE GRID?

Without question, the National Grid is a better option than latitude and longitude in an emergency response situation, but what about the rest of us? Why should the average citizen care? According to Swazee, there are two primary reasons: First of all, in a large-scale disaster zone, common geographic landmarks (streets signs and the like) are often obliterated. If you're familiar with the National Grid system, you can still reliably convey geographic information. This is important, because in many such disasters, the U.S. National Guard and other U.S. Armed Forces are often involved in the recovery effort, and they are well-versed in the National Grid system.

In addition, in many of the-end-of-the-world-as-we-know-it situations, it's not a given that GPS technology will survive. Like any other type of technology, it needs to be carefully maintained. Even if the system remains up and running, it's not necessarily a given that you'll be able to access it. After all, GPS units are power-hungry devices, and it's not a given that your hardware will survive a disaster or the rough-and-tumble-weeks and months after one.

More than anything, the biggest argument in favor of the National Grid is its simplicity. As a base-10 system, it's intuitive and easy to use. Better yet, it's free. You can download and print maps from the U.S. Geological Survey's National Map project at http://viewer.nationalmap.gov/viewer.

THE MINNESOTA MARKER SYSTEM AND IMPLEMENTATION OF THE NATIONAL GRID

Unfortunately, the National Grid System is not fully implemented nationwide. The U.S. Armed Services use it, but on the state and local level, there is a patchwork of different systems in place. According to Swazee, the biggest obstacle to its full-scale implantation is institutional inertia.

When organizations have used the same format for years—they are unlikely to change willingly.

Thanks to the benefits of the U.S. National Grid system, that's starting to change, however. Some states have begun adopting the U.S. National Grid as their preferred mapping system, and a pilot program in northern Minnesota has recently garnered a good deal of attention.

Launched in northern Minnesota's arrowhead region, the Minnesota Marker is a pilot program where signs with U.S. National Grid coordinates were placed on far-flung snowmobile trails. Stranded snowmobilers who happened upon the signs were instructed to call 911 and simply read the number on the sign. The project has received a good deal of positive attention, and has already aided in at least one rescue.

While Swazee emphasized that the program was only a trial, it is already serving as a model for several others, and it seems indicative for the future of the National Grid program as a whole. Given its power and simplicity, the U.S. National Grid seems destined to become a staple for emergency responders and preppers alike.

Smartphone Survival

TRICK OUT YOUR PHONE INTO A DIGITAL TOOLBOX AND SURVIVAL RESOURCE LIBRARY

BY BRETT ORTLER

Over the last 20 years, the cell phone has become a staple of everyday life. We use cellular technology for frivolous and serious reasons alike—everything from Angry Birds to dialing 911. Case in point: according to the FCC, about 70 percent of 911 calls originated from cell phones.

But given how dependent we are on cell phones, it's prudent to ask how the technology would fare in a disaster. After all, cell phone service is among the first pieces of infrastructure to fail in an emergency, and cell phones can be maddeningly power-hungry—not the ideal characteristic for technology in a blackout.

Nonetheless, if you prepare in advance, a cell phone can still be an invaluable tool in a wide variety of emergency situations, from run-of-the-mill severe weather to more widespread disasters like hurricanes and earthquakes. This is even true if your phone doesn't have service.

After all, cell phones aren't simply phones anymore. Even if cell service is knocked out, a cell phone can serve as a digital atlas, a survival library, a planting calendar, and an entertainment center; with a $5 app and some black tape, it can even serve as a makeshift radioactivity detector. With the right planning and some creativity, your cell phone can prove just as useful in a widespread crisis as it does on everyday errands.

IF YOU HAVE SERVICE…(APPS THAT REQUIRE CELL SERVICE)

If your phone has service, it's easy to stay abreast of the latest news and current events thanks to the Internet. A few apps go a bit further, however, and can warn you of potential dangers in advance.

WEATHER ALERTS AND LIVE RADAR

If you have cell service, there's no reason you should ever be surprised by the weather again. Thanks to the proliferation of weather apps, it's now easy to download free (or cheap) applications that can warn you about severe weather in advance (either via an alarm or by sending you a text message).

While the National Weather Service and the National Oceanic and Atmospheric Administration don't have a direct service that sends weather warnings, NOAA's webpage lists many providers of such services here: http://www.weather.gov/subscribe.

In addition, NOAA's website is easy to access from a mobile phone. If you enter a ZIP code in its search form, you'll get up-to-date weather information about that area, including active warnings and watches, live radar data and more.

If you want to see the radar for yourself, there are also many well-received radar applications that are easy to use. These include:

RADIO SCANNERS

As anyone with a police scanner knows, radio chatter can give you an on-the-ground view of what's going on in your area. While scanner information is neither definitive (not all areas are covered) nor always accurate, it's still a source of up-to-date information, which can be priceless in a fluid emergency situation. At the very least, it's a fascinating look into the response to a disaster.

FEMA

The Federal Emergency Management Agency (FEMA) also has a smartphone app, which can be used to locate open shelters and FEMA Disaster Recovery Centers.

FEMA also has a text-messaging service that allows users to receive information about open shelters and disaster recovery centers via text message. In the event of an emergency, users can text the following:

To search for open shelters: text SHELTER and a Zip Code to 43362 (4FEMA)

To search for open Disaster Recovery Centers, text: DRC and a ZIP Code to 43362 (4FEMA)

Note: Receiving a text message back doesn't guarantee you a place at a shelter or a center; it simply indicates that a shelter/center is available in your ZIP code.

IF YOU DON'T HAVE CELL SERVICE

Once the cellular network goes down, most people think their cell phone is useless. But if you plan ahead and download apps, maps and e-books, that's not true at

NOAA Weather Radio
itunes.com; play.google.com
Operating System(s): iOS, Android
Price: $3.99 on iOS, $0.99 on Android

RadarScope
www.radarscope.tv
Operating System(s): iOS, Android
Price: $9.99

MyRadar
itunes.com; play.google.com
Operating Systems(s): iOS, Android, Windows Phone
Price: Free

5-0 Police Scanner Lite
Operating System(s): iOS
Price: Free

Police Scanner
Radio Scanner
Operating System(s): Android
Price: Free

FEMA App
www.fema.gov/smartphone-app
Operating System(s): iOS, Android, Blackberry
Price: Free

Flashlight X
play.google.com; www.windowsphone.com/en-us/store
Operating System(s): Android, Windows Phone
Price: Free

Flashlight—4 in 1
itunes.com
Operating System: iOS
Price: $1.99

Google Maps
itunes.com; play.google.com
Operating System(s): iOS, Android
Price: Free

Stellarium Mobile
itunes.com; play.google.com
Operating System(s): iOS, Android
Price: $2.99 on iOS, $2.58 on Android

A NOTE ABOUT OPERATING SYSTEMS

As anyone who doesn't have an iPhone (me!) knows, not every cellular operating system offers the same amount of applications. Some, like iPhone's iOS and Google's Android, have thousands, whereas others seem to hardly have any. Obviously, you can't use applications designed for a system you don't have, so you won't be able to use all of the applications I'm including here. Given their dominant market share, I'm primarily focusing on iOS and Android phones. Nonetheless, there are similar programs for many of the other phone operating systems, and given the above, even the most basic cell phone can be quite useful in a survival situation.

all. There are many uses for a smartphone, even one that can never place a phone call again.

A FLASHLIGHT—AND A LOT MORE

Everyone has used their cell phone as a makeshift flashlight, and soon enough actual flashlight applications started cropping up. While they drain the phone's battery, they can work rather well as flashlights, and they can do more than just help you find your way through the dark. Some apps include S.O.S. buttons, emergency strobes, illuminated magnifying glasses and even Morse Code adaptors, enabling you to turn your cell phone into a signal lantern.

OFFLINE MAPS AND MORE

If you don't have cell service, you can't use Google maps, right? Wrong. Thanks to Google's upgraded Maps App for Android, you can now download maps for offline use.

ASTRONOMY

Of course, a map isn't much good if you can't find your way around. Thankfully, astronomy apps have got you covered.

Some of the first maps were of the stars—and there's a reason for that: if you know some basic astronomy, you can use your phone's astronomy app as a rudimentary compass.

Even if your phone's GPS no longer works, many programs let you designate a specific location (either a city or longitude/latitude coordinates). Once you choose a location and specify the date and time, the program does the rest, enabling you to see an up-to-the minute picture of the night sky, helping you find your way on a clear night. One of my favorite programs is Stellarium, but if it doesn't suit you, there are many high-quality astronomy apps available.

A SURVIVAL LIBRARY

One of the most useful survival aspects of smartphone technology is also one of the least obvious—e-reader technology enables anyone to carry a vast survival library with them at all times.

With a few software downloads, one's phone can carry everything from Powerpoint presentations about gardening from your local extension service to plant identification handouts from the USDA.

Kindle
amazon.com
Operating System(s): iOS, Android, Windows, Blackberry
Price: Free

Barnes and Noble
www.barnesandnoble.com
Operating System(s): iOS, Android
Price: Free

Adobe Reader
http://www.adobe.com/products/reader-mobile.html
Operating System(s): iOS, Android

Microsoft Office readers
or their equivalents are available for most operating systems.

Droid Timelapse
play.google.com
Operating System(s): Android
Price: Free

Lapse It
itunes.com
Operating System(s): iOS
Price: Free

Foodle
itunes.com
Operating System(s): iOS
Price: Free

Nutrition Facts
play.google.com
Operating System(s): Android
Price: Free

Garden Plan Pro
itunes.com
Operating System(s): iOS
Price: $9.99

Food Storage Calculator
Operating System(s): Windows Phone
Price: Free

Radioactivity Counter
play.google.com; itunes.com
Operating System(s): Android, iOS
Price: $4.49 for Android, $4.99 for iOS

THE USGS NATIONAL MAP

http://viewer.nationalmap.gov/viewer
Operating System(s): None, but PDF reader required
Price: Free
If you don't have an Android-based Smartphone, don't fret. It's simple—and free—to download maps from the USGS's National Map viewer, including maps with the ever-handy National Grid coordinates (an alternative to longitude and latitude). The site offers a myriad of other data sets you can overlay on the maps—helping you locate everything from the closest fire departments and the nearest hospital to satellite imagery and topographic maps.

Better yet, you can download as many maps as you want, as long as you do it before your service goes out.

PROTECT YOUR TOOLS AND YOUR PRIVACY

Even if you have your smartphone tricked out as a preparedness and survival toolbox, it's not going to do much good if it is broken. There are numerous hard-shell cases on the market that protect the phone from drops and some are even waterproof. The drawback is that they add a lot of bulk to an already sleek smartphone. One alternative is the aLOKSAK ($8), a resealable storage bag featuring a hermetic seal. Nothing gets in: no water, no air, no dust, or humidity. They are transparent and you can still hear a phone conversation through the bag along with being able to use your touch screen. The bags are flexible and have a slight rubbery toughness to them. Although they won't protect your phone from a hard drop, they will protect against dings and scratches. The same company makes SHIELDSAK ($65), a small Faraday pouch made of lightweight silk-like cloth that blocks all signals emitted from your phone and all signals trying to reach your phone and thus preventing any hacking attempts. The bag blocks everything. It blocks radio frequencies (RF), infrared, and skim/quick-scan technology—so along with your phone, drop in your credit cards, passports and anything that might be chipped (loksak.com).

In addition, thanks to e-readers like Amazon's Kindle App and Barnes and Noble's Nook App, you can purchase e-books and download them straight to your phone. While there aren't many high-quality field guides on the e-book market yet, non-fiction publishers are catching up and there are books and apps worth purchasing. (By all accounts: *Wilderness First Responder: How to Recognize, Treat, and Prevent Emergencies in the Backcountry* is one of them.)

In addition, thanks to sites like Project Gutenberg (http://www.gutenberg.org) and The Internet Archive (http://archive.org/details/internetarchivebooks), it's free to download a vast array of public domain books in various e-book formats. The selection is impressive and one can find everything from *Robinson Crusoe* to *Einstein's Theory of Relativity*. Some of these titles will be of interest to preppers, but there is also an impressive source of an array of reading material.

SURVIVAL USES FOR YOUR CAMERA
Plant ID & Time-Lapse Security Camera

Your phone's camera also can come in handy in a disaster situation. If you have to resort to foraging but are unfamiliar with wild plants, your phone's camera lets you record what those plants look like so you can consult with a reference material or show them to a more experienced forager. This enables you to shorten the learning curve and forage more safely.

You can also use your camera a bit more creatively. A time-lapse camera application can easily be adapted to become a makeshift security camera or a trail cam. All you have to do is have a full battery, position the camera surreptitiously, set the camera interval and hit the shutter. When you return, it's easy to simply review the video and single out individual frames.

SMARTPHONE CALCULATORS AND CALENDARS

A number of smartphone planting applications can help you plan your crops, get them in on schedule, and make the most of your fields. Some even include weather data that is tailored to your area.

Once that food is on your plate, nutrition calculators help you know exactly what you're getting out of your food and feature the nutritional and caloric content of more than 7,500 foods—including most of our everyday staples.

Given the number of available apps on the market, these suggestions are just the beginning. Clearly, if you prepare well in advance, creativity is the only limit on how useful your cell phone can be, even when the lights go out.

Buyer's Guide to GPS Smart-Phone Apps

Pricing key (based on manufacturer's suggested retail price):

$ = under $1
$$ = $1.99–$2.99
$$$ = $3–$4.99
$$$$ = over $5

Manufacturer/model: Big Air Software,
LLC / Park Maps
Price: $
Use: Outdoor
Type: Phone Application
Supported Phones: iPhone
Included maps: Base maps with hiking
and bike trails, campgrounds, rest-
rooms, parking, boat launches, fishing
areas and points of interest
Features: 250+ high resolution GPS
enabled maps which mark national
parks, monuments and recreational
areas. Once maps are downloaded, no
internet connection necessary

Manufacturer/model: AllTrails, Inc. /
Hiking & Mountain Biking Trails,
GPS Tracker, & Offline Topo Maps
Price: $
Use: Fitness, outdoor
Type: Phone application
Supported Phones: iPhone, Android
Included maps: 50,000 trail guides, topo-
graphic maps and routes for 5,000
popular trails
Features: Browse/search for trails close-
by, track activities, read and write trail
reviews, trails accessible without inter-
net, sync activity with AllTrails.com
account, compatible with Magellan
Echo smart sports watch

Manufacturer/model: MapMyFitness,
Inc. / iMapMyWalk App
Price: $

Use: Fitness, outdoor
Type: Phone Application
Supported Phones: iPhone, Android,
BlackBerry
Included maps: Interactive base maps
Features: Record detailed workouts
including duration, distance, pace,
speed, elevation, calories burned and
route traveled. Workout data can be
saved and uploaded to MapMyWalk

Manufacturer/model: Memory-Map
/ GPS Navigation with offline topo
maps and marine charts
Price: $
Use: Outdoor, marine
Type: Phone Application
Supported Phones: iPhone, Android,
Windows Mobile
Included maps: 250,000 topographic
maps, more detailed maps available
for download and purchase with PC
application
Features: Import/export GPX files,
speed/direction of travel, plan routes,
measure distance and bearings, shows
altitude, latitude/longitude, UTM and
British National Grid coordinates.
Once maps are downloaded, no inter-
net connection necessary

Manufacturer/model: Glacier Peak
Studios LLC / Topo Maps+
Price: $
Use: Outdoor
Type: Phone Application
Supported Phones: iPhone
Included maps: Detailed USGS and
Thunderforest maps, street maps,
aerial/satellite images
Features: Trace routes to find approxi-
mate distances and elevation profiles
between locations, traced maps
viewable on Satellite map, GPS and
compass functions without inter-

net, mark waypoints, sync routes,
trips, and waypoints between all iOS
devices. Once maps are downloaded,
no internet connection necessary

Manufacturer/model: Fullpower Tech-
nologies / MotionX-GPS Drive
Price: $
Use: Driving navigation
Type: Phone Application
Supported Phones: iPhone
Included maps: Base maps, street maps
Features: Visual lane assitance, speed
limis displayed with car's speed, maps
can be pre-loaded for offline use,
details provided for road constru-
crion, traffic accidents and events

Manufacturer/model: Backpacker magazine / Backpacker GPS Trails
Price: $
Use: Outdoor
Type: Phone Application
Supported Phones: iPhone, Android
Included maps: Aerial/Satellite images,
base maps, street maps, terrain maps,
USGS maps
Features: Record path, mark waypoints,
digital compass, latitude/longitude
coordinates, UTM coordinates, average speed/pace, elevation gain/loss/
net, geo-tagged photos/videos/audio,
in-app trip search, send pre-planned
trips from web to phone, save trips to
cloud on Backpacker.com. Once maps
are downloaded, no internet connection necessary

Manufacturer/model: Big Air Software,
LLC / iTrailMap
Price: $
Use: Fitness, outdoor
Type: Phone Application
Supported Phones: iPhone

Included maps: High resolution 750+ piste maps

Features: Maps downloaded directly to phone and usable without wifi or cellular service, upload tracks to Google Earth and online

Manufacturer/model: Trimble Outdoors / Trimble Outdoors MyTopo Maps

Price: $

Use: Outdoor

Type: Phone Application

Supported Phones: iPad, Android Tablets, Kindle Fire

Included maps: 68,000+ topographical maps of U.S. and Canada, aerial/Satellite images, street maps, terrain maps, hybrid maps

Features: Dual Map View allows user to fade between two different map types, latitude and longitude coordinates, mark and name waypoints, measure distance between waypoints, sync trips to Trimble Trip Cloud

Manufacturer/model: Fullpower Technologies / MotionX-GPS

Price: $$

Use: Fitness, geocaching, outdoor

Type: Phone Application

Supported Phones: iPhone

Included maps: Nine map choices, topographic/road maps, Apple Road, Satellite and Hybrid maps, NOAA marine charts

Features: iPhone magnetic compass integration, progress and ETA visualization during navigation, view cooridnates in UTM, MGRS, OSGB, Lat/Lon format, save up to 500 personal waypoints. Once maps are downloaded, no internet connection necessary

Manufacturer/model: Big Air Software, LLC / Topo 3D

Price: $$$

Use: Outdoor

Type: Phone Application

Supported Phones: iPhone

Included maps: 3-D topographic maps of U.S., terrain maps, USGS maps

Features: High resolution maps for hiking, mountain biking, cross country skiing, camping, RV travel, canoeing

Manufacturer/model: Trimble Outdoors / AllSport GPS

Price: $$$

Use: Fitness, outdoor

Type: Phone Application

Supported Phones: iPhone, Android

Included maps: Aerial/Satellite images, street maps, terrain maps, hyprid maps, topographical maps

Features: Audio alerts for stats, average speed/pace, calories burned, current speed/pace, direction of travel, distance, elevation gain/loss/net, max speed, rest time, total time, speed/elevation profile, weekly/monthly totals by stat and activity

Manufacturer/model: Trimble Outdoors / Trimble Outdoors Navigator

Price: $$$

Use: Outdoor

Type: Phone Application

Supported Phones: iPhone, Android, BlackBerry

Included maps: 68,000+ topographical maps of U.S. and Canada, aerial/Satellite images, street maps, terrain maps, hybrid maps , USGS maps

Features: Average speed/pace, marks waypoints, elevation gain/loss/net, distance, distance to next waypoint, compass bearing, geo-tag photos and audio, save trips to cloud, send pre-planned trips from web to phone. Once maps are downloaded, no internet connection necessary

Manufacturer/model: TrailBehind, Inc. / Offline Topo Maps

Price: $$$$

Use: Outdoor

Type: Phone Application

Supported Phones: iPhone, Android

Included maps: Downloadable maps of entire world, USGS topographical maps and aerial images, OpenStreet-Map-based topographical and road maps

Features: functional, stable and easy-to-use even for novice hikers, mark waypoints and receive guidance to and from distinations, coordinates display

Manufacturer/model: TrailBehind, Inc. / Gaia GPS

Price: $$$$

Use: Geocaching, outdoor

Type: Phone Application

Supported Phones: iPhone, Android

Included maps: Aerial/satellite images, USGS/USFS/ NRCan topographical maps of the U.S. and Canada

Features: GaiaCloud syncs tracks, photos, maps and waypoints to all devices, displays NEXRAD radar, track data and points of interes, imports/export GPX/KML files

Manufacturer/model: Backpacker magazine / Backpacker Map Maker

Price: $$$$

Use: Outdoor

Type: Phone Application

Supported Phones: iPad

Included maps: Aerial/Satellite images, base maps, street maps, terrain maps, USGS maps

Features: Electronic compass, map software included, saves waypoints, supports .gpx files, supports .kml files, touch screen, upgradable maps available, wireless upload to computer

Manufacturer/model: Garafa, LLC. / GPS Kit for iPhone & iPad

Price: $$$$

Use: Fitness, geocaching, outdoor

Type: Phone application

Supported Phones: iPhone, iPad

Included maps: Terrain maps, aerial/satellite images, street maps, cycling maps

Features: Offline mode, real-time friend tracking with "Squawk!"-shows others' position, speed and track, open KML, KMZ and GPX from Mail and Safari, attach KML and GPX files to email, export GPX and KML through iTunes, add photos and notes to waypoints, UTM, USNG, MGRS, magnetic compass, real-time distance to waypoint updates, create "weather stations" for point forecasts (U.S. only), specific data provided for fishing holes, ski tours, etc., real satellite positioning regardless of cellphone signal, latitude, longitude, UTM, MGRS, USNG coordinates, accuracy, speed, odometer, average/max speed, pace, average pace, background mode

Buyer's Guide to GPS Devices

HANDHELD DEVICES

Pricing key for handheld devices (based on manufacturer's suggested retail price):

$$$ = under $100
$$$$ = $101-$200
$$$$$$ = $201-$300
$$$$$$$ = $301+

Manufacturer/model: Brunton / Get-Back GPS
Price: $$$
Weight: 1.3 oz.
Use: Fitness, outdoor
Type: Handheld Device
Screen Size (diagonal): Contact manufacturer
Color screen: No
Included maps: N/a
Power source: Rechargeable battery. USB cable included
Features: Saves 3 waypoints, directs the fasted route back to selected waypoint, self-calibrating digital compass that does not require satellite

Manufacturer/model: Magellan / eXplorist GC North America
Price: $$$$
Weight: 5.2
Use: Primarily geocaching, outdoor, fitness
Type: Handheld Device
Screen Size (diagonal): 2.2"
Color screen: Yes
Included maps: Preloaded worldwide map with complete road network of North America and Western Europe, street maps of major roads in populated world, view parks, rivers, lakes, major city points and other landmarks around target geocaches
Power source: 2 AA
Features: connection to Geocaching. com user community, 30 Day trial premium Geocaching.com membership, preloaded popular geocaches, sulight readable screen, 10,000 stored geocaches, waterproof, picture viewer, saves 500 waypoints, logs total steps and track, average speed, elevation gain/descent, 500 MB of memory

Manufacturer/model: Garmin / Dakota 20
Price: $$$$
Weight: 5.25 oz.
Use: Fitness, geocaching, outdoor
Type: Handheld Device
Screen Size (diagonal): 2.6"
Color screen: Yes
Included maps: Base maps with the ability to add maps, built-in memory of 850 MB, compatible with microSD card for additional maps
Power source: 2 AA
Features: Saves 1,000 waypoints, 50 routes and 200 tracks, automatic routing, electronic compass, barometric altimeter, hunt/fish calendar, sun/moon information, tide tables, customizable points-of-interest, transfer data wirelessly with similar units

Manufacturer/model: Garmin / eTrex 20
Price: $$$$
Weight: 5 oz.
Use: Geocaching, outdoor
Type: Handheld Device
Screen Size (diagonal): 2.2"
Color screen: Yes
Included maps: Base maps with the ability to add maps, built-in memory of 1.7 GB, compatible with microSD card for additional maps
Power source: 2 AA
Features: Saves 2,000 waypoints, 200 routes and 200 tracks, waterproof, automatic routing, sun/moon information, tide tables, customizable points-of-interest, picture viewer

Manufacturer/model: DeLorme / Earthmate PN-60 with Topo North America
Price: $$$$
Weight: 7 oz.
Use: Geocaching, outdoor, fitness
Type: Handheld Device
Screen Size (diagonal): 2.2"
Color screen: Yes
Included maps: Aerial/satellite images, 3-D topographic maps of North America with 360-degree rotation, detailed U.S. trail information, Mexico's main roads, information on boat ramps, campgrounds, hunting and fishing spots, street maps, points-of-interest, compatible with microSD card for additional maps
Power source: AA

Features: Electronic compass, barometric altimeter, waterproof, built-in memory of 3.5 GB, unlimited waypoints and tracks (with purchases of memroy card), sunlight-readable screen, vibration/shock resistant, 11,000 U.S. national forest trails, odometer, trip time, speed

Manufacturer/model: Garmin / Oregon 650T
Price: $$$$$$$
Weight: 7.4 oz.
Use: Geocaching, outdoor
Type: Handheld Device
Screen Size (diagonal): 3"
Color screen: Yes
Included maps: Base maps with the ability to add maps, preloaded topographical maps, built-in memory of 4 GB, compatible with microSD card for additional maps
Power source: 2 AA or rechargeable NiMH pack (included)
Features: Saves 4,000 waypoints, 200 routes and 200 tracks, waterproof, automatic routing, electronic compass, barometric altimeter, 8 megapixel camera with autofocus and digital zoom, hunt/fish calendar, sun/moon information, tide tables, customizable points-of-interest, picture viewer, transfer data wirelessly with similar units

WRIST DEVICES

Pricing key for wrist devices (based on manufacturer's suggested retail price):

$$$$ = $100–$200
$$$$$ = $201–$300
$$$$$$= $301+

Manufacturer/model: Soleus / GPS Vibe
Price: $$$$
Weight: 2.3 oz.
Use: Outdoor, fitness
Type: Wrist Device
Screen Size (diagonal): N/a
Color screen: No
Included maps: N/a
Power source: Rechargeable battery
Features: vibration feedback, current/average pace and speed, 6 training interval timers, current/total calories burned, water resistant

Manufacturer/model: Garmin / Foretrex 401
Price: $$$$
Weight: 3.1 oz.
Use: Fitness, outdoor
Type: Wrist Device
Screen Size (diagonal): N/a
Color screen: No
Included maps: N/a
Power source: 2 AAA
Features: Saves 500 waypoints and 10 tracks, electronic compass, barometric altimeter, hunt/fish calendar, sun and moon information, transfer data wirelessly with similar units, waterproof

Manufacturer/model: TomTom / Runner
Price: $$$$
Weight : 1.75 oz.
Use: Fitness, Outdoor
Type: Wrist Device
Screen Size (diagonal): N/a
Color screen: No
Included maps: N/a
Power source: Rechargeable battery
Features: Measures pace, distance, calories burned and heart rate with optional accessory, compass, graphical training partner, waterproof, Quick GPSFix technology, indoor and outdoor tracking, sync and share stats on multiple running sites/apps

Manufacturer/model: Garmin / Forerunner 310XT
Price: $$$$$$
Weight: 2.5 oz.
Use: Fitness, outdoor, swimming
Type: Wrist Device
Screen Size (diagonal): N/a
Color screen: No
Included maps: N/a

Power source: Rechargeable battery
Features: Saves 1,000 laps and 100 waypoints, some versions have heart rate monitors, bike speed/cadence sensor, syncs automatically to computer, water resistant, train against virtual partner, compete against previous activities, multiple sport modes, customizable workouts, alerts user when goal is reached, customizable screens

Manufacturer/model: Suunto / Suunto Ambit2
Price: $$$$$$
Weight: 3.25 oz.
Use: Fitness, outdoor
Type: Wrist Device
Screen Size (diagonal): N/a
Color screen: No
Included maps: N/a
Power source: Rechargeable battery
Features: adjustable GPS recording interval, find location in multiple coordinate systems, waypoint and route navigation, point-of-interest creation, route planning, barometric altimeter, total ascent/descent, graphs altitude, temperature, manual and autolaps, countdown timer, interval timer, ability to change sport mode during workout, preconfigured multisport modes, sports comparison, track running speed/pace, bike lap, swimming time/lap/total, swimming pace/distance, swimming stroke rate/count/type, automatic intervals, dynamic lap table with strokes/pace/duration

The Day the Cell Phones Died

WHEN ALL ELSE FAILS, TWO-WAY RADIO STILL GETS THROUGH

BY COREY GRAFF

On the afternoon of Sunday, May 22, 2011, the residents of Joplin, Missouri, learned to distrust their cell phones. What convinced them were the hellish winds from a maximum-strength EF5 tornado that reached down from the heavens like a giant vacuum cleaner of death. It touched down just east of the Kansas state line and blazed a 22-mile path of death and destruction through the town — sucking, ripping and tearing the city's structures into mangled toothpicks and violently ending the lives of 158 people.

The monster mile-wide twister caused catastrophic damage in the neighborhood of $2.2 billion. And it knocked out cell phone communications for days. When the storm passed, 1,300 people were missing. The Show Me State learned a tough lesson that day: Don't rely on cell phones. While they're a great modern convenience, they're also the first to fail when high winds crush cell phone towers like pop cans.

It wasn't the first time. New York City, the morning of September 11, 2001. Ter-

rorists strike the World Trade Center. New Yorkers — and virtually everyone else in America — rush to their cell phones. They called to report smoke and fire. They called to request medical help. They called to check in on loved ones. And many just called because they needed to talk to someone, anyone who would listen, about the horrific scenes they saw on TV. It didn't matter why they called, as much as the fact that everyone called at the same time. The phone system locked up. There was too much data flooding

the network and not enough bandwidth. While some infrastructure damage could be blamed for the failure — several cell towers and connecting land lines were indeed destroyed — the real reason the networks failed was simply because they were overloaded.

"I walked from downtown to Lincoln Center (about 4.5 miles) before I was able to hail a cab with four strangers," said Andrea Mancuso as reported by CBS News ("Can We Count on Cell Networks?" September 7, 2011). Mancuso was working just north of the Trade Center. She was lucky; her phone worked. "Everyone was upset, and no one had a cell phone signal except me. I passed my phone around like a hot potato all the way to Harlem. Everyone including the cab driver graciously and tearfully called their families."

Since that day, cell phone networks have been tested and retested and they routinely fail when consumption demands exceed normal levels. Industry representatives claim providers are installing additional towers and built-in network redundancy to handle the volume spike during crises. But Telecomm Analyst Gerard Hallaren paints a different picture. In the CBS News story he revealed that networks are only designed to handle 20 to 40 percent of traffic, which includes phone calls and data modes such as wireless Internet and text messaging.

In the end, it may be business realities — as opposed to technical or infrastructure limitations — keeping cell networks lean and mean, susceptible to failure during extraordinary events. "It's just economic insanity for any carrier to try to solve the congestion problem," Hallaren said. "It's cost-prohibitive to build a network that could serve 330 million at the same time. A service like that would cost hundreds of dollars a month, and people are not willing to pay that much for cell phone service."

WHY RADIO WORKS WHEN CELL PHONES FAIL

The advantage of radio lies in its ability to send and receive a signal, with no help from others. Two-way radio has come a long way since the early days of Guglielmo Marconi's historic transatlantic wireless transmission that must have struck people in those days as nothing short of magic. Today, two-way radio transceivers (transmitter-receivers) are as technologically advanced as any other "tech gadget" — with amateur or ham radio leading the march toward integration with the Internet, GPS and exotic new data modes. But at its most basic level, radio is still radio. Like the basic Marconi set that transmitted the distress signal from the sinking Titanic, it works today for the same reason it worked then: It relies on no one else to get a message out. Thus it remains the best, most reliable form of communication for emergencies. Wireless two-way allows you to be a locally operated independent radio station. You are the network, in essence, and can take advantage of built-in network redundancy, communicating with other independent operators. If one operator loses capability, the network keeps chugging along. There is no middleman. And, other than initial equipment purchase and license fees, there is no cost, either.

Not so with commercial telecommunications systems. By their very nature, commercial communications are centralized. That means that all calls go through your service provider's network. If that system gets overloaded, which it will in the event of a widespread disaster, you're out. These systems are designed to make private companies money, not to ensure you can communicate during times of uncertainty. They are so fickle that any event that gets people talking can spark

POWER PACK CPR

BRING DEAD DEVICES BACK TO LIFE
One way to deal with low batteries while on the move or during a power outage is to have some portable power. Brunton's Resync uses a lithium battery to store enough juice to power up tablet computers, e-readers, GPS units and cell phones via USB ports. A quick test at the office revealed that an iPad can be charged in approximately two hours, a cell phone in about 30 minutes and an e-reader in less than an hour with plenty of juice leftover. The Resync can be recharged through a wall plug-in, a 12V DC charger in your car, a USB port or by solar panels. It has a waterproof rubberized shell for protection against foul weather and impacts. Bonus: it weighs 10 ounces.

⚠ High-performance transceivers like this Yaesu DX9000 transmit up to 400 watts, and can cover the full ham radio high frequency (HF) spectrum from 1.8 mhz (160 meters) up to 54 mhz (6 meters). Advanced filters allow you to pull weak signals from the static when atmospheric propagation isn't ideal.

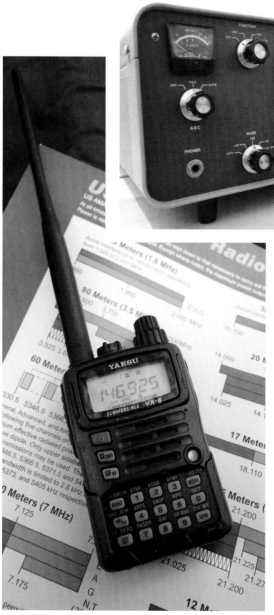

⚠ Another advantage of amateur radio is the option to run vintage equipment. These World War II-era radios use tubes, which allows them to keep working after an Electromagnetic Pulse (EMP), unlike solid-state electronics.

⚠ Today's small amateur radio "HTs" or handie-talkies, are incredibly advanced. This Yaesu VX-6R (pictured left) is a dual-band model transceiver that operates in the 70 cm (440 mhz) and 2m (144 mhz) bands FM. It also receives international shortwave AM transmissions and NOAA weather radio. While typically used for local emergency communications and weather spotting, it can access Internet-linked repeaters for international coverage.

telecomm gridlock. Equally troublesome is the weather: An ice storm or a wind event such as tornado or straight-line winds can twist lines into high voltage pretzels — rendering your smartphone into nothing more than a fancy-looking paperweight.

A LOOK AT THE RADIO SERVICES: THE AMATEUR "HAM RADIO" SERVICE

Arguably the most versatile of the radio services, amateur radio allows you to operate on all modes and bands, and push out a full legal limit of 1,500 watts. You'll need an amateur radio license to transmit. There are license classes — Technician, General and Extra Class and each requires a few weeks of study and gets progressively more difficult to ace. But with each new license upgrade, you attain access to more bands and modes. The Federal Communications Commission (FCC) administers licenses while testing is handled by certified Volunteer Examiners (VEs) through local ham radio clubs. Study manuals for each license class are available through the American Radio Relay League (www. arrl.org).

The benefits of ham radio for emergency communications include access to other local, state, national and global radio operators who are capable of staying on the air even during power outages and failures of the grid. You can operate FM, AM or Single Sideband (SSB) modes using voice, CW (morse code) and data modes from the high frequency (short-wave) bands through the ultra high frequency (UHF) spectrum for crystal clear local and statewide FM communications. You can find out what's happening. And you can get a signal out to get help.

PERSONAL RADIO SERVICES — CITIZEN'S BAND (CB)

You don't have to be a wayfaring trucker careening down the open road to realize the benefits of Citizen's Band or CB radio. While described by some as a "wasteland" — a reputation gained by rampant on-air vulgarity in some parts of the country — CB radio operates in the 11 meter band (26.965 – 27.405 MHz spectrum range) on 40 designated channels, and is quite useful for emergency use. Radios can receive and transmit in FM, AM or SSB modes but are limited to 4 watts (AM) or 12 watts (SSB). Unlike some of the other radio services, Citizen's Band no longer requires a license, though there are rules you need to follow. Amplifiers used to boost output power are prohibited and you must observe height restrictions on antennas. You are also required to assume a "handle," though it's a safe bet that "Rubber Duck" has already been taken.

PERSONAL RADIO SERVICES — GENERAL MOBILE RADIO SERVICE

The General Mobile Radio Service (GMRS) requires one adult, who is the head of the household, to obtain an FCC license. The license covers your immediate family, and gives you access to local- or intermediate-range communications between family members. Some hand-held GMRS radios claim up to a 36-mile range, but most GMRS units are hand-held "walkie-talkie" style and are limited to 5 watts, making them much shorter distance options. While the actual power limit is 50 watts for this service, there is

a loosely-scattered network of GMRS repeaters around the country (a repeater is a high powered station that receives weak signals and retransmits the signal on a different frequency at high power to cover a much greater distance) so if you need to stay in contact with family located over a few miles a way (but less than 50) GMRS may work for you.

PERSONAL RADIO SERVICES — FAMILY RADIO SERVICE (FRS)

Similar to the GMRS, the Family Radio Service, or FRS, is intended to keep, as its namesake implies, family members in contact with one another. You do not need a license to operate a radio in this service. However, FRS is considered a close-range proposition, due to the fact that radios are limited to one-half watt. In practical terms, FRS radio is a one-mile or less choice. One thing to note: Many FRS radios have GMRS capability, so be sure not to operate the radio outside of the FRS limits unless you have the GMRS license. That being said, one principle of preparedness is using gear that covers more than one use. Thus, one of the handiest units I've seen in this category is the Garmin Rino — a GMRS/FRS radio with full Garmin GPS capability. Not only do you get

two radio services covered with one transceiver, but you can find your way to safety (assuming the satellites are working).

PERSONAL RADIO SERVICES — LOW POWER (LPRS) AND MULTI-USE RADIO SERVICES (MURS)

Two final, less popular options are the Low Power Radio Service (LPRS) and Multi-Use Radio Service (MURS). The former uses one-way radio to transmit voice or data information to disabled persons. The latter, MURS, is a two-way service with five allocated channels in the VHF band. Radios used for this service are limited to 2 watts; a license is not required.

CONCLUSION

There's only one thing you can absolutely count on when it comes to your cell phone: It will fail — probably when you need it the most. However, long-range communication is still possible if you plan now to incorporate two-way radio into your family preparedness plan. Sometimes, your ability to get a signal out is your only lifeline to outside help. Don't entrust your family's safety to a telecomm company's flimsy cell phone network. Instead, get on the air now, while you still can — and stay on the air, when all else fails.

Getting to Point B
with or without Batteries

USE A MAP, COMPASS AND GPS IN TANDEM TO EMPOWER YOUR NAVIGATION SKILLS

NON-SIGNAL PHONE GPS

Over the past few years, phone GPS has gone from basic directions to full-blown maps on smartphones that show the user's exact location. While Google Maps is the preferred program for driving, the map portion requires a cell signal to properly work, which negates its usefulness in backcountry where reception can be spotty. There are, however, numerous apps for smartphones that allow users to download topographic maps. Prices range from $.99 to about $10 for both Android and iPhone versions that allow smartphones to be turned into a full-blown, handheld GPS unit. However, phone GPS have the same issues as handheld units; small screen size, limited battery life and potential for getting lost or damaged. Users should still carry a map and compass.

DIFFERENCE IN DATUM

Another issue with GPS units is Datum. A lot of USGS topographical maps are based on the NAD27 (North American Datum of 1924) Datum. However, most GPS units default to the WGS84 (World Geodetic System of 1984) Datum. These two systems have a difference of about 630 feet, or a tenth of a mile. Of course, some areas have been updated, while others haven't. It's important to know how to read a map legend, and how to change a GPS unit to match the map's Datum.

BY J. MARTIN

It wasn't that long ago when the idea of an electronic device determining a person's location down to a few yards was something out of a science fiction novel like Robert Heinlein's *Starship Troopers*. Today, however, global positioning satellite (GPS) is just a part of life.

Over the past few decades, GPS units have moved from military-only hardware to being carried by the "gadget guys" to pretty much universal use. GPS units are now used by many folks to make navigation easier by guiding them to everything from a popular deli for a pastrami sandwich, to a friend's house across the country and everything in between. There are numerous brands of portable units designed for vehicles, and few people head into the backcountry to hunt, fish or hike without a handheld GPS unit to guide their way. After September 11, Federal guidelines require that even cell phones activate a GPS chip when used to dial 911, and most of today's smartphones have GPS and mapping software to make traveling ultra-convenient.

The problem with this convenience is that people have become reliant on it and are quickly losing the ability to navigate. It's as if GPS has replaced conventional maps in many people's minds, even though the system was designed as a compliment, not a substitute.

"The utility of GPS receivers cannot be understated," said Jonathan Horne with Rocky Mountain Rescue in Boulder, Colo. "But relying on them as a sole navigational tool, especially in the backcountry, is dangerous."

GPS handheld units use either latitude/longitude lines or the Universal Transverse Mercator (UTM) grid coordinate system to show where the user is located pretty much anywhere on Earth. Longitude/latitude lines are listed on maps in degrees, minutes and seconds, while UTM grids are listed as a block number. Some maps list both longitude/latitude and UTM, while others only list one. Most GPS units can be programmed to either system, so users can swap to their preferred system or whichever system is listed on the map. Of course, to properly use a map and GPS together, one must understand how to read a map to obtain a location and plan a route.

"GPS is no replacement for map and compass," said Jeff Caulfield, Magellan Outdoor Products Trainer. "GPS navigates as the crow flies. Maps show lakes, mountains and other terrain features, and allow you to plan a safe, passable route. Maps allow you to see larger areas in just as good of detail. You can see the bigger picture and plan accordingly."

One benefit of GPS devices is magnetic declination. The difference between true north and magnetic north can be off by several degrees, depending on location. Maps are written on true north and provide the basic declination for the area that it lists so it can be adjusted for on a compass. With GPS units this is not a factor as the electronic compass can be

WORKING WITH A MAP AND GPS

To determine a route on a map and GPS unit together, first obtain your current location on the GPS. From there, orient the map to true north and mark your current location on the map. Then find the desired travel point on the map and figure the location's coordinates on the map and plot the general direction and measure the distance. Map scales range in size, USGS topographical maps are most often listed in 1:24,000 scale. This means 1 inch on the map equals to 24,000 inches, 1 centimeter equals 24,000 centimeters and 1 foot equals 24,000 feet on the ground. All this equals .378 miles. Usually, there is a distance scale in the key showing mile and half-mile increments.

Once distance has been determined, look at the contour lines to determine the best route, remembering that the closer the lines, the more steep the terrain. The preferred route can be loaded into a GPS unit, with multiple waypoints along the route to ensure that the user doesn't get off path.

Of course, some GPS units also allow maps to be downloaded and viewed on the unit in conjunction with points of interests and the user's location. This can be very useful for tracking distance traveled, speed and estimated time of arrival. Later that information can be uploaded to a computer to share with friends or to create custom maps.

However, the screens on most GPS units are three to four inches at most, meaning users must choose between viewing up close detail and the overall picture by zooming in or out on the unit. Maps have the ability to show both extreme detail as well as the overall picture. And while maps and compasses can become damaged or lost—just like GPS units—they don't run out of battery power.

programmed for either true north or magnetic north modes, depending on need.

By understanding how to read a map and compass, travelers can use a GPS units sparingly and save battery power for when the unit is truly needed, such as when hopelessly lost. Learning to combine the two is simple; the hard part is learning to properly use a map and compass. However, that only takes practice, which can be obtained by trekking into the woods.

Simply start at a trailhead and follow your progress on a map by marking land-marks that you can see. Once you have traveled a significant distance, determine your location on your map and use the GPS unit to discover your accuracy. If you're not correct, sit down and figure out why, and try again. Mentally retrace your route and visualize the landmarks you passed.

"There's no substitute for experience," said Horne. "Bunched-up contour lines take on a real significance when you're standing atop a cliff edge. Bring a map and compass. Bring a GPS. Learn how they work and how they work together."

Product Review

Eton FRX3 AM/FM/NOAA Weather Radio

BY COREY GRAFF

During times of disaster, you'll first want to find out what's happening. And today, radio remains the most reliable way to do that when normal services are snuffed out. In our modern gadget-centric world, the Eton FRX3 fills a unique role. It's a small, multi-use emergency radio ideal as a first line of defense for families.

The FRX3 is small, just 7.875" × 7" × 3.5", but it's packed with useful features, including a built-in solar panel and rechargeable Ni-MH battery (3.6V/600mAh) for extended use when grocery stores aren't stocking batteries. It also plays on 3 AAA batteries, for times when the sun isn't out. I tested the solar panel and it took a full day — about 10 hours — to charge the battery. You can keep the radio near an open window, though, and the thing will charge automatically so it's always ready to use. Another way to charge it is to connect to a laptop computer via the included USB cable.

The batteries can also be recharged with the big hand crank. It took me about two minutes of cranking to bring the charge up to full. The radio features an external, extendable antenna that pulls in broadcast AM and FM stations so you can get emergency messages through the Emergency Broadcast System. One thing to note: The FRX3 does not feature AM shortwave or single side band (SSB) reception.

FULL NOAA WEATHER RADIO

However, one of the most useful things about the FRX3 is its robust NOAA Weather Radio. It features pre-programmed frequencies so you can always find one NOAA signal in your area and an ALERT system that springs the radio to life when an emergency alert is issued. I found that the antenna was fine for the AM/FM broadcast station reception but only mediocre in pulling in the NOAA Weather repeaters — which operate in the 162.400- 162.550 MHz range, FM — out in the rural area in which I live. The signal was broken but readable.

If you live closer to a population center you should have no trouble in getting a strong NOAA signal. But just for comparison, I can receive the NOAA signal from a repeater station, which is located about 10 miles away, without any trouble using a small handheld amateur radio transceiver and minimal antenna. So the only improvement to the FRX3 would be to include a separate, internal antenna resonate for 162 MHz — it wouldn't need to be large or even external, just matched to the right frequencies.

PLAMPY / SHUTTERSTOCK.COM

Buyer's Guide to Weather Radios

Pricing key (based on manufacturer's suggested retail price):

$ = under $25
$$ = $26–$50
$$$ = $51–$100
$$$$ = $101–$150
$$$$$ = $151–$200

Manufacturer/model: Ambient Weather/ WR-090 Emergency Pocket AM/FM/ WB Weather Alert Radio with Digital Tuner and Flashlight
Price: $
Weight: Contact manufacturer
Power source: 3 AAA Batteries – can be powered from USB port
Tuning: AM/FM radio with Weather Band
Other Features: Alert system; LED flashlight; USB power cable; wrist lanyard

Manufacturer/model: Kaito/KA332W
Price: $
Weight: 7.6 oz.
Power source: 3 AAA batteries; built-in rechargeable Li-ion battery; solar; hand crank; adapter
Tuning: AM/FM radio; 7 NOAA Weather channels
Other Features: USB port; headset jack

Manufacturer/model: Kaito/KA210
Price: $
Weight: Contact manufacturer
Power source: 2 AA batteries
Tuning: AM/FM/NOAA
Other Features: high quality speaker; non-distortion sound for vocal and music

Manufacturer/model: Craftsman/C3 19.2 volt AM/FM/Weather Radio
Price: $$
Weight: Contact manufacturer
Power source: 19.2-Volt c3 Ni-Cd, removable/rechargeable battery pack
Tuning: AM/FM radio; weather bands
Other Features: Headphone jack; MP3 input and clip; LED backlit display

Manufacturer/model: Eton/FRX1
Price: $$
Weight: 8 oz.
Power source: Hand turbine power generator; mini USB cable can charge built-in rechargeable battery
Tuning: AM/FM analog radio with NOAA Weather Band
Other Features: LED flashlight; headphone jack; glow-in-the-dark locator

Manufacturer/model: Eton/FRX2
Price: $$
Weight: 9 oz.
Power source: Solar panel; dynamo motor/hand turbine; internal rechargeable battery; mini USB
Tuning: AM/FM analog radio with Weather Band
Other Features: Glow-in-the-dark locator; LED flashlight ; USB Smartphone charger; headphone jack

Manufacturer/model: Kaito/KA350 Dynamo & Solar Powered Radio
Price: $$
Weight: Contact manufacturer
Power source: Build-in replaceable/ rechargeable batteries; Dynamo hand-cranking; solar panel; 3 AAA batteries; USB port
Tuning: 5-way powered AM/FM/SW1 Shortwave Radio with 7 NOAA Weather Band channels
Other Features: 5-LED flashlight; earphones; USB jack

Manufacturer/model: Aervoe Industries Inc./Emergency Alert Radio & Flashlight
Price: $$$
Weight: 20 oz.
Power source: Solar, dynamo, USB, 120V AC and 12V DC, AAA batteries, rechargeable lithium ion battery
Tuning: AM/FM Radio Weather Band and NOAA hazards alert
Other Features: LED flashlight; cell phone charger, earphone jack, antenna

Manufacturer/model: Midland/ HH54VP2 Portable Weather Alert Radio
Price: $$$
Weight: Contact manufacturer
Power source: Rechargeable battery; 3 AA alkaline batteries
Tuning: S.A.M.E., receives over 60 alerts
Other Features: 9 programmable counties; single, multiple, or any SAME program settings; user selectable alert type-voice, display or tone; 10 viewable alerts

Manufacturer/model: Midland/ER102 Emergency Crank Weather Alert Radio
Price: $$$
Weight: Contact manufacturer
Power source: 3 AA alkaline batteries, AC adapter, crank, rechargeable battery
Tuning: AM/FM Radio; NOAA Weather alert
Other Features: Thermometer with freeze alert; alert override—automatically switches to emergency weather alerts; flashlight; clock with alarm; backlit LCD; water resistant; cell phone charger; visual alerts for hearing impaired

FER GREGORY / SHUTTERSTOCK.COM

Pricing key (based on manufacturer's suggested retail price):

$ = under $25
$$ = $26–$50
$$$ = $51–$100
$$$$ = $101–$150
$$$$$ = $151–$200

Manufacturer/model: Eton/FRX3 –
American Red Cross
Price: $$$
Weight: 21 oz.
Power source: Solar panel; hand crank;
built-in rechargeable battery; mini
USB cable; AAA batteries
Tuning: AM/FM digital radio with
NOAA Weather Band
Other Features: Alarm clock; AUX-
input; glow-in-the-dark locator; LED

flashlight; USB smartphone charger;
alert system; red LED flashing beacon
Manufacturer/model: Kaito KA550
Price: $$$
Weight: Contact manufacturer
Power source: Solar panel; Dynamo-
hank crank; 3 AA batteries; built-in
rechargeable battery pack; AC adap-
tor; USB port
Tuning: AM/FM/SW1/SW2 radio with
Weather Band
Other Features: 5-LED reading lamp;
multi-function LED flashlight; LED
flashing emergency signal; Weather
Alert

Manufacturer/model: C.Crane/Orphan
CC Pocket Radio w/ AM/FM/WX &
55 Presets
Price: $$$
Weight: 3.8 oz.

Power source: 2 AA batteries, recharge-
able batteries
Tuning: AM/FM/WX
Other Features: Headphone jack; sleep
timer; alarm clock; display light;
earbuds included

Manufacturer/model: RadioShack®/
SAME Weather Radio
Price: $$$
Weight: Contact manufacturer
Power source: 4 AA batteries
Tuning: Digital FM/AM radio with
7-channel weather
Other Features: Built-in alarm clock;
LCD display with touch panel;
pre-loaded FIPS codes by state and
county; selectable trilingual (English/
French/Spanish) system messages
display; signal loss and missed alert
reminder; LCD backlight and low-
battery indicator

Manufacturer/model: Uniden/Bearcat 40 Channel CB Radio
Price: $$$$
Weight: 5 lbs.
Power source: Transmission wattage-4 watts
Tuning: NOAA Weather Weather Alert; instant channel 9/19
Other Features: built-in SWR for perfect antenna matching, tone control for best sound, noise-cancelling microphone, mic gain adjust, RF gain adjust, automatic noise limiter and noise blanker for clearest reception

Manufacturer/model: Midland/75-822 Portable/mobile CB radio
Price: $$$$
Weight: Contact manufacturer
Power source: 4Watt output power; AC adapter; rechargeable batteries; AA Alkaline batteries
Tuning: NOAA Weather radio – access to emergency channel 9 and informational channel 19
Other Features: Backlit LCD display; last channel memory; 40-channels; flexible, removable antenna with BNC connector

Manufacturer/model: Eton/FRX5
Price: $$$$
Weight: Contact manufacturer
Power source: Rechargeable lithium battery; solar panel; hand crank power generator; 3 AAA Alkaline batteries; micro-USB cable
Tuning: AM/FM digital radio with NOAA Weather Band featuring S.A.M.E. technology
Other Features: Alarm clock; splash-proof (rating 2—fine in rain, sleet or snow but should not be submerged fully in water); smartphone or tablet charger; AUX-input; headphone jack; "alert" function – automatic broadcast of emergency weather alerts; LED flashlight; glow-in-the-dark locator; red emergency beacon; built-in, top mounted dimmable ambient light; drop-proof from a height of 3.3ft

Manufacturer/model: Eton/FRX5
Price: $$$$
Weight: Contact manufacturer
Power source: hank-crank turbine; micro-USB; rechargeable battery; 3 AAA batteries
Tuning: AM/FM/NOAA; S.A.M.E.

Other Features: LED flashlight, smart-phone charging, emergency beacon, alarm clock, dimmable ambient light

Manufacturer/model: Uniden/Solara D UM380BK Class D DSC Marine Radio
Price: $$$$
Weight: Contact manufacturer
Power source: 1 watt/25 watt transmit power
Tuning: All NOAA Weather Bands and SAME weather alert
Other Features: Waterproof, memory channel scan, backlit keypad and display, DSC

Manufacturer/model: Kaito/KA1121
Price: $$$$$
Weight: Contact manufacturer
Power source: Rechargeable batteries
Tuning: AM/FM/SW Radio with NOAA Weather Band; MP3 player included
Other Features: Recording features; play back MP3 music; Audio line-in (as an amplifier); software to program the preset stations; lyric edit program— shows the lyrics to music

CHAPTER EIGHT

Survival Knives and Cutting Tools

Knives are essential survival tools. They can be used in so many survival applications: cutting, hunting, dressing game, food preparation, making fire, self-defense, splitting/chopping, carving, building shelter, digging, and signaling just to name a few. This chapter teaches you the essential attributes of a survival knife so you can properly evaluated the suitability of any knife as a survival tool. You'll also find specs for many survival knives and an overview of the best survival knives from the annual BLADE show, the largest knife show in the world.

5 Features of the
Best Survival Knives

BY CREEK STEWART

Your survival knife is without question one of the top three most important items in your bug-out bag. (An ignition device and a metal container are the other top two.)

For many, choosing a survival knife is a very personal decision. With thousands of knives in the marketplace, the choices can be somewhat overwhelming. But remember that the best survival knife is the one that meets your individual needs.

Don't be fooled by what you see in the movies. The fancy knives seen in survival movies are more for prop collectors than for real survivalists. You don't know how much you need a good, sharp cutting tool in a survival situation until you don't have one.

I learned this firsthand on a three-day survival trip in which I was not able to bring a modern knife. I will never take my knife for granted again.

WHAT IT SHOULD DO

By design, a survival knife should be fairly simple. It should be about function not "flash." Below is a short list of tasks a survival knife should be able to assist you with:

- Cutting
- Hunting
- Dressing game
- Hammering shelter anchors
- Digging
- Self-defense
- Splitting/chopping
- Making fire
- Carving
- Signal mirror (if blade is polished steel)
- Building shelter
- Food preparation

Here are five features that are essential in a survival knife:

1. FIXED BLADE

The best survival knife in my opinion should have a fixed blade – not a folding or lockback style.

True, folding knives can be more convenient to carry, but strength is compromised at the folding joint. If the knife breaks during rigorous use, you are SOL.

If you really like folding knives, carry one as a backup, but not as your primary survival knife. I carry a Spyderco Native locking folder as my everyday carry knife and it will be my bug-out bag backup knife as well.

2. FULL TANG

The phrase "full tang" means the metal knife blade and handle are made from one solid piece of metal. The metal handle is then sandwiched with knife scales to form a grip.

The alternative to a full tang is a rat tail tang. A rat tail tang is much smaller and narrow.

A full tang blade is much more robust and stable. It can withstand incredible abuse from demanding tasks, such as splitting wood (often called "batoning" in the survival community).

3. SHARP

Your survival knife should be razor sharp. It should shave the hair off your forearm. If it doesn't, buy a whet stone and hone the blade until it does.

You should take pride in your knife's razor edge. A dull knife is more difficult and cumbersome to use effectively. It requires more effort and pressure to perform tasks, which leads to erratic carving and cutting.

Blackbird SK-5 Survival Knife

Becker BK2 Knife shown with the black nylon sheath that came with it and a custom Hedgehog Leatherworks leather sheath

A sharp knife is actually safer to use and is a more precise cutting tool that requires less energy and time as compared to using a dull knife.

4. SIZE DOES MATTER

As a rough estimate, the overall length of your knife should be in between 7"and 11". A knife that is much larger that 11" isn't practical for delicate and detailed tasks.

However, a knife smaller than 7" is less capable of performing tasks that require a larger blade, especially demanding jobs.

5. POINTED BLADE/SINGLE EDGE

Your knife needs to have a pointed blade tip. The point comes in handy for all kinds of chores.

I broke the point off of my favorite survival knife and it drastically impacted the

Gerber Big Rock Camp Knife

Mora 840MG Camp Knife

knife's effectiveness as a useful tool. I eventually had to replace it.

Also, the knife blade should not be double-sided. Choose a single-edged blade only. You won't have a need for two sharp edges. The flat back ridge of a knife blade can actually serve several functions.

Below are some of the most common:

- Striking a fire steel
- Used as a stabilizing platform for thumb or hand
- Pounding surface while splitting or "batoning" wood

The Anatomy of a
Survival Knife

BY JOHN D. MCCANN

HIGH CARBON STEEL
I prefer knives that are made from a high carbon steel, such as 1095 or 01. There are many, many quality steels when it comes to knives, but I feel that simple carbon steels work well for overall edge retention and toughness. A knife made with a high carbon steel that is fully hardened can also cast sparks with a piece of flint.

LANYARD HOLE
A hole near the butt of the knife to allow a safety cord (usually 550 paracord) that can be wrapped and secured around your wrist.

FULL TANG CONSTRUCTION
The blade and handle are made from a single piece of steel without joints or welds.

SQUARE SPINE
When the spine of the knife is square it may be used as a striker / scrapper on a ferrocium rod (aka firesteel or Mischmetal).

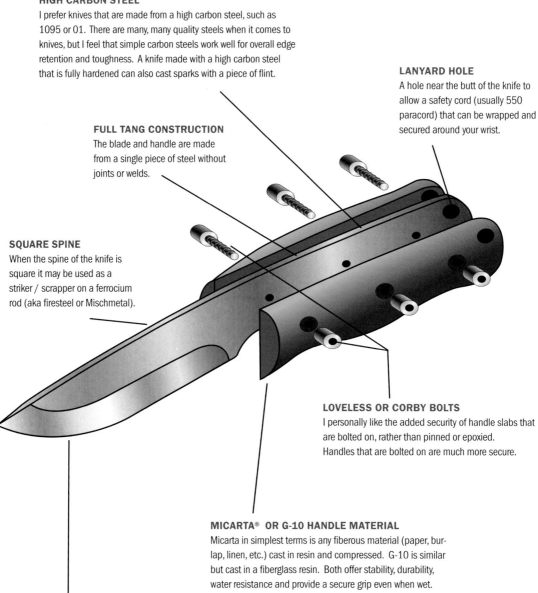

LOVELESS OR CORBY BOLTS
I personally like the added security of handle slabs that are bolted on, rather than pinned or epoxied. Handles that are bolted on are much more secure.

MICARTA® OR G-10 HANDLE MATERIAL
Micarta in simplest terms is any fiberous material (paper, burlap, linen, etc.) cast in resin and compressed. G-10 is similar but cast in a fiberglass resin. Both offer stability, durability, water resistance and provide a secure grip even when wet.

SCANDI / NORDIC GROUND EDGE
A Scandi ground edge consists of an edge with a single bevel and no secondary bevel and is the grind shown in the illustration. Other types of grinds such as convex, full flat with a secondary bevel are suitible and common grinds for a survival knife.

Illustration by: Rob L. Lyttle

Product Review
CRKT Guppie

BY STEVE SHACKLEFORD

There are plenty of multi-tools out there. The temptation is to focus on the number or kinds of features. There's plenty of value in that, but the platform those things sit on matters just as much.

Enter the patented Guppie, part of Columbia River Knife & Tool's innovative I.D. Works line of tools. Despite its "cute" appearance, designers Launce Barber and Tom Stokes created a hard-working carabiner tool with dozens of uses perfect for survival situations.

Much of that versatility comes from the adjustable wrench jaw. It opens to ½", making it ideal for all kinds of light repair and assembly jobs. That's helped by its

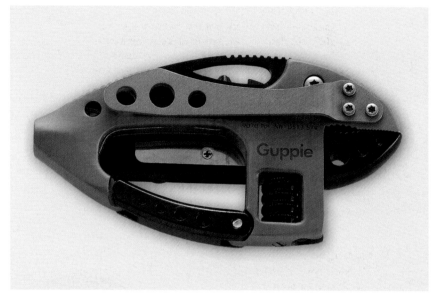

▲ CRKT Guppie

KEY POINTS

- Built on a carabiner platform
- Portable when attached to gear
- Versatile: Adjustable wrench jaw opens to ½"
- Winner: *BLADE* Magazine 2007 Best Buy of the Year

carabiner gate, which makes the Guppie easy to carry on a belt loop, D-ring, pack or rope. Keep in mind, though, it is not a weight-bearing carabiner.

Another highlight is the high-carbon, stainless steel 2" blade. It sports a Razor-Sharp edge, and can be opened or closed with one hand.

On the Guppie's left side is a removable bit carrier. It doubles as a high-intensity LED light with two strong magnets to hold it securely.

Outside of survival situations, the Guppie makes a great little money clip, too, for those who like to keep a thin wallet.

One more trick: The Guppie carabiner detent will open bottle caps and metal jar lids. (Note: Magnets may harm electronic media.)

Overall, there's a lot to like in this tool. No wonder it won the *Blade* 2007 Best Buy of the Year award.

Best Survival Knife of the BLADE Show

THE BEST BUSHCRAFT & SURVIVAL KNIVES AT THE WORLD'S LARGEST KNIFE SHOW

BY JOE KERTZMAN

With preparedness, survival and living ready at the forefront of the minds of individuals in any number of circles, it came as no surprise that bushcraft and survival knives were a hot category at the BLADE Show in Atlanta, Georgia, this past spring. For those unfamiliar, the BLADE Show (bladeshow.com) lives up to its billing as the "World's Largest Knife Show," with nearly every major knife manufacturer on the planet exhibiting annually, as well as hundreds of handmade knifemakers, dealers, collectors and purveyors.

It was a pleasure doing the footwork for Living Ready readers, visiting knife companies and choosing the best bushcraft and survival models from a wide range of knives. Following are what rose to the top as far as value, quality and practicality. For more on bushcraft and survival knives, visit blademag.com, or join the discussion forums at knifeforums.com.

SOG SPECIALTY KNIVES & TOOLS
Tangle
$80 /sogknives.com

The SOG "Tangle" integral fixed blade separates itself from the pack through simplicity of design and materials. One piece of stainless steel measures 8.75 inches from tip to handle butt. The grip is wrapped in seven feet of Paracord, proving useful unwrapped in case of an emergency.

It is lightweight, yet strong as a result of the one-piece, skeleton stainless steel handle.

The drop-point blade, with tip dropping below the center grind line, is a proven utilitarian design. The Tangle comes in a molded nylon sheath with belt loop and clip.

COLONIAL KNIFE CORP.
CE 200 Nomad
$200 /colonialknifecorp.com

Designed by Abe Elias, a teacher of survival skills, the Colonial Knife CE 200 Nomad is a no-nonsense, sturdy survival knife that looks the part in a choice of a Kydex or leather sheath. At 8.75 inches overall, it weighs 4 ounces and sports a 154CM stainless steel blade that holds an edge, yet remains relatively easy to sharpen, and a G-10 handle. It is a bushcraft and tactical blade rolled into one.

PREMIUM KNIFE SUPPLY
The Rival Knife
$225 /premiumknifesupply.com

Created as a working knife for law enforcement and military applications, and designed by Anglesey LLC, The Rival Knife has proven to be an excellent survival piece. "It weighs less than 10 ounces, and is strong enough to clear small branches, and big enough for self-defense and butchering," explains Jim Kumas of Premium Knife Supply. It is bead blasted for a non-reflective finish.

HALLMARK CUTLERY
BB0114 Jungle Commander
$62.49 /hallmarkcutlery.com

Jessica Hall of HallMark Cutlery says the non-slip Kraton handle of the Jungle Commander is engineered not to shrink or crack under extreme temperatures. She also indicates that the model is shorter than a regular machete, which gives it a heavier downward force for chopping with the 9-inch, black-coated 8Cr14 stainless steel blade. The Jungle Commander is 14.5 inches overall.

"It features a nylon sheath with MOLLE fittings, so it can easily attach to a pack or belt, and be strapped to your leg," Hall remarks. "The knife was originally designed by a former Navy SEAL for military applications, but it serves equally well in an outdoors or bush environment."

The large blade is suitable for a variety of bushcraft work. Since the handle is designed to endure extreme temperatures, it would make for a useful knife in an artic environment.

SPYDERCO, INC.
Bushcraft
$339.95 /spyderco.com

With a name like "Bushcraft," it's no secret what type of cutting chores the Spyderco knife is designed to perform—to be used for hunting, fishing, trapping, foraging, making fire, building shelter and thriving in a natural environment, according to company literature. Designed with input from Chris Claycomb and Bushcraft UK, the Spyderco Bushcraft has an O1 tool steel blade and excellent edge geometry, known as a "Scandi grind," allowing for easy sharpening in the field.

"It was designed to be used for prolonged periods of time," says Nicole Brandon of Spyderco. "The smooth, comfortable, contoured G-10 handle, complete with flush pins, palm swells and polished surfaces, makes it superior in comfort." The Bushcraft weighs 7.8 ounces and is delivered in a black leather sheath. The Bushcraft is a fine all-around choice for everyday carry in the field.

MISSION KNIVES
CSP—Chance Sanders Professional
$199.99 /missionknives.com

Urban survivalist Chance Sanders designed the CSP as an everyday-carry urban and wilderness survival blade. "The full-tang construction [with blade tang extending through and under the handle to the butt] of the CSP eliminates any possibility of failure during hard use," says Casey Hinckley of Mission Knives. "The straight back provides a reinforced tip without sacrificing blade shape."

"The robust design and construction allow the user to puncture and pry, with the blade still being effective in cleaning and skinning game," Hinckley adds. The CSP features a 4.75-inch A2 tool steel blade in a black-oxide finish, a black G-10 handle, titanium hardware and a Kydex sheath. While not stainless, tool steel is easier to sharpen in the field, but must be maintained, thus the black-oxide finish to help in rust prevention.

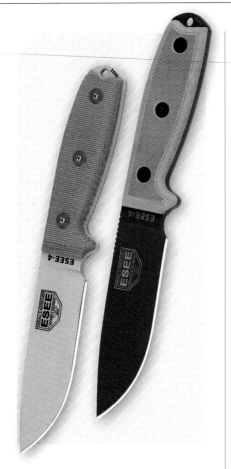

ESEE KNIVES
ESEE-4
$168 /www.eseeknives.com

Choices are good with any product, but particularly for need-specific bushcraft and survival knives. The ESEE-4 comes in a 4.1-inch, full-tang 440C stainless steel blade, or a black-coated 1095 high-carbon steel blade, in plain or semi-serrated configurations, and in a removable canvas-Micarta [thermoplastic and canvas composite] or an orange G-10 handle. Regardless of model, a rounded pommel with a lanyard hole, and a black Kydex sheath are part of the package.

"The blade is thick enough [.188"] to handle chopping through heavy wood to make feather sticks, without being too thick for tasks like cleaning game and making traps," says Patrick Rollins of ESEE Knives. "The knife is affordable for the average outdoorsman, costing a little more than the knives in 'big box stores,' but definitely worth it."

BEAR & SON CUTLERY
Bear Ops CC-600-B4-B Constant II
$130 /www.bearandsoncutlery.com or www.bearopsknives.com

The 4 1/8-inch, modified drop-point blade of the Bear Ops Constant II is fashioned from 1095 high-carbon steel, and is a solid .140" thick, bulky enough to handle tough jobs, according to company vice president Matt Griffey. He notes, "For those challenging situations you face, whether you're an adventurer in the wilderness or a law enforcement officer on the job, the strong, full-tang Constant II will handle them."

The blade comes in a choice of an uncoated or a non-reflective, black-powder-coated finish, and the handle is textured and finger-grooved G-10, a material Griffey notes is impervious to extreme hot or cold conditions. It is jump rated for the military and comes with a Kydex sheath.

SOUTHERN GRIND
Bad Monkey Folding Modified Tanto Serrated – Cerakote Armor Black
$225 /www.southerngrind.com

The Southern Grind Bad Monkey in a folding, modified-tanto blade coated in Cerakote Armor Black is an entire bushcraft and survival knife package. It opens via an Emerson Wave feature, which is a wave-looking extension over the top of the blade spine nearest the handle that can be used to catch onto a pants pocket so the blade opens while the folder is pulled from the pocket. It also includes a short pocket clip, and comes with a leather Koozie, keychain, and a black paracord bracelet.

The blade is Sandvik 14C-28N stainless steel in a conventional tanto style reminiscent of Japanese swords, but Americanized, and the handle is twill-weave carbon fiber in a textured, matte finish.

RAZOR REDUX
THE CLASSIC UTILITY RAZOR KNIFE GETS A REDESIGN

BY JAMES CARD

1. Stanley 99E Utility Knife. This utility knife is an essential tool on workbenches across America. The design is extemely simple with no frills. A simple push mechanism extends and retracts the razor blade. One screw holds the whole thing together and inside you can store more blades. It is a tough design to beat but three companies took the disposable razor knife concept and created them as folders.

2. Irwin FK 100 Folding Utility Knife. Irwin Tools created three types of folding utility razor knifes that use a locking technology to keep the blade secure. One model is a lightweight skeletonized version. Another has a compartment to hold spare blades, and the third one has a fold-out screwdriver and a space to store extra bits. All models have liner locks for quick one-handed operation and have pocket clips.

3. Piranta-EDGE by Havalon Knives. Havalon Knives produces razor blades so sharp they claim to be the "world's sharpest hunting knife." That could be heavily argued around a campfire but the blades are wickedly sharp. Think of these knives as surgical tools. If you butcher and field dress any kind of game or fish, this is the knife to use. The Piranta model is extremely lightweight and has a little nub on the blade for one-handed opening.

4. Outdoor Edge's Razor-Blaze. This knife bridges the gap between the heavy-duty Irwin and the delicate and lighweight Havalon. It is the all-around razor of the bunch. The razor locks into a metal slot that almost runs the length of the blade and that gives it more spine strength for cutting duties. The rubberized handle is a nice touch.

Folders vs. the Amazon

THE AMAZON JUNGLE OF PERU PROVED THE IDEAL TESTING GROUND FOR SIX HARD-USE FACTORY FOLDERS

BY KYLE VER STEEG II

The concept of hard-use folders is something that has developed rapidly. Sporting features like massive pivots, th▄▄▄ades, strong handles and nearl▄▄▄▄▄proof locking mechanisms, har▄▄▄ folders have started to push the boundaries of what is possible for a folding knife.

I decided to test the large blade/folding knife pairing myself on a trip to the Amazon jungle of Peru. I brought a half dozen hard-use folders and a parang-style machete I forged from a lawnmower blade.

I used each knife for about 24 hours to complete tasks like carving a spear, cleaning game, cutting rope and preparing

natural materials for making cordage. In addition, I did a few things that would be considered abuse. For instance, every knife was stuck into a tree at night. In the morning I would inspect it after the exposure to the elements. I also committed a cardinal sin and used each folder to split firewood. Do not try this at home. The knives were in and out of muddy swamp water all day long. They endured frequent rainstorms and the stifling humidity that followed.

DPX GEAR HEST 2.0

The day before I left for the jungle I received a DPx Gear HEST 2.0 folder in a left-hand-opening configuration. It came

with a tool to make adjustments, and I slightly tweaked the pivot tension. The ergonomics of the knife were the best for my hand of the folders tested. The blade arrived shaving sharp and stayed that way after much use. I liked the RotoBlock feature. When combined with the frame lock, the RotoBlock helps secure the blade in the open position. I have had the bad experience of a locking mechanism failing on a folder during use. The RotoBlock never failed and made me feel a little safer using the knife. The fit and finish were fantastic.

One feature I discovered accidentally during the trip is the groove atop the blade can be used to quickly open the knife while removing it from a pocket reminiscent of the Emerson Wave Remote Pocket Opener. I am far more likely to accidentally open the knife and injure myself than I am to actually need the feature.

I used the HEST 2.0 to prepare materials for a fire. It makes shavings and feather sticks almost as well as a blade with a Scandi grind. I found it useful in the kitchen.

THREE SISTERS FORGE BEAST
In January 2012 I bought a left-hand-opening Beast from Three Sisters Forge. My knife arrived extremely sharp and has held an edge despite daily use and abuse. I like small knives with slim profiles for daily pocket carry, so the Beast is ideal for me. The fit and finish are great and I like that the Beast is handmade by one guy in the United States.

The Beast took everything I threw at it and never exhibited any major problems in function. The blade is relatively thick for how wide from edge to spine it is, and as a result, the bevel is fairly steep. I found that it performed well on wood but not as well on slicing tasks because the blade binds a bit.

The blade is CPM-154 stainless steel. Over the course of the week it developed a small amount of surface rust. I spoke to the maker and he offered to replace the blade for free. Surface rust is not a big deal to me. A little rust and wear on a blade shows that I have used the knife.

SPYDERCO PARAMILITARY 2
I was shopping for a Spyderco Paramilitary 2 when I found a special edition with an orange handle. I favor orange-handle knives in the wilderness because the bright color makes them a lot easier to find when dropped or misplaced. The Paramilitary 2 has screw holes so you can attach the pocket clip in any of four positions. I try to buy left-hand-opening knives and I will not buy one that I cannot convert.

One feature I really liked about the Paramilitary 2 is the blade thickness and

From top: A parang the author forged from a lawnmower blade, the Zero Tolerance 0200, DPx Gear HEST 2.0, Spyderco Paramilitary 2, Ontario RAT 1, Three Sisters Forge Beast and a Benchmade 275 Adamas.

The Three Sisters Forge Beast developed a small amount of surface rust but proved to be an excellent performer.

The Ontario RAT 1 made short work of fashioning a fishing spear.

geometry. It achieves what I consider to be the perfect balance between sturdiness and usability. The Paramilitary 2 and the RAT 1 were the best of the knives at cleaning fish and slicing tasks.

My knife weighs only 3.9 ounces. The fact it is lightweight combined with a slim profile makes the Paramilitary 2 comfortable to carry. Despite being a large folder, it handles like a much smaller knife. Part of the weight reduction comes from using thin, embedded stainless steel liners within a G-10 handle. There were absolutely no problems with the Paramilitary 2, but I wonder about the thinness of the liners and handle scales.

ZERO TOLERANCE 0200
I used the Zero Tolerance 0200 a lot prior to the trip but was able to employ it only for a few hours in the jungle. I lost my passport in Iquitos. I gave the 0200 to a Peruvian Special Forces soldier who was instrumental in arranging the document I needed to fly to the U.S. Embassy in Lima. He came along to the jungle and used the knife every day, employing it to make a spear for caiman, to clean fish and to make natural cordage. He loved the knife and was grateful to receive it.

Like the soldier, I found the 0200 to be a good wood carver. It also did well in the kitchen and cleaning fish. He com-

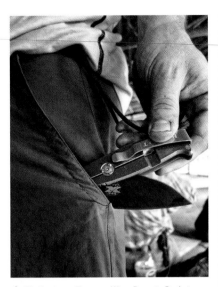

Similar to an Emerson Wave Remote Pocket Opener, the notch atop the HEST 2.0 blade can be used to quickly open the blade by purposely catching it on a pants pocket.

mented frequently about how sharp the 0200 remained throughout the tasks.

The ergonomics of the handle are good overall. One small problem I encountered was that my index finger rubbed against the flipper with the blade open. The flipper incorporates a finger groove at the front of the handle but it sweeps too far backward for my hand.

BENCHMADE 275 ADAMAS

The 275 Adamas did not disappoint. My favorite feature of the Adamas is the Axis Lock. It felt perfectly secure and never failed during use. If you pull back on the Axis Lock with the knife closed you can flip the blade open.

I used the Adamas more than any of the other knives for firewood prep. I could have used the machete to split the wood but I wanted to see if the folders could be carefully used without breaking or failing. The Adamas split a lot of wood and never had a single problem. The blade stayed

nice and sharp. The handle is comfortable. The only thing I would change is to round the top and bottom of the scales more instead of using flat slabs.

ONTARIO RAT 1

The best feature of the RAT 1 is the price. I bought mine for about $30. It is hard to argue that a $300 knife is better than a $30 knife when I can replace the RAT 1 10 times for the cost of a $300 knife. The RAT 1 is eminently comfortable to carry and use. The thickness of the blade is just about right for my tastes. Most of the tasks I use a knife for in the wilderness are of the slicing variety and the RAT 1 excels at slicing.

It performed well during my testing. The only problem the RAT 1 developed was a small amount of blade play at the pivot. Though it doesn't have the fit and finish of the other knives tested, it is nonetheless a good value if you are looking for a hard-use folder.

JUNGLE BLADE

BY JAMES CARD

Yea, though I walk through the valley of the swamp, I will fear no evil: for the Rodent Rucki is with me.

Machetes are the jungle standard and there are many variations of them. They are choppers and whackers but they give up nimbleness. Enter the Rodent Rucki by Swamp Rat Knife Works. It has the chopping and slashing power of a machete but with the feel of a well-balanced Japanese sword. It is based on a wakizashi design—the sword worn by samurai warriors as a back-up companion to their larger katana.

Essentially the Rodent Rucki is an Americanized version of the wakizashi: it is a unadorned utilitarian tool for heavy-duty use as opposed to a real made-in-Japan wakizashi which can cost thousands of dollars—not something you want to use for gritty bushcraft work. The Rucki can function like a machete for cutting, hacking and chopping duties but with the two-handed grip, it can also function as a pigsticker, snake stabber or as a formidable blade for self-defense.

SPECIFICATIONS
Overall Length: 25 ¼"
Blade Length: 15 ¼"
Thickness: ³⁄₁₆"
Blade Width: Approx. 1 ½"
Steel: SR-101 / 58-60 Rc
Blade Finish Options: Black, Desert Sage, Tanker Grey, Muddy Brown, Moss Green, Arctic White
Standard Handle Options: Black Canvas, Tan Canvas, Black Paper
G-10 Handles: Black, Red & Black, Blue & Black, Green & Black, Orange & Black, Tan and Black
MSRP: Starting at $298.95
Available: swampratknifeworks.com

Cutting Tools

KEEP A BLADE HANDY

BY STEPHEN GARGER

The idea of our car crashing into the water and sinking truly scares my wife. She fears the possibility similarly to the way a person afraid of flying worries the plane will crash. I had known of her concerns for some time but, when I saw her white knuckling the steering wheel while driving on a bridge over a lake in northern Idaho, it finally occurred to me to do something to ease her anxiety. After thinking about such things as the position in which the car could end up, potential injuries, water everywhere and the overall impact of the crash, I found the solution in knifemaker Bud Nealy's MCS II (for Multi-Carry System). Part of the MCS II is a strong adhesive material and

a sort of super fabric fastener, which can be used to firmly attach the Kydex sheath just about anywhere and in any position. I went through the vehicle and finally found a spot on the lower plastic part of the front driver's seat where I could reach the knife easily with either hand. The location also was situated so the knife could not be seen from the outside with the driver's door open during a rest or gasoline stop.

Jeff Hall of Nemesis Knives approached the idea of knives in unusual and easy reach from the point-of-view of where the knife replaces a firearm for home defense.

"Anywhere people would hide a gun they may hide a knife instead," said Hall. "Nobody's breaking any laws, and people uncomfortable with guns will have knives around the house—even the anti-gunners will have a knife. People keep knives in their refrigerator, in the bathroom behind the toilet, and hanging from the door knob or above the front door frame, since you don't always know who's at the door," Hall said. "I've also heard of knives between the bed linens, attached behind the TV, as well as between the cushions of the couch," said Hall.

▲ Tops Silver Bullet
The knife has a magnetic sheath to put it in those special "I-didn't-figure-to-find-a-knife-there" places, such as stuck to a refrigerator door. Blade steel: 154CM stainless. Blade length: 2 inches. The Micarta sheath is hollowed out in the shape of the blade profile so the blade fits down into it to protect the edge. MSRP: $99.

▲ The Hellion
Made by Nemesis Knives it sports a 1 ⅝-inch blade of VG-10 stainless and a Kydex® sheath with a bead chain and accessories. MSRP: $40.

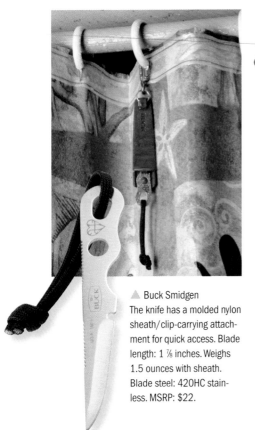

▲ Buck Smidgen
The knife has a molded nylon sheath/clip-carrying attachment for quick access. Blade length: 1 ⅞ inches. Weighs 1.5 ounces with sheath. Blade steel: 420HC stainless. MSRP: $22.

▲ Pro-Lite Pesh Kabz
The Kydex® dual-lock sheath of Bud Nealy's Pro-Lite Pesh Kabz has a strong adhesive material and a super fabric fastener, which can be used to attach it just about anywhere. Blade steel: CTS-XHP Grip/guard: G-10. Maker's list price: $199.

Notes on Neck Knives

BY STEPHEN GARGER

"When neck knives are designed and made properly, they will be minimal in size, yet easy and comfortable to use. They will be light enough around the neck to not be bothersome or noticeable and will be held safely and securely upside down in the sheath, but can be drawn and put into action with a minimum of effort," said master bladesmith Murray Carter. He knows a thing or two about neck knives since he forges nearly 40 varieties.

Given today's available neck knife choices, opting to wear one involves making decisions that include purpose, size, materials, design, or just about anything else you would consider when choosing a fixed blade, with the provision that the overall length will be naturally limited. I have worn a necker regularly for some time in perhaps the most common form—handle down in a Kydex sheath. It is easy enough to access under a shirt with the button closest to the handle open, though I exercise great care returning the blade to the sheath for reasons equally divided between my intense dislike of pain and a deep fear of embarrassment were I to stab myself in the chest. Along with using caution in re-sheathing, it is also important to remember a general rule of thumb: Any fixed blade may be considered "concealed" for legal purposes, so it is good to be familiar with pertinent state and local regulations.

Boker Plus Gnome
The full-tang design is 4 inches overall, which is somewhat smaller than most neck knives, and the 2 ⅛-inch blade of 12C27 stainless steel is relatively thin to enhance cutting ability. The Micarta handle is equipped with a hole for a lanyard. The knife also is available in a stag handle, and comes with a leather belt sheath.

CRKT Minimalist Tanto
An Alan Folts design, the Columbia River Knife & Tool Minimalist Tanto features a 2.125-inch blade of 5Cr15MoV stainless with a Rockwell hardness of 55-57 HRC. Weight: 1.6 ounces. Overall length: 5.13 inches. MSRP: $34.99

Ontario Ranger Neck Knife
Designed by Justin Gingrich, the Ontario Ranger Neck Knife has a 2.75-inch blade of 440 stainless with a brushed finish. Rockwell hardness: 54-56 HRC. Weight: 3 ounces. Overall length: 7 inches. Sheath: Kydex.

Nuclear Meltdown Fusion Battle Mistress. A knife for going to hell and back. Blade Length: 11.25 inches. Blade Stock: .270 inch.

The Busse Combat Knife Company

BY JAMES M. AYRES

A few years ago my son and I cut through an auto body with a Busse Steel Heart. There was no damage to the blade and it retained a usable edge afterward. Over a period of a few weeks we used the Steel Heart on about anything for which a big knife is suited. It was tough. It cut well. That was then. Do today's Busse knives perform as well? We aimed to find out.

Recently we tested four new Busse knives. In our review, we cut through heavy sheet metal or steel doors and auto bodies, drove blades into trees or wedged them between rocks, stone blocks or whatever is handy, and used them as climbing aids and self-arresting devices. The need for a knife that will bear the owner's

weight in an emergency is desirable. We use this test with a large measure of caution and consideration for the designed function of the knife. It is unreasonable to expect a Swiss Army knife to support the weight of a 270-pound linebacker, but it is well within reason to expect a survival/hard-use knife to support the weight of a 175-pound person.

We did all these things with the four Busse test knives. Moreover, we used all of them to cut roasts and ribs, a pile of cardboard, and 20 yards of hemp rope. We encountered one problem with the Busse knives: all of them performed so well the whole thing got kind of boring. Set up the object to be cut, apply edge to object,

object is cut. Denim, rubber sneaker soles, pork rib bones, tri-tip roasts, and stacks of wood fell to the Busse edge. The mid-sized, colorfully named Nuclear Meltdown Special Forces Natural Outlaw easily supported the weight of a 235-pound reviewer. During this field review we found the Busse knives perform at the top of their class in each size range. The slab handles are reasonably comfortable, if not totally ergonomic. The blades cut efficiently. They showed no signs of damage in extreme use. In sum, the big Busse knives chopped better than the little ones, and the latter were handier for whittling. All shared similar performance characteristics.

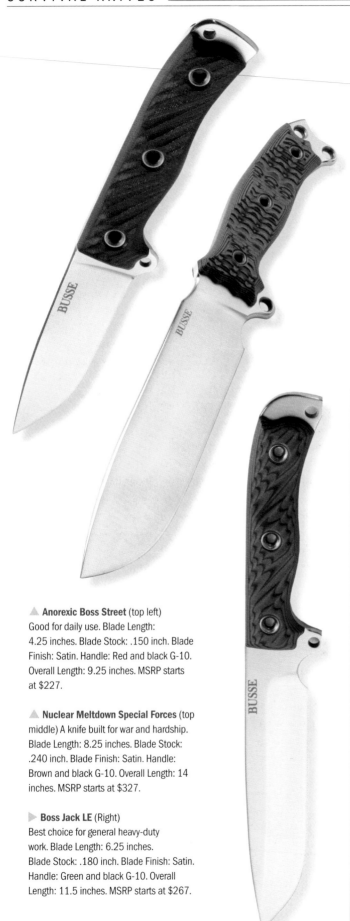

▲ The author's Gene Baskett Super Bolo boasts a 12 ⅛-inch blade of CPM-154 stainless with an extremely tough Moly Coat finish, and a horse-stall-mat rubber handle. The Moly Coat is by Richardson Gunsmithing. Overall length: 17 ⅝ inches. It comes with a Kydex® sheath.

▲ **Anorexic Boss Street** (top left) Good for daily use. Blade Length: 4.25 inches. Blade Stock: .150 inch. Blade Finish: Satin. Handle: Red and black G-10. Overall Length: 9.25 inches. MSRP starts at $227.

▲ **Nuclear Meltdown Special Forces** (top middle) A knife built for war and hardship. Blade Length: 8.25 inches. Blade Stock: .240 inch. Blade Finish: Satin. Handle: Brown and black G-10. Overall Length: 14 inches. MSRP starts at $327.

▶ **Boss Jack LE** (Right) Best choice for general heavy-duty work. Blade Length: 6.25 inches. Blade Stock: .180 inch. Blade Finish: Satin. Handle: Green and black G-10. Overall Length: 11.5 inches. MSRP starts at $267.

A Love Affair with Bolos

BY STEVE WATKINS

Operating as a Navy SEAL from 1988 to 1993 provided me with countless discussions of knives and guns. As basic tools of the trade, knives served various SEAL functions. One unforgettable experience involving knives happened in the Philippines.

Serving with my first SEAL platoon—Charlie Platoon, SEAL Team Five—I was introduced to the bolo. A veteran SEAL encouraged me to buy one of the inexpensive knives as he said it would serve multiple purposes in the triple-canopy jungle.

The bolo is a thick-blade machete Filipinos have used for a very long time. Made by Negrito natives, the knife is known to be durable and sharp. It has been an essential tool for jungle applications for over a century. Bolo is a general term referring to a heavy, machete-style knife with numerous stylistic nuances. The weight and design of the blade make it perfect for slashing through dense jungle. Philippine bolos were and still are often made from the leaf springs of discarded heavy trucks. Used throughout the Philippines and Indonesia, the bolo is somewhat analogous to the Nepalese kukri and, to some degree, the pha-huatad of Thailand. While the kukri is legendary for its ability to lop heavy vegetation, I have found the bolo an equal match for such tasks.

One of the most impressive displays of the bolo's versatility took place at a jungle survival course on the old Subic Bay Naval Base, now the Subic Bay Freeport Zone, in Olongapo, Zambales, Philippines. Jungle escape and survival training (JEST) was a weeklong immersion into various jungle survival techniques. The knowledgeable Negritos pointed out edible plants as well as those to avoid. They demonstrated such tasks as making fire using only bamboo, and constructing a rice cooker out of 4-to-6 inch bamboo sections. The common denominator in all the demonstrations was the use of the bolo.

In 1992, my third SEAL platoon traveled to Malaysia to cross train with the Malaysian Special Forces. The dense Malaysian jungle was among the harshest I had ever encountered. The Malaysian soldiers demonstrated many techniques specific to that environment. One such demonstration was the killing and cooking of an enormous monitor lizard. In most all the exhibitions by the Malaysian soldiers, one knife emerged—the bolo. I was especially impressed when one soldier, who had been born and raised in the jungles of Borneo, cut down a palm tree and extracted and cooked the palm heart over an open fire. From start to finish, he used nothing but a bolo. The palm heart was delicious, by the way.

Nearly 20 years later and with my original bolo in disrepair, I thought it time to replace it with an updated and more technologically sophisticated design. My goal was to find a knifemaker from my home state of Kentucky who would be capable and willing to collaborate on the project. It was not long before several members of the Knifemakers' Guild recommended Gene Baskett (www.baskettknives.com). A Guild member since 1981, Gene has proved to be one of Kentucky's finest custom knifemakers and has earned the respect of his peers for the quality work he produces.

He and I based the knife's design on the old bolo I had used when I served in the SEALs. Our decision was to go with CPM-154 stainless steel, and Gene made several blade adjustments. We experimented with a rubber handle made from extremely durable horse matting material—a perfect Bluegrass State touch, and a substance also favored by a number of makers and contestants in the cutting competitions. The resulting grip is firm yet shock absorbing. The handle can also be securely grasped when wet. My concerns were simple: durability and performance. I wanted a knife that would withstand a heavy amount of punishment and still perform well.

Both Gene and I agree that the knife has exceeded our expectations. Its cutting ability is just plain scary. Without honing the original edge applied by Gene, I put the knife to the test. He already had whacked through 1-inch saplings, and still the blade was gliding through blades of grass and straw. My test consisted of saplings, 1-inch tree branches and wild

The author somewhere in the Philippines in 1992. Note the handle of his old sheathed bolo just to the left of his right shoulder on his pack. The firearm is a Heckler & Koch MP5 9mm. (photo courtesy of Steve Watkins)

grape vines. All were easily severed with one clean hit.

After 20-to-30 strikes on branches and vines, I moved on to a grass mat wrap 4 inches in diameter. The grass mat was wrapped tightly around a 1-inch piece of dried bamboo. One diagonal strike went completely through. I finished the test with a piece of quarter-inch tanned cowhide. With only slight pressure, the bolo sank through the hide from tip to handle. Drawing the blade out and away left a clean, effortless cut through 8 inches of hide. The blade was still quite sharp afterward.

Our completed knife has an extremely tough Moly Coat finish and is paired with a Kydex sheath. The bolo is both tactical and durable. In the unthinkable scenario of being banished to the wilds and given only one knife to take with me, this would be it. It is capable of building a shelter, hunting and serving as a self-defense weapon. Gene's expertise and craftsmanship, coupled with the finest materials and technologies for knifemaking, has produced a nearly indestructible product: the Super Bolo.

THE BOLO AS A SPEAR

At least one advantage the Baskett bolo has over the kukri and pha-huatad is its pointed leading edge. You can use the bolo as a spear if necessary. The knife contains rivets, which provide holes through the handle. The holes enable you to lash the knife to a longer staff. This would provide a frontward stabbing potential for the bolo that pha-huatad would be incapable of and awkward for the kukri.

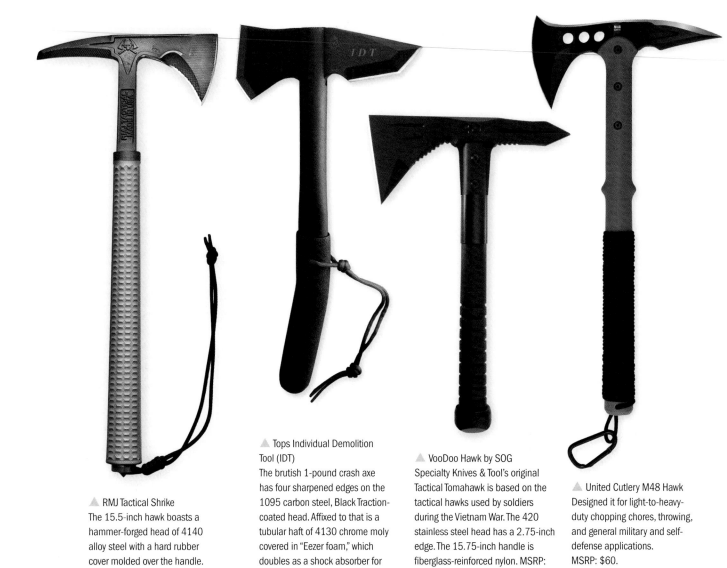

▲ RMJ Tactical Shrike
The 15.5-inch hawk boasts a
hammer-forged head of 4140
alloy steel with a hard rubber
cover molded over the handle.
Weight: 27 ounces. MSRP: $395.

▲ Tops Individual Demolition
Tool (IDT)
The brutish 1-pound crash axe
has four sharpened edges on the
1095 carbon steel, Black Traction-
coated head. Affixed to that is a
tubular haft of 4130 chrome moly
covered in "Eezer foam," which
doubles as a shock absorber for
the user. MSRP: $175.95.

▲ VooDoo Hawk by SOG
Specialty Knives & Tool's original
Tactical Tomahawk is based on the
tactical hawks used by soldiers
during the Vietnam War. The 420
stainless steel head has a 2.75-inch
edge. The 15.75-inch handle is
fiberglass-reinforced nylon. MSRP:
$64.24 and $50.

▲ United Cutlery M48 Hawk
Designed it for light-to-heavy-
duty chopping chores, throwing,
and general military and self-
defense applications.
MSRP: $60.

Classic Design: Tomahawks

BY DAVE RHEA

Owner of RMJ Tactical, Ryan Johnson builds modern tomahawks used in the field by soldiers who need absolute reliability and durability. He is a student of tomahawk history, having appeared on an episode about axes on the History Channel's "Modern Marvels," as well as creating his own high-end, period-accurate reproductions. "I was originally tasked in 2001 to design and build a tactical tomahawk for members of the special operations

community," said Johnson. "The design was to be based on a French and Indian War-era spike tomahawk." However, Johnson said eventually it dawned on him his customers were not interested in the hawk being historically accurate but rather in it providing superior performance. "With this in mind I took the aspects of the historical design that made it work well and scrapped the rest, rethinking how the design could be improved." Johnson

added that when he designs a tomahawk, breaching and ease of carry are his two main concerns. "Yes, one of our hawks will still punch through body armor," he said. "But more importantly, it will pop a Master Lock in 10 seconds, rake and break glass, puncture tires, cut through sheet metal, break chain—and do all this in a small footprint that's easy to carry and lightweight."

What to Know When You Carry a Knife

SINCE THE STONE AGE, THE KNIFE HAS HELPED MANKIND TO SURVIVE FOR CENTURIES. NOW SOME STATE AND LOCAL GOVERNMENTS WANT TO PREVENT YOU FROM CARRYING THE ULTIMATE PREPAREDNESS TOOL.

BY MIKE HASKEW

When carrying a knife, you must know what's legal and what's not, how to reply when a law enforcement official asks why you carry a knife, and other important considerations. Such knowledge can keep you from being arrested, paying a fine, serving a jail sentence or worse.

In your hometown, or in any jurisdiction for that matter, it pays to be familiar with local laws regulating the length of the blade, overall length, opening and closing mechanisms, methods of carry, and more. Understanding the basic knife laws in any location can prevent major headaches and unintended consequences.

The most readily accessible source for information on local knife laws is the Internet, where the websites of state legislatures are searchable. Federal law is searchable as well; however, it focuses mostly on interstate commerce. Generally, beware of legal interpretations of such items as "illegal" knives, automatics, bowies, daggers, gravity knives, ballistic knives, shurikens (throwing stars) and butterfly knives/balisongs, among others. The websites of the American Knife & Tool Institute (AKTI) and Knife Rights provide advice on dealing with knife laws and their enforcement.

Even then, the possibility of an encounter with law enforcement officers is ever present. Know and understand the law. Then, remember that appropriate conduct, or knife etiquette, is essential.

"A knife owner needs to be polite and respectful when carrying a knife in public," advised AKTI Executive Director Jan Billeb. "Avoid any unnecessary flourishing movements or anything that could be misconceived as 'brandishing.' Don't start demonstrating how quickly you can open your knife."

Billeb says that maintaining a respectful attitude toward law enforcement personnel is the key to avoiding an unfortunate situation. "You need to understand the law and know whether open carry is legal or not, and if a pocket clip showing is considered open carry where you are or will be traveling," she added. "If you are arrested for carrying an 'illegal weapon,' it's best not to argue with or try to persuade a law enforcement officer. It's in your best interests to say nothing and ask for an attorney."

Evan Nappen, an attorney who specializes in gun and knife law, has written extensively regarding knife laws while practicing criminal defense for 26 years. He suggests avoiding the obvious conduct that could prompt an inquiry from law enforcement.

"Unless you are absolutely certain about the law, be discreet," he offered. "Do not use a pocket clip. That is the number one trigger to be searched for a knife, and it's

▲ When you carry a knife, attorney Dan Lawson said one with a blade less than 2.5 inches long will be legal in many, though not all, jurisdictions. A 1 ⅞-inch blade of 420HC stainless and a glass-reinforced-nylon handle top off the Buck Nano Bantam Viper. MSRP: $22.

in plain view. The clip means that you have a knife, and an officer will use that as probable cause. Depending on the circumstances, he may assert that just seeing the clip is enough. The universal belief that there's any comprehensive blade-length law is a myth, and three inches is an arbitrary number. Actually, the blade-inch-length number varies. It depends on the jurisdiction."

5 KEYS TO KNIFE CARRY

1. Be polite and respectful when carrying a knife.
2. Avoid unnecessary flipping/quick opening of folders in public.
3. Don't wear a pocket clip in New York City.
4. Carry a knife that does not leave an imprint on the outside of your pocket.
5. The less aggressive the knife—in other words, the more it looks like something your grandfather carried—the better.

TOOL, NOT A WEAPON

The dialogue between an individual and a questioning police officer often leads to the purpose of the knife being carried. When the topic comes up, the appropriate response to the question "Why are you carrying a knife?" depends on just how assertive either party becomes during the encounter. Nappen advises against trying to prove that you are smarter than the officer, antagonizing him or her, and risking "contempt of cop."

Doug Ritter of Knife Rights advocates a forthright answer. "If they take notice of a knife you have and ask why you're carrying it, the only safe answer is to say because it is a tool," he advised. "Saying that it's for self-defense is problematic in some jurisdictions, and that's absurd despite the provisions of the Second Amendment. Carrying a knife for self-defense can get you in trouble, particularly in urban areas. Billeb agreed, adding, "If stopped by a law enforcement officer, you don't have to answer any questions, and you do not have to consent to a search without a warrant."

Varying knife laws compound the difficulty for a knife-carrying individual to actually comply, especially when traveling. According to Ritter, in New York City a knife clipped to a pocket is a violation of city code, which actually requires that any knife being carried must be concealed.

"The reality is that each individual must make a choice about what they're comfortable with, and a 3-inch blade may not be legal in some areas," Ritter continued. "Most of us don't go looking for difficult

MYTH

There is no such thing as an always-legal blade length; the law varies by jurisdiction. While 2.5 inches or less generally is within the parameters of blade-length limits of most jurisdictions, there no doubt are exceptions.

Blade-length limits vary from jurisdiction to jurisdiction. When measuring, measure the blade from where it meets the handle to the blade tip. If you must err, err on the long side rather than the short.

If asked, always say you carry a knife because it's a tool for opening boxes, envelopes, etc. Never say it's for self-defense or is a weapon.

circumstances and couldn't see ourselves in such a situation because we are law-abiding citizens. In most circumstances with a typical folding knife, the best way not to come to the attention of the authorities is to have the knife completely sealed so it doesn't make an imprint on the outside of the pocket. The smaller and less-aggressive looking the knife is, the less likely you will have a problem unless a cop is looking for an excuse—and then too often it doesn't matter what the law says."

Carrying a knife does require the owner to do a little expecting of the unexpected. While profiling is considered a "politically incorrect" term by many, the fact remains it does occur. Despite freedom of expression, those who carry knives and choose to dress a certain way or behave in a certain manner are more likely to attract the attention of law enforcement. That's life. If such an encounter occurs, knowledge is power.

THE TERRY STOP

Attorney Dan Lawson of Pittsburgh, Pennsylvania, warns of the prospect of an encounter referred to as a Terry Stop. In such a situation, a law enforcement officer may detain an individual on suspicion that the person is involved in criminal activity or that a crime is being, is about to be, or has been committed. The officer is allowed by law to conduct a limited search of a person's outer garments if possession of a weapon is suspected. Such a search is commonly known as a "stop and frisk."

In reference to the New York City pocket-clip law, Lawson commented, "In most cases this does not appear to be a Terry situation. If the officer asks to see your knife, I don't think you have to show it to him if there is no probable cause. The only place the pocket clip search is happening is New York City. The Terry Stop happens if an officer observes unusual conduct and concludes that criminal

activity is afoot. Then they can search your outer clothing."

Carrying a knife requires responsibility and an understanding that the possibility of an encounter with law enforcement exists at any time. "Law enforcement officers have a tough job to do," Nappen observed. "Have the mindset that you are carrying a knife that could be construed as a weapon. People often forget that if they use a knife for deadly force, it's the same as using a gun. Deadly force is deadly force. The laws of self-defense apply to your knife the same way as a gun because a knife can inflict bodily harm or death just like a gun. Viewing your knife as a tool is fine, but if it ends up in a circumstance as a weapon because it's used in self-defense, then be sure you know the laws of self-defense."

UNIVERSALLY LEGAL?

For those interested in carrying a knife that is universally legal, the task is difficult. However, Lawson's experience sets some parameters.

"I do believe that if one wants a knife that will be legal in almost all situations, the maximum blade length should be 2.5 inches," he remarked. "A slip-joint design is going to be less likely to cause alarm on the part of law enforcement than a framelock with a blade of equal length. The same applies to a blackened blade as opposed to a polished one, or jigged-bone handle slabs as opposed to green canvas Micarta."

Knife carriers beware. The more your knife looks like something your grandfather carried, Lawson concluded, the less likely it will offend the sensibilities of a police officer, judge or jury. Use common sense and keep your knife and knowledge of knife laws sharp.

CHAPTER NINE

Survival Guns

Guns are practical self-defense tools to include in a preparedness plan. They can also be used for hunting to help supplement your emergency food supply following a long-term disaster.

This chapter explains the essential attributes of a survival gun. It details attributes of revolvers, shotguns, and air rifles. Plus it also includes profiles of guns you can choose to include in your bug-out bag and instructions on how to chose the best gun for concealed carry. Plus you'll find ammo storage tips to help you build your stockpile.

▲ Wagner with the Ithaca 37 Defense pump-action shotgun. Rifled slugs are in the carrier on the stock.

Six Essential Attributes of Survival Guns

BY SCOTT W. WAGNER

1. RELIABILITY

To put it succinctly, your tactical preparation guns must, I repeat must, be absolutely drop-dead reliable. Every time you pull the trigger, you must get the proper bang with the appropriate projectiles leaving the muzzle. Reliable right out of the box the gun came in is best. I don't like guns that take a relatively long break-in period before they can be considered reliable. In this age of CNC machining and with the modern materials that are available, I don't feel there's a lot of legitimate excuse for break-in periods. Give me a weapon that runs flawlessly, right from the box, without doing anything to it. I don't care how trendy or popular the gun is in whatever circle or how much of a status symbol it may be to own, neither is of value for this purpose. If you have to make an emergency evacuation, who are you going to get to fix that fancy (or extremely inexpensive) gun when it goes down? It isn't likely there will be a gun-smith in the crowd of angry, dangerous people attempting to surround you and your family who will volunteer to fix your weapon so that you can go ahead and defend yourself with it.

2. RUGGEDNESS

Your preparation gun needs to be able to take a beating without functional damage, especially guns intended for evacuation or travel. They need to hold up to lowered levels of maintenance by you, because, unlike our military, you won't have an unlimited supply line from a rear echelon to keep you and your gear up and running. Your weapon choices should not be a type that will require replacement parts like new springs every few thousand rounds or other specialized service for the duration of the conditions.

3. PORTABILITY

When I talk about survival conditions, I don't mean conditions one might encounter on a weekend Audubon Society bird-watching hike. I am taking about dirty, dangerous, painfully brutal conditions, conditions where you will be short of food, water, and medical supplies because of limited carry capacity. Too, you may be injured or ill.

I will be 55 later this year. While I feel I am still in good shape, carrying heavy things around on foot over long distances in terrible conditions doesn't appeal to me much anymore. So, do you think I'm going to want to lug around a fancy, piston-driven, heavy-barreled M4-type carbine with its acres of Picatinny rail and every accessory under the sun mounted on it for hours per day, maybe for multiple days? How about the excellent and capable Springfield Armory M1A SOCOM II, which weighs in at 10 pounds without anything attached to the rails? You think you can handle it now, sitting there reading this from the comfort of your armchair, but check with me after a day or two of dragging around these kinds of guns under the conditions I'm describing.

4. SIMPLICITY

The tactical preparation gun needs to be simple to operate in all facets, including loading, clearing, making safe, and firing. This is especially important in terms of getting the weapon to run from an empty and unloaded state, if that's how it's stored. Is there anything in the "make ready" process that you'll easily screw up? There is always something that someone can mess up, but let's choose a system that keeps that potential to a minimum.

So, how quickly can you go from empty to boom without injuring yourself or someone else? For me, simplicity also means you aren't hanging bucketfuls of equipment from your tactical preparation firearm. That includes flashlights and most electronic sights. I know I'll catch flack over that statement, but I think that the K.I.S.S. principle reigns supreme here. The more electronic equipment you have on your weapon to rely on, the more likely it is to break under extreme conditions. Yes, I know we use these items on S.W.A.T., and the military makes extensive use of these items in combat, but both

those circumstances are supported circumstances. You won't be supported in the same way. Your supplies will be finite, and unlike S.W.A.T., your weapons will be in use constantly (even in terms of just being carried). How many different types of batteries do you want stored at your home or lug around during travel? How much benefit do you really get from that red dot sight?

Don't get me wrong, during normal societal conditions for law enforcement or civilian use and where resupply is not a problem, add whatever additional pieces of equipment you feel you need. But weap-

▲ The Marlin Model 1894C lever-action rifle and the Mossberg 590A1 pump-action shotgun are good for travel in areas where semi-auto firearms may not be welcome because of local laws.

ons selected for use in conditions of complete societal disruption should be capable of being brought to ready instantly, with minimum action needed on the part of the operator. There should be no knobs to fool with, buttons to push, systems to check, or batteries to test. This is the same principle I use when it comes to recommending police patrol rifles and shotguns for department-wide issue. The guns stay in their basic iron sight format. No electronics are allowed unless the weapon is personally owned and departmentally approved. This way the individual officers not only can decide what and how many accessories they feel will be beneficial to them, but how much additional gear they want to be responsible for. Want this in simpler terms? Your survival gun, unless it is for shelter-in-place long-range preci-

sion, should be one you would be able to bury in the ground (in a protective container, of course), come back to months later, dig up, and be able to fire without failure.

5. EFFECTIVENESS

Survival guns must be effective in terms of completing the task assigned to them. This means that you can only evaluate a particular weapon based upon what it is designed to do in order to judge effectiveness. For example, the 5.56mm AR-15 and its variants work very well for a number of tactical purposes. In terms of dealing with single or multiple aggressors within 300 meters, it is generally very effective. However, if a 5.56mm AR is the weapon you choose to take with you for protection against grizzly bears in the wilds of Alaska,

then its effectiveness rating, and your I.Q., would be very low. If your primary mission is to address single/multiple human threats at ranges within 300 meters, there are a number of possible weapons choices for this purpose. Of course, some choices will be better than others, and there are also weapons that may be selected for this purpose that are totally unsuitable, and that's what we are trying to avoid. Effectiveness in terms of a survival firearm used for defensive/assault purposes includes its potential ability to hold off, stop, or turn away large masses of people.

Some weapons are extremely effective in stopping single offenders, due to the amount of destructive energy each particular round puts out, but, due to lower ammunition capacities, would not be effective in dealing with larger groups of

THE LAYERED DEFENSE

Layering your defense is a basic principle as old as armed combat itself. It simply means that, ideally, we have different weapons that are particularly effective for different distances. This is likely of greatest importance as you set up your plan for long-term sheltering-in-place. If you are going the emergency evacuation route instead, it will mean that you have fewer specialized weapons that you will need to make work in a wider variety of circumstances, unless you have an exceptional transportation system. Ideally, the weapons selected should cover these basic ranges/conditions:

LONG-RANGE

While our modern military snipers are getting kills out to 2,000 yards or so, this is performance reserved for a few highly trained and exceptional individuals with very specialized rifles, mostly bolt guns. For the average shooter or law enforcement officer, "long range" is anything beyond 100 yards, especially when one considers we're talking about being on the "two-way range," where targets shoot back. In these situations, a semi-automatic rifle equipped with a lighted reticle variable scope of no more than 15-power works extremely well, although certain battle rifles with precision iron sights are also effective. Full-power battle cartridges on the order of .308 or .30-06 are excellent performers for this challenge.

MID-RANGE

Anything from 100 yards down to about 25 yards. Several weapon types come to mind, but basically a high-cap semi-automatic rifle of intermediate caliber reigns supreme.

CQB Close Quarter Battle, or 25 yards down to eye-gouging distance. High-cap semi-automatic rifles, shotguns, pistols, pistol-caliber carbines, and edged weapons are at the forefront here. The intermediate semi-auto rifle, especially with a bayonet affixed, is an excellent choice as well.

viduals. The lesson here is that, in order for a weapon to be effective for survival, it must have the highest magazine capacity possible.

6. SUSTAINABILITY

While shelter-in-place guns can be of a wide variety of calibers since you will have room to store plenty of ammo, any evacuation gun should be chambered for calibers commonly available and popular in any locale, in case you are forced to resupply on the move. I love the 6.8 SPC. In fact, my department sniper rifle is chambered in that caliber. But it is not the gun I am going to take with me when I evacuate, even if I had an M4 carbine chambered for it. Stick with the calibers that are popular with civilian shooters, law enforcement, and military users, where not only ammunition is more likely to be available, but also magazines for your weapons.

Find detailed survival gun information in *Gun Digest Book of Survival Guns* by Scott W. Wagner, available at www.gundigeststore.com.

assailants. For example, in the incident portrayed in the movie *Black Hawk Down*, two Delta sniper team members, SFC Randy Shugart and MSG Gary Gordon lost their lives after they volunteered to protect downed chopper pilot Michael Durant (who was later captured), from hordes of Somali assailants. At least as depicted in the motion picture, the two Delta Operators were armed with 1911 .45s as their secondary weapons, but the ammo supply for the pistols was exhausted in short order. The .45 was very effective in its basic mission of personal-defense, but not in terms of being able to hold off large masses of angry, determined indi-

What Gun is in Your Bug-Out Bag?

BY COREY GRAFF

It was to be an interesting project: Crowd-source material for a book about what everyday people put into their bug-out bags. Through Living Ready's social media network, we asked our readers what the contents of their bug-out bags looked like and their rationale for including the items that they carefully picked. The participants were asked to break down the contents into the following categories: the type of bag used, food and water; clothing, shelter and bedding; fire and lighting; first aid and hygiene; tools, communications, and protection and self-defense.

The most noteworthy lesson of the book was that everyone is different along with their needs and perceptions of just what they might actually be bugging out from. Many people were concerned about natural disasters in the area where the live. Often the bug-out bags reflected the climate where they lived. People in northern regions tended to have more to carry to ward off the colder temperatures. Just about everyone's bug-out bag contained some nifty item that most people never considered. Assembling a bug-out bag is a matter of many personal decisions that reflects your goals and plans. Here are some examples of the kinds of firearms people have picked to go with their bug-out bags.

JJ SWIONTEK

Guns of Choice: The Walther PK 380 holds nine rounds of .380 ACP in a compact package. For self-defense it's a good choice. He keeps spare mags for the Walther with 200 rounds. He also has a Springfield Armory XD-45 with spare mags that also add up to 200 rounds. The Walther is JJ's concealed-carry weapon and the XD-45 is for larger threats.

Bug-Out Bag Philosophy: "At first I focused more on self-defense than medicine. I learned from others and their ideas. I picked a 3-day weekend and turned off the power and used my bag to survive. After I found a few holes in my plan, I corrected and tried again. I found more holes, and corrected again. I feel confident that I can survive and help others if need be. My wife has her own bag, as does my son. Each is armed. My wife has more freeze-dried food than I do, and my son has more ammo."

JOHN FARKAS

Guns of Choice: The Ruger Mark II rimfire pistol holds ten rounds of .22LR and is perfect as a lightweight hunting pistol. As an added bonus, ammo is cheap and plentiful. John hopes that he will have a full-size pistol, or better yet, a rifle with him if the bag is ever needed. He keeps the Ruger in his bag as a backup.

Bug-Out Bag Philosophy: "I clean and refill my canteens every week. Clothing depends on the time of year. I try to keep this a 3-day bag. Weight is always a concern. I want to be as comfortable as possible, but still able to carry over long distances. The contents change from time to time, but these are the basics that I always keep. I take this bag with me to work and vacation (as long as I'm not flying). My wife and two children (9 and 10) each have a bag. They each contain basic clothing, canteens, food, first aid items, hygiene items, GPS radio, poncho and casualty blanket."

CURT CARLSON

Guns of Choice: It's hard to beat a bolt-action rifle for game-getting when the going gets tough. And the Winchester Model 70 is one of the best all-around rifles, especially when chambered in the common and very effective .308 Winchester round. For optics he has a 2 × 7 power Leupold scope mounted on the rifle and he uses 165-grain premium handloads for ammo.

For a sidearm he carries a .357 magnum revolver. Curt says that his .308 Winchester is plenty of gun to defeat any wild beast and certainly adept for self-defense. The .357 magnum is just big enough to take care of medium-size critters that happen to wake him.

Bug-Out Bag Philosophy: "My bug-out bag was put together over the years through many trials and errors made while hunting the high country. I tried to get it down to the basics where I could spend the night away from camp if needed. You may be miles from camp at 4:30 p.m. and the shot of a lifetime presents itself."

WILLIAM "AZBILL" JOHNSON

Guns of Choice: William's personal protection kit includes the Henry U.S. Survival AR-7, a break-down .22 rifle that holds 8 rounds — just enough for shooting some small game for supper.

The AR-7 folds up to fit inside the backpack. It is accurate, quiet and lightweight. The Taurus Judge is very effective at short range and extremely effective when loaded with 45 Long Colts or .410 shotshells. He would also carry anything he had time to grab from the gun safe.

Bug-Out Bag Philosophy: "I put my pack together based on what I'd like to have with me if for any reason I was pulled from my home and dropped in the middle of the wilderness. I set my own limits as to total weight and the amount of consumables I was willing to deal with. My limit is 20 pounds for the bag (minus the sidearm). My bag currently weighs in at 17.6 lbs. Knowing 72 hours may stretch into 72 days, I packed a minimal amount of protein bars and hunting/fishing gear instead of MREs. I also included local maps and a compass. Overall, I feel safe with what I have."

GEORGE LAWALL

Guns of Choice: George has a Browning URX .22 pistol. He says his wife is a fine shot and will bring home a squirrel or rabbit with no trouble at all. "She is a much better shot than me," George says. "I would have to carry a shotgun to hit anything. A shotgun adds weight and I don't feel the need for one."

Bug-Out Bag Philosophy: "I went the surplus route for things I didn't have at home. A lot of time was spent on keeping the weight down. I'm a disabled vet and hopefully the bag would be in the back of my FJ Cruiser instead of on my back. At 50 pounds now, a lot of time in the woods would be hard. My wife and I would probably have to cut a sapling and carry it on our shoulders but I believe in having enough to last three days. My wife has a separate bag with a couple of water bottles and all of our paperwork that we might need."

BRIAN FITZPATRICK

Guns of Choice: Brian has a Glock 19 with Trijicon sights. He keeps 15-round mags loaded with Speer Gold Dot 147-grain GDHP. One mag is in the pistol, two are in a fanny pack and two are in the bug-out bag. The fanny pack holster is not the ideal fashion statement but it can sit on the outside of most any garment Brian is wearing.

Bug-Out Bag Philosophy: "If I am leaving my house, I am doing so under the assumption that I will return one day. I want to be able to prove who I am while I am away and when I return, prove what was mine and prove who owes me when it is time to clean up and get on with life. I am also prepared for the ATM/banking network to be down but cash to still be legal tender, if only for a limited time."

For this kind of situation, Brian has two duplicate 32 GB thumb drives with scans of every document that is important in his life: bills, certificates, licenses, identification, etc.

Choosing the Best Conceal Carry Gun

BY COREY GRAFF

In the blink of an eye your concealed carry gun could be the one thing standing between you and a threat. Therefore you need to be sure you're carrying the absolute best handgun that you possibly can. But that doesn't mean you need the most expensive handgun. Or the most fancy. You don't necessarily need a hand-fitted custom pistol, but you do need one that is reliable.

CONCEALED GUNS TO FIT YOUR LIFESTYLE

As a general rule, choose a carry gun that will fit with your lifestyle most of the time. If you live in a warm part of the United States, you might gravitate toward thinner designs with shorter barrels, such as the mid-sized 1911, or the single-stack polymer handguns on the market like the Springfield XDs, Smith & Wesson M&P Shield, Ruger SR9, Sig Sauer P239, Kahr CW9 or Glock Model 36.

In those warmer parts of the country, you'll normally wear t-shirts and the like, thus you don't want your gun to bulge or "print" through your shirt. A slimmer, more mid-sized handgun will make it easier to conceal. However, if you're a woman, there are specialty purses on the market for concealing a full-size handgun. In fact, some men use fanny packs for concealed carry for just this very reason.

On the other hand, if you live in the north where cold weather dictates wearing jackets and heavy shirts for most of the year, consider the full-sized handgun. There are advantages in doing so. A full-size gun carries more rounds and that's a good thing. They also have longer barrels (wider sight radius) making them easier

to shoot accurately. And a bigger gun will tend to tame recoil more effectively (thanks to its mass) than will a smaller, lighter pistol.

Good choices for full-sized carry guns include the Glock 17 or Glock 22, the Kimber Super Carry Custom HD or Rock Island Armory Standard 1911, Springfield XDm, Browning Hi-Power, CZ P-07 or Heckler & Koch P2000.

While it may seem counterintuitive, one of the mistakes that well-meaning boyfriends and husbands routinely make when buying their ladies a concealed carry handgun is choosing a small, lightweight

revolver, usually in .38 Special. Don't do it. The truth is, these cute little guns are among the hardest to shoot — even for large-fisted men — with intense recoil that will discourage new shooters. If you're buying a handgun for a lady, a full-sized (or possibly mid-sized) semi-automatic is a much better choice. It'll be much easier to shoot. And for that she'll thank you.

REVOLVER VS. SEMI-AUTOMATIC

With advances in semi-automatic handgun design, you might wonder why anyone would still want to carry a revolver for concealed carry. After all, this isn't the

A PISTOL IN THE PURSE

It all started at a handgun training class for women. They showed up with guns stuck in their bras, in cumbersome holsters and in ugly tactical handbags.

"The handbags looked hideous," says Leslie Deets, founder of Concealed Carrie (www.concealedcarrie.com), a maker of fashionable handbags that can conceal handguns.

The other women in the class agreed: the current concealed carry options for women were pretty unfashionable and that gave Deets the sudden inspiration to start her new business. A designer by trade, she studied trends in high-end handbags, drew up her own designs with a separate compartment that conceals a handgun securely, yet allows for quick access.

Each handbag has a removable and adjustable holster so users can arrange the way they draw their handgun according to their liking. The line of handbags includes totes, satchels, hobos and computer carry-alls that come in ostrich and crocodile prints and smooth and distressed leather.

"We had a lot of men purchasing these handbags for their wives over the holidays," said Deets. Her philosophy is that fashion should not be completely sacrificed to function. She even believes her handbags will encourage women to carry a handgun more often since many fashion-conscious women would rather not carry any handgun at all if it means lugging around a military-styled man purse or having to wear a holster that sticks out in the wrong places. Prices range from $249 to $299.

Wild West. But the double-action revolver is simple in design. And simple promotes reliability. There are less parts to clean and maintain on a revolver, and as such less can go wrong should the need to draw the gun ever arise.

Small snubnose revolvers, while more difficult to shoot, make excellent backup guns. Police experience proves that a second backup gun can make all the difference between winning or losing in a gunfight. Think about a revolver in an ankle holster or pocket holster on a jacket. You won't notice it's there, but it's extra insurance should your main weapon jam or be inaccessible for some reason.

A few excellent choices of revolvers for concealed carry include the Smith & Wesson Bodyguard or Night Guard, Ruger LCR or Taurus Model 605PLYB2.

Semi-automatics are faster to reload — you simply dump the spent magazine and insert a new one and you're back in the game. Revolvers are a bit trickier in this area. Not only that, semi-autos tend to be nicer to shoot. Whereas all of the recoil energy in a revolver comes back into your hand, in a semi-automatic some of that energy is dissipated by the slide action, which uses some of the energy to chamber another round.

BEST CALIBER FOR A CONCEALED CARRY GUN

The best caliber for a concealed carry handgun is the one that allows you to shoot well and often and carries enough punch to do the job. For me it's the 9mm (9X19, 9mm Parabellum).

While the .40 S&W is a bit bigger, and the .45 ACP even more so, 9mm ammo is simply more affordable. Which means you'll shoot more. And the key to choosing a concealed carry handgun is to pick one you'll be able to shoot often enough to become proficient.

Much debate has been made about "stopping power" but the fact remains that the 9mm is still one of the most popular calibers in use by police agencies and armed citizens. However, should other factors compel you to settle on a small revolver, the .38 special is probably the

most manageable to learn how to shoot, provided you get good instruction and spend lots of range time to tame that hot little cartridge.

No matter what caliber you choose, be sure your gun and ammo combination

is comfortable and affordable to shoot. When you enjoy shooting your concealed carry gun, you'll shoot more often. And that's key to being sure you're ready when faced with the unthinkable.

CONCEALED CARRY FOR BACKPACKERS

BY JAMES CARD

If you are committed to responsibly carrying a sidearm for personal protection, you most likely have a holster that has been carefully chosen. It fits your handgun perfectly and it rides comfortably on your body. But there is one problem: backpacks, and chances are, your bug-out bag is a backpack since that is the best load-bearing system out there.

When you put on a large backpack there is usually a padded lumbar strap that snaps around your waist and bears much of the load. If you carry your sidearm on your waist, the strap will cover up your handgun and probably pinch it against your body. Likewise, if you carry a shoulder holster rig, the shoulder straps of the backpack will cinch down against the holster, either making it uncomfortable or unreachable. There is a chance that you could attach your handgun holster on the outer side of one of

the straps but that depends on how the holster and backpack are designed. And since it is exposed on the outside it is no longer a concealed weapon.

One answer is the Kit Bag by Hill People Gear. It is a chest rig that keeps your handgun (and other essential items) within quick reach as it rides right on the center of your chest while carrying a backpack. The design is smart and simple and the construction is rugged. The Kit Bag stays secure on your chest by an H-harness that goes over your shoulders and under your armpits. It is lightweight and is hard to notice once you get used to it. There are four models, from the Snubby, a small minimalist bag large enough for a Glock, to the Recon bag model which has a PALS grid (Pouch Attachment Ladder System) for adding on accessories. ($85, hillpeoplegear.com)

Why the Revolver?

THE SIMPLICITY AND RELIABILITY OF A CLASSIC HANDGUN

BY GRANT CUNNINGHAM

The revolver is generally more reliable than an autoloader of similar quality. This isn't to that malfunctions can't occur with a revolver, only that they are less common. What malfunctions do occur are almost always a function of improper reloading technique or poor quality ammunition. A malfunction that needs clearing is quite rare. The most common problem, a failure to fire, is usually solved by stroking the trigger again and using better ammo. Another common malfunction is a case caught under the extractor, which ren-ders the gun inoperative until fixed. It is prevented by proper reloading techniques.

There is a malfunction clearing process for the very rare instances not covered above, but needing to perform the drill is quite rare. Because of this inherent reliability, less training time is expended in malfunction drills, which means more for learning the important task of shooting.

A revolver doesn't need just the right grip to keep it running; there are no "limp wrist" malfunctions with a wheelgun. Shooting from disadvantaged positions or while injured won't stop the gun from operating.

During an actual defensive encounter, the revolver is more resistant to induced failures. The revolver isn't jammed by clothing or incompletely ejected cases. With an autoloader, slight contact can actually slow the slide enough to induce a malfunction. That's not an issue with the revolver, making it ideal for close-quarters defensive duties. The shrouded or concealed hammer models are about as immune to such problems as can be imagined.

It is also possible to fire a revolver from inside a pocket without fear of malfunction. Shooting the revolver from inside a purse holster is also doable. An autoloader wouldn't be a reliable under those circumstances.

A revolver is easier to fit to the hand. An autoloader, even one of the few that feature interchangeable backstraps, is still limited by the dimensions of its magazine well. A revolver's grip can be easily changed to be longer, shorter, deeper, shallower, wider or thinner. The angle at which the gun sits in the hand can even be altered on some models. In most cases it's easy to make the revolver fit the hand perfectly.

One overlooked feature of the revolver is that it operates without ammunition. While I'm not a big proponent of extensive dry fire, the fact that the revolver is fully functional without ammo means that dry fire training is more useful than it is with an autoloader. There's no interruption in the firing cycle, so trigger control is learned faster that if you had to stop to constantly rack a slide.

The revolver is not only less expensive to purchase, it's less expensive to operate as well. The gun itself tends to be less expensive than an auto of equal quality, but that's just the start. If you have a defensive autoloader, it's imperative that you test its function with the ammunition you plan to carry. Recommendations vary but the most common is that you shoot 200 rounds of that ammunition through one gun. If you've priced ammunition lately you know how much that can cost.

With a revolver, you need to test your ammunition primarily to adjust the sights or to verify that the bullet impact matches your non-adjustable sights. A couple of cylinders are all that takes and you can then substitute cheaper practice or range ammo.

There are no expensive magazines to buy. If you shoot your autoloader a lot, most authorities recommend that you have a half-dozen magazines for that gun. That's a lot of money and magazines are disposable parts: they wear out or can

THE TAURUS JUDGE

BY DAVE WORKMAN

Taurus introduced this awesome five-shot revolver in 2008, and it is gaining traction among people who want a close-range fight-stopper. Built from stainless steel with a matte finish, fiber optic front sight on the 3-inch barrel, it is a double-action wheelgun that chambers both .45 Colt cartridges and 3-inch magnum .410 shells. By no coincidence, I suspect, Federal Cartridge had just introduced a couple of Personal Defense .410 shotshell loads for use in a handgun—and this being the only .410 revolver around specifically designed for that purpose—it seemed like a good combination. One load fires a charge of No. 4 shot while the other is loaded with four 000 buckshot pellets. At close range, either round will make an immediate impression.

On the other hand, if this revolver is loaded with .45 Colt cartridges, it can put an abrupt end to a criminal attack. Some people load up with a shotshell and a .45 in alternating chambers, and my experience at the range involved shooting with just such a setup. This seems to be a smart way to load up. I noticed immediately how advantageous alternating rounds would be in the event of an emergency situation.

There are other models with 2 ½-inch chambers for standard .410 shotshells that will still handle the .45 Colt round, in blue or matte stainless finish. There is one model made from Ultra-Lite alloy. Taurus offers the Tracker version with a 6 ½-inch barrel, also in blue or matte stainless. Depending upon the model, guns weigh anywhere from 22.4 ounces to more than 36 ounces. One model has a very deeply blued finish, almost a royal blue/black that is one of the more handsome models in the line.

To my liking, Taurus has fitted The Judge with its famously comfortable ribbed rubber grip, and this really tames the recoil. This Ribber grip also fits the hand very well.

I loaded up and cut loose at targets from about seven yards, and the Judge held on target very well. The shot patterns it produced were convincing. Taurus cuts the barrel with six lands and grooves on a 1:12-inch twist on a couple of models, while others have smooth barrels with no rifling, according to the company website. According to Taurus publicity, this handgun was dubbed The Judge because several judges now carry it into the courtroom. This does not surprise me, considering the occasional tale one hears about a suspect going berserk in court. Taurus designed this gun with a transfer bar so that an accidental discharge if the revolver is dropped with the hammer down is virtually impossible.

The hammer is checkered for positive cocking while the trigger is smooth to allow for a gliding trigger stroke when shooting double action. A traditional thumb-type latch is located on the left side of the frame to release the cylinder. The rear sight is a notch on the frame, but the Judge is not designed for long-range target shooting, so the sight setup is quite adequate for its intended purpose.

The Judge is not awkward, and should be an easy firearm for even an amateur to master. For home defense, hiking or backpacking, roaming around in snake country, and even taking a grouse at close range, The Judge certainly has what it takes. Loaded up with .45 Colt loads and either soft lead or JHP bullets, this is one defense handgun that is a stout piece of defensive hardware.

be damaged relatively easily. That's an expense the revolver doesn't have.

Speaking of magazines, on of my favorite revolver attributes is that there are none. Sometimes I go to the range with several guns and when I'm dealing with autoloaders, more than once I've forgotten to bring a magazine. The revolver doesn't have that problem because the magazine is part and parcel of the gun. Even many years from now a revolver bought today will still be operational, while I've run into many autoloaders over the years that are missing their magazines.

I know I'm picking on the magazine issue, but another point is that it's impos-

sible to load rounds into a revolver backwards. I've seen more than one person load a round into a magazine backwards, and that causes a heck of a jam. Admittedly the incidence goes down with the familiarization but I remember one match I shot where a seasoned competitor loaded a round backwards into the middle of his magazine.

There is another advantage: should you need to pick your gun up from a table (or even the ground), the protruding cylinder makes a small gap between the gun and the surface on which it is resting. This makes it a bit easier to retrieve than an autoloader that rests flat on the sur-

face. A small difference to be sure but one that could prove valuable in the event you must pick up yours in a hurry.

Many people say they pick a revolver because it's easier to manipulate: no confusing buttons or levers, and a direct and unambiguous loading and unloading procedure. This makes it a superb choice for a home defense gun in those cases where one person is an enthusiast but his or her partner may not be. Any one can pick up a revolver and shoot it. For the overwhelming majority of double-action revolvers in circulation, all of the controls are in the same place and do pretty much the same thing. If you know how to run a Ruger,

.45 COLT

Historical Notes: This was introduced, in 1873, by Colt's as one of the cartridges for its famous Peacemaker single-action revolver. Both the cartridge and the revolver were adopted by  the U.S. Army, in 1875. This served as the official handgun cartridge of the Army, until 1892 (some 17 years), when it was replaced by the .38 Long Colt. The .45 Colt is one of the cartridges that helped civilize and settle the American West. It was originally a blackpowder number, loaded with 40 grains of FFg powder and a 255-grain lead bullet. Testing has demonstrated that muzzle velocity of the original loading almost certainly exceeded 900 fps in the original revolvers. Various importers offer excellent Italian-made replicas of the original Colt's model, and Ruger and several other makes of more modern single-action revolvers are currently chambered in .45 Colt.

General Comments: This is one of the most famous American handgun cartridges and still a favorite with big-bore advo-

cates. It is extremely accurate and has more knockdown and stopping power than nearly any common handgun cartridge, except the .44 Magnum. It is a popular field cartridge and can be safely handloaded to velocities in excess of 1000 fps with 250-grain cast bullets. Blackpowder revolvers should not be used with any load developing more than about 800 fps muzzle velocity. Although the .45 Colt has a larger case than the .45 Automatic or the .45 Auto-Rim, it is not quite as efficient with factory-duplicating loads using smokeless powder. Using special revolvers, some very heavy loads have been established for the .45 Colt case. These put it in almost the same class as the .44 Magnum. Such loads should not be attempted except by an experienced person who fully understands what he is doing and who will ensure that those loads are only used in a revolver that will withstand the pressures generated. This is another cartridge that has developed a rebirth of interest. Federal, Remington, Winchester, Black Hills Ammunition, CorBon, and others all offer .45 Colt loads.

.410-BORE

Historical Notes: Though gun and load selection are somewhat limited, the .410-bore (12mm) is a perfectly good dove and  quail chambering and can be argued to be the ideal small-game shell. A light, handy, .410-bore breech-break shotgun is a pleasure to carry on long hunts, and top three-inch loads deliver all the punch necessary to cleanly anchor rabbits and smaller species. Many use this

diminutive chambering for breaking clay pigeons. Interestingly, it is possible to fire .410-bore shells in .45/70-chambered rifles. There are also a slug load and one in 000 Buck (a three-pellet load in the three-inch shell) as alternate home-defense rounds. The .410-bore follows the 12- and 20-gauge in popularity. Many young shooters have learned to shoot with a .410-bore, and that tradition continues. The .410-inch bore would be called 68-gauge.

being handed a Smith & Wesson is not going to make you stop and scratch your head in confusion.

Since the revolver has a heavy trigger it's more immune to adrenaline-induced accidental discharge. While most trainers (including me) stress that the finger should be outside of the triggerguard unless actually shooting, we must acknowledge that not everyone does this. In such hands, after being startled out of bed or in a stressful confrontation, it's probably better that the gun require significant effort to shoot.

While many revolvers today have built-in locks, it's a simple matter to lock up any revolver: simply open the cylinder and hook a padlock through the frame opening. If you have a long-shackle lock, you can even run it through one of the chambers. It's a simple matter to lock the gun into something immovable, making it safe from accidents and from theft as well.

One benefit that doesn't seem like a benefit is that the revolver isn't an easy gun to master. I've said for many years that the revolver is the easiest gun to shoot but the hardest gun to shoot well. There is a personal satisfaction to shooting a revolver well, and it's magnified when you can do it to the point that you can beat people who insist on using those newfangled self-shucking things.

I'm a partisan of the revolver yet the revolver isn't right for every shooter or every application. First, there are those situations where capacity is important. The double-action revolver is a great tool for personal defense but the limited ammunition capacity makes it unsuitable for military use. While many people tout the revolver as being a good choice for those with limited upper-body strength, I'm not sure it's always practical. Those people I've encountered who have strength issues with their arms or hands, such that they can't operate an autoloading pistol, often lack the strength or range of movement to operate a revolver's heavy double-action trigger. While gunsmithing can help this to some degree, I've observed many folks who just couldn't handle the trigger weight. With proper technique those same people often were often able to use an autoloader and for them it was a better choice.

Revolvers aren't well suited to the mounting and use of weapon lights. The presence of the ejector rod generally requires that the light be mounted very far forward where it is difficult to actuate with the hands in a shooting position. There are revolvers on the market with mounting rails near the muzzle but the ease of operation issues has limited their popularity.

A revolver does recoil more with any given level of cartridge power than an equivalent autoloader. There have been revolvers chambered in 9mm, for instance, and they display markedly more recoil than that same cartridge in an auto of equal weight. This is because there is no reciprocating slide and recoil spring to use up any of the recoil energy. With a revolver, it's all transmitted straight into the shooter's hands. For those who are recoil sensitive, or whose hand strength presents control issues, the revolver is much less pleasant to shoot.

The Versatile Shotgun

A BULLDOG DEFENDER AND AN ALL-PURPOSE HUNTER, THE SHOTGUN IS A MUST-HAVE IN THE PREPAREDNESS TOOLBOX

BY SCOTT WAGNER

The shotgun is a legendary arm, and rightfully so. It has a tremendous amount of close range power, as suggested by the very large hole in the end of the barrel. It is not difficult to shoot with the right training, attitude and equipment. It is versatile and useful for a wide range of tasks. If you purchase a gun that allows for the use of different length/type barrels and chokes, you can use it for anything from hunting birds or clay pigeons to hunting bear and everything in between, for home defense, law enforcement and military situations, including lethal and less-than-lethal interactions. Ammo is abundantly available and I would speculate that 80-90 percent of the jobs that need to be done can be done with some form of the shotgun.

Home defense is probably one of primary uses of a shotgun. From the days where farmers once loaded shotgun shells to fire "rock salt" to irritate and scatter interlopers on their property, hopefully without killing them, to 21st-century defense against home invaders where some form of lead shot is the load of choice. Even though its popularity is being supplanted by the meteoric rise of the AR-15, the shotgun still has a place in self-defense. Really, the shotgun exists outside

---

WHAT IS A TACTICAL SHOTGUN?

If a product is to be considered truly "tactical" (and not just an average everyday product just spray painted black- such as a "tactical sledgehammer" originally purchased at Home Depot) it must:

1. Be reliable and of high quality. After all, we are talking about products designed for person-to-person fighting situations. It must work each time, every time.
2. Be of such a configuration that it is currently useful in combat-type operations, whether that means military, law enforcement or civilian operations. The configuration of the item cannot, due to complexity or poor design, impede the basic reason for which the product was designed.
3. Possess features that give it an advantage in use over the standard version of that product. Why pay more for something that is marketed as being "tactical" when the standard version will suffice?

---

of the basic self-defense arena, which is dominated by the handgun. Because of its legendary reputation and brute power, the shotgun is more of an offensive weapon. It has been used in warfare since the invention of the powder which powers it, and the military is not usually in a defensive mission. I believe it was Clint Smith who said that the handgun exists to allow you to fight your way to a bigger weapon, and that's the shotgun.

A home defense shotgun can take several forms, and also serve as a multi-role tool, especially if one lives on a farm or ranch, where it can serve animal control duties as well. When we talk about defending the home, we can also mean defending the camper trailer or RV. Traditionally a standard hunting shotgun is used for this purpose, such as a Remington® 870 Wingmaster, loaded with hunting loads, since the concept of a tactical shotgun is relatively new. While a weapon like this can suffice, there are some better shotgun configurations to work with.

THE BASICS OF A MODERN TACTICAL SHOTGUN

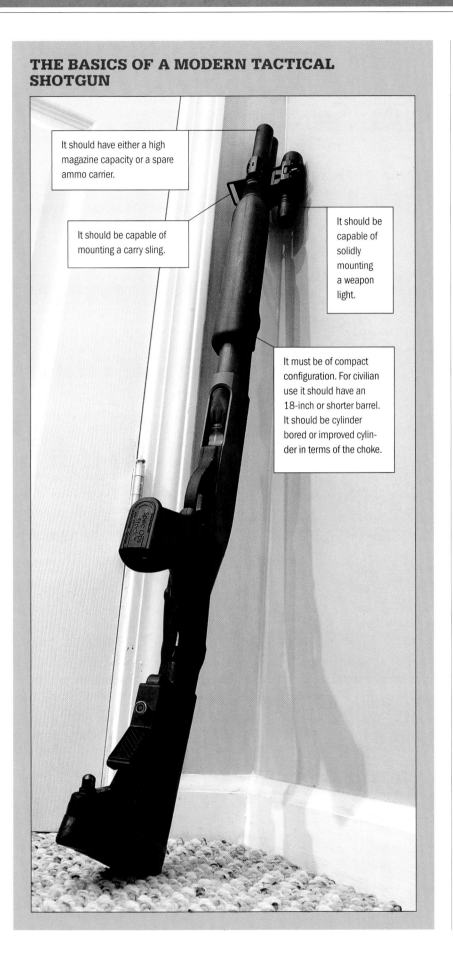

It should have either a high magazine capacity or a spare ammo carrier.

It should be capable of mounting a carry sling.

It should be capable of solidly mounting a weapon light.

It must be of compact configuration. For civilian use it should have an 18-inch or shorter barrel. It should be cylinder bored or improved cylinder in terms of the choke.

MAKING THE SWITCH: THE OPTIONS

STOCKS
- Length of pull of the available stocks range from 12 ½ to 14 ¼ inches.
- Camouflage standard stock
- Matte black standard stock
- Camouflage adjustable dual comb stock
- Matte black adjustable dual comb stock
- Pistol grip
- Adjustable tactical with telescoping stock with a pistol grip

BARRELS
- 26-inch barrel
- 28-inch barrel
- 28-inch ventilated rib
- 18 ½-inch close-quarters barrel
- Cantilever rifled
- Iron-sight rifled
- Stand-off breaching barrel

FOREARMS
- Matte black
- Camo patterns
- Black with Picatinny rails

Product Review
The Mossberg Flex

BY M.D. JOHNSON

Flex is short for flexible, meaning the shotgun can be quickly and easily modified to fit the situation at hand, be that bagging waterfowl, gobblers, or protecting your home. Mossberg refers to the Flex as the "ultimate adaptive shotgun platform." The shotgun starts as Mossberg's well-recognized M500 pump-action 12-gauge, 3-inch shotgun, and morphs from that foundation through the Tool-Less Locking System (TLS).

The TLS works in two ways. The first are button-like releases on both the toe of the stock and the underside of the forearm. When pressed, they allow the shooter to remove and replace the recoil pad and forearm almost instantly. Replacement options include pads ranging from ¾ to 1 ½ inches, and forearms in different camouflage patterns and one incorporating Picatinny style rails for mounting lights and secondary sighting devices.

The second type of release in the TLS is a T-shaped recessed latch located at the upper junction of the receiver and stock. Shooters simply pull upward on the grooved sides of the T, and turn the latch 90 degrees in either direction to unlock; the stock can now be easily removed and replaced with one of several choices. Select Flex models feature Mossberg's Lightning Pump Action (LPA) trigger, easily adjustable with only an Allen wrench from 3 to 8 pounds. The Flex System is offered in two basic configurations—a M500, with a 28-inch ported vent-rib barrel sporting a 3mm white front bead and small brass mid-bead ($600), and a military style OD version with a 20-inch barrel, ghost ring sights, and an integral Picatinny rail system atop the receiver and in the forearm ($900).

I will tip my hat to Mossberg's LPA trigger, an excellent, easily adjustable instrument that truly takes the Flex to the next level, particularly if one wishes to use the piece as a whitetail gun. And finally, there's the foundation for the Flex, the M500, a reliable, rugged, undeniably versatile shotgun in and of itself.

Double-Barreled Shotguns

KICKING ASS SINCE THE INVENTION OF GUNPOWDER

BY CHAD LOVE

One of the more interesting firearms fads in the past few years is the rise of the post-apocalyptic, tactical or "survival" shotgun. These imposing-looking weapons have serious-sounding names and bristle with the latest accoutrements desired by the ever-expanding "SHTF" set. Admittedly, these flavors of the month do have a very high cool factor, and many of them have a correspondingly (and shockingly) high price tag. And if you're into that sort of thing, that's perfectly fine. The zombies will, I'm sure, give you a wide berth. But for those of us who inhabit the world of the living and desire a simple, rugged, reliable do-it-all shotgun, preferably one not endorsed by an action figure, is there an alternative?

The original do-it-all shotgun, the classic side-by-side, have been reliably serving their self-reliant owners for centuries, with nary a hollow plastic tactical stock, picatinny rail or a laser sight to be found anywhere. No, they don't hold 10 rounds, so you are at a distinct disadvantage in a charging squirrel situation, and the lack of laser sights means you do have to, you know, practice a bit. And the lack of a radiation-and-rust-proof finish means that you will, on occasion, have to actually engage in a minimum level of maintenance.

But if you can get past these glaring deficiencies, you may find that your

Double-Barreled Shotgun

grandfather may have been onto something. You would be hard-pressed to find a gun more likely to go "bang" when you squeeze the trigger than a double gun. They are simple, reliable, and extremely easy for even the non-gun nuts among us to understand and operate.

Better still, good used examples, from simple, unadorned low-end models to exquisitely made English game guns, are easily found in today's tactical-crazy gun market. You can still find basic, lower-end American side-by-side shotguns from makers like L.C. Smith, Fox, Ithaca and Winchester, among others, for around the same price range of those clunky,

ugly, modern plastic shotguns that feel and handle like injection-molded 2 × 4s.

For the ultimate in simple ruggedness, a double-trigger, boxlock gun with extractors is hard to beat, but any of the various incarnations (boxlock, sidelock, single or double trigger) make good choices. Obviously, when you're talking about buying a used gun, getting it checked out by a gunsmith is a good idea. There's a reason these guns have been around for so long. Side-by-sides have served as a "survival" gun for generations of farmers, ranchers, peasants and lords alike. They just work, and unlike the modern cartoon guns of Zombie Nation, they look good doing it.

The Amazing Modern Air Rifle

THE AIR WE BREATHE POWERS THE PROJECTILE AT 1,000 FEET PER SECOND. IT IS QUIET, EFFICIENT, AND ACCURATE. IT ALSO IS ECO-FRIENDLY AND SUSTAINABLE.

BY JAMES CARD

WHICH TYPE OF AIR RIFLE?

There are multiple ways the air is compressed into the rifle and each has benefits and drawbacks. First are the multi-stroke pneumatic airguns. These are the ones many people grew up with and to power the gun you simply cock a lever mechanism which is usually the forestock. Cock it once; you have a little bit of air inside the gun. Cock it more and more air goes inside. Usually the limit is around eight to ten pumps before the gun can no longer hold any more air. These are basic air rifles and can be lots of fun but the main drawback is constantly pumping the gun back up after every single shot.

Single-stroke pneumatic air rifles require only one cocking motion. Typically, the rifle breaks in half near the forestock and you crank the barrel backwards as it compresses air into the gun. As it requires only one pump, more muscle is needed to push the barrel back to compress the air. Once cocked, the barrel snaps back into place and the rifle is pressurized. These types of rifles are often used in competitive air gun markmanship events.

Spring-piston air rifles have a lever to cock back a spring that pushes down a piston. Upon firing, the spring blasts forward hitting the piston that shoots a burst of air that propels the pellet.

Cartridge-powered air guns use cartridges that are like mini-CO2 tanks (sometimes called powerlets). You load one into the air gun and the powerlet disperses the pressured air for you. No cocking or pumping needed. The drawback: you have to keep buying the cartridges and with lots of target shooting, they can go pretty fast. They also don't work well in cold weather.

Precharged pneumatic air rifles are loaded with air from an outside source. Air is pumped into a cylinder on the gun that holds a supply of air. Since the air is already inside the gun there is no cocking. There is a control regulator that can be tweaked to adjust the power of each shot. The gun can be loaded by either a hand pump, an air compressor or a Scuba-like air tank. These air rifles pack a lot of power for hunting and are used in world-class air rifle competitions. They are also quieter than other types of air rifles. If you are interested in pushing the limits of distance, these are the rifles to experiment with. The drawback: you are dependent on an outside piece of equipment (air tank or pump) to power the rifle and they are the most expensive types of air rifles in the market.

So of these types of air rifles, which is the best choice as a survival-utility gun? The winner is the single-stroke pneumatic air rifle (along with the spring-piston types) as it is completely self-contained. With one cocking motion, the rifle is charged. The multi-stroke air rifle isn't the best for small game hunting as cocking the rifle ten times is a jerky, noisy affair that will tip off the game animals being pursued. Also having to pump the gun multiple times after shooting doesn't help with taking a quick follow-up shot. The guns powered by CO2 cartridges are a money drain and unsustainable. You are left with empty cartridges to recycle or deal with. The precharged rifles are incredibly accurate and powerful but you have to haul around the equipment to pump the gun. The single-stroke air rifle is truly the grab-and-go rifle of the air gun family.

WHICH CALIBER?

Air rifles come in a number of calibers but the two main ones are .177 and .22. The .22 caliber is larger and heavier and thus, is slower than the .177. Both are powerful enough to take down small game but the .22 is the best choice if you plan to do a lot of hunting with your air rifle.

BEGINNERS AND EXPERTS

Air rifles are a great way to teach a beginner the fundamentals of marksmanship. With almost zero recoil, the new shooter will not develop a flinch. There is also no intimidating report like one coming from a deer-hunting rifle. Likewise, no ear protection is needed although safety glasses are necessary. Since the ammo is inexpensive, the beginner can practice for a long time before the pellet stash runs empty.

For those that are already expert rifle shooters, air rifles are excellent practice surrogates for regular rifles for the same

▲ Trail NP All Weather with Realtree APG

reasons stated above. The basic skills of breathing, steadiness, focus, stance and posture do not change.

SELF DEFENSE

Is an air rifle a viable weapon for defensive use? The first rule of a gunfight is to have a gun and if an air rifle is the only thing you have then it is better than nothing. The single shot that you are limited to before reloading again may be enough for you to get to another more powerful gun, to escape, take cover or call for help.

While testing the featured air rifles, I nailed a piece of half-inch plywood to a tree and stapled paper targets to it. After a couple of hours of shooting, I was chainging the targets and I happened to look on the backside of the plywood. It was an enlightening and horrifying sight. The plywood was chewed and splintered and cracked apart. Some pellets were still embedded in the wood and others blasted right through into the tree. I asked myself if an air rifle can to that to plywood, what would it do to human flesh?

A British study published in the Journal of Clinical Pathology in 1998 looked into the damage an air rifle could do to the human body. Here is a brief sum-

mary of the abstract: "Five cases of fatal airgun injury were identified by forensic pathologists and histopathologists. Three of the victims were adult men, one was a 16-year-old boy, and one an eight-year-old child. Four of the airguns were .22 air rifles, the other a .177 air rifle. Two committed suicide, one person shooting himself in the head, the other in the chest. In both cases the guns were fired at contact range. Three of the cases were classified as accidents: in two the pellet penetrated into the head and in one the chest."

The researchers also noted that one person dies each year in the United Kingdom. An Internet search reveals that air rifle fatalities throughout the world are not uncommon.

The British study, which included some gruesome photos, concluded: "Non-fatal injuries following airgun pellet penetration include significant brain damage leaving permanent impairment. Those involving damage to eyes may result in blindness . . . Penetration into the chest or abdomen may require surgical intervention . . . A retained airgun pellet may raise concerns about lead poisoning. . . The adult skull is vulnerable to penetration by airgun pellets, and if the temple

TRAIL NP ALL WEATHER WITH REALTREE APG SPECS

Caliber: .22
Velocity: 950 fps
Barrel Length: 15.25 inches
Overall Length: 43.0 inches
Shot Capacity: 1
Cocking Effort: 33 lbs.
Barrel: Rifled
Front Sights: None
Rear Sights: None
Buttplate: Ventilated rubber
Trigger Pull: 3.5 lbs.
Action: Break barrel
Safety: Manual
Power: Gas piston
Weight: 8.0 lbs.
Optics: 3-9x40mm
Price: $279.95
www.crosman.com

region is chosen as the entry site, suicide may be achieved."

Although that may seem obvious to experienced shooters of air rifles and mothers (That thing will poke your eye out!), it is nice to know that if you were

RWS Pro 34 P Compact

in a self-defense situation you might not be as undergunned as you think you are.

COST-EFFECTIVE SHOOTING

Air rifle pellets are usually sold in hockey puck-sized tin canisters that hold 500 pellets. For the common calibers they cost around $8 to $15 depending on the design. Some hunting pellets have plastic pointed tips designed to penetrate small game. Other lower-end pellets are just meant for backyard plinking. Flat-headed pellets are useful for rodents and practice shooting. Round-headed pellets are good for longer ranges and penetration. If one were to buy $200 worth of pellets at $10 per canister that would be 10,000 pellets. Even .22 rimfire ammunition, the cheapest of all firearms ammo, doesn't come close to such a bargain. If you stockpile the pellets, they will never go bad. Under the right circumstances, firearms ammunition can last for decades, but there are many environmental factors that can make them become duds. Pellets have an infinite shelf life.

LEGALITY AND POLITICS

Although there may be some restrictions in certain areas, air rifles are largely unregulated. Unlike other firearms, there is no background check and no three-day waiting period. The government does not care if you own one. You can usually keep one where other firearms are not allowed and may even be able to fire one where other types of recreational shooting is forbidden. Check your local laws and see if anything applies to your personal situation involving air gun ownership.

MAINTENANCE

I've always liked cleaning guns. It is part of the process of mastering them and getting to know how they work. But consider what happens inside of a conventional firearm: the gunpowder creates an explosion and that leaves traces of fouling that builds up after every shot. The more you shoot, the filthier the gun becomes. Some ammo burns clean and other ammo burns dirty. The residue requires solvents and there is an entire cottage industry that supplies all kinds of gun solvents, lubricants, preservatives and cleaners to keep firearms functioning. For air rifles, the care is minimal. The only explosion is one of air. Think about it: every time you shoot, you are blowing tiny particles out of the barrel of the rifle. It almost cleans itself. Other than an occasional lubricating of some parts and cleaning the barrel

RWS PRO 34 P COMPACT SPECS

Caliber: .177
Velocity: 1,000 fps
Barrel Length: 15.75 inches
Overall Length: 42.13 inches
Shot Capacity: 1
Cocking Effort: 33 lbs.
Barrel: Rifled
Front Sights: None
Rear Sights: None
Trigger: Two-stage adjustable
Buttplate: Plastic
Trigger Pull: 3.3 lbs.
Action: Break barrel
Safety: Automatic
Power: Spring-piston
Weight: 8.0 lbs.
Optics: 3-9x40
Price: $267.75
www.umarexusa.com

as directed in the owner's manual, maintenance of an air rifle is nothing compared to shotguns, rifles and pistols firing gunpowder cartridges and shells. For the outside finish, a couple drops of oil on a rag is enough to give the rifle a wipe down that will protect the metal parts from rust.

Gamo Silent Stalker Whisper

Some manufacturers also sell specialized cleaning kits for their line of air rifles.

QUIET

Break-barrel air rifles are pretty quiet yet they do make a distinctive sound that is a cross between a thwack, ponk, or crack. It is not as loud as a .22 nor is it obvious and distinctive as a gunshot. Some air rifle manufactures are building suppressors into their barrel to make them quieter. Unlike suppressors for regular firearms, there are no restrictions on suppressors for air rifles. This quietness is very much appreciated when you do not want to disturb your neighbors when taking out a varmint in your garden or when you are out hunting and do not want to giveaway your position.

FOR HUNTING

For years air rifles have been used to take all kinds of small game animals, with squirrels and rabbits as the most common. Farm boys have used them to take barn pigeons to make squab and they can easily take down a crow (yes, you can eat crow and with the right recipe it can be delicious). The key for a clean kill is shot placement and for small game, the vital area may be only an inch in diameter.

Practice is essential and there is no excuse not to practice as the ammo is so cheap. Also, air rifles do not have the range of other firearms, hence, you need to get closer to your prey and that makes you a better hunter. The maximum range for hunting is about 50 yards. Shots around 30 yards or closer are ideal for the best shot placement and penetration.

I've heard of turkeys being taken with headshots and ground sluicing all types of gamebirds such as pheasants or grouse is easily done if you can get into range before the bird flushes. Jeff Foiles, a former waterfowl hunting guide, once used an air rifle to "park" geese. He would head to a park and shoot the suburban geese to collect their waterfowl leg bands. He is now in prison on multiple wildlife violations. As with any kind of hunting, be sure to check the regulations to see if air rifles are permissible on the species that you want to hunt.

SUSTAINABLE

When shooting air rifles, you leave a pretty small footprint. Other than the tiny lead pellet (to wit, some pellets are made of other metals), there is only the air. There are no plastic hulls, no gunpowder, no spent brass cases, and few chemicals

GAMO SILENT STALKER WHISPER SPECS

Caliber: .177
Velocity: 1300 fps
Loudness: 3-Medium
Barrel Length: 18.0
Overall Length: 43.0
Shot Capacity: 1
Cocking Effort: 32 lbs.
Barrel: Rifled
Front Sights: Fiber Optic
Rear Sights: Fiber Optic
Trigger: Two-stage adjustable
Buttplate: Rubber
Trigger Pull: 3.74 lbs.
Action: Break barrel
Safety: Manual
Power: Gas piston
Weight: 7.15 lbs.
Optics: 3-9X40
Price: $249.95
www.gamousa.com

used for cleaning. It is a lean, frugal, and efficient form of shooting and an air rifle has a spot among those firearms deemed as "survival guns."

A Case for the .22

WHY EVERYONE SHOULD OWN A GUN IN AMERICA'S FAVORITE CALIBER

BY JAMES M. AYRES

Your first gun should be a target-grade rifle or handgun chambered for the .22 long rifle cartridge. This principle used to be gospel. All new shooters were advised to start with the little rimfire. Then something changed; I'm not sure what. This now appears to be a minority opinion, one that many experts today disagree with. I have read that some think it's best to go right to the gun and caliber the new shooter intends to use for big game or self-defense, especially if the object is self-defense.

I believe a foundation of marksmanship laid down with a .22 will better serve a shooter than any other introduction to shooting. About the only exception I can think of would be the shooter who plans to shoot only trap or skeet and never intends to do any other kind of shooting. Even then, starting with a .22 is not a bad thing.

A strong and solid foundation for marksmanship is best built on a few thousand rounds of .22 ammunition, expended in both fun and in serious practice. There's a good deal more to shooting than hunting and self-defense, but if either of these endeavors is your goal, you won't go wrong starting with a .22. Target shooting, from plinking to Olympic level, bench rest, trap and skeet are only a few of the shooting sports that have occupied and entertained millions. Virtually all of these activities can be built on a foundation laid down with the lowly .22 rimfire. Further, the twenty-two is more than a training round. It is a useful and versatile cartridge. I know more than one person who relies on a .22 for subsistence hunting, and others who, for various reasons, have used it for self defense.

FUN TO SHOOT

Twenty-twos are just plain fun to shoot. They have none of the muzzle blast and recoil that intimidate so many new shooters. I have seen more than one first-time shooter try his hand with a large-caliber rifle or pistol only to be driven away from the sport forever with ringing ears and a sore shoulder from a monster magnum rifle, or a stinging palm from that Dirty Harry special. There's no excuse to not use good ear and eye protection when shooting. However, even with the proper protection, the kick of a full power .44 Magnum revolver can be a bit much for a new shooter, or even some experienced shooters to deal with.

ACCURACY

Accuracy always matters. But it can be especially important when you're learning to shoot. A new shooter should expect to make many mistakes as part of the learning process. He or she will not benefit from a firearm that cannot be relied upon to produce consistent, excellent accuracy. With an inaccurate firearm a new shooter cannot be sure if a miss is his fault or that of the gun. With a "no excuses" gun, you can focus on improving your marksmanship and not worry about the gun.

COST

Twenty-twos have the virtue of being inexpensive to buy and to shoot. A thousand rounds of .22 long rifle ammo costs less than dinner in a cheap restaurant, less than a car wash in Los Angeles, less than…well, you get the idea. Twenty-twos are cheap to shoot, even if you're buying top quality ammo. The guns are also inexpensive to purchase. Unless you go for a top match-quality pistol or rifle, or a highly decorated one, you can get a .22 that will shoot the ears off a rattlesnake at fifty yards.

EFFECTIVENESS OF THE .22

Make no mistake; the .22 is far more than a training round. It is effective beyond what its limits would appear to be. In part this is due to good sectional density, which enables it to penetrate well. There are subsistence hunters the world over who use the .22 to take whatever game is available, including large game.

One of my friends is an Inuit from Alaska and uses a .22 rifle to hunt caribou and moose to feed his family and to kill marauding walrus when they destroy his nets and eat his fish. Caribou and moose are very large animals. The technique Mike uses for caribou and moose is to get very close and shoot a burst of at least five rounds into the heart and lungs. He shoots walrus, which can weigh four hundred pounds and have sharp tusks, from about

.22 LONG RIFLE

Historical Notes: Information available indicates that the .22 Long Rifle was developed by the J. Stevens Arms & Tool Co., in 1887. It is the .22 Long case with a five-grain blackpowder charge (likely with a granulation similar to what we would now call FFFFg), and a 40-grain bullet instead of the original 29-grain. The Peters Cartridge Co. is supposed to have first manufactured it, specifically for Stevens. If this is true, then why does the 1888 Stevens catalog refer to a UMC .22-caliber Long rimfire rifle cartridge? This would be a gross ingratitude, at best. This 1888 catalog lists the Nos. 1, 2, 9, and 10 model break-open rifles as available in the new chambering with increased rifling twist. The New Model Pocket or Bicycle rifle also chambered it. The 1888 Marlin-Ballard catalog recommends the new .22 Long "Rifle" cartridge for its No. 3 Gallery rifle as being more accurate than the common .22 Long or Extra Long.

At one time, the .22 Long Rifle was available in blackpowder, semi-smokeless, and smokeless powder loads. Remington introduced the first high-velocity type, in 1930. The 40-grain solid and 36- and 38-grain hollowpoint bullet have been available for many years. The original case was not crimped, a feature that finally appeared in 1900. Space does not permit a full discussion of the different loads and types of .22 Long Rifle cartridges or the rifles and handguns that chamber it. Suffice to say, it is the most accurate and highly developed of any rimfire cartridge ever.

General Comments: The .22 Long Rifle is the most popular match cartridge in existence, and also the most widely used small-game and varmint cartridge. The high-velocity hollowpoint is the best field load and will do a good job on rabbit-sized animals out to 75 yards. Beyond that, it is unreliable. The Long Rifle is a great favorite of poachers for killing game out of season with close-up head shots. The

modest report does not alarm or alert passersby or officials. At close range, the high-velocity load with the solid-lead bullet will penetrate six inches of soft pine board and has a maximum range of nearly two miles. Maximum range is achieved at the relatively low angle of between 25 and 30 degrees, so one must be very careful. Humans shot with the .22 Long Rifle often show little immediate distress, survive without complications for several days, then die very suddenly. This is mentioned because many individuals regard .22 rimfires as play things not powerful enough to be dangerous. Careless shooting with the .22 rimfire has probably led to the closure of more areas to hunting and caused more trouble than any other cartridge. Use your head and be careful! There is also a .22 Long Rifle shot cartridge, loaded by most companies and useful mostly for rat and other pest control.

ten feet using headshots. The point is that the .22 is much more effective than most people think it is.

The military and various other government agencies also use the .22 to good effect. I was taught to always keep a Bug-Out Bag (BOB) close at hand to be used in the event I had to E&E (Escape & Evade) and found myself in a survival situation. I was to always keep in my BOB, a target-grade .22 pistol and 200 rounds of ammunition. The reasoning for this specific handgun was that it would take any reasonable game; it was effective as a self-defense weapon; its report was relatively quiet; and, the entire package, pistol and ammunition, weighed very little.

Today this kind of training is called Survival Escape Rescue Evasion (SERE) and is taught to elite units, covert agents, and pilots. In one military school I am aware of the trainers and students take everything from frogs to deer with .22 handguns as part of their SERE training. They do so legally on a military reservation.

The .22 is an effective all-around cartridge. It's good to know that in a survival situation, you can take large game with a .22. However, do not go out in search of your autumn whitetail with your new .22 pistol or rifle. Be sure to check regulations with your local fish and game authorities to learn which firearms are legal for the game you pursue. In general, small game is fair game for a .22, but check and make sure.

When you select your .22, be aware that performance will vary with various brands of ammo. You should try as many different variations as you can find in order to determine which one groups best and which is most reliable in your gun.

Without exception, everyone in my Basic Training and Advanced Infantry Training classes who qualified as Expert, which none of us considered a major accomplishment, had owned and shot a .22 since they were kids.

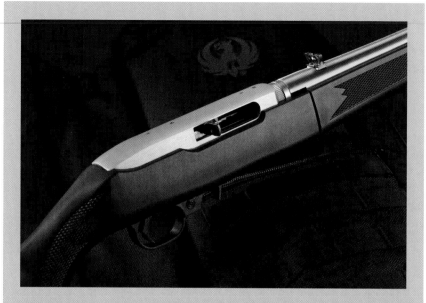

RUGER'S 10/22 TAKEDOWN

BY JAMES CARD

I like gear that breaks down. To put it more specifically, gear that is designed to disassemble into separate parts for convenient storage and transport. One of my favorite fly rods breaks down into seven pieces and fits into a small tube. My recurve bow is of the take-down kind: unbolt the two limbs from the riser and other than those three pieces, all I need are arrows, the bowstring and my shooting glove. Ruger's 10/22 Takedown gives me the same satisfaction: the barrel twists off a locking mechanism and in the other hand is the stock and action. Combine that with the fly rod and recurve bow and you're set for a great backcountry outing.

There is a creeping feeling about take-down gear items: a sense that they are not built solid enough as their one-unit counterparts. This perception of quality can range from items that at first seem nifty but are really pieces of junk to take-down equipment that equals or surpasses their solid-state competitors. With the Ruger Takedown (the company spells it as one word) there is no doubt that the rifle functions as well as all other 10/22 rifles. And that says a lot since the 10/22 has been in production since 1964 and it is one of the finest semi-auto rifle designs ever produced.

When I first picked up the Takedown, the locking mechanism was so intuitive that I was able to take apart and reattach the barrel without looking at the user's manual. It locks with an affirmative twist and unlocks with a twist and a push of a nub-like lever. It's that simple. Other than that, it has all the great qualities one would expect from a 10/22. The black synthetic stock is plain and simple and that might turn off some shooters but to me it is a virtue: this is a gun designed to be a traveling companion. A few scratches accumulated during your adventures is little to fret about for a tool that is meant to be used often.

Ammo Storage Tips

BY WALT HAMPTON

We've seen prices on ammo and components rise, supply shrink, and the ever-present threat of some type of government clamp-down on firearms-related products; serious shooters, hunters and ordinary gun-owning citizens need to protect their stocks of these items. With the current political situation in mind, here are a few tips for keeping your handloads and other ammunition safe and reliable.

Modern primers and gun powder, if properly stored, have a nearly infinite shelf life. These items need to be stored with the three watchwords of care; cool, dry and dark. By cool we mean stable temperature in the 50 to 80 degree Fahrenheit range. Extreme high temperature can cause the deterioration of gun powders over long exposure; we've seen it time and again, ammo left on the dashboard and heated to extreme temperatures or frozen and re-heated.

"Keep your powder dry" is a phrase all shooters have heard and comes from the days when flintlock firearms ruled the field; it is just as important today as it was 200 years ago. Temperature swings from very low to high and back again cause condensation within modern brass-cased cartridges and renders ammunition inert. It doesn't take much moisture to ruin a primer and this is one reason I usually don't recommend the basement for ammo storage, unless some type of dehumidifier is present to balance the humidity.

While the sun is the engine that drives all life it can be the worst enemy of ammunition and gunpowder by virtue of its heating ability. I keep my ammunition in cabinets away from sun exposure for this reason. For obvious reasons don't leave your ammo on the dashboard of the truck and if you have a window in your hand-

Until Further Notice
Handgun Ammo is
Limited to 2-Boxes Per
Visit

There has been no change in price

loading room make sure the sun doesn't settle on your supply of powder and primers while you're away.

If you are going to put your ammunition away for a period of time look into the military surplus ammo cans with the neoprene seal rings, these work great if they are kept in a dry environment and protected from sudden swings in temperature. The military powder cans that have the same rubber seal rings also work great, but don't hold a heck of a lot.

I'm reminded of the Confederate command that stored a few hundred muskets for future use in caves in southwest Virginia, a damp and gunmetal-unfriendly environment, that were lost and later discovered in the early 1940s, still operational and indeed in wonderful condition. The guns were heavily greased before storage, metal and wood, and stored in wooden barrels sealed with a mixture of wax and tallow. Gunpowder kegs had been stored within larger wooden barrels, also sealed with the wax/tallow, and the outside of the kegs themselves had been coated with the wax/tallow mixture. The powder was just as good as the day it was stored.

DIY Camouflage for Your Gun

BY TIGER MCKEE

There is nothing that visually stands out more than a rifle. It can be a modern urban environment, a dusty village in Iraq, or the middle of dense bush and the first thing that will grab someone's eye will be the shape of a rifle.

Camouflaging your equipment can be accomplished in a variety of ways. Tape, cloth, and burlap are temporary measures that can be changed to fit different environments. There are professional systems that use two part paints and provide durable long lasting finishes. And then there's my favorite friend, the spray can. Spray paint is cheap, available almost anywhere, and it's easy and quick; using a few simple materials, some imagination, and a little spare time, you can create professional-looking camo jobs.

The basic principles of camouflaging are to blend into the environment to create concealment and to disguise your gear, making it appear to be something else. The eye is quick to pick up on anything abnormal, so we need a few tricks to fool it.

First, avoid pure black. Few things in nature or man-made environments are pure black. If you examine these environments, you'll see the dark areas are just the same colors darkened by shadows or the lack of light. (My grandfather taught me at an early age not to look for the rabbit, but to spot its round black eyes.)

Next, try to create depth by incorporating blurry areas underneath sharply defined areas. Even if you focus on the object, blurry areas give it the appearance of being "deeper" than it really is.

⚠ This is the sponging technique pictured in stages. The AR is taped to protect the barrel, receiver and the light's lens. The stock, handguards, light, and grip have been sprayed with the base colors, blending them together. The handguard, light, and grip have already been sponged.

Finally, we want to trick the eye by making the object appear to be upside down. If you study an area, you'll notice that the tops of objects are usually lighter in color than the bottom. In nature animals reverse this out; the top of a deer is brown while its underside is white. Doing the same thing with your gear makes it appear to be a different shape as opposed to something the eye is familiar with.

The materials you'll need are easy to obtain. For paint, go for flat colors that won't dry with a shiny finish. I normally work with camo paints from Brownells. Brownells offers a variety of high-density colors, which means they cover really well without having to apply multiple coats. You can also pick up other brands of camo paint at most shops that sell hunting sup-

plies, and larger hardware stores will have some in stock.

You'll want a mask to reduce inhaling fumes and overspray and a set of safety glasses. I wear latex gloves to keep paint off my hands and prevent oil on my hands from transferring to the gear during handling.

A degreaser, such as acetone or Brownells TCE degreaser, is highly recommended to remove oil from the weapon. Scuff pads or sandpaper are used to prep the surfaces.

Masking tape — the expensive good blue stuff made specifically for painting — is needed to cover important areas that you don't want painted. You may also need a sharp utility knife for trimming tape or making stencils.

A stand or some way to hang your gear allows you to work around all sides while painting.

Those are the basics; you may need to pick up other materials depending on the technique you use.

When working with firearms, the first step is to make sure the weapon is clear and unloaded. The safety rules still apply, and I'm always careful of where I point the muzzle. Any loose ammo is secured. If I leave the work area, I recheck once I return to make sure the weapon is still empty. I also don't take any chances with my eyes, so as soon as I enter the shop I slap on a pair of safety glasses.

SPONGING

Sponging, using a rough sponge to blot on color, is one of the easiest techniques to use when painting your gun. Most people who have painted the inside of a home are familiar with this interior decorating standard.

The first step is to tape off any areas that you don't want to be painted or damaged, such as the lens and dials on optics, and iron sights. Make sure you cover other areas that are critical to its operations, such as the muzzle crown or bolt.

After donning a pair of gloves, I degrease the weapon to ensure there isn't any oil present. Depending on the weapon, you may need to prep the surface by lightly scuffing the parts. If you have wood stocks — especially anything with a slick clear finish — you may need to take extra time and sand it. Once you've prepared the surface, degrease again.

Spray a base coat using at least two colors, and blend one into the other to create the "blurring" effect. Then, taking a coarse painting sponge (available at any major hardware store or craft shop), sponge the next color onto the areas where the base colors meet.

I cut the sponge into different sizes and shapes and constantly rotate the shapes so I don't end up with a repetitive pattern. To apply the paint to the sponge, just spray it until it's good and moist, then sponge until it's dry. Then repeat. Once this is done, I'll sometimes use a fourth color and sponge on the highlights using a lighter color, or create shadowed areas using a darker paint.

STENCILING

Stenciling is about as easy as the sponging method. The prepping process is the same.

Again, start by laying down a base coat using at least two colors. Once it's dry, use a stencil to add more defined patterns.

Stencils can either be positive — such as a section of fake plastic plant — or negative, created by cutting patterns from cardstock to create a silhouette or a negative stencil.

Attach the stencil to the rifle by the stencil to conform to the weapon's shape, and tape it to the rifle. It doesn't have to be perfectly formed to fit the rifle; anywhere the stencil is not touching will create a blurry area to provide a sense of depth.

With the stencil attached, spray the next color, being careful not to spray too heavily (once you remove the stencil, there's usually too much contrast). Then move the stencil to a different location or attach another stencil and repeat the process.

Using different colors or stencil shapes will create a more random pattern. This technique works really well for field environments where you're trying to reproduce the chaos found in nature. Let your wild side guide you.

MASKING

Masking is a little more complicated and time-consuming, but also produces some of the best results.

Use masking tape to create shapes as you layer on your paint. I recommend starting with your darkest color and working your way to the lightest. You can always blend colors for depth.

Begin with your base color. Cut out masking tape to cover the areas that you want to remain that color. Any areas left uncovered will be painted over, so advance planning is necessary — especially if you're trying to reproduce or match an existing camo pattern.

Once you have the areas masked off, apply the next color. Let it dry. Mask off the areas you want to remain that color and spray again. After completing all the masks and colors, remove the tape to reveal the finished product.

The cool thing about these techniques is that you can combine them to obtain a variety of results. Consider the environment in which you're most likely to use your weapon and use colors and shapes that match that area. When in doubt, use lighter colors rather than darker.

For practice, use wood 2 × 4s until you have your technique squared away. If you run a paint application on your weapon you don't like, you can always scuff it up and paint it over again. If you're a little squeamish about painting your weapon, just paint the "furniture" (stocks, grips, and handguards), leaving the receiver and barrel plain.

CAMO TIME

The amount of time it takes to complete your camo job depends on the complexity of the pattern or technique used. A complicated masking technique will take more time just to cut out the patterns. The sponging technique takes about 30 minutes; maybe a little longer, depending on how quick your paint dries.

The good thing about most camo paint is that it dries quickly unless it's a cold or humid day. I normally paint outside so the sun helps with the drying process.

Just remember that even though it may be dry to the touch, it will take a day or so for the paint to fully cure, so avoid handling the weapon any more than necessary until it's fully cured.

Think about the practical field applications of camouflage: Don't stand out and draw attention. For the sniper, this means blending into the environment for a successful mission. For a hunter, it can be the difference between putting meat in the freezer and just spending a nice day in the field.

Index

"postal drop", 191
power, 152–159
    loss of, 50–51
    portable, 189
PowerPot portable generator, 153
propane lanterns, 142

R
radios
    two-way, 165, 188–191
    weather, 194–197
rain, 103
rifles, 17, 244–246
rule of threes, 26, 48, 94

S
safety issues. *See also* water, purification
    in the cold, 51
    with lanterns and lamps, 140
seed stock, 115
shelter. *See also* tents
    options for bug-out bags, 66
shemagh, 63–64
shotguns, 30, 236–237, 239
sleep pads, buyer's guide, 86–93
sleeping bags, 74–76
    buyer's guide, 77–85
smartphones, 180–183
snares, 121
snow, 103
snowmobile/ATV survival kits, 17–18
socks, 62
solar power, 142, 154–155
    buyer's guide, 156–159

SolarWrap, 155
space blankets, 74–76
storage, for back-up bikes, 45
stoves. See food preparation
summer survival kits, 22
sunlight
    for heat, 51
    protection from, 51
survival kits
    automobile, 75–76
    bug-out kits, 37–39
    ditch bags, 21
    everyday carry gear (EDC), 14
    fire-making kits, 38
    first aid kits, 38
    fishing kits, 38
    food for, 123
    for back-up bikes, 46–47
    general survival, 35–37
    go bags, 13
    home survival kits, 10–12
    pet first aid kits, 38
    ready-made, buyer's guide, 35–39
    summer, 22
    vehicle kits, 15–20
survival supplies, 162, 166–167

T
tarps, 66
tents, 66
    buyer's guide, 67–73
tinder, 58–59
toilet access, 171
tomahawks, 216
tools, 160
tools, 150, 160, 164–165, 167
    multi-tools, 203
traps, 121
truck survival kits, 16–17

V
vacuum sealers, 124
vehicle survival kits
    aircraft survival kits, 17–18
    automobile survival kits, 15–16
    boat survival kits, 17, 21
    packing for temperature variation, 19

    snowmobile/ATV survival kits, 17–18
    truck survival kits, 16–17
vehicles, for bugging out, 27
vitamins, 111

W
water. *See also* water bottles
    on the back-up bike, 46
    buyer's guide for filters and purifiers, 104–107
    chemical treatment, 98–99
    containers for bug-out bag, 100

    for cooling and hydration, 51, 94, 97
    filtering, 98
    home storage options, 101–102
    natural sources for, 103
    pre-filtering, 97–98
    purification, 94, 96–99
    purifiers for, 99, 107
water bottles, 97, 100–101, 167
    with built-in filters, 105–106
water filter straws, 106
waterbricks, 101–102
weather alerts, 181
weather radios, 194
    buyer's guide, 195–197
wild hogs, 119–121
winter driving kit, 20
women
    backpacks for, 33–35
    sleeping bags for, 83–84
wood stoves, 50, 52–53
wool fabric, 61

About the Contributors

James M. Ayres is the author of *The Complete Gun Owner*. He served in the Green Berets and the 42nd Airborne. He has taught at survival schools for over two decades.

James Card is the Editor of *Living Ready Magazine*.

Grant Cunningham is a world-renowned revolversmith and shooting instructor. He is the author of *Book of the Revolver*.

Jill J. Easton helps control the hog population in the Ozark Mountains of Arkansas.

Stephen Garger is a knife aficionados and long-time contributor to *BLADE* magazine.

Corey Graff is the Online Editor for Living Ready and operates the U.S. Amateur Radio Station W9NSE, a two-generation station formerly owned by his father, Clarence, on the air since 1939.

Walt Hampton is a professional gunsmith and writer from Virginia.

Stacy Harris is the author of *Recipes & Tips for Sustainable Living*. Her website is www.gameandgarden.com.

Mike Haskew is an author and journalist from Tennessee.

Charley Hogwood is the owner of P.R.E.P. Personal Readiness Education Programs. His website is readygoprep.com.

James Hubbard, M.D., M.P.H., is the author of *Living Ready Pocket Manual First Aid*. His website is thesurvivaldoctor.com.

M.D. Johnson lives in eastern Iowa and is a contributor to many outdoor publications as well as the author of numerous books about hunting topics.

Joe Kertzman is the Managing Editor of *BLADE* magazine.

Brett Laidlaw is the author of *Trout Caviar: Recipes from a Northern Forager*.

Chad Love is an award-winning full-time freelance writer and photographer based in western Oklahoma.

John D. McCann is the author of *Build the Perfect Survival Kit*.

Pat McHugh is a woodsman and outdoor safety expert that writers about outdoor survival topics.

J. Martin is a freelance journalist and editor that has written for many nationally recognized outdoor magazines.

Tiger McKee is director of Shootrite Firearms Academy, located in north Alabama, and author of *The Book of Two Guns*. His website is www.shootrite.org.

Dave Morelli is a retired Las Vegas police officer and SWAT sniper now living in Idaho. He regularly writes on topics pertaining to law enforcement, search and rescue and precision marksmanship.

Dave Mull is a freelance writer and the editor/publisher of Great Lakes Sportfish Digital Magazine. He is an avid angler, kayaker and hunter and lives with his family, six dogs and countless chickens on a hobby farm in Paw Paw, Michigan.

James D. Nowka is the author of *Prepper's Guide to Surviving Natural Disasters*.

Brett Ortler is a writer and editor based in Minnesota.

Angela Paskett is the author of *Food Storage for Self-Sufficiency and Survival*. Her website is foodstorageandsurvival.com.

Dave Rhea is the Field Editor of *BLADE* magaizne and contributing writer to *Outdoor Life Magazine*.

Tom Sciacca is a former US Marine, a veteran of the Gulf War, a survival enthusiast and President of CampingSurvival.com.

Steve Shackleford is the Editor of *BLADE* magazine.

Ben Sobiek is the online Product Manager of Living Ready.

Creek Stewart is the author of *Build the Perfect Bug Out Bag, Build the Perfect Bug Out Vehicle* and *The Unofficial Hunger Games Wilderness Survival Guide*. His website is willowhavenoutdoor.com.

Kyle Ver Steeg II is a medical doctor and an outdoorsman interested in survival topics.

Scott W. Wagner is the author of *Gun Digest Book of Survival Guns*.

Steve Watkins is a knife aficionados and long-time contributor to *BLADE* magazine.

Dave Workman is a reporter, editor and author of several books, an award-winning outdoor writer and a firearms instructor.

Other fine Living Ready books are available from your local bookstore and online suppliers. Visit our website, www.livingreadyonline.com. Living Ready® is a registered trademark of F+W Media.

18 17 16 15 14   5 4 3 2 1

ISBN-13: 978-1-4403-3744-4

Distributed in Canada by Fraser Direct
100 Armstrong Avenue
Georgetown, Ontario, Canada L7G 5S4
Tel: (905) 877-4411

Distributed in the U.K. and Europe by F&W Media International, LTD
Brunel House, Forde Close, Newton Abbot, TQ12 4PU, UK
Tel: (+44) 1626 323200
Fax: (+44) 1626 323319
E-mail: enquiries@fwmedia.com

Distributed in Australia by Capricorn Link
P.O. Box 704, S. Windsor NSW, 2756 Australia
Tel: (02) 4560-1600
Fax: (02) 4577-5288
E-mail: books@capricornlink.com.au

Edited by Jacqueline Musser and Kelsea Daulton
Designed by Clare Finney
Production coordinated by Debbie Thomas

Hone your preparedness skills with these two FREE downloads

FREE

1. Bug Out Bag Inventory Review Sheet

This five-page Bug Out Bag inventory Review Sheet will make packing and reviewing your Bug Out Bag's contents efficient and foolproof. Download it for free at **livingreadyonline.com/bug-out-bag-packing-list**

Bug Out Bag Inventory Review Sheet

*NOTE: Print in LANDSCAPE mode

BOB Pack Item (Write in other items as necessary)	Quantity	Review Date					Notes
Water and Hydration							
Fresh Drinking Water							
Collapsible Water Bottle							
Nalgene Style Water Bottle							
Metal Canteen							
Water Purification Tablets							
Water Filter/Purification System							
Food and Food Preparation							
Open and Eat Bars							
MRE Meals or Dehydrated Meals							
Metal Cook Pot							
Metal Cup							
Spork							
P-38 Can Opener							
Pot Scrubber							
Portable Pack Stove							
Fuel for Portable Pack Stove							

2. How to Make Emergency Shelters

This guide provides instruction on making emergency shelters during wilderness survival situations. Download it for free at **livingreadyonline.com/free-download-how-to-make-emergency-shelters**

STAY ALIVE! SURVIVAL SHELTER AND PROTECTION FROM THE ELEMENTS

From the author of Build The Perfect Survival Kit

John D. McCann

eShort

More Books on Survival and Preparedness

Build the Perfect Bug Out Bag
by Creek Stewart

Living Ready Pocket Manual
First Aid
by James Hubbard,
The Survival Doctor™

Food Storage for Self-Sufficiency
and Survival by Angela Paskett

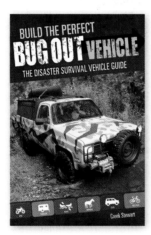

Build the Perfect Bug Out Vehicle
by Creek Stewart

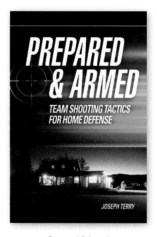

Prepared & Armed
by Joseph Terry

AVAILABLE ONLINE AND IN BOOKSTORES EVERYWHERE!
Get free survival and preparedness tips! Join our mailing list at livingreadyonline.com.

Become a fan of our Facebook page: facebook.com/LivingReady